D1461923

TO THE LAST ROUND

The Leicestershire and Rutland Home Guard 1940–1945

This book is dedicated to the memory of the 18 Leicestershire
Home Guards who died while serving their country,
and to the thousands of Home Guards in Leicestershire and Rutland
who answered the call and were prepared to make the ultimate sacrifice
to serve and protect their fellow citizens in the war against fascism 1939–1945.

TO THE LAST ROUND

The Leicestershire and Rutland Home Guard 1940–1945

AUSTIN J. RUDDY

Leicester Mercury

breedon **books**
PUBLISHING

First published in Great Britain in 2007 by

The Breedon Books Publishing Company Limited

Breedon House, 3 The Parker Centre, Derby, DE21 4SZ.

To my Grandfather, Private Frank Leslie Tagg of D. Napier and Son Ltd Platoon,
7th (Acton) Battalion, Middlesex Home Guard and my Great Uncle,
Company Sergeant Major John Oliver Smith of 5th (St Marylebone) Battalion,
County of London Home Guard.

The author's research into the Leicestershire and Rutland Home Guard is an
on-going project that does not end with the publication of this book. Any readers
with further information, photographs or ephemera are cordially invited to contact
the author via the *Leicester Mercury* Newspaper, St George Street, Leicester LE1 9FQ.

Most of the photographs in this book are available to purchase by telephoning
Leicester Mercury Photosales on 0116 222 4256.

ISBN 978-1-85983-559-3

Printed and bound by Cromwell Press, Trowbridge, Wiltshire

CONTENTS

'All ranks in this Sector will defend their allotted post to the last man and the last round. There will be no withdrawal from positions which they have been ordered to hold.'

Defensive Policy of Leicester Sector Defence Scheme
November 1941

'If, and when, the balloon goes up, we are all in this for one common and sole purpose, and that is the total destruction of the enemy.'

Lieutenant Charles W. Thornton,
CO No. 13 (Quorn) Platoon, 'D' Company, 10th (Charnwood) Battalion
Leicestershire Home Guard
June 1943

Orderly Room Ode

When we stand on Keyham Hill and look with admiration
On rolling Uplands spread before our eyes,
Emotions stir within our hearts, and in our adulation
We thank our God for such a peaceful prize.

We know these lands in many moods all changing with the seasons,
When rounded hill tops are so coldly bared.
Where furrows of the plow share shew designed reason
Of men whom for these lands have cared.

We know the hedge rows in the Spring with their flow'ring May,
When birds do sing so blythly as they mate.
When the dews with diamond sparkle all so lightly weigh
On nodding flowers which for the sunrise wait.

We know the sylvan summer with trees in dress'd array,
When fledglings leave their nests and take to wing.
When flow'ring fields are filled with scent of luscious hay,
And God looks down and blesses everything.

We know the coloured Autumn which decorates our trees,
In tinted yellows, russet browns and gold.
When early morning mists will liberate the leaves,
Which flutter to the earth to die and mold.

We love this blessed Leicestershire – this County of our own,
We venerate these uplands of our birth.
Her deeds of stirring glory to all afar are known.
We knew her sons will always prove their worth.

So should some dark invader dare to cross our shore,
In plane or 'chute or tank or armoured car,
We'll quickly man our trenches, and shoot at once to score,
For none shall pass. Their progress we shall bar.

May then we stand on Keyham Hill and look with admiration
On rolling uplands spreading far and wide.
Our God we'll praise in prayer and humble supplication
For keeping safe our blessed countryside.

'R.W.S.'
Orderly Room Sergeant
'C' (Keyham) Company
6th (Quorn) Battalion
Leicestershire Home Guard

FOREWORD

It is quite remarkable that some 60 to 65 years later, there should appear such a detailed and fascinating account as that now contained in this book, which is the result of much meticulous research and painstaking investigation.

I suppose that those of us who were privileged to serve in the Home Guard will recollect similar stories to those recounted by Mr Ruddy.

As the book explains, we were serious in our training and exercises, and doubtless fortunate that we were not called upon to face the enemy.

But as time went by, our confidence grew, and we would, with our Sten guns and grenades, have given good account of ourselves whatever the situation.

However, there was one occasion which I remember as the 'Battle of Showell Gravel Pits,' where I had orders to outflank and attack an imaginary foe, eventually only to find that we were facing the CO and firing live rounds, fortunately out of range.

More often, it seems in retrospect, we occupied our Sunday mornings with a route march planned to finish close to the Denbigh Arms in Lutterworth before closing time.

Reverting to the book, its stories and records can only be described as worthy of a place in any library. Although concerned with Leicestershire and Rutland, it could relate to most other parts of the country and is therefore to be highly valued as the story of the Home Guard.

Lieutenant John A. Bennett-Powell,
Commander of Lutterworth Platoon 1942–1944,
7th (Market Harborough) Battalion,
Leicestershire Home Guard
February 2007

Lt John Bennett-Powell, seated centre front, with his Lutterworth Home Guard Platoon, 1944.

ACKNOWLEDGEMENTS

Interviewees:

The Home Guards:

Ken Allsopp, Sir David Attenborough, Norman Bazeley, Robert Beardsley, John Bennett-Powell, John Bevis, Dennis Booth, Jim Bradley, David Brookman, Roy Burton, Alan Clare, J.T. Clarke, Frank Cooke, Jack Cox, Edith Eayrs, Raymond Elgood, Les Forryan, Horace Gamble, Frederick Gerrard, John Greaves, Harry Gudger, Sidney Guest, Leslie Hales, Roy Hanley, Allan Hopcraft, Peter James, Les Jeffcoat, Arthur Kirkpatrick, Ron Lambell, Chris Long, Duncan Lucas, Derrick G. Malyon, Cyril Mee, Aneurin Owen, Fred Parr, Albert Purchase, Robert Reay, Arthur Russell, David Salmon, Henry Shipley, Eric Smith, Bernard Spiers, Bill Stevenson, John Swan, Jim Tailby, Bill Tollington, Dennis Underwood, Dennis H. Ward.

Also **Kay Staddon** and **Wendy Warren**.

Assistance:

Captain Bob Allen of the **Leicestershire Regiment Association**; **Sir Edmund Baker**; **Ron Bodicoat**; **Kerry Bodycote**: my *ex-officio* chauffeur who, through default, probably knows more about World War Two than any other woman in the East Midlands; **Richard Bradley**; **Jim Briggs**; **Steve Caron, Michelle Grainger** and all the **team at Breedon Books Publishing**; The late **Terence C**. **Cartwright and family**, particularly his son **Clive**; **John Cooke**; **Karenna Galer Coombes** of the *Quorndon Magazine* for the papers of Lt C.W. Thornton, CO of Quorn HG; **Anne Cooper**; **Terry Cox** of **Hathern Local History Society**; **Tom** and **Dick Elliott**; **Alison England**, Local Studies Librarian, **Wisbech Library**; **Jim Ford**; **Martin and Barbara Foster**; **Sue Hollins**; **Linda Jones** of the Licensing Team at **Ordnance Survey** maps, Southampton; **Roger Killingley**; *Leicester Mercury* **staff**: Editor **Nick Carter**; The **Picturedesk** and **Photographers**; **Scanning Department**; Editorial Artist **Ian Franklin**; Librarian **Steve England**; **Peter Walker** aka 'Mr Leicester'; staff of **The Record Office for Leicestershire, Leicester and Rutland**; **Martin Mace** of **Historic Military Press**; George McGilvery, Head of the Secretariat, **Royal British Legion**, London; **Judith Mileham**; **Roger Miles**; **Jon Mills**; **Ather Mirza** of **Leicester University**; N. **Moseley**; **Newarke Houses Museum, Leicester**; **Dr Philip Oddy**; My former tutor, **Professor Marilyn Palmer MA PhD FSA** of the **School of Archaeology, Leicester University**; **Robert Ovens**; **Hugh Purcell**; **Mark Sansom**; **Eileen Smith**; **W. Ruth Smith**; **Tony Smith** of Oadby RBL; **Mavis Squires**; **Professor Penny Summerfield**, Modern History Dept, **University of Manchester**; **Richard Tyler**; **Maureen Walker**; **Wendy Warren**; **Mo Watson** of **Leicestershire and Rutland Royal British Legion**, all the Branch Secretaries who responded to my appeal for information; **Adrian Westwood**; **Fred and Bernard Whitford**; and **Charles Yeates**.

INTRODUCTION

For over four long, dark years during World War Two, around 50,000 men and women served in the Leicestershire and Rutland Home Guard. After hard days in factories, fields and offices contributing to the war effort on the Home Front, men and women of all ages and abilities offered their services to defend their homes, families and fellow citizens. Armed with mediocre weaponry, they faced a well-equipped, ruthless and tyrannical Nazi enemy poised just across the Channel. Though this enemy never came, the Home Guard stood to, watched and waited. With this in mind, this book has been written as a tribute and salute to the men and women of the Leicestershire and Rutland Home Guard.

Two Counties, One Fight
Although geographically Leicestershire and Rutland are two separate counties, during the war they were combined to form a defensive Sub-Area and were administered by the Leicestershire and Rutland Territorial Army Association. Nonetheless, Rutlanders maintained their well-known proud independence from their larger neighbour by producing their own Home Guard cap badge, rather than wearing that of the Leicestershire Regiment. This book tells the story of the Home Guard in both counties, although its overall balance is tilted towards Leicestershire. This is deliberate and proportional to the size of the force in both counties: Leicestershire had 14 Home Guard battalions, whereas its little neighbour had just one.

A Story Almost Lost
At the war's end, many Home Guard units published biographical histories of limited print runs, mainly intended as souvenirs for their members. Colonel Ogilvy-Dalgleish, commander of the Rutland Home Guard, wrote a brief history of his battalion in 1955, but it, too, had a limited print run and is now practically unobtainable. The Colonel revealed his battalion's records were lost in transit when the Home Guard disbanded. Although Leicestershire comprised of 14 battalions, it appears not one unit history was ever widely published.

Now, over 60 years on, this book uses a plethora of previously unpublished – and in some cases recently declassified – records, documents and photographs gathered from all over Britain to tell the belated history of the Home Guard in Leicestershire and Rutland. More than 50 of the last Home Guards have shared their memories, some sad, some funny, to explain first hand the importance of the force.

Setting the Record Straight
Nowadays, the Home Guard has become synonymous with *Dad's Army* and is rarely mentioned without reference to its satirical offspring. The much-loved, classic BBC sitcom has become as much a part of British folklore as the organisation it mimicked. And not without reason. Many Home Guard veterans recall amusing anecdotes that would not have been out of place in *Dad's Army*. Likewise, nearly all platoons seem to have had more than their fair share of Mainwarings, Wilsons, Joneses, Walkers, Pikes and Godfreys.[1] But the comparison ends there. *Dad's Army* was conceived with comic intent; the Home Guard was conceived in desperate times with deadly-serious intent. This key point seems to have been all but lost and forgotten in the shadow of the programme's success and, to a certain degree, has tarnished the Home Guard as a light-hearted joke itself. But this is far from the truth. Had the German invaders reached Leicestershire or Rutland, it would have been no laughing matter.

Many Home Guard histories written in the immediate post-war years are largely fawning, glossing over the darker and more uncomfortable realities of the force, contributing to the now established idea it was all a 'jolly boys' outing'. In this book, I attempt to tell the whole story of the Home Guard, not only of its accomplishments and lighter moments but also its adversities. The Home Guard was a civilian army and as such comprised all sections of society. Thus, Home Guards ended up in court for various misdemeanours. A minority of the civilian population also acted less than honourably while under the threat of invasion. Brushing aside this part of the story would merely continue the misrepresentation of the Home Guard and, in the long run, prove a disservice to the men and the women of the force. I hope Home Guards, or their relatives, understand this is the reason why I have included the more graphic and less admirable moments in the narrative.

The history of the Leicestershire and Rutland Home Guard is a great human story. It tells of a strong bond and comradeship forged through the impact of war. It also tells of great altruism: how men and women were prepared to defend their families, friends and homes – with their lives if need be: no greater honour or token of respect can be made by one person to another. Eighteen of Leicestershire's Home Guards made that ultimate sacrifice while serving in the force.

The title – *To The Last Round* – has a double meaning, reflecting both the military and social aspects of this book.

Official local defence policy stated 'All ranks in this Sector will defend their allotted post to the last man and the last round.'

However, by most accounts, Home Guard activities tended to revolve around the local pub! Battalion, company and platoon meetings, officially and unofficially, occurred at the pub; Sunday manoeuvres usually finished at the pub and on more than one major exercise a pub was commandeered as a Home Guard battle headquarters!

When interviewed, John Greaves, formerly of the Husbands Bosworth Home Guard, said glumly 'The Home Guard is a bit of a forgotten army now. A lot of the youngsters these days don't know what it was all about.' Harry Gudger, formerly of the Birstall Home Guard, said 'Although it had its moments, when looking back, in reality, it was not very funny, but actually quite serious.' He was saddened the force did not even get a mention at local Remembrance Day services and felt the Home Guard had become forgotten and misunderstood over the years. I would feel most honoured if this book went some way to redressing the balance.

Austin J. Ruddy
Leicester Mercury
December 2006
62nd Anniversary of the Home Guard's Stand Down

CHAPTER 1:

IT ALL HAPPENED BEFORE: THE HOME GUARD THROUGH THE AGES

'The Home Guard stands in the direct line of the various bodies of militia, trained bands, fencibles, and volunteers, the records of whose fine spirit and military aptitude adorn many a page of our history.'

King George VI, First Anniversary of the Home Guard, 14 May 1941

The famous Home Guard of 1940–1945 was the largest and best armed volunteer home defence army in history, but cannot claim to be the first. However, the Home Guard forms the most important milestone in the long tradition of British amateur volunteer armies, particularly seen in Leicestershire and Rutland.

At this stage, it is not proposed to retell the full story of the military volunteer tradition in Leicestershire and Rutland: this has already been expertly covered in G.A. Steppler's 'Britons, To Arms!' However, a brief background will illustrate how the two counties led the way in the formation of the nation's volunteer defence forces.

Militias versus Volunteer Forces

For over a thousand years, ever since Anglo-Saxon times, there had been a civilian militia raised to defend hearth and home and sometimes further afield. In 1642 both Royalists and Parliamentarians raised militia and volunteer forces in Leicestershire for the impending Civil War. However, it was not until the late 18th century that the first true volunteer forces appeared.

Although similar to militias, volunteer forces are almost diametrically opposite. Volunteer forces were raised spontaneously on a local basis and, as the name suggests, were composed solely of volunteers. Militias were generally organised by central government, composed of conscripts and could serve outside their own county, even abroad. Compared to the militia's direct governmental control, the volunteer forces were raised via a certain degree of anarchical local democracy. Due to their voluntary nature, both the decision-making process and the choice of leadership was generally driven from grass roots upwards. As with all the volunteer forces, this invariably led to a power struggle with central government, which inevitably the latter always won, reining in the independence and at times the enthusiasm of the volunteers.

1794–1899: Leicestershire and Rutland Lead the Way

Arguably the first proper organised volunteer force in the two counties dates back to 1794, when the Loyal Corps of Leicester Volunteer Infantry was formed to counter the threat of a French invasion. Rutland, meanwhile, carved its name in British military history as the first county to produce a complete unit of Yeomanry – essentially volunteer cavalry.

In 1859 renewed fears over France's military ambitions gave birth to the new Rifle Volunteers Corps. Leicester claimed to be one of the first counties to raise a corps, forming the 31st Regiment of Volunteers. As the crisis subsided, the Volunteers Corps continued, until 1877 when they were eventually absorbed into the Leicestershire Regiment.

Following the outbreak of the Boer War in 1899, the law was modified so volunteer forces could

Four days before the outbreak of World War Two, aging volunteers of the National Defence Corps parade at the Magazine square, Leicester, wearing their newly-issued greatcoats, 31 August 1939.

serve overseas. The Leicestershire Volunteers joined the 1st (Regular) Battalion, The Leicestershire Regiment, engaging in fighting but fortunately suffering only minimal casualties. On their return, they were welcomed through the streets as heroes.

20th-Century Challenges

The Volunteers ever closer links with the regular military led to the end of their true independence when, in 1908, they were absorbed into the new Territorial Force (Territorial Army from 1921). The government finally stamped their control on the volunteers, but in return they became better organised and equipped.

At the outbreak of World War One in 1914 most of the Leicestershire Yeomanry volunteered for service abroad, leaving few men to defend the Home Fires. The threat of invasion was limited due to the stalemate of the Western Front, but a threat was still perceived. Although now largely forgotten, the immediate precursor to the Home Guard was formed in November 1914, called the Volunteer Training Corps, and was the first major volunteer anti-invasion corps of the 20th century. Although it shared only a fraction of the success of its successor, both forces were very similar, having the same role and receiving the same reception.

From the start, the government worried the VTC would compete with the Regular Forces for manpower, and they did little to encourage the force. Under grass-roots pressure, the government eventually relented a little, and in 1915 Leicester's Civic Defence Corps totalled around 3,000 men. A letter from 'An Old V.T.C. Ranker' to the *Loughborough Monitor* in August 1940, recalled:

'There were great occasions with field days and sham fights in the [Charnwood] Forest district, as well as ceremonial parades and inspections. Then there were those two memorable Sundays in April 1916, after the great blizzard, when we were of some service to the postal authorities clearing up the tangled mess of broken wires on the Leicester Road and the canal bank. Nor shall we forget, while memory lasts, the Brush [factory] guard, whose duty was, of course, not to be compared with the strenuous work of the Home Guard today. Yes, those were great days...'[2]

As with all British volunteer forces, the VTC endured a certain amount of ridicule, their 'GR' (Georgius Rex) armlet attracting comment that the initials stood for 'George's (W)Recks', 'Genuine Relics' or 'Granpapa's Regiment'.[3] When the VTC finally stood down in February 1919, it had attracted 230,000 members.

Recruitment into the TA between the two world wars was very slow. The bloody battlefields of France and the pitiful return of often disabled troops – or rather the lack of survivors – was the biggest discouragement to potential volunteers. This general anti-war sentiment pervaded throughout the interwar period. It took the arrival of Hitler in 1933 to nudge recruitment, and from 1936 the new local 44th AA Battalion attracted many new recruits due to the mounting fear of air raids.

In 1936 the TA began to recruit older ex-servicemen over 45 for part-time service into a new National Defence Corps. During a national emergency, they would serve near their homes as part of their local NDC company. However, with the lack of any immediate invasion threat, the NDC never really took off and didn't attract more than 6,000 volunteers nationwide.[4]

Soon after the outbreak of World War Two in September 1939, the TA's Leicestershire Yeomanry moved out of the county and within six months had been split into two separate regiments. As in World War One, mass conscription meant the home defence cupboard was left bare, with only a few Regular Army and TA troops available to defend the country. Unexpectedly, the conflict immediately flopped into a Phoney War stalemate, barely making headlines in the newspapers. As a result there was no perceived threat of invasion and consequently no need to raise a volunteer home defence corps – or was there...?

CHAPTER 2:

LEICESTERSHIRE AND RUTLAND HOME GUARD WAR DIARY 1940–1945

From Western Front to Home Front

To understand why the Home Guard was formed, it is important to know the immediate history of the period.

As in World War One, Britain relied on the buffer countries of France, Holland and Belgium. So when Britain declared war on Germany on 3 September 1939, the prospect of Britain's invasion seemed nil. The mass superpower of France with its impressive Maginot defence line, coupled with the British Expeditionary Force guarding the borders of Germany, mixed with the stagnancy of the Phoney War, created a complacent attitude towards home defence.

In April 1940 the Germans made a surprise invasion of Norway, which was met by an ill-equipped British expeditionary force who were rebuffed back to Britain. National thinking seemed to be that this was just a setback, but very few Britons realised a giant trap was slowly being sprung.

So when the German Blitzkrieg ('Lightning War') exploded across the length of the Allied lines on 10 May 1940, the Allies were violently woken from their military slumber. Advancing north westerly, the Germans completely bypassed the Maginot Line, instantly invalidating it, and stormed on through Belgium. This simple tactical masterstroke seems to have been completely unaccounted for by Allied planners, who seem to have relied on the Germans being 'good sports' and 'playing the game'. In weeks, the large but antiquated French army and smaller B.E.F. were pushed back as the Germans bulldozed on.

In Britain, the first reaction on the day the Germans attacked was the resignation of Prime Minister Neville Chamberlain and the instalment of his worthy successor Winston Churchill, who offered the nation his 'blood, toil, tears and sweat'. Britain was finally waking up to the threat.

A Fifth Column in our Midst?

The speed with which the Germans had stormed through Europe shocked the world, who failed to understand how two of the most powerful armies could be defeated so rapidly. The blame was instantly put on a dastardly and mysterious Fifth Column of spies and saboteurs, who it was believed betrayed and undermined nations.

The phrase 'Fifth Column' originated in 1936 during the Spanish Civil War when General Mola of the fascist Nationalist forces claimed he had four columns of troops outside Madrid and another secret fifth column inside.[5] In reality, there were no Fifth Column agents freely active in Britain, yet fear of the unknown overcame the population. Even Churchill believed 'there were 20,000 organised Nazis in Britain'.[6]

Within weeks, 'spy mania' erupted with various acts of alleged treachery blamed on the 'Fifth Column'. However, there was always a more rational answer.

At the end of May 1940, sabotage was alleged at M. Wright and Sons factory in Quorn. The factory was engaged in vital war work by making army webbing equipment and five looms were sabotaged. Subsequently, a 19-year-old weaver from Thringstone was arrested. He admitted sabotaging the machinery by dropping screws in the cogwheels – but not through pro-Nazi sentiment: because 'they would not give me a pay rise' said the disgraced employee.[7]

Likewise, a 21-year-old mechanic of Wigston Magna was arrested on a spying charge for photographing an aeroplane without a permit at a RAF airfield. The Chairman of the Bench said he 'took a very serious view of the case'. The accused was fined £5 with 17s 6d [£160] costs[8] and ordered to surrender his camera together with a collection of 1,100 aircraft photos and was banned from using a camera for the rest of the war. The accused was no spy but a rather over-enthusiastic planespotter. Although the airfield was not named, it would not have taken the greatest masterspy to work out it was probably RAF Desford, as the article stated the case was heard at Market Bosworth Police Court![9] Strangely, 61 years later another Leicestershire man, Gary Fagan, was also arrested for 'planespotting' while in Greece.

'War jitters' even led to violence on the streets of Leicester. A railway porter from Raymond Road was fined for assaulting a disabled man after accusing him of being a German spy. On 30 May 1940 the disabled man was returning from a Leicester City match when the porter accosted him at Welford Place. He asked the disabled man if he could walk without his stick, to which he replied he could. Immediately the porter punched him on the jaw and shouted to passers-by to help him capture 'a German spy'. The porter accused the disabled man of having just 'come down in a parachute' and a crowd soon formed. The porter, after being fined £1 [£31], apologised to his victim. The magistrate told the porter he had 'a touch of war jitters'.[10]

Despite the lack of any Fifth Column in Leicestershire, ironically, German Military Intelligence (the Abwehr) certainly thought there was. An Abwehr report from January 1941 stated they had 'heard via Spain that members of the IRA had blown up a munitions train in the county of Leicester'.[11] However, no records state such a memorable event to be true. This probably suggests the report was sent by a 'turned' German agent, passing back disinformation on behalf of MI5's Double-Cross Committee.

The chief result of this Fifth Column fever was the rounding up under Defence Regulation 18B, those immigrants considered to be 'enemy aliens': a harsh term that reflected the prevailing attitude. But there was no sure way of telling friend from foe, and between 16 May and 21 June 1940 many of Leicestershire's foreign guests were rounded up and sent to internment camps 'for the duration'. Many had fled Nazi Germany thinking they had escaped life behind barbed wire. Churchill later expressed regret at this 'executive detention', which he called 'in the highest degree odious'.

LDV: The Call to No Arms

Nonetheless, despite the illusory nature of the Fifth Column, the British populace demanded an active role in the defence of the nation. First World War veteran, 44-year-old Paul Stuart Wakefield, was the chief turbine designer at Brush Electrical Engineering Works in Loughborough. He kept a diary capturing the feelings of the time.

'Sunday 12:5:40. Over 100 Parachutists have been dropped in Brussels alone. They must have been training thousands of them and I read some British Legion clubs are asking for rifles and ammunition to help deal with any dropped in this country.'[12]

In neighbouring Northamptonshire one man 'incited' villagers to form their own defence force.[13] The national tabloid press jumped on this populist bandwagon, with calls to 'arm the people'. But the last thing the government wanted was reckless vigilante groups roaming the country. But public clamouring and the invasion threat forced the government's hand. Having only had one day to draw up

Volunteers for the Local Defence Volunteers parade at the Magazine square, Leicester, the first day after the call to arms, 15 May 1940. Most appear to be World War One veterans.

tentative plans and with no organisation or weapons to equip any new force, at 9pm on 14 May 1940 Secretary of State for War Anthony Eden broadcast:

'Since the war began the Government have received countless enquiries from all over the Kingdom from men of all ages, who, for one reason or another, are not at present engaged in military service and who wish to do something for the defence of their country. Now is your opportunity. We want large numbers of such men, who are British subjects, between the ages of 17 and 65...to come forward now and offer their services in order to make assurance doubly sure. The name of the new force which is to be raised will be the "Local Defence Volunteers". This name describes its duties in three words. In order to volunteer, give in your name at your local Police Station...Your loyal help, added to the arrangements which already exist, will keep our country safe.'[14]

The Call is Answered
Ten minutes after Eden's broadcast, the first recruit walked in to Leicester City Police Headquarters on Charles Street. Within the hour, 30 more men presented themselves and a steady stream of recruits attended police stations and village police houses throughout the two counties. Quorn resident Allan Hopcraft must have been one of the first to sign up,

'I was 18 at the time and rushed to the local police station, which was just down the road from where I lived. Bobby Norman was in charge. I said "I hear they want volunteers". "Oh" he says, "You're the first one". This was straight after the radio call. He took my name and said "we'll get in touch later on".'[15]

By lunchtime the next day over 200 men had enrolled at Loughborough police station, the majority being ex-servicemen. After 24 hours, 1,300 had registered in Leicester with a total of 3,000 in Leicestershire.

Little was demanded of the volunteers. No medical was required: the volunteers just had to be 'capable of free movement'. At this stage, the force was truly voluntary: no one was paid or under regular military law. The only stipulation was that volunteers had to give a fortnight's notice to resign, nicknamed 'the housemaid's clause'.[16]

'Franc-tireurs' and 'Murder bands'
German reaction to the formation of the LDV was of dissuasion. On 16 May 1940 German radio threatened:

'The British Government is committing the worst crime of all. Evidently it permits open preparation for the formation of murder bands. German official quarters warn the misled British public and remind them of the fate of the Polish franc-tireurs...Civilians who take up arms against German soldiers are, under international law, no better than murderers. British people, you will do well to heed our warning.'[17]

'Leicestershire Parashooters' and 'Parashots'
The local press heralded the LDV's arrival with prosaic and Victorian-sounding unofficial titles, including 'anti-parachutists', 'Leicestershire Parashooters' or 'parashots'. These titles reflected the LDV's generally perceived role, although at this stage they had little to 'shoot' 'paras' with. Nationally, the LDV's monikers were a little harsher, including 'Last Ditch Venture' or 'Look, Duck and Vanish', although in the cold light of day both these nicknames had a ring of truth. The last sobriquet was the most accurate, as the WO planned observation rather than combat as the LDV's chief role. The LDV's strength was its valuable local knowledge. It could report, harass and delay the invader wherever possible until the Regular Forces arrived.

Something From Nothing
The speed with which the LDV was formed meant its structure was only created *after* its birth. On 15 May Anthony Eden sent a telegram to the county Lord Lieutenants asking for their help, and the WO sent similar telegrams to the TA associations.[18]

GHQ Home Forces and the various Army Commands already had their hands full preparing for the invasion of Britain and did not have time to deal with this whole new level of bureaucracy, so the full weight was dropped on the county TA associations. The British Legion also lent a hand.

As had been the case for over 400 years, the Lord Lieutenant was automatically the Chairman of the county volunteer force, which, in 1940, was the TA association. He helped choose the LDV's officers. They were prominent men in local society, usually with previous military experience, often in World War One or earlier, or had served in the Empire. It was noted in Leicestershire 'there has been a big response from ex-officers of 60 and 65, who will be valuable for their ability in leadership'.

Within a week of the LDV's formation, the counties' structure had been created. The two counties' Lord Lieutenants chose the LDV County Commandants (soon renamed Zone Commanders). In Leicestershire, Sir Arthur Hazlerigg of Noseley Hall, Billesdon, chose Brigadier-General Sir Thomas Cope of Market Bosworth as Leicestershire's Commandant. In turn, Cope chose seven Area Commandants. These Areas, or Groups to give them their official name, were based on police districts. In Leicestershire, these were based on the principal centres:[19]

> Leicester Group: Col. H.W.H. Tyler
> Leicester (County Area): Lt-Col. H.E. Noel
> Market Harborough Group: Brig-Gen. J.L. Jack
> Loughborough Group: Major C.H. Martin (Chairman of Leics. Yeomanry OCA)
> Ashby Group: Major W.H. Sowter
> Melton Group: Brig.-Gen. George Paynter
> Market Bosworth Group: Lt-Col. J.L. Griffiths

In Rutland, Lord Lieutenant Lord Ancaster chose his 68-year-old brother, Lt-Col. the Hon. C.H.D. Willoughby of Prebendal House, Empingham, as County Commandant. Willoughby resigned in July and was replaced by former naval Wing-Commander J.W. Ogilvy-Dalgleish OBE of Springfield House, Ashwell Road, Oakham. The Area/Group Commandants were:

> North-Eastern Area: Vere Chaplin
> Oakham and District: W.J. Baird
> Uppingham and District: Major J. Sterndale Bennett
> Rest of County: Major H.E. Whaley[20]

The 'Tremendously Popular' LDV

Meanwhile, volunteers still came. By 17 May enrolment had slowed, but, nonetheless, in two days 6,000 men had volunteered in Leicestershire. In Hinckley 650 registered, while in Ashby over 200 had come forward, with 60 in New Lount Colliery alone.[21] By a week later, 250 men had volunteered in Melton Mowbray[22] and so great was the final response at Loughborough that recruiting had to be closed.[23] As the county TA minutes recorded 'From the first this new force proved tremendously popular and when it can be said that its strength in Leicestershire is equal to that of about a division, it will be seen what a simple matter recruiting has proved.'[24]

If anything, it was too simple, as their ARP colleagues noted disparagingly. The growing threat of invasion made air raids more likely. An appeal for more ARP workers was made, but only 139 new recruits responded and the council's Emergency Committee had to plead to existing ARP workers not to join the newer and slightly more exciting LDV. At the end of May 1940 the Chief Constable and ARP Officer C.E. Lynch-Blosse complained in a confidential ARP report 'The introduction of the LDV has had rather an upsetting effect in some areas on ARP personnel; a rifle and uniform was very attractive...'[25]

Nationally, it had been hoped a total of 500,000 volunteers would answer Eden's appeal. Within 24 hours some 250,000 had enrolled, and by the end of June this total had risen to a staggering 1,456,000, almost three times the target figure.[26]

The First 'Ragtime Parades'

In his diaries, Wakefield aired a commonly-heard complaint about the lack of immediate organisation. It was almost two weeks after many volunteers had first signed up before they were summoned for their first meeting.

'Sunday 26:5:40. Attended the most ragtime parade I have ever seen at the College Stadium [Loughborough] at 6pm today. Nothing happened until 6.20 when about 800 men were divided into ex-service men and others. The others were sent home. Why they were asked to be there I don't know, because the organisers knew from the Police Station registers how many were ex-service men and how many not! Individual inspection and interview took place while we stood in the ranks for about an hour. By 8.30 a number who had been inspected were marched inside to enrol. The remainder were then told to come back at 7.30 Wednesday! [Incidentally] when I talk about a ragtime parade I refer, of course, to its organisation. There is nothing ragtime about 400 ex-service men of all ages. The men will be all right.'[27]

At first, the LDV was divided into companies of about 1,600 men, which were, in turn, divided into four platoons of 400 men and sections of 100 men, though these groupings were significantly lower in more rural areas.[28]

Margaret Sparrow (née Hoden) remembers seeing the first LDV meeting at Stanton-under-Bardon, near Coalville, in a scene that was commonplace,

'The very first meeting was held one Sunday morning in the field at the back of our house. About 20 men turned up, including my dad. They were drilled and marched up and down armed with brush handles, garden rakes, spades and hoes, carried on their shoulders like rifles. Mr Johnson, who had been a sergeant in the First War, was giving the orders…Their headquarters were in the old school…The ARP shared the same building.'[29]

Broomstick Army

Despite now being seen as bit of a myth, at first the LDV really were a 'broomstick army'. Former Wigston Home Guard CSM Arthur Mitchell later recalled 'In May 1940 we had only broomsticks for weapons and I used to ask gardeners if we could borrow rakes. If Jerry had caught us in those first few weeks we would have been battling him with saucepans…'[30] John Smith remembered Thornton's early LDV 'I remember seeing some of their first drills, which included charging in unison into the allotment hedge, in bayonet-like stance with broom handles.'[31]

The severe shortage of arms following Dunkirk left the Local Defence Volunteers weaponless. A public appeal was made for the donation of shotguns and these were handed in to Leicester police station on 17 June 1940.

Any Guns Will Do

The situation became more desperate as the Allies fell back in the face of the German onslaught. The foreboding threat of invasion loomed larger. With no arms at all, on 21 May police visited gunsmiths in Leicester and commandeered firearms.[32] A request was also made to the public for shotguns, sporting rifles and cartridges for the LDV.[33]

Wot No Guns?

In May 1940 there were only 70,000 rifles left in the whole country.[34] In perspective, Leicestershire and Rutland alone required 22,000 weapons. The first recorded issue of proper firearms occurred in Rutland at the end of May when 135.303 P14 rifles were delivered to Oakham police station with 50 rounds per rifle. These weapons were immediately distributed proportionately, their usage taught by World War One veterans.[35] Nonetheless, the vast majority of LDVs were still unarmed.

First Patrols

Rifles or no rifles, the LDV still went on patrol. An example of how the LDV was organised on a local basis can be seen in North Leicester. The Birstall platoon first started patrolling on 24 May, with four patrols covering Birstall, Wanlip, Thurcaston and Cropston.[36]

The LDV's almost completely passive observational role during that tense summer can be seen in the notes of Sgt C.W. Thornton of Quorn's LDV, whose first patrol was a week later.

'Instructions and General Information for Sections:
Observation Posts must be fully manned from 8.45pm to 10pm. There are three OPs:
Along hedge parallel to the farm building.
At the farm gate leading to the farm.
Along the path between beans and corn fields.
Three men are to be stationed on these posts between 8.45pm and 10pm and from 1am to 5.30am.

Between the hours of 10pm and 4am it is only necessary to have two men on patrol. The suggested patrol is from the rick-yard through the gate leading to the cornfield.

In case of an attack, ring up NOTTINGHAM 77841 stating "First Priority – War Office Call". State as briefly as possible the positions of Parachutists etc. and state that a guide will be at such and such a point to conduct the Military to their objectives.

Note. Always have two pennies in your possession in case of telephoning from a call box.'[37]

Starting later, 1,300 volunteers of the 1st Loughborough LDV Battalion first mounted guard in civilian clothes, including bowler hats with only armlets for identification, armed with shotguns and sticks.[38] Wakefield recorded:
'Saturday 1:6:40. Our first two posts at the Brush were manned tonight by Mr Blunt's section. Mercer (68) looked a fine old soldier even in his ill-fitting uniform. He and Urquhart were like old dogs with 10 tails when they had their rifles loaded. P- and C- weren't trusted with live rounds at first, their ammunition was kept in the pockets of their old soldier comrades! The "armoury", for the present, is the big cupboard in TBK's office. The RAF had the big meadow strewn with old trucks and derelict lorries during the afternoon to make it less desirable as a landing place for troop-carrying aeroplanes.'[39]

'Shiver Sisters' and 'Jitter Bugs'

Heightened public anxiety led to panicked rumourmongering. One such rumour was that the authorities had decided not to give any warning if there was an air raid on Loughborough. A commentator in the *Loughborough Monitor* berated:

'At this very moment, sane men and women in this town are spreading entirely false rumours about the war that are doing incalculable harm…Such pitiful alarm has it already caused and will cause in the future unless it is stopped, it has been made necessary for the authorities to ask the *Loughborough Monitor* to refute it.'

The commentator went on to call the rumourmongers 'Shiver Sisters' and 'Jitter Bugs', adding 'they deserve far worse titles than these'.[40] Wakefield noted further nicknames, including 'Dismal Jimmies' and 'Melancholy Michaels'.[41]

Cross-Dressing Parachutists

The parachutist, a novel new form of warfare, became chief bogeyman of 1940. Nationally, the most common rumour was that cunning, burly parachutists would land dressed as clergymen or even more bizarrely, cross-dress and attack in nuns' habits. In an attempt to scotch such obscure rumours, Harold Nicolson, the Parliamentary Secretary to the Ministry of Information and MP for Leicester West, broadcast a special warning on 'chatterbugs':

'He will say that his brother-in-law – chatterbugs always have innumerable brothers-in-law – was in the train from Derby when a nun entered and started to read a religious book. The book dropped from her lap, and as she stooped to retrieve it she disclosed a manly wrist complete with a tattooed inset of Adolf Hitler.'[42]

Only adding to the melee, the Home Office warned parachutists might even land disguised as policemen or air raid wardens.[43]

The Government even misled themselves with speculative advice. Lord Croft, the Under Secretary for War, informed Churchill that Britain should expect an attack by 100,000 German airborne troops. Yet the Germans had no more than 7,000 paratroopers available. Europe had mainly been conquered by tanks and infantry, a much greater threat than the limited numbers of paratroopers used. Indeed, the number imagined never existed in the first place and, despite their skill, they had suffered heavy casualties.

With hindsight, belief in such rumours and poor advice may seem naïve, but the hurried atmosphere of hysteria, together with the fear of the unknown, made the unbelievable believable.

The 'Chicken's Neck'

By the end of the month it was apparent the Allies' stand in Europe was now untenable. On 28 May 1940 Belgium surrendered. Valerie Tedder (née Gisborn), then six years old, lived on Leopold Street, South Wigston.

'High up on the wall of the corner house was the street name. The wall was thickly splattered with mud where people had thrown it in anger and blamed King Leopold of Belgium for capitulating and giving in to Hitler's demands. No one climbed up to clean it off and it stayed there, an ugly mess, until the weather and rain removed it.'[44]

Allied troops evaporated back to the French coast for evacuation to England. In what has become known as the Miracle of Dunkirk, between 27 May and 4 June a mixed flotilla of ships bravely rescued a rag-tag assortment of 338,226 tired and weaponless Allied troops. But the miracle ended there. In less than a month Britain's buffer countries had evaporated. Britain was now faced the Nazis alone.

To oppose 134 victorious divisions, Britain only had 27 tattered divisions with scarcely enough arms to equip two divisions. The defeated French army predicted within three weeks that England's 'neck' would be 'wrung like a chicken's.'

Dunkirk – 'The Wonderful Retirement'?

Yet for once, the public misjudgement of the situation, together with the British character of stubborn pig-headedness under pressure, combined to form a fiery, stoic national outlook. Even the minutes of the county TA association read like a piece of upbeat propaganda, 'Three of the [county] TA units took part in the wonderful retirement through Dunkirk.'[45] However, the shine was somewhat tarnished when the bedraggled troops arrived in the county. Tired but smiling soldiers alighted at Leicester railway station and slowly marched to Victoria Park, where, ironically, they rested near to the War Memorial. Elsewhere in the county, Allan Hopcraft felt the strange combination of shock and stoicism,

'It was very serious. Trains stopped at the Great Central Railway station at Quorn. People were rushing up with sandwiches and buckets of tea for the returning troops. It was an atmosphere of great togetherness: everybody was willing to help each other out and there was no antagonism. The threat of invasion seemed very real when you saw the troops coming back on the train, shattered. You wondered what the hell was happening and thought "Oh well, we'll just have to soldier on".'[46]

In Rutland, the HQ and two companies of the 4th Cheshires arrived at Burley where they pitched tents at the Rectory. There were also 200 gunners, without guns, billeted at the Oakham Drill Hall and in Uppingham.[47]

Putting a brave face on it. Four Leicester soldiers stand in Leicester, having just disembarked from the train after returning from Dunkirk, Monday 3 June 1940. Their uniforms tell the real story of the state of the British Army at the time: shabby and torn. The soldier on the right has lost his army boots and is wearing plimsolls instead.

Invasion Scare: Summer 1940
On the Nazi 'Black List'

Over 60 years on it is difficult to envisage how the invasion scare gripped the nation. There was an overall fever of worried anticipation, more pressing than that felt by those who lived through the Cold War and the threat of nuclear annihilation.

The scare gripped all levels of society. Harold Nicolson firmly believed Britain would be invaded.[48] Fearing he would be a target for the Gestapo, Nicolson made a suicide pact with his wife, author Vita Sackville-West. Both kept suicide pills, which they called 'bare bodkins'. As early as 26 May 1940, Nicolson wrote to his wife in his diary:

'I don't think that even if the Germans occupied [Britain] they would harm you, in spite of the horrified dislike which they feel for me. But to be quite sure that you are not put to any humiliation, I think you really ought to have a "bare bodkin" handy so you can take your quietus when necessary. I shall have one also. I am not in the least afraid of such sudden and honourable death. What I dread is being tortured and humiliated.'[49]

Nicolson was right to be concerned. After the war it was revealed that his name was on the *Sonderfahndungsliste-GB*, the SS post-invasion 'Special Wanted List GB' of 2,820 persons most wanted by the Gestapo. Compiled in May 1940 by SS-General Walter Schellenberg, of the Nazi counter-espionage unit, the 'Black List' carries the names of persons to be 'taken into protective custody'. The arrest operations were to be headed by the sinister SS Colonel Professor Frank Six, who was later responsible for massacres in Russia. From London, Six would have commanded six units of 'search and destroy' *Einsatzkommandos* (Action Commandos), the nearest based in Birmingham. Several other persons from Leicestershire were also included on the list:

'Burt, Ronald, 27.10.20. Leichester [sic], Ringstead, Knigton [sic], RSHA IV E4, Stapo Frankfurt/M.'[50]

Burt was a 20-year-old from Knighton, but the exact reason why unit RSHA IV E4, who were assigned to deal with counter-espionage in Northern Britain, were so interested in him is a mystery.

Professor John Erickson of Edinburgh University believes Burt may have come under suspicion if he had visited Germany before the war, perhaps on a school trip to Frankfurt, as the last part of the entry suggests: 'Perhaps he had got into trouble with the authorities or they had seen something they didn't like about his passport. They certainly wanted to speak to him quite badly. I'm sure it wouldn't have been a pleasant experience.' Tragically, Burt was killed in 1941 while training to become an RAF pilot. His name does not appear on the Commonwealth War Graves Commission records, but interestingly several other Burts do, including one who was a high-ranking intelligence officer likely to be known to the Germans.[51] As can be seen from the entry, the *Sonderfahndungsliste-GB* was hurriedly composed and is full of mistakes: could it be Burt's entry is a case of mistaken identity?

Two more entries read:

'Kreissl, Johann, 18.6.93 Christophhammer, Eisendreher, Leichester/England, RSHA IV E4, Stapo Chemnitz.'

'Kreissl, Werner, 18.6.22 Christophhammer, vermutl. Leichester, RSHA IV A1.'[52]

Johann and Werner Kreissl were both wanted by the Nazis, the older by 'counter-espionage' and the younger as an 'opponent of the regime'. It is possible they were father and son and had also fled Germany.

The Black List was actually only part of a larger guidebook about Britain, named *Informationsheft GrossBritannien* or Information Handbook Great Britain. The handbook was prepared for those setting up a Nazi regime in Britain and explained how the Germans believed Britain was run. So, for example, in the List of Principal Cities in England and Wales, Leicester is listed as 15th out of 48 largest conurbations, with a population of 239,000.[53] The handbook also lists target organisations that were to be dismantled, such as the English Trade Unions of Marxist Foundation, which included the Amalgamated National Union of Quarryworkers and Settmakers of 167 Hinckley Road, Leicester.[54]

As Professor Erickson explains, the *Informationsheft GB* '…was a manual for total occupation, for the ruthless elimination of any who stood in its way or who had shown any propensity to opposition, resistance or revulsion at the sights and sounds of National Socialism…'[55]

Watching the Skies

The LDV stepped up their patrols and observational duties. A dusk to dawn watch was kept, watching for individual saboteurs parachuting in or whole hoards of steel-helmeted paratroopers. Immediately, on the last day of the Dunkirk evacuation, reports of paratroop landings started to reach the authorities. More worryingly, the confusion almost led to 'friendly fire' incidents, as Thornton LDV John Smith explains:

'One night when the workers from Leicester came home on the 6.45pm bus, a parachutist was seen on the other side of the reservoir. By the time the bus arrived at Bagworth, rumour had it that the Germans had landed at Thornton. Someone rushed to tell Harry, who was shaving. I personally witnessed the resultant action. Harry went down the reservoir hill, face half shaved, half lathered, rifle across the handlebars. Finally he reached Old Hayes Farm, to find the farmer already had the airman, who could not speak any English, cornered in the stockyard with a shotgun aimed at him. The airman turned out to be a Polish trainee pilot, learning to fly Tigermoth aircraft at RAF Desford.'[56]

Front of If the invader comes leaflet, which, according to his diary, is believed to be written by Harold Nicolson, Labour MP for West Leicester and Parliamentary Secretary to the Ministry of Information.

Anti-Invasion Preparations

An announcement was made on 13 June 1940 that henceforth church bells would remain silent except as a warning to announce the landing of enemy paratroopers in that parish.[57] But not everyone took the scheme seriously, particularly the bellringers of Emmanuel Parish Church, Loughborough.

'It appears some of the Home Guard are unable to tell the difference between the agitated pulling of bells to announce the arrival of the Hun and the more measured beating and mingling of the Grammar School and Emmanuel clocks. This being so, we have bowed to the wish of the authority, though with a certain amount of amusement in our minds.'[58]

The Stay where you are *leaflet was delivered to every household in July/August 1940.*

'There Is Not An Hour To Waste'

On 22 June 1940 local newspapers published silhouettes of German troop-carrying aircraft, under such alarming titles as 'THESE PLANES MEAN INVASION', urging readers to hang the illustrations in prominent places.[59] Two weeks later, the Regional Commissioner for the North Midland area appealed to the 'patriotism as well as the instinct of self-preservation of the farming community', by ordering farmers to obstruct all fields over 300 yards long at once, to prevent invading aircraft using them as landing grounds – otherwise the military would implement the obstructions themselves. 'The need for this precaution against the threatened invasion of this part of England is so vitally urgent, even the presence of growing crops cannot be regarded as an excuse.' Old farm carts and machinery or strong upright posts were said to be the best obstructions suitable for damaging landing aircraft.[60]

The Leicestershire 'Paraslasher'

Meanwhile, others thought about defeating the parachutists before they had even landed. In the August 1975 issue of *Pilot* magazine, a locally-produced, Heath-Robinson invention was described:

'Most bizarre of all was a device called Paraslasher, which was invented by George Reid of the Reid and Sigrist Training School, Desford. Pure *Dad's Army* in conception, the Paraslasher was a farmer's hand scythe attached to an eight-foot pole projecting through a Tiger Moth's [biplane] floor so that it lay flat along the fuselage but could be swung down vertically when required. The Tiger Moths, it was thought, would fly among invading German paratroops cutting canopies and shroudlines and further harassing those who made it safely to the ground, and was enthusiastically demonstrated by chief flying officer George Lowdell, wheeling around Desford like a demented Dervish, slashing away at life-sized effigies of Hitler and Mussolini...The prospect of being split asunder by 18-inches of cold steel travelling at 90-odd mph was scarcely relishing, and it might just have worked...'[61]

But it does not take much to realise a slow biplane hitting another object at 90mph would probably be enough to bring them both crashing down. Also, would the far more adept German fighter escorts have been sitting back and watching all this happen?

All Roads Lead To...?

Had the invader reached Leicester, it was planned he would not know he was here. On 19 June 1940 'a big army of painters and sign erectors' went around blotting out the word 'Leicester' from signs, even from the sides of city buses and trams. The police made an inspection the following day. But as a columnist in the *Illustrated Leicester Chronicle* noted, the name blackout was far from perfect.

'Concealing place names out in the country was a stiff enough task, but when it comes to hiding the identity of a city of the size of Leicester – well, it just can't be done with any completeness. I do not think it advisable to discuss unexpected places in which you may find the word LEICESTER visible to the naked eye just in case these lines should find their way into Germany, but, believe me, if you look around you, you will find a score or more.

Some concealment of placenames has its moments of humour, too. One signpost, not many miles out of Leicester, has had its four arms chopped off, but a wag has nailed on to the post of a single board, bearing the inscription 'To Berlin'...an excellent way of confusing the enemy.'[62]

Preparations were also made by the WVS to receive families evacuated from coastal areas in the event of a seaborne invasion. The WVS checked all available accommodation around Leicester. One school in each city ward would be used as a 'clearing house', from where the evacuees would be distributed to billets around Leicester. Part of the plan was to requisition and open empty houses.[63]

Getting Organised

The first proper attempt to organise the LDV was made on 24 June 1940, when local TA associations were made responsible for the administration of the force. They took on the responsibility for receiving and distributing all of the LDV's clothing, equipment and arms. At first, this was not particularly onerous, but as supplies became available it became all-consuming. As most TA staff had been called-up there were now fewer to handle this task, as the minutes of the Leicestershire and Rutland TA Association record: 'Since the last meeting of the Joint committee…a new formation [the LDV] has now come into being, which has more than taken up any time they had to spare through the disappearance of these TA units.'[64]

Getting Active

Patrolling became the main activity, as Quorn LDV Chris Long remembers:

'We used to patrol at night in twos along the railway to Rabbit Bridge, near Swithland reservoir, because they thought the Germans would land and put poison in the water. But there was that much undergrowth, we would never have seen them.'[65]

However, the LDV's keenness could lead to unfortunate incidents. Fred Parr, formerly a sergeant in Ab Kettleby Platoon, 5th (Belvoir) Battalion, remembers his platoon apprehending a 'spy':

'We had a report a suspicious-looking man had been seen walking about the village. One Sunday morning, we spotted him wandering about the cemetery and we got him. We questioned him but he didn't talk. Perhaps he was a foreigner? So we called the police and they drew us aside and told us "He's quite harmless. He's from Melton". He was a simple lad.'[66]

LDV Roadblocks

One of the main duties the LDV undertook was manning roadblocks. The ardour with which the LDV manned these roadblocks made them particularly unpopular with the motorist. Paul Billings remembers 'defending' Stoughton aerodrome,

'[We had] one Martini-Henry gun, which had been in service in the Boer War, and one rifle. Every time we set up a roadblock, we used to quarrel over who should hold the rifle. The main activity for

An RAF 'Queen Mary' transporter carrying newly made wing sections, most probably from Brush Works, Loughborough, passes through an improvised roadblock at the junction of Loughborough Road and Greengate Lane, Birstall. Meanwhile, a steam-powered lorry unloads further concrete sewer pipe sections as the roadblock is built, summer 1940.

the Home Guard on the road to Stoughton aerodrome was checking passes. Most of our business came from doctors and their girlfriends. One of the doctors used to get really angry, so he was the one we stopped each time.'[67]

And it wasn't just civilians that were inconvenienced, as Robert Beardsley, then of Quorn LDV, recalls: 'We stopped one officer in his car on the way to Beaumanor and he was so furious he said he'd have us shot!'[68]

But Frederick Gerrard remembers the job did have its perks:

The original caption states 'A Leicester Home Guard anti-tank section capture their first "Nazi" Whippet tank, Thursday 5 September 1940.' The tank is made from corrugated iron sheeting and an oil drum, while the driver wears a miner's helmet backwards. If only it would have been this easy in real life...

'I worked as a butcher's boy and joined the Groby LDV at the time of Dunkirk. I was 16, but I had to put 17 on the form and altered my date of birth. We used to stand guard at a roadblock on the A50 bridge over the Glenfield brook. One day a busload of women arrived, out on the drink. Us lads checked their identity cards – among other things!'[69]

But it wasn't all light-hearted, particularly at night. On 3 June 1940 PC T.D. Bingham was manning a road barricade with LDVs when he saw headlights approaching. An LDV advanced carrying a hurricane lamp with a bright red light, which he waved horizontally to signal the driver to stop. But the LDV had to jump out of the way as the driver did not slow and struck another LDV with the wing of his car, slightly injuring him. Another LDV tried to jump out of the way but was pinned against the barrier by the car, badly injured. PC Bingham challenged the driver, a 36-year-old doctor from Whitwick, who was clearly drunk. While travelling under arrest he became abusive and wanted to fight. He was fined £20 (£620) with £3 2s (£93) costs and banned from driving for 10 years. In court, he suggested he would be more use to the country if he joined the services rather than go to prison. The magistrates agreed and the doctor undertook to join the army immediately.[70]

It was not until November 1940, with the onset of winter and a reduced threat of invasion, that the LDV's enthusiastic patrolling and roadblocking was relaxed.

Early Exercises

Even though the LDV were still evolving, full field exercises were undertaken. Plans survive showing No. 6 Platoon (Braunstone Aero Club), 'B' (West City) Company, Leicester LDV staged a tactical exercise in the defence of Braunstone Aerodrome on 18 July 1940. Their basic nature is apparent:

'No. 6 Platoon, 'B' Company, LDV
PROPOSED TACTICAL EXERCISE

DIRECTIONS: The enemy will be represented by individuals carrying white flags, which will be raised and moved from point to point to convey the position of landings. Each flag should be assumed to be 24 of the enemy. After the landings the white flags and rattles will represent machine gun fire. Troop carrier planes will be represented by motor cars with a white flag.

The Group Commander of Kirby District will be advised so that sections under his command may take part. Umpires will be with each section to advise what is actually happening, as it may not be possible for them to see what is happening, whereas in the real thing they would obviously see planes dropping the parachutists.

ZERO 0.00.   3 groups of parachutists land at various points NW and within 700 yards of the 'drome gates. They proceed to move in the direction of the 'drome.

.05	No. 6 Platoon occupy Action Station No. 3. Reports are transmitted, telephones destroyed and HQ established at 'drome gates.
.10	Parachutists press up road from Kirby and across fields NW forcing platoon to withdraw to position at "Airman's Rest". 2 groups of parachutists land N of 'drome and occupy northern boundary of 'drome.
.15	One group of parachutists lands west of "Airman's Rest" and advances to occupy buildings. No. 6 Platoon withdraws and occupies position west of road on the south end of the spinney south of the "Airmen's Rest" and also holds road.
.20	Enemy occupies 'drome and advances down western boundary.
.24 Approx.	Military arrive at Braunstone crossroads. The enemy position will be roughly indicated by the white flags.
.30 Approx.	Two carrier planes land on 'drome. Their personnel coming under fire from the east end of the 'drome. They proceed to consolidate the west end with a view to providing a defence for further landings at this end of the 'drome.
1.00	Exercise complete – Stand Fast – Commanders' conference.'[71]

Defeatist Talk

While the majority of the population did their utmost to help the country, there were those whose words did otherwise. In response, the Defence Regulations even clamped down on free speech, prohibiting defeatist talk.

On 17 July 1940 a 31-year-old teacher of Ratcliffe Road, Leicester, from a well-known Loughborough family, was sentenced to two months' imprisonment and fined £20 (£620) for 'endeavouring to cause disaffection among army officers' with whom she shared a house, in the first case of its kind in Leicester.

On the subject of the war, she 'expressed most violently pro-Nazi and anti-British views,' such as 'To be quite frank, I think you are a lot of BFs to wear that uniform. All army officers are fools to take part in war against Hitler,' 'if Hitler thinks he is right, he is right,' 'the English have no guts. The Germans are highly cultured people,' and 'if the Germans came here I should not resist them.' On 18 June, after listening to Churchill's famous Finest Hour speech, she remarked 'What utter tripe!' She said she had visited Germany, admired that country and said the Nazi regime was 'a fine thing,' and 'a good thing for England if it came here'.

In court she denied she was pro-Nazi, her solicitor stating she was naturally argumentative, neurotic 'and a very foolish person'. He suggested 'sometimes women were not so careful as men in these matters, and did not realise the seriousness'. When her father was called as witness, she began to cry and had to be assisted from the court on the passing of the sentence.[72]

Defeatist talk was also reported in Ashby, leading to the summonsing of an Appleby Magna farmer on 20 July 1940 for 'making a statement likely to cause alarm'. A police detective overheard three farmers in the smoke room of the Queens Hotel, Ashby. The Appleby Magna farmer said 'They will beat us easily. They have taken all the countries they wanted so far, and a small country like this cannot stop them coming here.' One of the other farmers told the defendant to be 'more optimistic,' but he replied 'They have only sent one or two 'planes over, but wait until they send a thousand or two.' At that point several people walked out of the room. Another witness said the defendant stated about a dozen times the Germans would win. In his defence, the defendant's legal adviser said the farmer had 'been a fool'. Fining the defendant 25 guineas, the Chairman of the Bench said 'If you had been in Germany you would not come before a Bench, but been put against a wall.'[73]

'An Intolerable State of Affairs'

Nearly two months had elapsed since the LDV's formation, but still little headway had been made in equipping them. In lieu of uniforms, a locally-produced LDV armlet was issued. Doreen Boulter remembers:

'Father went out and joined the LDV and came home with an armband. Mother gave one look and said "What are you going to do with that if the Jerries come? Choke 'em with yer armband?"'[74]

This was a measly stopgap: an armlet was no uniform. And they still had very few weapons; an NCO in Fleckney LDV 'discovering a shortage of arms, sent one of his men on duty with a .22 rifle and a bandolier of .303 ammunition'.[75]

Throughout the country there was a desperate lack of arms. Wakefield bemoaned:
'Sunday 24:6:40. The LDV want to withdraw our four rifles and give us shotguns instead. Shotguns won't be much use for dealing with landings on the meadow and L.G.R. has refused to hand over our little armoury without a written order from the company commander.'[76]

Circumstances in Leicester were little better. The first 40 Ross rifles reached North Leicester's 'D' Company LDV on 4 July 1940.[77] But this still meant there was an approximate ratio of only one rifle to every 35 men. To some, the inadequate situation reached boiling point, and they complained forcefully to their superiors

'To O.C. 'B' Company from R. Eric Pochin, No. 6 Platoon [Braunstone Aero Club Platoon, West Leicester], 5.7.1940: Sir, I have the honour to bring to your notice the following facts and to request representation be made to the necessary higher authority that instant action should be taken.

In the first inadequate issue of rifles there was no equipment for cleaning, nor were the arms provided with slings, with the consequence the members of the Platoon under my command were compelled to extemporise. In fact, what can only be described as a "slip-shod" method of equipping this force has been aggravated by the provision of bayonets without any means of wearing them.

This means the men will have to resort to any temporary expedient they can manage, such as pieces of rope or string, and I venture to suggest this is an intolerable state of affairs and one which never need exist had efficient organisation prevailed…It not only detracts from the efficiency of the corps but brings ridicule upon it, which is resented by the ex-service members who naturally expect to be provided with such gear as will enable them to maintain the dignity of the British Army.

I trust immediate steps may be taken to rectify this matter.

I have the honour to be, Sir, your obedient servant…'[78]

But the reply received five days later was curt and to the point 'With reference to your memo of the 5th inst. Frequent representations are being made to higher authorities for better equipment, and while the position is very unsatisfactory, as far as I can ascertain, we are receiving our fair share…G. Russell, OC Coy.'[79]

In essence, there were more needy vulnerable areas such as the coast, rather than land-locked Leicestershire!

Between 579 LDVs in Rutland there were 135 P14 rifles, 85 Canadian Ross rifles and 30 12-bore shotguns. Authority was received in late July for Rutland LDV to become a battalion with a strength of 850, 'which gave hope of more arms…[but] the men were becoming very weapon hungry and it was difficult to convince them that no more were available'.[80]

It was now up to the WO to at least partially meet the volunteers' demands, otherwise despondency and apathy, or alternatively vigilantism, would set in. As Platoon leader Pochin wrote to accept the current limitations would be 'almost treasonable'.[81] The volunteers began to doubt how seriously the government were taking them.

A section of Groby Home Guard, outside Stamford Arms on the corner of Markfield Road and Ratby Road, late 1940. No wonder they do not look very happy: the ninth and 10th Home Guards have no weapons. The eighth Home Guard has a dummy wooden rifle, as does the third, partially hidden by the Home Guard kneeling with the Lewis machine gun. (Jim Briggs)

From LDVs to Home Guards

The government responded slowly. On 14 July 1940 Churchill referred to the LDV as the 'Home Guard'.[82] In response, Nazi Propaganda Minister Doctor Goebbels spoke some truth for once, although his vituperation was somewhat lost in translation, 'Churchill has spoken of Home Guards under arms. We ask what arms? Broomsticks or the arms of the local pub, with pots of beer and darts in their hands?'[83] Nonetheless, the new name was an improvement on the officious and nondescript Local Defence Volunteers, which Churchill thought 'uninspiring'.[84]

Although the Home Guard name is now generally associated with Churchill – he had used the phrase in 1939 – he did not invent it; Confederate Home Guard militia units had been founded in 1862 and participated in the American Civil War.[85] The LDV officially became the Home Guard on 23 July 1940, but locally the transition occurred on 31 July.[86]

Over the coming weeks, further small but important morale-boosting improvements were made, such as the issue of some uniforms, albeit often ill-fitting and sporadic. At the start of August 1940 the Home Guard were affiliated to their local regiments and allowed to wear the regimental badge.

There were now 18,495 men in Leicestershire Home Guard and 604 in Rutland. In Leicester alone, 8,283 men had come forward.[87] Their commanders held 'many conferences' to discuss the 'most effective operational use of…an ill-armed, semi-trained but enthusiastic body of men, spread over a large area'.[88] Most importantly, throughout August stocks of rifles and new instructions giving the Home Guard a more aggressive role were received.[89] At last, the men began to feel they were beginning to be taken more seriously.

Arms at Last

Although British weapon production grew steadily, the government appealed to the US for arms to replace those lost in Europe. The US officially remained neutral, but stated they wished to support democratic nations, so they supplied Britain with 75,000 mothballed Ross rifles and 100,000 P17 rifles. It took until July for the weapons to reach Britain. It appears Leicestershire's first P17s arrived a month later, with 490 reaching the 1st (North Leicester) Battalion on the 14 August 1940.[90] Col. Ogilvy-Dalgleish records Rutland had to hold on to their P14s and Ross rifles until November 1940, when they were replaced by 610 P17 Springfield rifles with bayonets.[91] Due to the rushed nature of supply, 'Arms and equipment began to arrive by lorry in large quantities without warning, usually at the most inconvenient times.'[92]

The Home Guards' joy at finally receiving these weapons was not diminished by the messy task of degreasing the crated rifles. Leslie Furnival, formerly a corporal in Croft Platoon, 3rd (West Leicester) Battalion, recalls the rifles 'had to be put in a tub by the fire to melt the grease off before they could be used'.[93] The new delivery meant that now one in three Home Guards were armed: not brilliant, but at least some could now put up a fight.

But no amount of enthusiasm could make up for lack of experience, as Robert Beardsley, formerly of the Quorn Home Guard, explains:

'I remember when one young fellow first received his rifle, he didn't realise the kick it had and got a bloody nose. Later, when I was first issued with a Lewis gun, I took it home and placed it on the kitchen table. I blindfolded myself and reassembled the pieces "in the dark". We were finally issued with ammunition and I ran through the procedure for if the gun jammed. Well, I did this and there was a big bang and puff of smoke! My old mum came dashing in and asked what had happened. My father didn't hear anything as he was fast asleep! The result was a mangled piece of lead and a hole the size of my fist in the kitchen cupboard!'[94]

Fined for Leaving the Enemy Transport

On 28 August 1940 the first case was heard under the new order, compelling the immobilisation of motor vehicles. A 40-year-old haulage contractor from Leicester was fined 20s, after leaving the keys in his car's ignition and the doors unlocked in Narborough.[95]

'Parachute Fever'

As summer drew out and no invasion materialised, rather than having a deflationary effect, the public grew more anxious and wondered why Hitler had not come. Ever on the lookout, their increased vigilance led to 'parachute fever'. Preceding the UFO sightings of the following 60 years, any unidentified object in the sky was more often than not reported to the authorities as paratroops landing. The Home Guard engaged on several wild-goose chases, notably on 20 August 1940. Parachutists were reported at Coalville and Loughborough.[96] Wakefield responded to the call:

'Tuesday 20:8:40. All quiet today until 5pm when Capt. Lewis rang up telling us to take special precautions, as parachutists had landed at Quorn and surrounding district. It was an inconvenient time of day but I managed to collect 14 others as a scratch section to man our fire posts and the two main gates. We hadn't

HOME GUARD
INSTRUCTION No. 15—1940

COMMON GERMAN MILITARY EXPRESSIONS

English	German	Pronunciation
Halt! Who goes there?	Halt! Wer da?	HARLT. VAIR DAR?
Hands up!	Hände hoch!	HENDER HOCH.
Come closer!	Kommt hierher!	KOMMT HEAR-HAIR
Surrender.	Ergebt euch	AIRGAYBT OICK.
Do not shoot.	Nicht schiessen	NICKT SHEESSEN.
Throw down your arms.	Waffen hinlegen.	VAFFEN HIN-LAYGEN.
Stand still.	Stehen bleiben.	SHTAYEN BLYBEN.
Go in front of me.	Vorausgehen.	FOR-OWSE-GAYEN.
Forward!	Vorwärts!	FOR-VAIRTS.
At once!	Sofort!	SOFORT.
Double!	Marsch! Marsch!	MARSH MARSH.
Faster!	Schneller!	SHNELLAIR.
Slower!	Langsam!	LUNGSUM.
Left!	Links!	LINKS.
Right!	Rechts!	WRECHTS.
Stop!	Halt!	HARLT.
Come back!	Kommt zurück!	KOMMT TSOORICK.

NOTE.—The pronunciation given in Column 3 is the nearest English equivalent to the German sounds. The exact pronunciation can only be learned from a German speaker.

Prepared under the direction of The Chief of the Imperial General Staff.

THE WAR OFFICE,
20th September, 1940.

Official Home Guard Instruction Common German Military Expressions, dated September 1940. Phrases included are: 'Hande hoch!' (hands up); 'Ergebt Euch' (surrender) and 'Kommt zuruck' (come back)!

been there very long before Section Leader Van Zwannenberg reported he had seen a parachute come down in the Normanton direction. L.G. Reid arrived, got in touch with Capt. C.K. Lewis our Company Commander. The three of us with W. Mercer drove over the hills to where the parachute had been reported. Nothing was to be seen until a huge barrage balloon came blowing along in the wind. Until it was quite near it looked remarkably like a parachute with a man on it, but balloon it was. After shorting the grid wires with its trailing wire it shot up and disappeared into the clouds.'[97]

Such episodes may seem risible now, yet they were not completely without basis, as Col. Ogilvy-Dalgleish explained, 'Later on, enemy agents were dropped in different parts of the country to report on the general situation in Britain, one was picked up by a Home Guard over the border in Northamptonshire, complete with W/T transmitter. We and the Police had to be particularly alert for these agents.'[98]

'CROMWELL': The Invasion Scare Peaks

Without warning, on Saturday 7 September 1940 the Luftwaffe suddenly blitzed London. This surprise move at first confused the defenders and then worried them: was this the precursor to invasion? Nationally, the codeword CROMWELL was issued, meaning 'conditions suitable for invasion'. However, in the heightened panic, many misunderstood CROMWELL, believing its announcement actually heralded invasion.

Leicestershire and Rutland received CROMWELL at 21.25 hrs from Northern Command. Tom Elliott recalls his father, Major C.A.B. Elliott, the Deputy Group Commander of the Leicester Home Guard, reacting to the alert:

'When CROMWELL came through, my father was rung up at our home – by the Oadby manual telephone exchange. In those days every time you wanted to make a phone call, you had to wind a handle to get through to the exchange and the operator would phone the number for you. However, my father was so anxious to get through to all the numbers on his Home Guard phone list that he told the operator to keep the line open for him, so all he had to do was lift the phone after each call and he would have the operator.'[99]

Throughout both counties Home Guards were 'standing to'. It may well have been this night Monica Turner, then a seven-year-old schoolgirl living in Stonesby, remembered. Her father, Cecil Branston, was called out:

'My brother and I were awakened by a thumping on our cottage door. It was dad's boss in the Home Guard. "Cis, come on, they've landed." Well, mum got we kids up, wellies on, the lot. Dad came downstairs in his uniform. I say "uniform" in the mild sense because his issue only got as far as a cap, a battledress about three sizes too big, and farm leggings. Dad said "All I've got is my hay fork." He never got as far as a rifle issue. I will remember to this day my dad and his mate going off, as they thought, to meet Jerry with a hay fork and a shepherd's crook to fight their own private war while we kids were congregating on the cricket field.'[100]

Many Home Guards lost a night's sleep as they peered up into the inky darkness looking for burly Nazi paratroopers descending from the night sky, but, as the dawn rose, the early light revealed no German boots had set foot on British soil – it had all been a false alarm. Locally, CROMWELL was cancelled later that day.[101]

In a strategic mistake of epic proportions, the Luftwaffe relieved the pressure on the battered RAF airfields and switched their campaign to London. As long as the RAF remained flying, the Luftwaffe would be unable to gain mastery of the British skies, without which there could be no invasion of Britain. But at this stage the British population were unaware of the significance of the recent events. In the days following, Britons remained on high alert.

At 00.02 hours on 16 September 1940 the Leicestershire Home Guard reported to the 50th Leicestershire Regiment that parachute troops had landed in the Highcross area on the A5. Two platoons of Regular troops were sent to meet the invaders, but instead found a crashed German bomber over the county border in Warwickshire, containing two dead.[102]

The Junkers Ju88 had flown into the Coventry balloon barrage, striking a cable. The bomber exploded over Hopsford Hall Farm, Withybrook. Two of the crew managed to bale out and were captured injured. The pilot and flight mechanic were killed in the explosion and buried in Nuneaton.[103] Two barrage balloons were found entwined around the wreckage, and it had probably been the sight of them descending with the falling bomber that had prompted the Home Guard to think they had seen paratroopers descending.

On 18 September 1940 the Home Guard were warned 'Cobweb-like material dropped from enemy aircraft: must not be handled.' What ghastly German chemical warfare trick was this? Wakefield was warned it was '...netting looking like cobwebs, which burns or blisters when touched'.[104] The truth was revealed six days later, when Northern Command reported the 'cobweblike material' was 'innocuous'. The mysterious Nazi secret weapon was just spider cobwebs, commonly found across meadows during late summer.[105]

Chasing CROMWELL'S Ghosts

As the summer faded into autumn, invasion jitters continued and, rather like the Keystone Cops, the Home Guard rushed to attend many false alarms. Len Hill, then a corporal in Scraptoft Platoon, recalled 'one night, one of our members came rushing in to say the Germans had landed, but when we went to investigate the huge "parachutes" they were really clouds of lime scattered on the fields'.[106]

Anstey Home Guard received a similar dramatic message: parachutes had been sighted in a field just outside the village. 'We duly arrived at the field and peered gingerly over the hedge' recalled Fred Jones. 'Sure enough, there on the grass lay haphazard shapes of fabric, evidence of the enemy's descent from the skies. Abandoned parachutes? No, it had been a windy night and bed linen and clothes had been blown from a washing line.'[107]

On Guard?

The partially-trained Home Guards continued to guard against invasion, but at times their inexperience with weaponry was revealed. Les Cook was in the Shepshed Home Guard: 'Our HQ was the boardroom at the Reservoir Houses, we were guarding the dam. One time, some of the lads had come up on relief, they were in high spirits, and there was a bit of larking about, one of them bumped his rifle on the floor and it fired. The incredible thing was that the bullet went through the ceiling and the bed occupied by the reservoir keeper and his wife, passing between them as they lay there!'[108]

Former Husbands Bosworth Home Guard Aneurin Owen recalls 'We used to patrol down to the Sibbertoft crossroads and then on to Cote Hill. One night, we heard a horse coming. One old boy jumped into a ditch by the track and said "I'll deal with this". When the horse reached him, he shouted "Halt! Who goes there or I fire! Advance and be recognised!" It turned out to be Lt-Col. Jack, CO of the 7th (Market Harborough) Battalion, coming from his manor to go on Home Guard duty. But the old boy still did not recognise him in the dark. Brigadier-General Jack said to him "What would you have done if I had not stopped?" The old boy unfortunately replied "I would have shot you up the bloody backside!" For which the old boy was reported for bad language!'[109]

Former Groby Home Guard N. Jarvis remembers the Home Guard causing an invasion scare themselves 'One night I was on duty with my mate. As the guards handed the gun over one of them accidentally pulled the trigger and the bullet went through the window of the fire station. The firemen ran out really frightened thinking the Germans had come.'[110]

Leicestershire Home Guard's First Fatal Casualty

On 17 September 1940, a warm, late-summer's day, the village Home Guard platoon were carrying out manoeuvres on Hall Field, Sutton Bonington. As part of the exercise, they advanced and then dived down into the corn. However, when they rose, one man was missing: Section Leader George Monk, who ran the saw mill, had collapsed and died from a heart attack. A Nottingham evacuee saw Monk being carried out of the field on a gate.[111] Mr Monk's funeral was held five days later at St Anne's Church, Sutton Bonington. A detachment of the Home Guard under Mr H.G. Robinson escorted the coffin, which was draped with a Union Jack and carried by Mr Monk's workmen. A member of the Home Guard carried his World War One medals. The whole village turned out for the funeral.[112] George Monk had the dubious honour of being the county's first Home Guard fatality; sadly, he would not be the last.

The Homeless Home Guard

The Home Guard was now up and running, yet they had no home. Due to the population's transient nature, plus billeted evacuees and troops, accommodation was short. In Oakham, the Home Guard struggled to find a home, as Ogilvy-Dalgleish explains:

'During the first five months or so the Bn had no satisfactory HQ, the first issue of rifles and ammunition and driblets of equipment were dumped at the Old Police Station, which was very cramped. I remember checking ammunition, etc, with Cahusac in a cell. By June 1940 the Drill Hall was vacant and we were allowed the use of one room officially and the rest of the building unofficially, and on sufferance with the liability of immediate eviction. I therefore had two HQs, the Drill Hall normally and, at action stations, my house, where there was plenty of space and whence we should not be turned out by Authority. By degrees as men and equipment increased, we were using the Drill Hall fully, though unofficially...The Drill Hall was quite essential as Bn HQ and training quarters in a country area where no other suitable building was available...'[113]

Sutton Bonington Home Guard lead the funeral cortège to St Anne's Church of Section Leader George Monk who collapsed and died during an exercise on Tuesday 17 September 1940. Tragically he became the first of 18 known Leicestershire Home Guards to lose their lives while serving in the force.

However, not all Home Guard units were so fortunate, and even if they did possess quarters they were not always satisfactory, as No. 16 Platoon, 1st (North Leicester) Battalion, noted in April 1941: 'One bed collapsed, others need overhaul, hut telephone not working, ammo box lock not working, no key for side gate, tea supply exhausted – nothing further to report.'

The trouble persisted a month later, although this time the occurrence seemed to be somewhat malicious!

'Situation report: Several blankets were found to be in a dirty and fouled condition and unfit for use owing to a hedgehog having been placed within the pile.' [114]

Blackouts and Red Faces

From late 1940 German bombers were seen more frequently over the Midlands. As a result, ARP blackout measures became more important and householders could be fined for showing lights. Previously, the preserve of ARP Wardens, now Home Guards, also looked out for blackout breaches and vigorously enforced the law.

A householder from Broom Leys Road, Coalville, was fined 30s with 5s costs after 'allowing a light to be seen from his house'. Local Home Guard Frank Smith found there was no one in the house so had smashed his way in with his rifle and put the light out.[115]

However, much to their embarrassment, the Home Guard could not afford to be too pious. On 26 October 1940 Lt-Col. Packe, Second in Command of the Leicestershire Home Guard, appeared in court for breaching the blackout at his mansion, Great Glen Hall, Great Glen. A Special Constable and ARP warden had spotted four windows improperly blacked-out on one side of the hall, three more on the other side and a further two with no blackout at all. The warden said he had previously informed the Colonel his lights could be seen for 200 yards. The Colonel had argued the lights could not be seen from the air.

In his defence, Colonel Packe stated his home had 43 windows and some awkward corridors to blackout. Spreading the blame, he said there was 'a certain number of irresponsible people living at the hall, and he felt he was not altogether responsible for what happened'. Rancorously, he stated 'I have never been charged with anything before in my life and I rather resent being summoned now on the present charge, as it seems to imply I am failing in my duty.' Reminding him the law applied to all, the Court Chairman fined him £2 [£62] with 15s costs.[116]

Home Guard Blackout Tragedy

The blackout caused the Leicestershire Home Guard further grief on 5 October 1940. Home Guard Bert Martin, of Derby Road, Hinckley, an electrician at the Leicestershire and North Warwickshire Power Station, Hinckley, fell seven feet into an ash pit while patrolling in the blackout with a 16-year-old Home Guard. An inquest heard the 42-year-old suffered an injury to his spine and died two weeks later at the Leicester Royal Infirmary. The Coroner recorded a verdict of accidental death.[117]

The Leicestershire Blitz

For almost two months the Luftwaffe had concentrated their Blitz on London. Recently, however, raiders had dropped bombs locally. During one such raid on 4 November 1940, 30-year-old Home Guard Sidney Smith, of Albert Street, Melton Mowbray, was one of the fatalities when a German lone-raider targeted the town's Brook Street gasworks.

War grave of Home Guard Bert Martin of A6 (North Leicestershire & Warwickshire Electric Power Company) Platoon, 8th (Market Bosworth) Battalion, who died on Saturday 19 October 1940.

Ten days later, the Luftwaffe switched their bombing campaign from the capital to the industrial provinces to target war production. Leicestershire residents watched the fiery sky as 449 bombers raided Coventry. That night, Germans did land in Leicestershire, but they no longer posed a danger. At 22.00 hrs a Dornier Do17Z crashed in flames at Prestwold Hall, Burton-on-the-Wolds, killing all four crew.[118] Local Home Guards, ARP and Police rushed to the scene but there was little they could do.[119]

On 19 November 1940 the Germans again invaded Leicestershire by air, when Leicester suffered its main 'Blitz Night'. Hundreds of high explosive bombs, incendiaries and parachute mines crashed down on the city, seriously damaging industrial and domestic property and killing 108 people. Two Leicester Home Guards were among the fatalities: Walter Alexander, 32, of Samuel Street, was killed at Southampton Street. John Stansfield, 28, was killed at his home on Allandale Road. It is not thought they were on Home Guard duty. [120]

However, the value of the Home Guard was shown when Kirby Muxloe was blitzed that night. 'The area of serious damage was cordoned off, the Home Guard giving valuable help…'[121] During air raids, Home Guards often helped shift rubble, rescue casualties and guard properties from looters. They cordoned off and guarded incidents and UXBs, keeping the public away from danger areas

The Home Guard: 'A Free People at War'?

On 1 December 1940 the Leicester Group Home Guard took part in a march past parade, with the salute taken by Lt-Gen. George Paynter. Afterwards, Mr Harold Nicolson, MP for West Leicester, addressed the parade at the Corn Exchange, Leicester. He gave a rousing speech, praising the Home Guard.

Harold Nicolson, Labour MP for Leicester West and Parliamentary Secretary to the Ministry of Information, talks to Colonel Copeman during the Home Guard's parade through Leicester on Sunday 1 December 1940. Mr Nicolson carries a boxed gasmask. The poster behind Colonel Copeman tells what motorists must do during an air raid.

'Mr Nicolson said it was an "astonishing tribute to the self-sacrifice and patriotism of the men of this country that within six months, the Home Guard had approached the great figure of one million seven hundred thousand – more than seventeen times in excess of what Mr Eden had originally hoped." That invasion was intended and indeed imminent was beyond question….The moral effect of the Home Guard is enormous. And they give to the world an example which is inspiring and impressive: the example, not of a mass of conscripts herded into battle, but of a free people at war.'[122]

But was this really the case? The two counties' Home Guard now totalled 22,000 men.[123] Yet, as the force developed, more and more control was rested from local Home Guard commanders to the WO. As with the Home Guard's Volunteer predecessors, the force had originally been formed and organised from grass-root level. But, increasingly, orders from above started to curtail this autonomy, as the WO reined the power of the Home Guard back in. In November 1940 orders were received that battalions were to be numbered consecutively and, soon, standard army ranks would be introduced in place of the Home Guard's original system of appointments. This was not such a bad thing. Standardisation with the Regular Army gave the Home Guard a more official military feel. Not veering off in its own direction also saved money and resources. Despite losing their original independence, the Home Guard were now being treated as a proper fighting force.

Lieutenant-General George Paynter takes the salute as Home Guards march past Leicester's Lancaster Road fire station, Sunday 1 December 1940.

Listening for the Christmas Bells

Some, such as P.S. Wakefield, chose to remain vigilant in case the Germans chose to exploit the Christmas lull. Others, to Wakefield's chagrin, took full advantage of the rest period.

'Xmas Day: Wednesday 25:12:40. No raids last night and no sirens today yet, but most of us Home Guards are spending the holiday in uniform ready to turn out on "man posts" or the sound of church bells. I have promised to go and see Cpl Bennets's section on guard tonight.

Boxing Day: Thursday 26:12:40. Went with Ryan to visit the Morris South Works. Found Cpl Nix and one man! His other five had failed to report for duty. Called round to PC Cumberlands's house in the dark and fog and told him. Spent the day with the family. Am keeping uniform handy these nights and sometimes dream I'm hearing church bells!'[124]

1941: 'Let Us Prepare'

'The year 1940, with its cares, its sorrows and its joys, has gone – gone – but not forgotten. We shall never forget one thing, and that is how unprepared we were.

The New Year – 1941 – is now here, and are we – are you yourself – satisfied that we are fully prepared? Prepared to meet a fully-trained enemy face to face, even at the point of a bayonet. Don't let us underestimate his skill and cunning. Don't imagine because you have a suit of denim overalls, and a rifle and a few rounds of ammunition, you are a fully trained soldier…

Now lads, let us forget how many parades we missed in 1940 and seriously get down to it in 1941. It is serious. Don't let us have to wait for a bomb, or a thousand incendiaries to drop, or a few troop carriers to arrive in Loughborough to make us realise how serious it is.

Motto for 1941: If a thing's worth doing, it's worth doing well.'

'ELECTRA'
'B' Company, 9th (Loughborough) Battalion,
Leicestershire Home Guard,
January 1941.[125]

Loughborough Home Guard Accidentally Killed By 'Bosom Pal'

On 26 February 1941 19-year-old Loughborough College student Owen John Hale was accidentally shot dead by a fellow student.[126] The two Home Guards, described as 'bosom pals', were on duty at a house in Ashby Road.

That night, Hale had been armed with a revolver and the other Home Guard with a Ross rifle and five rounds of ammunition. They decided to practise aiming, one sitting either side of a table. Hale apparently sat behind the target and looked through a small hole in it 'to check the alignment of the sights of the rifle' held by the other Home Guard. Hale's face was about a foot away from the rifle muzzle. When asked by the Coroner if he remembered snapping the trigger, the young Home Guard broke down and sobbed. He was horrified at what had happened and he had not realised the rifle had been loaded. In witness, Loughborough Home Guard Battalion Commander Lt-Col. S.K. Lewis stated Home Guards had been told rifles were not to be loaded without orders. John A. Choate, a tutor at the college and also the Platoon Commander, held up the rifle in court and showed the safety catch worked. The College Principal, Dr Herbert Schofield, stated Hale had been a student of whom any college could be proud and never since Loughborough College had been founded had it been so moved as by this tragic event.

The inquest jury returned a verdict of accidental death, but also severely censured the Home Guard who fired the fatal shot for disobeying Home Guard standing orders.[127] Volunteer Hale was buried at Minehead Cemetery in his native Somerset.[128]

Memorable March

Several notable events happened in March 1941. The first list of Home Guard Officer commissions was published on 20 March.[129] The Home Guard was now no longer ranked by 'appointments' but army commissions. In the first six months of 1941, a total of 730 officers were commissioned in Leicestershire and Rutland, including 3 colonels, 15 lt.-colonels, 78 majors, 80 captains, 297 lieutenants and 257 2nd lieutenants.[130] The force could now stand on its own two feet.

On 4 March the Duke of Kent, accompanied by the Regional Commissioner Lord Trent, visited Leicester and Loughborough, inspecting the Home Guard, among other services, at the Brush Works in Loughborough. The Duke was received by the heads of the firm, Mayor Councillor G. Hill and Town Clerk A. Gwynne Davies.[131] Newly-promoted Captain P.S. Wakefield eagerly recorded the Duke's tour of the Brush Works:

'Wednesday 5:3:41. Well, the great day is over and I have commanded a Royal Guard of Honour. We had 60 NCOs and men in a preliminary parade on the tip at 4pm yesterday. Then, off we marched at the slope with bayonets fixed, halted in front of the main steps and were ready with officers in position by 4.35. HRH was late, so we had a few minutes' practice salutes, including one (given by LGR) for the Chairman, Sir Ronald Matthews, who inspected the guard and then at 5.15 – about – the gates opened, the car rolled in, I gave "Guard Shun! Slope Arms!" facing them, then turned to the front and gave "Present Arms!" as HRH stepped out of his car. He kept me at the present rather longer than he ought, I think, by receiving the Directors and the Mayor on the steps instead of returning the guard salute first and it was only as he approached the guard that I asked the ADC whether I should slope! All went well, both ranks were inspected, then LGR presented Blunt Mears and myself. A short chat about our Home Guard Company and the Royal Party turned away. That left me free to march the guard off to the tip again, unfix, slope

HRH the Duke of Kent talks to Home Guard Volunteer Mumford during the royal visit to the Brush Works, Loughborough, on 4 March 1941. Major P.S. Wakefield stands in the centre. (Martin Foster)

again, "fall out the officers" and dismiss. Then tea! Mr Midgley rang me up again this morning to tell me that HRH and ADC had told the Directors just before leaving how pleased they were with us.'[132]

Inter-County Rivalry

Despite Leicestershire and Rutland's traditional rivalry, both counties' Home Guard co-operated well. However, the same cannot be said about their larger neighbour Northamptonshire, as former Oadby Home Guard Bernard Elliott recalls:

'LEICESTERSHIRE v NORTHAMPTONSHIRE: – or how a bus-load of dead men saved Leicester

On April 5th and 6th 1941 I, myself, took part in a manoeuvre. The plan was for the Northamptonshire Home Guard to capture Leicester. This meant the HGs of Market Harborough, Kibworth and Oadby had to stop the "enemy" from reaching their objective.

The Oadby HG, of which I was an insignificant member, was ordered to report to Wistow Park, which was to be its area of operations. On arrival there about 11 o'clock on the Saturday morning, we took up our stations behind the hedgerows in the park ready to repel the enemy.

The day wore on but no enemy appeared in sight, so about eight o'clock in the evening the sergeant in charge, Sergeant Shute, decided on a route march to see if they could be located.

The march took us through Great Glen and as we were passing the local pub, Sergeant Shute suddenly conceived the idea the enemy might have sought shelter therein.

The patrol entered The Greyhound to see if the idea was correct, but it was not. The only occupant was the landlord, who greeted us with the remark "Have you caught any Germans today?"

Ignoring his impertinence, our sergeant asked if he had seen anything of the Northamptonshire HG.

"No" he replied sardonically, "the only people who have been in here tonight were a couple of proper soldiers."

Having quenched our thirst with half a pint each (beer was in short supply at that time), we made our way back to Wistow Park. Then we bedded down for the night…

That Sunday morning we took up our positions once more in the park, hoping the enemy would soon arrive, but, as on the previous day, he did not. We were getting thoroughly browned off when suddenly it happened – a Rolls-Royce entered Wistow Park with a red flag on its bonnet. This was clearly the car of the officer who was officiating as umpire.

Indeed, an officer, with red braid around his cap, alighted from the car, and in a stentorian voice shouted "Who is in charge here?" Sergeant Shute replied that he was, as the Oadby officer in command,

Major Hind, had recently been summoned to his HQ in The Crown at Glen. There followed a prolonged silence, after which the umpire looked Sergeant Shute straight in the eyes and said "You're dead. For the past two hours your company has been bombarded with artillery fire from the Gumley Heights"...

At this point, another member of the Oadby HG (an innkeeper) whispered to Sergeant Shute. Shute, having regained his usual composure, asked the umpire "Sir, if we are dead, can we go home?"

This unmilitary request took the officer by surprise, and he said he would have to consult a superior authority before answering the request. He promised to return with an answer in a short time.

He had not returned after half an hour, so Shute rang up the Midland Red and asked them to send a bus to Wistow Park as soon as possible. It soon arrived and the "dead men" of Oadby embarked. Shute asked the driver to return to Oadby via Wigston in case the umpire returned and, having found we had gone, set out for us on the usual road.

Just before reaching Wigston we noticed some army trucks on the side of the road, and coming nearer we suddenly realised that these were the enemy whose approach we had hourly expected when we were "alive".

On reaching them, Shute stopped the bus, jumped out and asked them if he could be of any assistance. The Northamptonshire HG officer replied that they were somewhat lost. At that time all signposts had been removed. The sergeant volunteered to help them find their way to Leicester. "You see that cross-roads in the distance," he said. "Well, when you get there, turn left and you will be in Leicester in an hour."

Thanking the sergeant for his help, the officer climbed into his truck and continued on the way the sergeant had directed.

What he and his men said when they realised they had been wrongly directed and should have turned right instead of left can be best left to the imagination. The Northamptonshire Home Guard never reached the centre of Leicester...but neither, for that matter, did the Germans.'[133]

Leicestershire and Rutland Home Guard Capture Nazi Airmen as Two Bombers are Shot Down in Two Days

No. 1: Ratby Home Guard Trio Capture 'Nasty' Luftwaffe Duo

On the night of 8-9 April 1941, a heavy raid developed against Coventry. A Hurricane nightfighter of No. 151 Squadron, flown by Pilot Officer Richard Stevens, based at Wittering, was sent to intercept German bombers heading for the battered city. At 01.15 hrs, P/O Stevens shot down a Heinkel 111 over Warwickshire. Half an hour later, he shot down another Heinkel 111 G1+DL of 3/KG55. The bomber crashed in flames at Roes Rest Farm, Desford.[134] Despite strict wartime censorship, this dramatic story was too good for the local press to ignore.

'Hearing a crash during the night, a Leicestershire farmer, Mr Falder, looked out of the window of his lonely home and was astonished to find a tree in front of it had disappeared...in place of it were the remains of a German bomber. The tail, with its swastika tail marking, lay in the farmer's stockyard. The rest of the machine was 20 or 30 yards away in a little apple orchard right in front of the house...The crew of four were all captured, although two were injured. One officer, who was wounded, was wearing the Iron Cross [probably Hauptmann Otto Bodemeyer].' [135]

Two of the crew who bailed out were captured by Home Guards some miles away. One was the sergeant pilot, Oberfeldwebel Heinz Sollner, while the other was navigating officer Hauptmann Otto Bodemeyer, a valuable catch, as he was the Gruppenkommandeur of 1/KG55. Former Rothley Home Guard Sergeant F.W. Newcombe recalled:

'...while on duty at Rothley Temple [now Rothley Court Hotel]...three of my men were patrolling the lane towards Cropston, in the early morning, when they saw two men approaching them in grey uniform, who put their hands above their heads. They turned out to be a sergeant and a lieutenant of the German air force, who had crashed and had wandered along the country lanes until they reached Rothley.

I often thought this story would make a good *Dad's Army* tale because one of the men was walking behind the Germans with his rifle cocked and "one up the spout". The police came to the Temple with a car and took the captives to Loughborough, the unarmed policemen sitting in the front with the two Germans at the back – a bit risky because the sergeant [Oberfeldwebel Heinz Sollner] was quite a nasty piece of work!'[136]

Apparently, one of the Home Guards who captured the German aircrew was Sid Harris, a quiet man who was jokingly nicknamed Sharp Shot Sid forever afterwards. He had called 'Who goes there?' At which point the airmen had surrendered. Sid later recalled one of the Germans spoke perfect English and had apparently attended Manchester University before the war.[137] It is believed another of the Home Guards was John Henry Hill.[138]

The other two crew were fortunate to be thrown clear when the tail section broke away on impact. The first, Feldwebel Herbert Link, had been wounded in the attack by the RAF nightfighter and was the most badly injured. He was found by the farmer near the wreckage. The other injured airman, Feldwebel Hans Kaufold, was concussed and suffered minor burns. He later stated he managed to follow a minor path to a road but heard footsteps and hid behind a bush over a ditch. He heard shouting and barking as soldiers (Home Guards) searched for him and so he 'sat as still as a rabbit in the ditch and the seekers passed me by'. The bomber's fuel tanks and ammunition started to explode and soon the Fire Brigade arrived. After a while, Kaufhold noticed it was quieter and limped down the road. A car suddenly came around the corner and braked. A RAF officer stepped out and raised his revolver, shouting at Kaufhold to put his hands up. For Kaufhold the war was over.[139]

Following the incident, the *Leicester Mercury* presented Lt-Col. J.T.L. Baxter, CO of the 8th (Market Bosworth) Battalion, with souvenir photos of the crashed bomber, as he had been the first officer on the scene.

No. 2: Embarrassing Farce as Luftwaffe Airman Roams Rutland

The following night, on 9 April 1941, at 20.00 hrs, a fiercely-armed Junkers Ju88 C-4 nightfighter R4+CM of 4/NJG 2 took off from its Dutch base on an intruder sortie, hunting for RAF airbases. In the dark night sky, he failed to notice an equally-lethal RAF Beaufighter nightfighter, flown by Sgt S. Bennett and Sgt Curtiss of No. 25 Squadron from nearby RAF Wittering, gaining on him. At 22.10hrs, when the intruder was close to Oakham, all hell broke loose as the hunter became the hunted and the Beaufighter's cannon and machine guns ripped into its Junkers prey. Ironically, the aircraft crashed behind Rutland Home Guard Commander Col. Ogilvy-Dalgleish's home, Springfield House, by the Burley-Langham Road, towards the current site of Ashwell Prison. British Air Intelligence AI1 (g) officers examined the wreckage for clues.[140] Again, the *Leicester Mercury* reported 'Two Germans bailed out of the raider that was shot down in a Rutland town, but a third [pilot Gefreiter Franz Brotz] perished in the burnt-out wreckage.

Local farmer Mr Purrott, from a neighbouring village, said the plane was flying low over the rooftops. He rushed out and saw the plane crash with flames spurting from it. He looked into the sky and saw a parachute drifting down towards a wood at Barleythorpe. At the same time he saw another white object, which he thought was another parachute, drifting towards the town. He told wardens what he had seen and they walked across a field, but could find nothing. Purrott

Enemy Uniforms at a Glance leaflet, August 1941. A Home Guard has drawn some smiley faces on the German Paratroopers!

himself then took a shotgun, began a search in the fields and saw a parachute rolled up on the ground.

'As he drew near, [Gefreiter Ewald Gorlt] called out and raised his hands above his head. Mr Purrott kept him covered, but there was little need for that, for the man was injured and indicated he was suffering from a broken left leg on landing. Mr Purrott took from him an eight-inch clasp knife, which he had in his hip pocket.

'He then called out to Home Guards who were in the vicinity, and, with their aid, carried the man back to the village on a gate. He was then taken by ambulance to the Police Station and later to Ashwell Camp, where he was treated by a doctor, and then onto hospital.'

The first the Rutland Home Guard heard of the incident at their Oakham Drill Hall HQ is recalled by Burley Platoon Home Guard Jim Bradley:

'I was about 18. I cycled to the Drill Hall for night duty. I was told I would be on duty with a fellow Home Guard. But when I got there, there were several officers and sergeants waiting around and they said "Sorry, the other chap has not turned up, perhaps he'll turn up later. There is the telephone, but it never rings, so you needn't worry. In the meantime, you will have to guard the drill hall alone." And then they left me. Much later on, this blessed phone started to ring! I picked it up and I got this horrendous message that parachutists were landing at Barleythorpe. I was very raw at the time and didn't feel I could cope on my own, so I rang one of the top Home Guard officers. He was surprised by what I told him. He asked if I had told the police, which I thought was funny because I thought surely that's our job to be defending England? Anyway, it wasn't long before all the top officers arrived at the drill hall. I got an ear-bashing off one, who said I should have called him not the top man. This turned out because he had also been promised a financial incentive to catch the first German!'[141]

Meanwhile, Unteroffizier Willi Lindla, the radio operator, had landed safely by parachute in a field next to the Burley Road, where he buried his W/T notebook. Lindla had lost his flying boots while jumping out of the aircraft. Nonetheless, he decided to walk in his flying suit and socks to the nearest settlement, Langham, complete with his pistol still stuck in his belt.

In an episode that would have seemed implausible even in a *Dad's Army* storyline, Lindla passed several people, including a British soldier who bade him goodnight, but no one seemed to realise who Lindla was. A signalman at the Burley Road signalbox opened the level crossing gates for him and he walked into Langham where he asked in broken English where the police station was. When the locals finally realised who Lindla was, they asked him to wait a moment while the Home Guard were sought, who finally accompanied him to the police station. Lindla's notebook was later recovered and carefully examined by British Air Intelligence.[142]

The story passed into local folklore. However, as with many great tales, rumour and hearsay mythologised the incident. Mr Barratt of Gaul Street, Leicester, recorded one version in his diary: 'Mr Dawson, a lorry driver, was away on Home Guard duty that night, but his wife was at home when there was a knock at the door. She said later, whoever she asked was there gave such a strange-sounding reply that she didn't open the door. It turned out to be the "Nazi" trying to give himself up. The German airman then went further down the street and spoke to a firewatcher who couldn't understand him either, but, grasping the situation, called two fellow firewatchers and they escorted the "enemy" to the police station.'[143]

Not unsurprisingly, Col. Ogilvy-Dalgleish omitted all the farcical aspects with a calmer, sanitised version, 'One evening, in the Spring of 1941, an enemy bomber was shot down over Oakham by our fighters [sic]. I was returning from a training night at Hambleton when I saw the bomber, out of control and on fire, just clear the chimneys of Springfield and crash in flames with bursting ammunition west of the railway, near the Langham crossing. I walked over to see if a guard was required...By the time I reached the spot, officers and men from the S.L. Regt. at Ashwell Camp were there and their CO undertook to find the guard. Meanwhile, two of the crew had bailed out and Stanley Johnson, then 2nd i/c of "C" Coy, was informed by a member of the Civil Defence that a parachutist was drifting towards Braunston, the local platoon was called out and, as a result, a German prisoner was brought in by Lieut.

S.S. Watson and handed over to the Police; the parachute and other equipment were recovered by Corpl. D.E. O'N. Johnson, who set off at dawn along the estimated track of the parachute. Another member of the crew came down, injured, at Barleythorpe and was taken to hospital.'[144]

Lying in the National Archives, Kew, are the wartime Home Office Intelligence Summaries. In Report No. 48, Unteroffizier Lindla provided an even more astonishing : 'A wireless operator (in uniform), of a German night fighter, which was shot down on the 9 April, according to his own account after the crash, was passed by a soldier who bade him "goodnight" and then had to wait at a level crossing, at which the gates were shut. The signalman eventually came to open the gates, but took no notice of him. Several other people did the same and he was finally obliged to ask a civilian, in broken English, the way to the police station. The latter requested him to wait while he went round the corner to fetch a Home Guard, who finally accompanied him to the police station. The prisoner concluded that in these conditions, parachute troops would have little difficulty in effecting a landing and carrying out their tasks.'[145]

This damning critique at the state of the defences, whereby a German pilot had difficulty in surrendering and no Home Guards could immediately be found, coupled with the perceived ease with which German paratroopers could invade the county, make this a stinging indictment of the defences, and it is not surprising Col. Ogilvy-Dalgleish chose to recall an edited version of events.

Picking Up the Pieces

Nonetheless, the Home Guard did play a valuable role when an Allied aircraft crashed. At Illston-on-the-Hill, a lone Home Guard came to the rescue, 'For the most part the defenders of Illston spent their time watching for aircraft in distress and aircrew dropping to safety by parachute. But one night, in September 1941, a British bomber crash landed in a field on the edge of the village. Volunteer Clarence Jones was quick on the scene; he helped the crew to safety and then cycled to nearby Billesdon for a doctor.'[146]

Jim Briggs remembers when his father, who was in the Ratby Home Guard, responded to an RAF Blenheim that was in distress in March 1942:

'I was only about five at the time, but I remember it very well. This aircraft flew down in front of the houses on Markfield Road and was dropping flares. I think it was a training plane in a bit of trouble looking for Desford airfield. These flares were lighting the place up and my dad suddenly jumped out of bed and pulled his trousers on and ran across to the window to see what were what. He opened the curtains and looked out. He then turned round and tucked the back of his shirt into his trousers – and part of the blackout as well. As he went away, he pulled the whole lot down and lit the whole room up. My mother was scared because she thought we were gonna be bombed! My dad then went out somewhere. The next morning, he took me up to see the plane and it was on its belly being guarded by Thornton Home Guard, who wouldn't let us anywhere near it.'[147]

First Anniversary of the Home Guard

The first anniversary of the Home Guard in May 1941 was a subdued affair, because of the uncertainties of the war. Nonetheless, the C.-in-C., Northern Command, Lt-Gen. Sir T.R. Eastwood, KCB, DSO, MC, briefly toured Leicester and Oakham at the end of the month.[148]

The Invasion Threat Renewed

Britain was isolated in Europe and retreating throughout the Mediterranean and North Africa. Matters were made worse that month when Crete was captured by German paratroopers and a whole new parachute scare started again. Although Hitler surprised everyone by suddenly invading Russia in June 1941, this provided little relief. Russia was viewed as weak, and it was generally believed Hitler would triumph in a few weeks. He would then be free to return to finish off Britain.

Fortunately for the British, the war on the Eastern Front developed into a painful battle of attrition

Beating the Invader leaflet delivered to all homes in May 1941.

that drained 'Aryan' blood, bogging down forces that could have been used against Britain. However, Britain's defenders did not have the privilege of hindsight. Due to the supposed threat, the Home Guard started their first proper large-scale field exercises with the Regular Army in July 1941.

The Battle of Kilby Bridge

On 27 July 1941 the Leicestershire Home Guard conducted a large anti-invasion exercise that centred on Kilby Bridge, just south of Leicester, testing the city's perimeter roadblock defences situated there,

'Realistic Invasion Exercises – Home Guard's Invention Wrecks "Enemy" Tanks:

Perched on a hen house that gave them a grandstand view of the countryside, a group of villagers saw an "invasion party" mopped up on Sunday morning. It was a realistic episode in part of the vast exercises being carried out by the Home Guard and army units extending over the whole country.

Secret devices, cleverly concealed bomb throwers and picked men armed with tommy guns were effectively used by men of the No. 2 Battalion Leicestershire Home Guard, to frustrate this attack on a village and bridge over a canal. The attacking party, consisting of members of the ITC, Leicestershire Regiment, were reported landed by enemy planes in the neighbourhood of Lutterworth and North Kilworth. Large planes had also landed armoured fighting vehicles.

First sign of the attacking force was a despatch rider, who careered past a spinney and came to grief in a minefield set by Home Guards further along the road. A second despatch rider, seeing his companion's fate, turned back, but was shot when passing the spinney.

A light enemy tank [Bren Gun Carrier] then appeared on the scene and its occupants set about exploding the mines in the road when a secret electrical device – the invention of a local Home Guardsman – enveloped the tank in flames and smoke and put it out of action.

Enemy troops following the tank, however, succeeded in clearing the wood, and some went forward on the main road in armoured fighting vehicles while others carried out a flanking movement. The final assault on the [roadblock on the] bridge was a spectacular affair. Flaming sacks suspended across the road held up vehicles and, as the occupants dismounted, cleverly concealed bomb throwers took a heavy toll. The party which undertook the flanking movement were surprised by Home Guards armed with tommy guns and eventually rounded up at the point of a bayonet.

Officers watching the exercises were warm in their praise for the high standard of efficiency shown by the Home Guard, a large proportion of which consisted of men who saw service in the last war.'[149]

Chasing Shadows

A new spy scare accompanied the renewed invasion fear. 'On August 26th, 1941, the Chief Constable, A. Bond, rang me up at 11pm to say that two suspected enemy agents, possibly of the kind referred to earlier, had last been reported going towards Tolethorpe Oaks, an isolated wood about three miles East of the North Road [A1], and he asked men to assist in drawing the wood at first light. The hour was late, but Bolton, 2nd in Command of 'A' Coy with 25 HG, met the Chief Constable and his men, and some Airmen, at dawn the next morning and every yard of the wood was drawn, blank.'[150]

The results of the 1st (North Leicester) Battalion's vigilance were rather more amusing as the Orderly Officer reported '23.25 hrs: flashing light seen near Platoon HQ; patrol sent out and brought in a civilian and girl. Civilian claimed he was lighting his pipe – duly warned and allowed to go.'[151]

Officers on exercise at Kilby Bridge, 27 July 1941.

A motorcyclist is stopped at the Kilby Bridge checkpoint during the defence exercise, Sunday 27 July 1941. Although he has shown his 'E.L.' (Emergency Label) pass, the Home Guards still detain him, much to his visible frustration.

Men of the Leicestershire Home Guard man a Mk 1 Northover Projector while on exercise, believed to be by the Grand Union Canal near Wigston, probably during the attack on Kilby Bridge, Sunday 27 July 1941.

The Real Cost of the Invasion Threat

The renewed anti-invasion exercises were not without cost, as seen on 7 September 1941. While taking part in manoeuvres, Home Guard Horace Brant, 42, a van driver of Nottingham Road, Loughborough, collapsed, dying a few hours later at Loughborough Hospital. At the inquest, Home Guard Corporal George A. Rutherford described the exercises as being 'very strenuous', which necessitated crawling some distance with full equipment. Dr Stephanie Lichenstein said Brant had been admitted to hospital in a state of coma and died without regaining consciousness. Although Mrs Brant said her husband was 'strong and wiry,' the doctor said there had been a relic of old meningitis. A rupture might have resulted from the great exertion. The coroner recorded a verdict of death from natural causes.[152]

On 3 October 1941 tragedy struck yet again, as reported in the *Hinckley Times and Guardian*, 'The death occurred very unexpectedly on Friday of Mr Albert Charles Haywood, of Shilton Road, Barwell. Deceased who was 55… developed a chill and his end came with tragic swiftness. He leaves a widow and a daughter, his son being in the army. Mr Haywood was a very popular member of the Home Guard, a number of whom attended the funeral in the Barwell cemetery on Tuesday afternoon. Deceased, who was a shoe operative, was very well known and highly respected throughout the Barwell locality and there were many expressions of regret at his passing. Among the Home Guard who attended his funeral were Capt. A.F. Castle (Adjutant), Lieut. L.W. Harvey and a number of men of the platoon.'[153]

Two months later, on 2 November 1941, 15-year-old Home Guard Cadet Kenneth Burnard of Bembridge Road, Leicester, also collapsed during an exercise and died before the ambulance reached Leicester Royal Infirmary.[154]

This was not the first time strenuous exercises had taken a fatal toll. But it would take another year and a half before the matter was properly addressed by the WO, when a circular was sent to all Home Guard commanders reminding them 'men of low medical standard should not be employed on duties beyond their powers.'[155]

Home Guard Jet Off on a Secret Delivery Mission

For the past five years, Frank Whittle's Power Jets team had been working hard, with little financial support, to create Britain's first jet engine. By the end of 1941 they had successfully completed the W1X experimental engine. In his book *Jet*, Whittle recalls how, on 29 September 1941, a W1X engine was disassembled and packed in crates.[156] It was then sent by road, with an armed escort of Power Jets'

Home Guards, probably in the firm's only 3-ton Austin lorry, to Prestwick, Scotland. From there, the engine was flown to the General Electric Co, in Massachusetts, US, in a stripped-out Liberator bomber. Power Jets' fitters, some of whom were also Home Guards, escorted the engine on the long flight and on their return told 'lurid stories' about how basic the conditions were aboard the fully-loaded aircraft.[157] Thanks to Whittle's work, the US created their own jet engine, which became operational a year later. This was a very important and controversial mission. Not only was Whittle's jet technology 'top secret', but the US were still not officially involved in the war. Although the Nazis knew America favoured the Allies, they could have embarrassed the US government in front of its still largely isolationist population, had they discovered Britain was sharing such key technology. The Power Jets Home Guard section had played an important part in this mission.[158]

Head of Britain's Home Guard Visits Leicester
Following on from his visit to Rutland in May, Lt-Gen. T.R. Eastwood, C-in-C Northern Command and now the Director-General of the Home Guard, inspected men of the 2nd (South Leicester) Battalion, when they paraded at Wigston on 16 November 1941. There was also a church parade at St Margaret's, Leicester.[159]

Goodbye to the Sons and the Dads
The manpower problem deepened towards the end of 1941. The Countesthorpe Home Guard roll book reveals many of the younger members were now leaving to join the services or moving away due to war work. Many platoons stretched the 17–65 age boundaries, turning a blind eye towards those members younger or older.

But the Home Guard were becoming a source of amusement for music hall comedians, damaging their public image. As a result, the rules were tightened with a WO edict stating 'All Area, Zone, Group and Battalion Commanders over the age of 65 will have their appointments terminated by 31 January 1942,' with no appeal allowed.[160] This move attempted to rid the 'Colonel Blimp' image associated with many officers. ORs over 65 years, however, were quietly allowed to stay on with six-month reviews.

This improved the overall fitness of the force, so by 1943 the Home Guard were more capable, composed mainly of teenagers awaiting call up and younger men in reserved occupations. The force actually weighted more towards the younger generations than the stereotypical aged image of *Dad's Army*, but the image stuck. But at a time when manpower was already falling, this only accelerated the drop. The WO would have to urgently find another way to consolidate the force if it was still to be effective.

1942: The 'Hornet's Nest'

'If in 1940 the enemy had descended suddenly in large numbers from the sky…he would have found only little clusters of men, mostly armed with shotguns…

But now, whenever he comes – if ever he comes – he will find wherever he should place his foot, he will immediately be attacked by resolute, determined men who have a perfectly-clear intention and resolve – namely, to put him to death or compel his immediate surrender. Therefore, to invade this island by air…is to descend into a hornet's nest.'

Winston Churchill, 14 May 1942, on the second anniversary of the Home Guard.

A Bad Start to the Year

The opening of 1942 did not bode well for the Leicestershire Home Guard.

On 30 January 1942, while on Home Guard duty, Private D.H. Henson of Birstall passed away in his sleep. Born in Newtown Linford, Henson had a distinguished military career. After serving as a member of Canada's North West Mounted Police in the Yukon goldfields, he went on to fight in the Boer War and later with the RASC during World War One. He commanded the 2/1 North Midland Mounted Brigade and also served in Dublin District between 1918–1920.[161]

Although not perfect, the Home Guard were now equipped with better weapons. A new ruling forbade the Home Guard from making any more home-made devices.[162] Nonetheless, on 8 February 1942 a corporal in 11th (Ashby-de-la-Zouch) Battalion was killed demonstrating an improvised device at Measham.

The inquest heard they had paraded on a Sunday morning. The senior NCO attending Corporal William Hodson Williamson, 25, a colliery underground official of Bosworth Road, Measham, arrived carrying a home-made bomb, saying he wanted to try it out. The men marched to the top of a nearby hill, but a couple of minutes later the bomb suddenly exploded while Corporal Williamson was holding it, blowing off both his hands.

Lt J.A.H. Sutton, a Home Guard bombing officer, said the manufacture of home-made bombs had never been discussed. If he had seen any experimenting he would have stopped it. PC Jesson said he had made many inquiries to find where the explosive came from and had interviewed most of the platoon, but obtained no information. The deceased's connection with the colliery may have provided the source of the explosive.

In returning a verdict of accidental death, the coroner said it was 'fairly obvious in a village like Measham someone knew something, but no one had come forward'.[163]

New Home Guard Chief Visits Rutland

'The Director-General of the Home Guard, Major-General Lord Bridgeman, C.B., D.S.O., M.C., made a brief visit to the Rutland Bn HQ in February 1942; all available officers were assembled in the Drill Hall and the DG gave an interesting talk on subjects of interest to the HG at the time.'[164]

The End of the Home Guard Volunteer Spirit?

Despite the entry of the US, the war was going far from well for Britain. The Afrika Korps had reversed British successes in North Africa. The Germans had almost reached Moscow and were expected to finish off Russia soon. In the Far East, British and Commonwealth forces were retreating in the face of the Japanese and Singapore was about to fall.

These war reverses had caused high British casualties and the ensuing conscription to replenish numbers had drastically taken its toll on the Home Guard. This could not be allowed to continue, as by late 1941 the Home Guard were providing the main defence of the country.

Also, the voluntary nature of Home Guard service meant officers could do little when men shirked. Captain P.S. Wakefield regularly checked attendance of the Brush Works Home Guard in Loughborough. His diary records his frustration at the levels of absenteeism.

'Sunday 1:12:40. Zwannenberg in this evening to tell me only four volunteers turned up today to help him and Ryan and Sgt Mercer clean and degrease the rifles. The work of this Home Guard is all being done by a very few members of it.

Wednesday 24:9:41. We are warned of the danger of silent glider attack at last nights battalion meeting. There was nobody on the Morris guard until 9.30pm...'[165]

To check this absenteeism and the ebbing numbers in the Home Front services, the government introduced the National Service (No.2) Act in December 1941, making it compulsory for all adults to perform national service for the war effort. All men aged 18–51 not already on national service were now liable to be called-up – or 'directed' as it was officially called – to perform a minimum 48 hours service per month in the Home Guard. If they failed to carry out their duty, they could be fined £10 (£310) or spend a month in gaol. Serving Home Guards were given the option of resignation from the force before the Act was implemented on 16 February 1942, but, ironically, under the terms of the Act, they could be redirected straight back into the Home Guard.[166] The right to resign from the force was also rescinded and Home Guards had to serve until the war ended or they reached the age of 65.

However, by 1942, for much of the population, enthusiasm for national service was beginning to wear thin. The nation was now working very long hours and the last thing many wanted to do afterwards was crawl through wet fields on night exercise, stand out in the cold on sentry duty or be shouted at while square-bashing.

The conscripts did not have the same volunteer spirit as the original volunteers and, technically, the Home Guard became a militia. The title 'Volunteer' was replaced by 'Private'. But direction was not without its benefits. The flood of new manpower greatly boosted numbers, gaining 263,000 in the space of three months, taking the Home Guard's total strength to 1,793,000 in March 1942. Direction particularly helped the sparser rural areas, such as in Rutland, where flagging numbers were boosted and the battalion's ceiling was raised from 850 to 1,100.[167]

Melton's Home Guard Accused of 'Gross Negligence' Over Child's Death

In April 1942 the father of a schoolboy killed by a grenade, while playing in pits used for bombing practice by the Home Guard, told the Melton District Deputy Coroner Mr H.K. Barker there had been 'gross negligence'.

A verdict of accidental death was recorded on Ivor Scolley, the eight-year-old son of Archie Scolley, munition worker, of the council houses, Waltham. A playmate denied the children had been warned in school against going to the pits. He gave evidence of going to the practice range with his chum that Sunday morning: 'Ivor picked up the bomb and said, "Is this a live one?" I told him I did not know. He said "Smell at it." I smelt it and I could smell gunpowder' said the playmate. He did not think it was safe to be near it and went a little distance off. Ivor took hold of the grenade's pin and there was an explosion.

Three Melton Home Guard officers gave evidence of visiting the pits on Saturday afternoon for grenade practice, but were emphatic they could account for each grenade. At the inquiry's conclusion, Mr Scolley stated 'I wish to make protest. I think there has been gross negligence on somebody's part and I want a further inquiry.'[168]

Young Leicester Home Guard's Sad Death

'Don't let my dad know' said Albert Stanley Pratt, 19, a boot and shoe finisher of Overton Road, Leicester, to his friend, both Home Guards, when he bought from him for £2 (£62) a revolver and ammunition. The weapon and ammunition was brought home from Egypt by Pratt's father after World War One.

An inquest at Leicester Royal Infirmary heard that when Pratt's younger sister came home on 10 April, she talked and joked with her brother until she retired. A quarter of an hour later she heard a sharp report. She called three times, 'Are you all right?' without reply, but the fourth time Albert answered, 'I'm all right'. However, she went downstairs and saw her brother standing on the living room hearth with his face covered in blood. 'I said, "What have you done?"' continued the witness. 'He replied, "Oh, the rotten thing," meaning the revolver, and then fell to the floor.'

The father said he was a widower with four children. His son, Albert, was a normal youth of a bright disposition. The revolver was lying on the floor in a pool of blood when he was called to the scene by his daughter. He added his son was wearing a belt and holster at the time. A surgeon at the Royal Infirmary said an operation was performed two hours after admission and three fragments of bullet removed from the skull. Death occurred a week later due to contusion of the brain following the bullet wound. The coroner, Mr E.G.B. Fowler, returned a verdict of accidental death.[169]

The Home Guard's Second Birthday

On 14 May 1942 the Home Guard celebrated its second anniversary. Again, due to the poor military situation abroad, there were few celebrations; however, in a bid to boost the force's morale, King George VI assumed appointment as Colonel-in-Chief of the Home Guard.

Barwell Home Guard's Sudden Death Following Exercise

On 19 June 1942 the *Hinckley Times and Guardian* had the sad duty to report yet another Home Guard fatality.

'Barwell people learned with much regret of the death, which occurred very suddenly on Sunday, of Stanley Marvin, of Stapleton Road, Barwell. Mr Marvin, 43, was a popular Home Guard and had been out on duty during Sunday morning. He took ill while at exercise and was conveyed home in a colleague's car, but died shortly afterwards. He had not been in the best of health for some time, but he appeared to be all right when he left to take part in the Home Guard practice. He was a hosiery operative and leaves a wife, a son and a daughter, to whom much sympathy is extended. The funeral took place on Wednesday afternoon. Members of the local Home Guard formed a Guard of Honour.'[170]

Too Keen? The Home Guard Who Bought His Own Tommy Gun

'A tommy gun, which, according to his statement, he acquired from a man evacuated from Dunkirk, landed a HG corporal in to County Police Court today. The 43-year-old haulage contractor from Leicester Road, Glen Parva, summoned for possessing the weapon without authority, was fined £5 [£155] and the gun was confiscated. He was also fined 10s for using obscene language at Whetstone earlier the same day. Defendant said he used the gun for HG practice. PC Bestwick deposed to going to Blaby, where defendant was seated in a motorcar. The defendant at first said he had no firearm in his possession, but the tommy gun was found in the car.'[171]

Gas Mask Saves Home Guard's Life – But No Gas

'The story was told at Ashby-de-la-Zouch Police Court today of how an Ibstock member of the Home Guard, while on duty at Heather, was struck by a bullet that had been fired at a bird. Luckily, he was wearing a gas mask at the time and escaped serious injury, except for a dented respirator. A Heather man pleaded guilty to possessing firearms without a licence. PC Parker said the rifle was a Winchester repeater. He had bought the gun for his son, 18, as he was a member of the HG and had not been issued with a rifle. The Bench, imposing a fine of 10s, said they understood the rifle would be handed over to the HG.'[172]

Exercise LEICESTER: The First Major Test of Leicester's Defences

On Sunday 5 July 1942 Leicester's Home Guard and CD services took part in Exercise LEICESTER. This important exercise was the first major test of the city's latest defence scheme following its introduction in November 1941 (see page 97) and proved very useful.

Captured Home Guard prisoners are marched through the centre of Ratby, during Exercise LEICESTER, Sunday 5 July 1942. The second Home Guard from the front is Bob Geary. The participants don't look particularly upset at being captured.

'Battle For Leicester Was Realistic Test:
Leicester was "invaded" yesterday when the HG and CD co-operated in the biggest exercise yet held. It brought into action a great section of the defence strength of Leicester Sub-Area, which includes a considerable strength beyond the city boundary.

The object was the co-ordination of military and civil plans for defence against invasion, particularly a test on the function of all casualty services. In Leicester there was a CD turn out of about 2,000, with all vehicles manned. The 72 incidents staged were all concerned with high explosives and fire. The County Civil Defence personnel engaged made another 2,000 in addition to the HG.

Paratroops outside City
The assumption was that paratroops and airborne troops had been dropped outside the city and were trying to take Leicester. British troops wore service caps and the enemy steel helmets. The HG manned roadblocks, organised strong points in farmsteads and village streets, and were backed up by Special Police, Wardens, AFS and First Aid Parties. It was the first time such extensive co-operation had been attempted, and the whole exercise was a most valuable and worthwhile effort.

Planes Dive-Bombed
The exercise started in the city just after 9 o'clock, with incidents in various quarters – in London Road at the corner of Highfield Street, in Southgate Street etc. There, wounded citizens could be seen labelled and lying around with the FAP attending them amid the noise of thunder flashes (large-sized crackers) and pall of smoke bombs, while overhead trainer planes dive-bombed to the very house tops. At the same time, the HG was fighting on the outskirts.

Many Challenges
There was a codeword for those entitled to use it, but the real word for the day was "Security". There was never in the Leicester area such a day of showing identity cards and challenges in general. This possibly irritated some people – it should not have done, had they but reflected that it was a serious test of the city's defence system and that those on duty were on trial.

The defenders had to stop infiltration and were prepared to expect some tricks in the way of surprise. For instance, just outside main control in Leicester an army despatch rider was "captured". His paybook disclosed him as "Private Boloney, height 3ft 9in, weight 350lbs, place of birth Berlin".

No wonder the HG, Police and Wardens felt constant scrutiny was important. So suspicious were the HG that for a time they even held an umpire under arrest! 'Do not trust anybody' had to be the motto on an invasion occasion.

As far as could be gathered, the HG held the outer defences, but as, in many cases, prisoners taken early in the day were released so they could see what they could do against the inner defences. In that way certain depots were captured by small groups and sometimes retaken. Main Control itself was captured just a few minutes before action was due to cease. There will, of course, be an "inquest" on the whole operation, but the verdict won't be made public.'[173]

'Unusual Accident' Hospitalises Four Young Braunstone Home Guards

'Four young Leicester Home Guards, travelling with a party in an army lorry towards Kibworth [probably to the rifle range], were the victims of an unusual accident. They were sitting on one side of the lorry inside the tarpaulin top. As the lorry was proceeding near to the side of the road, the camber tilted the top and it caught a telegraph pole set in the verge. The four lads were swept into the bottom of the lorry, where they lay unconscious. Services of a nearby doctor were procured and an ambulance answered a call with speed. The youths, who regained consciousness, were taken to the Leicester Royal Infirmary.

All live on the Braunstone Estate. They are: Harold Mortimer, 16, of Gutheridge Crescent, who suffered back and shoulder injuries; Eric Brewin, 17, of Chartley Road, who suffered abdominal injuries; Anthony Dawkins, 18, of Rose Farm Close, who suffered internal injuries and a damaged left shoulder, and Walter Stretton, 19, of Valence Road, who suffered back and chest injuries. Brewin was the most seriously hurt and was described as very ill. The other three were said to be progressing satisfactorily.'[174]

Lord Lieutenant of Leicestershire Sir Arthur Hazlerigg inspects Home Guards of the Leicester Group on Victoria Park, Leicester, Sunday 9 August 1942. Home Guards of the 1st (North Leicester) and 2nd (South Leicester) Battalions are seen nearest the camera.

The 'Pride of Leicester': Home Guard's Big Review

With flags of all the Allied nations fluttering around the saluting base and a crowd of spectators numbering several thousand, the Lord Lieutenant Sir Arthur Hazlerigg attended a review of the Leicester Group Home Guard on 9 August 1942, at Victoria Park, Leicester.

'It was the first full group assembly the Leicester area HG has made. The parade was under Group Commander Col. H.W.H. Tyler, and bands of the Leicestershire Regiment and the HG took part. On arrival, the Lord Lieutenant took the salute and then with Col. Tyler, Zone Commander Sir Thomas Cope, Lt-Col. C.A.B. Elliott, Sir Robert Martin, Lt-Col. A Halkyard of the Cadet Corps and Lt-Col. S.B. Harrison, passed along the length of the parade. When they then returned to the saluting base, where, among others, were the Lord Mayor (Councillor E.R. Frisby) and the Lady Mayoress (Miss Jessie Frisby), the Lord Lieutenant addressed the parade. Sir Arthur spoke of the tremendous and patient work done by officers and NCOs in training the HG, and the willing response by the men in turning out after their day's work. Leicester was proud of the Leicestershire HG and of the Leicester HG Group.'[175]

Invasion Committees Keep Up the Pressure

Despite the assumption the invasion threat had receded, Leicestershire's newly-formed Invasion Committees toured the county's cinemas showing films portraying what invasion by the Nazis has meant for other countries. Starting at the Empire Cinema, Loughborough, on 20 September 1942, they then visited 800 people in Hinckley,[176] then Leicester,[177] and finally Melton Mowbray on 17 October 1942.[178] Forms were also distributed throughout Leicestershire asking what residents would do to help in an invasion.

Rutland also took part in anti-invasion preparations in September 1942, named Exercise LIBERATOR. British paratroopers dropped from USAAF aircraft and tried to capture RAF Cottesmore, but umpires decided the defenders successfully held off the attackers.[179]

Example Made of Young Miner as Warning to Others

A 22-year-old miner from Ibstock pleaded guilty at Market Bosworth for failing to obey a direction of a National Service officer to join the HG. The case was the first of its kind in Leicestershire. The defendant, a pony driver at Bagworth Colliery, said he worked seven days and had to do his garden and had no time for training.

'The Ministry has brought this case as a warning to all other young men who are doing nothing. This man thinks he can flaunt the law. Other young men from the same colliery are members of the Home Guard. The case was adjourned for 14 days to give the miner an opportunity to join the HG.'[180]

With the recent introduction of compulsory service into the Home Guard, it was perhaps inevitable a public example would be made of the first person to breach the new ruling. At first sight, such public vilification of a young man who clearly was not idle may seem harsh, but both the court and the Ministry of National Service showed total war called for all-out effort from everyone.

The PARTRIDGE Has Landed

Exercise PARTRIDGE, on Saturday 10 and Sunday 11 October 1942, was the largest county exercise yet and the second major exercise of 1942.

The exercises were important at all levels. At North Midland District and above, the military could see how strong this particular area of the nation's defence network was. For the Sector Commander and senior staff, this was the first major test of the defence schemes and Invasion Committees in that area. This was also the closest staff could get to test whether their plans would work under combat conditions. At the end of the exercise, any weak spots could be noted and rectified. Officers and NCOs could also test how well the command structure worked and Home Guard Privates on the ground could put their training into practice.

The initial premise of the exercise was that German invaders had captured Leicester and were advancing in an attempt to capture Loughborough, Kegworth and Coalville, plus all the airfields in that area. The opposing forces were:

'Enemy Attacking Force ("German"):
Tylerforce
Commander: "Oberst" Tyler
Hitchings Column: 1st (North Leicester) Bn = c. 750 men and 4th Bn.
1st Inman Column: 80 men
2nd Inman Column: 80 men
Dunn Column: c. 350 men
Group Mobile Column: c. 80 men with Group Guard: c. 20 men
Objective: Loughborough and Coalville.

Elliottforce
Commander: "Oberst" Elliott
2nd (South Leicester) Bn: c. 500 men and 3rd (West Leicester) Bn: c. 770 men with three companies of Derby RAOC OCTU known as the Primary Training Company and 30th Foresters (possibly at Rearsby).

Total strength: 9,000 men.
Each of the five Home Guard attacking battalions will have ten 3-ton lorries marked with yellow crosses. Total = 50 lorries. Enemy Attacking Force wears steel helmets.

Defending Force ("British"):
Commander: Col. Studd.
8th (Hinckley and Market Bosworth) Bn
9th (Loughborough) Bn
10th (Charnwood) Bn
11th (Ashby) Bn
12th (Motor Reconnaissance) Bn
and Striking Force at Desford RAPC
with RAF Regt troops at RAF Wymeswold, RAF Desford and RAF Castle Donington. The latter defended by Castle Donington and Long Whatton Home Guard and section of mobile 9th (Loughborough) Battalion, known as Mobile Striking Force.

The Defending Force wears field service caps turned down.
Every man involved in the exercise issued with one pint of tea and a haversack ration. Umpires wear white armbands and carry white flags on vehicles. All troops issued with cracker blanks.
Areas Out of Bounds: Garendon Park POW Camp, Beaumanor Park Y Station and Ratcliffe Air Transport Auxiliary Airfield.' [181]

How the Battle Went
Tylerforce (part of the Enemy Attacking Force) started at Bradgate Park and advanced north overnight, capturing Nanpantan by 09.00hrs Sunday. At 10.30hrs, having regrouped, they advanced to attack Loughborough using Burleigh Brook as a covered line of approach.

Meanwhile, at 03.10hrs, the 3rd Battalion (part of 'enemy' Elliottforce) set up HQ at the Red Cow Inn [!], Leicester Forest East. At 10.30hrs Elliottforce attacked Hinckley from the north east and south. By 11.30hrs they had captured the market place and most of the town in spite of stiff resistance. The town was finally captured at 12.00hrs. RAF Desford was also captured. The *Hinckley Times and Guardian* explained how Hinckley was captured:

'Final Assault on Town
So far as Hinckley and district was concerned, the main attack came from the east by Stoney Stanton, Sapcote and Sharnford, proceeding on either side of the Sapcote Road, Aston Flamville and Burbage Woods, to a line in front of the Burbage Woods

A member of the forces on his motorcycle is held up by a patrol of 10th (Charnwood) Battalion Home Guard during Exercise PARTRIDGE, Sunday 11 October 1942.

from where a final assault was made on the town. In a smaller diversionary attack from the south-west around the Lime Kilns, the enemy was considered by umpires to have been annihilated, and a platoon of defenders in the London Road and Lash Hill area were also counted successful.

Elsewhere, the enemy succeeded in penetrating defences and the exercise was called off when large numbers rushed various objectives in the town at a time when close combat appeared imminent.

Other schemes operated on a line north-west of Desford via Kirkby Mallory, and Cadeby to Sutton Cheney and beyond. Further afield an enemy column approached from the north-west and encountered strong opposition at Sheepy Magna, but eventually got through into the Market Bosworth area, which they attacked and stormed well into Sunday morning. Other incidents occurred in the area of Bagworth and Ellistown Colliery.'[182]

The *Leicester Mercury* reported the battle in fine detail, despite wartime censorship:
'The "Enemy"
At the Leicester end of Loughborough, a mechanised unit was assembled under camouflage to attack the town, but an umpire decided a railway bridge had been hit from the air and the Bren-guns and various motor vehicles had to make their approach by a more circuitous route.

On the Nanpantan Road and its vicinity, there was much activity. Defenders used cover from spinneys and gardens and smoke bombs were employed. A feature of the work on both sides was the contact by motorcycle and cycle messengers.

Coalville people took a keen interest in the invasion exercises, several hundred taking part. There was a striking demonstration of street fighting in the centre of the town as troops, armed with rifles and automatic weapons, tackled an "invading" force.

Effective roadblocks were erected after dark, and motorists were stopped by troops and questioned. As dawn broke, the "battle" began in earnest. As the "invading" force neared the outskirts of the town, the military took up positions at vantage points, shop entrances, road junctions and behind any effective cover, while other defenders were cunningly hidden in the centre of the town. Scores passed by a spot near the Memorial Square, without noticing troops with a machine gun [*sic*: actually a Northover Projector] between shrubs, covered with camouflage netting.

Rather confused-looking locals observe as umpires examine a camouflaged Mk II Northover Projector position located in a flowerbed around Coalville War Memorial during Exercise PARTRIDGE on Sunday 11 October 1942.

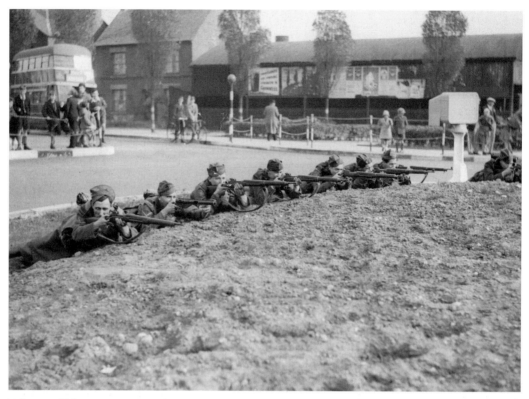

Defending Home Guards take cover behind the Coalville War Memorial traffic island during Exercise PARTRIDGE, Sunday 11 October 1942.

Prisoners Taken

An army officer told the *Mercury* the exercise proved of great value. It was the first time there had been co-operation between military and Civil Defence authorities, combined under one head, through the Invasion Committee, which functioned with the military. The attacking forces found many of the smaller villages put up a good defence and they mainly suffered 'heavy casualties' through ambushes.

Home Guard Injured

One incident brought a regrettable accident. Home Guard Donald Greenacre of Station Road, South Wigston, met with an eye and facial injury, which necessitated his removal to the Leicester Royal Infirmary.' [183] (It is said he was advancing alongside a lorry when somebody in the back of it fired a blank from close range, blinding him in one eye.)

It is thought former Wigston Home Guard Arthur Kirkpatrick took part in this exercise, probably as part of Elliottforce,

A defending Home Guard 'sniper', wearing a camouflaged veil and armed with a Mk II Sten gun, fires from cover at the corner of Outwoods Drive during the attack on Loughborough, in Exercise PARTRIDGE, Sunday 11 October 1942.

'We took part in a big weekend exercise attacking Bruntingthorpe aerodrome, testing the RAF defences. However, it was far from easy – they had aircraft! The planes were flying so low, if you didn't drop your head they would have chopped it off! An umpire who had been watching our assault on the aerodrome told us we had all been defeated!' [184]

Ibstock resident W. Ruth Smith

A Home Guard defender retreats after throwing a smoke bomb at attacking Regular troops, at the junction of Barrow Road and Loughborough Road, Quorn, during Exercise PARTRIDGE, Sunday 11 October 1942.

remembers the exercise as a young girl '…Our house, which was on the edge of the village, was being used as a checkpoint and I remember being so excited, watching from bedroom windows as khaki figures crawled from bush to bush. When I saw one of "ours" approaching, I crept outside behind a brick pillar to await his arrival and when he saw me, he said something to the effect "Thank God it's you Ruth. What the 'ell's the password? Is it sparrer?" It was in fact Partridge!'[185]

After the exercise there was some clearing up to do. Quorn Home Guard records show the local platoon commander had to pay farmer Geoffrey Fisher of Moorfields Farm, Quorn, £5 (£155) for damage caused after 'a Bren gun carrier smashed down the gate… releasing into the field a lot of cows,' which damaged the crops. Three horses also escaped and ended up in Woodthorpe.[186]

Richard Tyler recalls his father Col. H.W.H. Tyler, who was leading part of the 'German' attacking Tylerforce, had painted white swastikas on his staff car for the exercise. However, once the exercise was over he found the paint would not come off![187]

Exercise Marred by Fatality

Almost two weeks previously, Major P.S. Wakefield recorded his concerns surrounding such a big exercise:

'Wednesday 30:9:42. Meeting at Coy HQ tonight to discuss a few things relative to exercise "Partridge"…Hope we don't have any serious accidents. It's rather much to hope with 10 battalions and more out on a pitch black moonless night.'[188]

Prophetically, the day before the exercise the *Leicester Mercury* had warned 'It may be there will be a considerable amount of traffic on the roads without lights and other road users should take special care.'[189]

Sadly, Major Wakefield's fears were met. Despite all the warnings, there was a fatal accident. At 6am on the Sunday morning a miner from Bagworth Colliery, Sidney Allen, 41, of Shaw Lane, Markfield, was motorcycling to work in the darkness when he collided with a stationary military bus used by the Home Guard. He received serious head injuries and was taken to the Leicester Royal Infirmary, where he died two hours later. The military vehicle, driven by a corporal in the RASC, had a defective rear light. A verdict of accidental death was given.[190]

Bells Ring – But No Invasion

On the evening of Sunday 15 November 1942 bells rang out across both counties for the first time in over two years. Had this happened before, mass panic may well have ensued and the Home Guard would have mustered. But on this day the bells rang out in jubilation, not warning. The Allies had scored a significant victory over Rommel's Afrika Korps at El Alamein and Churchill ordered that bells be rung across the land in celebration. On the Eastern Front, the German advance had ground to a halt at Stalingrad and was about to face annihilation. This was the turning point in the war, which Churchill labelled 'The End of the Beginning'.

'Dodging the Column'

Perhaps the first case in Leicestershire of absenteeism from Home Guard service without reasonable excuse was reported in November 1942. A 17-year-old from Ashby Road, Loughborough, was fined £5 (£155) at Loughborough Police Court.

Superintendent Darling stated 'This man appears to be bone idle'. The defendant had been sacked from several jobs through absenteeism and when seen by the Police had only just got out of bed. He had been in the Home Guard since August 1941 but told 2nd Lieutenant Cutter he had been 'working away'. When asked where, he replied 'Round about'. When asked the name of his employer, he said 'Find out'. When asked why he had not attended any parades for 10 months, he replied that every time he went it was 'lectures, lectures, lectures'. He had joined to learn to use a rifle and he had not used one yet. The Magistrate stated 'You are a very young man, but your record is an extremely bad one. It's about time you turned over a new leaf.'[191]

A week later, a 40-year-old engineer in the Home Guard from Hazel Street, Leicester, became Leicester's first prosecution for absence. In defence, he said 'it was raining very hard and he did not think he was fit.' He had lost nearly a stone in weight. However, the Magistrate said 'it was grossly unfair to others, as well as unpatriotic, for men to be guilty of what was known as "dodging the column".'[192]

Through compulsion, the Home Guard reached its peak at the end of 1942, with 1,850,757 members.[193] However, the nation was now working harder than ever in the face of an ever-receding invasion threat. To many, Home Guard service was becoming a chore. In the coming year, the authorities would have to think of ways to prevent absenteeism, while maintaining the morale of the Home Guard.

Major General Viscount Bridgeman, Director General of Britain's Home Guard, takes the salute as 'A' Company, 1st (North Leicester) Battalion, march past, at the Greengate Lane/Loughborough Road crossroads roadblock, Sunday 21 February 1943.

1943: No Slackening

'The danger of invasion has by no means passed. England remains the main forward base of Allied operations against Germany and that "aircraft carrier off the coasts of Europe," of which Ribbentrop spoke venemously [sic] in a recent speech. Even if there is no attempt at full-scale invasion by the enemy, it is quite possible that he may seek to do damage by substantial raids, which may be sea-borne or air-borne, or both together.

In these circumstances, the Government could not agree to slackening in any degree of the precautions against invasion. The home defence forces, including the Home Guard, are very much on the alert, and the civil population will receive no official advice other than to observe that example.'

J. Bruce Galloway, Leicestershire County Controller to Invasion Committees, December 1942.

AWOL

The vast majority of Home Guard absence without leave was due to work-related pressure, not idleness. In these cases, the courts took this into consideration.

When a 40-year-old Nailstone miner was fined at Market Bosworth Police Court in March 1943 for failing to report for duty without reasonable excuse, the case aroused considerable interest in the coalfield. The defendant pleaded not guilty. Superintendent E. Mason said it was a bad case because the defendant, who was a Private in the Nailstone Home Guard, was 'only doing about 45 hours a week in the mine'. He had failed to attend four parades, during one of which he had been found in the pub. The defendant said he would be ready if the invader came.

Joseph Smith, the colliery timekeeper, said the defendant was doing an important job on the conveyor and was one of the finest workmen at the pit, who had not missed a single shift since the war started. In his defence, the miner said that during World War One he had joined the army at 15 and served overseas. In 1939 he volunteered again, but was told that, as a miner, he was in a reserved occupation. He had volunteered for the Home Guard from the start. His parades were in the morning and he could not attend every one because he had to return home to change, have dinner, then cycle for half an hour to reach the colliery for his shift. Sometimes he had gone without dinner. Fining him £3 5s (£95) for all four cases of absenteeism, the Chairman said the Bench had taken his good record into consideration.[194]

Home Guard Chief Visits Leicester

On 21 February 1943 Major-General Viscount Bridgeman, the Director General of the Home Guard, visited Leicester.[195] He arrived at 10am at the Greengate Lane/Loughborough Road crossroads, Birstall, and took the salute of 'A' Company, 1st (North Leicester) Battalion as they marched past with their band. At 10.30am he arrived at their Nissen hut by the crossroads north east of Cropston, where he watched battle drill. At 11am he went to the Dixie Arms in Market Bosworth and watched a demonstration of mustering, the mobile section and movement by the 8th (Market Bosworth) and 11th (Ashby-de-la-Zouch) Battalions.[196]

Young Home Guard Lieutenant Killed at Wanlip

There was no slackening in exercises during the first part of 1943, an example being the 1st (North Leicester) Battalion. On 7 February 1943 they took part in Exercise BLUEBELLS, a joint manoeuvre with various other Home Guard mobile sections and the 106th Bridging Company RASC. The following Sunday, the 1st Battalion also took part in Exercise SNOOKER.[197]

Lt Jack Moffat.
(Judith Mileham)

Sadly, it was during this period of continued pressure that 23-year-old Home Guard Lt Jack Moffat, of St. Saviour's Road, Leicester, was tragically killed on 7 March 1943. To make training more realistic, from September 1942 live-firing 'battle inoculation' exercises had been introduced, and it was during one such exercise that Moffat was killed at Wanlip.

The youngest of 11 children, Lt Moffat was a draughtsman at Messrs Wadkin Ltd, Green Lane Road Works, Leicester. He was a Territorial in the RAMC and had been called-up when war broke out. However, as he was in a reserved occupation, he was returned to industry after six months in the army. He was very disappointed and made several failed attempts to rejoin. Instead, he joined the Home Guard and received his commission only a few weeks before his death. His senior officer stated Moffat was very keen on Home Guard duty, training several days as week.[198]

It was revealed during the inquest Lt Moffat, OC of the Pioneer unit of HQ Company, 1st (North Leicester) Battalion, had been left in charge and was observing the exercise. This involved a platoon of Home Guards crossing the River Soar under simulated battle conditions, which included live rounds fired overhead. Five gelignite charges were submerged in the river and detonated from the riverbank, creating large waterspouts.

As a corporal in HQ Company, 1st (North Leicester) Battalion, it was Ray Elgood's job to set up the training courses. He recalls:

'We had a course set out at Wanlip with all sorts of obstacles, such as barrels with planks across they had to run over, plus fences, crawls etc. There was one or two ounce charges buried to simulate fire. We had also had two army snipers that were licensed to ping about low velocity ammunition. This made the Home Guards all get their heads down and stick their bums up – and we had a job stopping the snipers putting one in there!

There was a small stream that widened out and we put charges on the bottom and it was all banging off. The whole exercise went perfectly all right and then, while clearing up at the end, they found a couple of misfires, including one in the river.'

The dud charge was removed from the river, checked, then put back. The Sergeant in charge returned to the firing point 20 yards away. By unfortunate coincidence, at the same time Lt Moffat and Corporal Squire decided to cross the river in a canoe. Bushes on the riverbank obscured the view of their approach and they were over the mine precisely at the time the Sergeant instructed a private to fire the charge. Lt Moffat was blown in two, his lower half never found, while Corporal Squire was left shocked and stunned in the shattered canoe. Other Home Guards were left distressed and shocked, with the Sergeant 'looking very white and upset' standing on the bank. The canoe then suddenly submerged.

'Corporal Squire was relatively physically unharmed, except the explosion affected his memory and he was never the same again' recalls Ray Elgood.[199]

Six charges had been in the river 'for some time' and previously one had spontaneously 'exploded while there was no one there'. Gelignite can become highly unstable when left in water and the electrical fuses can also malfunction. Returning a verdict of accidental death, the Coroner stated there 'was always a certain element of risk quite inseparable from exercises of this kind'.[200]

Blaming himself for Lt Moffat's death, the Sergeant was so upset he had a memorial bishop's chair made at Wadkins works, which he presented to St. Saviour's Church six months later.[201] Lt Moffat's mother was so saddened by her son's death, it is said she wore mourning black for the rest of her life.[202]

The author is currently working with Lt Moffat's niece, Judith Mileham, and the Royal Tigers' Association to have the memorial chair placed in either the Regimental Chapel at Leicester Cathedral or in the new Regimental Museum at Newarke Houses, Leicester.

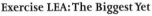

Jack Moffat's memorial bishop's chair. The inscription on the head reads 'A tribute to Lt Jack Moffat, OC Pioneers, HQ Coy, 1st Bn Lei Home Guard, who lost his life while engaged on manoeuvres 7.3.1943 – from comrades in the Pioneers.'
(Judith Mileham)

Exercise LEA: The Biggest Yet

Exercise LEA, held between 06.30 hrs to 16.00 hrs on Sunday 28 March 1943, covered the largest area and involved the greatest number of troops yet. There were, in all, 30,000 men engaged, the majority being Home Guards. The exercise tested the defence of the Trent River crossings and the outer defences of Nottingham and Leicester, as well as the Home Guard mobile columns. As such, Home Guards from Leicestershire, Derbyshire and Nottinghamshire took part, plus Regular troops.

The premise of the exercise was that invading German forces had occupied southern England and had reached a line from Worcester to The Wash. They were advancing north-westerly, apparently to seize

Home Guards of the 'enemy' attacking Symonsforce assemble in the farmyard of Bloomhills Farm, Dunton Bassett, before setting off to attack Leicester's defences, during Exercise LEA, Sunday 28 March 1943. Lt-Col. Symons briefs despatch riders of the 12th (Motor Reconnaissance) Battalion before the exercise begins. They have yellow crosses marked on their crash helmets signifying they are the 'enemy'. This truck is a mobile command and control post. Also, notice the CO's Rolls-Royce covered with camouflage net at the back!

the River Trent's crossings. On the left flank they were being held at Birmingham and on the right in the Grantham area. However, they had made a breakthrough in the centre, overrunning Rutland and southern Leicestershire with the exception of Leicester, which was holding out.

Enemy Attacking Force ('Germans'):
Winterforce
Commander: Lt-Col. C.E. Winter
Including companies of the RAOC, 10th (Charnwood), 5th (Belvoir) and 6th (Quorn) Battalions Leicestershire Home Guard.
Objective: Attack and capture bridgeheads on the River Trent at Gunthorpe, Radcliffe and Nottingham, plus three airfields.

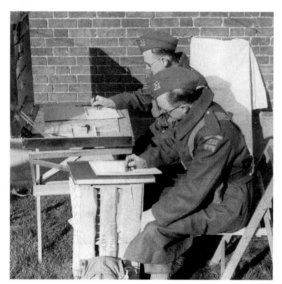

Home Guards of the 12th (Motor Reconnaissance) Battalion work at a battleboard in the farmyard of Bloomhills Farm, Dunton Bassett, during Exercise LEA, Sunday 28 March 1943.

Symonsforce
Commander: Lt-Col. W.J. Symons VC
Comprising three companies of the 4th (Central Leicester), the 8th (Market Bosworth) (less 'B' Company), 'C' Company 6th (Quorn) and two companies of the 7th (Market Harborough) Battalions Leicestershire Home Guard.
Objective: Attack and test Leicester's defences.

Defending Force ('British'):
Elliottforce
Due to be commanded by Lt-Col. C.A.B. Elliott, but, due to illness, replaced by Col. H.W.H. Tyler MC.
Role: Defence of Leicester.
Taylorforce
Commander: Major R.B. Taylor MC
Comprising the 9th (Loughborough) and 'C' Company of 11th (Ashby) Battalions Leicestershire Home Guard, with 11th (Repton and Woodville) and 13th (Derby and Borough) Battalions Derbyshire Home Guard.
Role: Defend and engage the enemy at bridgeheads in the Sawley and Cavendish areas, and then launch a detachment towards Draycott.

The western side of Nottingham was defended by two battalions of the Nottinghamshire Home Guard under Lt-Col. D.E. Williams.
The Leicester Sub-Area Commander was in control of the whole exercise in the Leicester area. Smoke bombs, clay grenades, thunderflashes, rifle and cracker blanks were used.

The *Leicester Mercury* reported the exercise in great detail

'The Opening of the Home Guards' Spring Offensive in the Midlands

The Leicestershire Home Guard, with several companies of Servicemen supporting, had a considerable share in the combined civil-military exercise. It was, as it were, the opening of the Home Guards' spring offensive in the Midlands. Throughout the winter the Home Guard has been tackling the science of battle-drill, which teaches fighting by squads, sections and platoons, and this was the first big field practice.

The Battle Plan

In order to prevent interference from strong HG units in the cities of Leicester and Nottingham, parachute troops were landed on the outskirts of these cities to attack vulnerable points and centres of communication. Leicester is unique in that it has a mobile battalion, although Nottingham might set against that its "navy" – the HG's Trent River Patrol was due to be afloat in this particular exercise guarding Holme Lock.

Col. Symon's job was to contain the local HG and keep them from going to the aid of the British forces at the Trent. From a farmstead [Bloomhills Farm] at Dunton Bassett, he and his officers controlled their forces, linked by wireless. There they had a lorried infantry force to be rushed off to any strong point that might be secured. The holding force had mobile columns on tap too – at Victoria Park and Abbey Park, Leicester.

There were "landings" west of Syston at 07.00 hours, Swithland 08.00, Kilworth 08.30, Broughton Astley 10.00, west of Huncote 07.00, Desford 08.30 and near Thornton 10.00. In open country the Home Guard certainly does understand the art of concealment. It was really difficult to pick out advancing groups, so well did they make use of ground contour and hedge bottoms.

Convenient Capture

A minor incident, but worth mention, was the assault and capture of a "pub" that happened to be a headquarters for the day – the timing looked good indeed. The Police, Civil Defence and NFS communications were available, and the Home Guard in many cases were fed by the WVS. Some Army Cadets and ATC gave good assistance as messengers and signal personnel.'[203]

A Nottinghamshire newspaper explained the results:

'Major-General Harter issued a statement for the press, in which he said that while certain sections of the attackers gained their objective, he was on the whole satisfied the defenders had won the battle.

The attackers undertook quite considerable operations, and a Leicestershire battalion, forming one of the groups converging on Trent Bridge and nearby industrial undertakings, must have marched 10 miles at least before going into battle and made a most violent assault on the defenders. The Loughborough battalion succeeded in their attack on the Sawley bridge and went on to infiltrate across the Trent towards Derby.'[204]

Maurice Woodward, formerly a Private in the Snibston Colliery Platoon of 11th (Ashby-de-la-Zouch) Battalion, later merrily recalled:

'We arrived at the destination near Kegworth and got posted near a river's edge, told to use the long grass at the side to make us less conspicuous and wait. We crouched and lay in the tall grass for nearly two hours and then it became apparent to all of us that coming down the river were Royal Engineers with their floating pontoon bridges.

Before they manoeuvred their sections into position to exactly where we were, the object of the exercise was spelt out clearly to us: we were to make a large-scale assault across the river using the pontoon bridges. Once the bridges were erected, the order soon came through to advance, which, after waiting all that time, was quite a relief. We crossed the river to the same old jokes and advanced through the same old smoke, until, after no more than 20 minutes after we had crossed the river, an umpire showed up to tell us we were all supposedly "dead".

'Enemy paratroopers' (Home Guards of the 8th (Market Bosworth) Battalion lie in wait for a counter-attack on the road they have just taken, during Exercise LEA, Sunday 28 March 1943.

Burly 'enemy paratroopers' (Home Guards of the 12th (Motor Reconnaissance) Battalion) relax at the end of Exercise LEA, Sunday 28 March 1943. They are distinguished from the defending troops by the string tied around their weapons, their black face paint and bayonet slung as a fighting knife.

Being "dead", the next "objective" was "captured" without much difficulty – a public house. I do know they opened before time that morning – maybe it was all part of the exercise, so we relaxed, for we'd got another long wait, only this time more enjoyable. I was just a 20-year-old boy then and what was to follow made it all the worth while being in Dad's Army: it was the most happiest and hilarious time of the whole five years.

First one and then another got on the piano. The party commenced and soon we were joined by others who had suffered the same "fate". It took off and as more and more joined us and spilled out onto the lawns, it became one hell of a party. The entertainment was terrific and the friendship and comradeship was all there. They say "dead men tell no tales" but "dead" men drank some beer that morning.'[205]

Captain William Stanley Yeates, of the 9th (Loughborough) Battalion, Leicestershire Home Guard, killed on manoeuvres, Sunday 28 March 1943.

Loughborough Home Guard Captain Killed By 'Enthusiasm'

However, all had not been fun and games: the exercise was marred by an accident at Sawley, which led to the death of 43-year-old Captain William Stanley Yeates, of the 9th (Loughborough) Battalion.

Captain Yeates was head of the commercial motor agents W.S. Yeates and Co, of Derby Road, Loughborough, and he lived on Knightthorpe Road. He had joined the Home Guard in June 1940 and was a popular member of his battalion. His promotion to Major had been expected that week. Captain Yeates was originally from London and was married with three children.

On the Sunday morning, the 9th (Loughborough) Battalion had been on exercise at Hemington. At about 11.30am Captain Yeates was part of a group attacking a trench by Sawley Lock. He was crouched in a hedgerow, with Home Guard Derek Barker kneeling beside him. Captain Yeates was holding a mortar firework, the fuse of which he had lit. He held the 'bomb' in both hands by his left side, while pointing it at the trench. In seconds, it fired like a Chinese cracker before erupting in a large explosion and something appeared to fly into the air. Captain Yeates toppled backwards into Barker's lap.

Bill Tollington, of Hathern Home Guard, took part in the exercise:

'I was about 100 yards away when Captain Yeates was killed, just before I got to Sawley Bridge. We heard this "bang". Captain Yeates had camouflaged his face with dark green facepaint. He looked a right mess with blood all over his khaki. We didn't know he was dead, although he looked it to me. They yelled for stretcher bearers and took him away. We didn't get word he was dead till we were over the bridge into Sawley.' [206]

Major Harry Murray, second in command of 9th Battalion, said the bomb was not authorised issue, but had been bought by Captain Yeates at his own expense. The base of this bomb had blown out, suggesting perhaps the propelling charge had become displaced during manufacture, causing it to misfire.

The Coroner Mr H.J. Deane, stated Captain Yeates was 'exceedingly keen on the training of himself and his men, and in order to add to the reality of the proceedings he had with him a number of these…mortar mines of shrapnel, causing a rattling fusillade in the air. On each of these mortars is, in type of considerable size, instructions…that it was to be partially buried. Then it should be lighted with a light on the end of a 5ft stick, and that person should get away quickly. What Captain Yeates did this day in enthusiasm was to have a number of these mortars with him, one of which he had previously let off without any ill effects. But the second time he did so this exploded and in consequence he died.' In recording a verdict of accidental death, Deane said Captain Yeates died from 'suffocation from deflation of the lungs caused by the blast'.[207]

This was not the only accident of this type. David Salmon, then a boy messenger for the Market Bosworth Home Guard, remembers one man lost his hand when a thunderflash he was holding exploded during an exercise. The battalion held a raffle to buy the Home Guard an artificial hand.[208]

Captain Yeates was buried with full military honours on 31 March 1943. A contingent of 200 Loughborough Home Guards paraded outside All Saint's Church before attending a service by Archdeacon W.J. Lyon. Captain Yeates's coffin was draped with the Union Jack and six officers from his company acted as bearers. After the service, the Home Guard marched behind the cortege along Leicester Road to Shelthorpe. A firing party then presented arms while the officers gave the salute before breaking away, the body proceeding to Leicester for cremation.[209]

Once again, another Home Guard exercise had ended with a fatality.

Dambusters Alert!
One evening in May 1943, a Home Guard patrol at Stoughton Aerodrome were alarmed to see low-flying aircraft rapidly approaching Leicester. Beneath each aircraft were two lights, focused on the ground. The patrol reported back and an alert was immediately sounded with air raid sirens wailing out across the city. However, at the last minute, the aircraft banked away from Leicester and flew back towards the coast. After the war, it was revealed that the first practice flights of 617 Squadron's 'Dambuster' Lancasters had been over the North Sea, followed by a 100 mile sweep inland to the Leicester city boundary. The vigilant watchers over Leicester East aerodrome had witnessed the first experiments in 617's height-fixing. The squadron also used Eyebrook Reservoir during the exercises.[210]

Thousands Join the Home Guard's Third Birthday
To boost the force's morale, the Home Guard's third anniversary in May 1943 was the biggest and most publicised event yet. Leicester Home Guards marched in a national parade in London watched by ambassadors of all the Allied nations. The main day of celebrations was called Home Guard Sunday and the public were invited to join in the festivities, as the *Leicester Mercury* reported:

'Between 25-30,000 people went to Victoria Park, Leicester, on Sunday 16 May 1943 to see the Leicester Sector battalions celebrate the third anniversary of the Home Guard.

It was the largest crowd seen at a wartime ceremony in the city. A full half hour before activity was due to start, the spectators were lined four and five deep around the great arena of the cricket ground. They stayed two hours – and their frequent applause showed they felt their patience was being fully rewarded.

The saluting base was on the main pathway directly opposite the War Memorial. Inside the enclosure of the War Memorial was the band of the Leicestershire Regiment and on the pathway the guard of honour furnished by the 1st Battalion Home Guard, under the command of Captain J. Rowlett.

General Salute
First there arrived the Lord and Lady Mayoress Alderman S. Taylor and Mrs Taylor. Then came the Lord Lieutenant Sir Arthur Hazlerigg, his car escorted by Home Guard motorcycle outriders. He was met by the Area Commander. The Lord Lieutenant, having inspected the guard of honour, went to the saluting base with the Lord Mayor, the Sub Area Commander and Col. H.W.H. Tyler MC. The Home Guard (1st North Leicester Battalion) Band led the way at the head of Serial 1, the RAOC heading Serial II.

In contrast to last year's parade, a noticeable feature was the number of young men, the 18-20s. They showed good discipline and steadiness. Another contrast was the increased number of Sten gun parties: the public also saw some of the machinery that a year ago, was still just the pet dream of almost any Home Guard.

Members of the Home Guard march past the saluting base during Oadby's Wings for Victory parade, 1943. Sir Arthur Hazlerigg, Lord Lieutenant of Leicestershire, stands framed between the first two Home Guards.

Battle Exercises

Five up-to-date exercises were gone through on the cricket ground. Captain Harry Fine MC gave a running commentary. This certainly helped the crowd to a better appreciation of the fine fighting machine that the Home Guard has made itself. First, there was a final assault on battledrill lines. Then came the Spigot mortar teams, followed by a mobile force battle platoon's attack on an observation post, an exciting show with the "enemy" paratroops in special uniform. Field communications was an exercise that showed the use of the telephone system and pigeons. The show closed with a Smith Gun demonstration.

The Only Mishap

At one point an aeroplane flew over. In it was Captain J.A.V. Boddy, who gave a short talk fitting to the occasion, believing it had reached the crowd below by wireless telephone and amplifier. But for some reason it did not. This was the only mishap at an otherwise perfect show.'[211]

Eyes right! Sir Arthur Hazlerigg, Lord Lieutenant of Leicestershire, taking the salute at a march past of Leicester Home Guards at Victoria Park, Leicester, Sunday 16 May 1943, commemorating the third anniversary of the founding of the Home Guard.

Other celebrations occurred across both counties. Meanwhile, filmmaker Frank Attfield captured the parade at Ashby Magna using rare colour film. Rob Foxon of the Leicestershire Film Archive restored the original footage and it was once again shown to the people of Leicestershire in 1990, almost 50 years after it was made.[212]

Exercise UMBRELLA: 'Nazi' Airmen Captured in Leicestershire

On 23 May 1943 north-west Leicestershire Home Guards took part in an exercise with a difference. Not altogether surprisingly in wartime, the *Loughborough Monitor* reported the exercise in a cheery manner,

'One of the most thrilling combined exercises took place in the Loughborough Division. It was the first time no warning call was given to the several thousand men engaged.

Fifty-five members of flying crews stationed at Midland aerodromes posed as German airmen evading capture in hostile territory. The efficiency of members of the Services concerned is shown by the fact that out of 55 airmen trying to reach their objective undetected, two only managed to, and one of these had to swim the River Soar. Five others became lost and gave up, and of the remainder Special Constables captured 28, Home Guards 15 and Wardens 5.

A car in which were members of the Regular Force and specials was driving along a certain road some miles from the town when one special fancied he saw a movement in the hedge. The car was stopped and the area searched.

"Nothing here" was the verdict of all but the man who had caused the car to be stopped. He moved some vegetation that covered a ditch and at the bottom of it lay one of the "enemy". He was very disappointed at his capture.

"I escaped from Narvik" he said, disgustedly, "and I got away all right from Dunkirk, only to be caught here by a blooming special." Heads of all Services were all of the opinion valuable experience had been gained.'[213]

UMBRELLA's Private Post-Mortem: 'Leave the killing to me'

Publicly the verdict may have been upbeat, but a surviving document reveals privately that it was a different story altogether.

A week after the exercise, Lt Thornton, CO of No 13 (Quorn) Platoon, was invited to give his observations in a private talk to the village's various services. The assembled audience could not have sat comfortably as Thornton angrily ranted. He was scathing of all that took part – including his own platoon.

Despite previous orders, the CD did not know where his Battle HQ was so that 'in not one instance did I have a message from the CD Services to the correct place'. He criticised his own platoon's messages for long-windedness and taking too long to communicate. His men also took too long to report for duty. It also seems not everyone took the exercise seriously,

'While on Sunday we were all patrolling and enjoying it, it would be an entirely different proposition if machine guns and tommy guns were being fired and I can assure you it would not be quite so funny… One of my friends always said to me "Charles, I consider 1 in 10 of blank ammunition should be a live one," although I do not altogether agree with all he said, I think at times this would perform a useful object lesson.'

The Home Guard patrols seemed to stroll nonchalantly through the village, much to Thornton's disgust:

'You are in uniform and if an enemy paratroop observes you in the distance, he probably does not know what uniform it is [but] will have a crack at you, and "then there would be flowers in your bedroom in the morning, but you would not smell them." The point I am bringing out here is, at all times wherever possible, take as much cover as you can, bearing in mind that as soon as ever you are a casualty, you are a liability.'

Although he said 'Quorn achieved quite good results' by capturing eight prisoners, 'had they been real paratroops, Ladies and Gentlemen, I am certain Quorn would have suffered quite a few casualties.'

Mainly addressing the village's CD Services, he said '…it is not an earthly bit of use chasing paratroops unless you are armed and I want to stress this very particularly, I want you to leave the killing to me, that is my job and my job only'.[214]

By mid-1943 the invasion threat had all but disappeared. Never again would there be the costly, time-consuming, countywide exercises. Instead, the Home Guard started to step down a rung on the alert ladder and, as Col. Ogilvy-Dalgleish describes, find other things to do. 'We did, however, relax somewhat by holding fewer exercises and later in that fine summer most of the HG were busy getting in a good harvest.'[215]

Home Guard Spend the 'Holiday at Home'

With Britain now on an all-out war effort, the public were encouraged to spend their August holidays at home, thereby saving fuel and saving the railways for war industry. Various events across the counties encouraged people to participate in the campaign. The Home Guard also played their part:
'10,000 Saw Leicester "Into Battle" Show
A team from the 3rd (West Leicester) Battalion, Leicester Home Guard, were the winners of the Assault Course competition staged at the Oval, Abbey Grounds. They scored 627 points, second came the 13th (Post Office) Battalion 586 points and third the 2nd (South Leicester) Battalion 566 points. Cups were presented to the winners by the Lord Mayor Alderman S. Taylor.

The Assault Course event had thrilled the 10,000 crowd. There was also a display by Home Guard motorcycle despatch riders, plus a sub-artillery action by a Smith Gun section and, as the item of the afternoon, the Into Battle, 1943 show.'[216]

Arthur Kirkpatrick, formerly of Wigston Home Guard, remembers taking part. During the assault course, Home Guards had to climb over a wall carrying rifles with fixed bayonets. One Home Guard propped his rifle up on the other side just as another jumped over, the bayonet going right through his hand. Less serious was the result of the 'how to cross barbed wire' demonstration. One Home Guard threw himself on the wire while others ran over him. After they crossed, the man tried to get up and tore his battledress trousers to shreds![217] On 14 August 1943 the Home Guard took part in a large 'Holidays at Home' parade, with various uniformed Home Front organisations, down London Road, finishing in Abbey Park.[218]

Mystery Death of Leicester Home Guard Instructor

On the morning of 11 August 1943, James Bristow, 39, a Home Guard sergeant-instructor, was found fatally wounded in the cellar of his house in Danes Hill Road, Leicester. His wife heard a single shot and discovered him lying on his back. In court, Dr D.J. Smith showed how the Sten gun found by Mrs Bristow might have been fired. The doctor held the gun at arm's length, pointing towards his right temple and stated Bristow had a small circular wound at this point. Mrs Bristow said her husband, a Sten gun instructor, never seemed worried and knew of no reason why he should take his own life. The Coroner said there was not sufficient evidence to show if death was accidental and returned an open verdict.[219]

Colonel Ogilvy-Dalgleish Bows Out

Colonel Ogilvy-Dalgleish, Zone Commander and head of the Rutland Home Guard, suddenly retired, as he explained:
'My health had been indifferent latterly and in August 1943, it broke down altogether. I had been invalided to the retired list of the RAF in 1921 through ill health resulting from earlier naval service in the Far East, necessitating two major operations, so I suppose I had lasted fairly well considering the strain…of over three years with the Home Guard.

I was sorry to leave the Rutland Bn with which I had been so closely concerned from the start and whose members of all ranks had co-operated so loyally, in spite of the pressure of greatly-increased civilian work.

Major H.E. Whaley succeeded to the Command of the Bn with the rank of Lt-Col.; it was consoling to me to know… the Bn could not be in better hands.'[220]

Loughborough Home Guard's Flying Boot Bomber

Smaller exercises continued towards the end of the year with Exercise GEORGE in the Melton Mowbray area on 3 October 1943.

About the same time, the 9th (Loughborough) Battalion tested the defences of their hometown using somewhat unusual methods. It was assumed Loughborough was being attacked by paratroops and by road. Police at various vantage points informed the defending Home Guard on 'enemy' movements. The enemy did not take Loughborough, although several parties managed to enter the town. One lesson learned was that body searches had to be more thorough, after one prisoner exploded a 'grenade' in the defenders' HQ. The attacking troops came from Leicester City and Ashby, and there were two mobile columns from the north-west. It was the first time Loughborough used an aircraft for reconnaissance and the adjutant of the 9th (Loughborough) Battalion had some bombing practice dropping messages to his men in Home Guard boots! A mobile column found itself fighting on two fronts when it pursued an 'enemy' column, only to find another column was following it from behind.[221]

'Perfect Boys' Cause 'Considerable Damage' to Home Guard HQ

By 1943 the Leicestershire and Rutland Home Guard occupied 241 requisitioned premises, 210 hirings for winter training, 70 explosive stores, two huts and a further nine TA premises.[222] For the majority of the time, these buildings were unused and locked, so it was almost inevitable some would be disturbed.

'On 6 October 1943 three Secondary Schoolboys appeared at Leicester County Juvenile court, charged with breaking into a Home Guard store and stealing a rifle and other articles valued at £7 2s and 4d [£220].

One had such a good character at school that his headmaster said he was "about the last boy he would expect to do anything of this sort". The other two boys – one of whom was said by his father to have been a "perfect boy," also admitted breaking into a house while the occupier was away and stealing £4 [£124].

This father was asked if any steps had been taken to bring home the seriousness of the offences. He replied "He has had his money restricted and been ostracised at home, but no corporal punishment has been given pending the hearing of this case."

The boys were stated to have hidden the Home Guard rifle in a wood. They gained access to different rooms of the Home Guard premises by burrowing holes in the ceilings. A Sten gun and two bayonets were also said to have been missed, but defendants denied any knowledge of these. One boy was placed on probation for a year and the other two for two years. They had to pay costs and the boys who stole the money were ordered to refund it.'[223]

Home Guard Chief's Loughborough Lecture

On 18 December 1943 the Director-General of the Home Guard and army cadets, Major-General Lord Bridgeman DSO MC, met all commanding officers of all local Home Guard and cadet units at Loughborough Town Hall. He had come to talk about the WO's policy on the Home Guard and army cadets.[224]

Carrot and Stick

Absenteeism continued throughout Leicestershire and courts still dealt out hefty fines. However, magistrates adopted a 'carrot and stick' approach. They were more lenient towards cases they thought more deserving, often dismissing them. Fining hard-working men for missing a couple of hours square-bashing was almost a waste of time itself and court was only a last resort.

The 'D' team of the 1st (North Leicester) Battalion Leicestershire Home Guard, winners of the Silver Challenge Bowl in the final of the Leicester Sub-District miniature rifle competition, Saturday 5 February 1944. They defeated the Leicester city police team by one point, scoring 470 out of 480.

The court tended to make a few strong examples as a warning to other potential absentees, knowing the cases would be reported in the local press. Yet behind this strict face, there was an understanding the majority of cases were not through laziness but through work pressure. With the coming Second Front and the evaporating invasion threat, Home Guards would serve the country better at the workplace aiding production than standing guard at the gatepost. In essence, the Home Guard was now becoming second fiddle. Aware of the growing problem, Churchill sent a message to the Secretary of State for War:

'We should make every effort to ease the lot of the Home Guard, whose duties are more exhausting than those of any form of Civil Defence…Many of these men have had little free time for more than three years and compulsory parades, with fines, sometimes ending in imprisonment, for non-attendance, can cause considerable industrial unrest. Guards and strenuous exercises should be cut to a minimum…'[225]

Sad Goodbye to a Popular Leicester Home Guard

The year ended sadly for the Leicester Home Guard with the death of one of their well-known members. Captain Arthur S. George, 47, of Southmeads Road, was Quartermaster of the 1st (North Leicester) Battalion. He had been with the Home Guard from the start and was well known in many circles of city life. He died at a Lincoln Hospital on 23 December 1943 through an illness associated with his Home Guard service.[226]

1944: From Front-line Fighters to Rearguard Home Guard

'It is unfortunate that there should be village idiots and more unfortunate that they are not confined to villages. These are the ignorant, who called the Home Guard useless in their early unarmed days and see no useful purpose in the Force when Germany has been pushed back to the defensive. Such people have not read enough military history to realise that this country must have a large defence force until the enemy is not only down, but out.

Britain may no longer be the front line in the next campaign, but it will be the advance base to the Western Front. German counter-attacks and raids on that base must be expected, and…the Home Guard must be fit and ready to destroy these raids with speed and efficiency before they reach their objectives.'

Home Guard Instruction No. 64: Notes on Summer Training March 1944

'Mein Pal': Home Guards Helping Hitler?

Despite the continued problem of absenteeism, it was in real terms a very limited problem, with around one court case a month. Bearing in mind there were 22,000 Home Guards in both counties, reported cases of absenteeism ran to approximately 0.0005% of the total force – almost immeasurable.

With Britain on all-out effort for the coming Second Front, the Home Guard top brass did their utmost to dispel the notion that they harboured shirkers. So, bearing in mind the actual level of absenteeism was very low, it did not help in April 1944 when a damaging poster appeared on the streets appearing to accuse the whole force of being shirkers. Home Guards were even more shocked to discover this had been an attack from the rear – from the Home Guard Directorate themselves.[227] It was not surprising many Home Guards found the poster offensive; entitled 'Mein Pal!', the picture showed Hitler embracing a Home Guard with the word 'absentee' scrawled on his back. The poster was a sledgehammer to crack a nut, exaggerating the scale of the problem and, at worse, implying at first glance all Home Guards were absentees from 'proper' service.

Fortunately, after much criticism, the poster campaign was hurriedly withdrawn a few days after it had started, before it could do any further damage. Nonetheless, this had been an own goal against the morale of men who felt they were less appreciated than ever.

Moral Objections to Home Guard Service

The most common reason for objection to Home Guard service was a lack of time due to long work hours. However, in February 1944 a 47-year-old man from the Grange Farmhouse, Leicester Forest East, appeared before the Leicester Conscientious Objectors' Tribunal, objecting to Home Guard service because of his Christadelphian beliefs. He said he was partially disabled, but was willing to do ambulance work, but 'would not take up arms'. His name was placed on the CO register.[228]

'Ten-Footed' Home Guards On Theft Charges

On 12 February 1944 two Home Guards, a 32-year-old of Holden Street, Belgrave, and a 30-year-old of Surrey Street, Belgrave, were fined £5 (£155) each for stealing army boots from their HQ. After they had been on duty, a window was found smashed and the lock on a cupboard broken. Ten pairs of boots were missing, worth approximately £50 (£1,550). Some of the boots were recovered at the men's homes. Both defendants claimed they had taken them for their own use on Home Guard duty – but could not explain why they needed five pairs each![229]

Over Here

American troops had been based in Leicestershire since around 1943. In preparation for the coming Allied invasion of Europe, US paratroopers appeared locally in February 1944. When the US 82nd Airborne arrived in Mountsorrel, they parked on the outskirts of the village and looked somewhat forbidding figures in their deep, rounded helmets. According to Mr D.R. Taylor, whose father was Mountsorrel's village bobby, one horrified Rothley lady telephoned the police to warn the Germans had landed![230] Former Ibstock Home Guard Albert Squires remembers joint American and Home Guard exercises:

'From early 1944 we spent a lot of nights helping the US forces, namely the 82nd Airborne Division which was stationed near Leicester and the American Rangers, the equivalent of our Commandos, stationed at Gopsall Hall. We would defend the objectives and they had to attack under the cover of darkness. I now know this was the rehearsals for D-Day itself. But the Americans didn't take the exercises very seriously. They would walk up and practically give themselves up and then find somewhere to sleep the night away until their transport picked them up in the morning!'[231]

Relations between the Home Guard and their new American comrades-in-arms were largely very good. Sadly, however, the Americans did not endear themselves to everyone, as Major P.S. Wakefield recorded:

'Monday 6:3:44. Quorn is full of US paratroops. They and other Americans walk around Loughborough with the air of an occupying army in a conquered country. They certainly are not endearing themselves to the local people.'[232]

America's racial problems were also imported, as Ray Elgood, then a corporal in HQ Company, 1st (North Leicester) Battalion, experienced first hand:

'We used to go to Stoughton aerodrome and guard things. One duty, us four Home Guards went into the canteen. There was only about two people in the whole place and in the corner was this black chap eating his dinner. All of a sudden, in comes these four white blokes and kicked his chair from under him and threw his dinner all over him. I looked at Johnno and Johnno looked at me and I thought "this is not on" so I went over and belted this thug. There was 200 quids worth of damage done to the tables and I got a black eye and finished up in the police station at Charles Street.'[233]

At the end of March 1944, the Duke of Gloucester inspected the Whitwick Colliery Home Guard.[234]

Bravery of Mystery Home Guard

On 18 April 1944 an unknown Home Guard made a gallant attempt to save two dogs trapped in a blazing store room at Messrs Healeys, salvage waste merchants of Bow Street, Leicester. The fire broke out at 7.30pm and Mrs Storer, who lived opposite, raised the alarm, then fetched buckets of water from her house and handed them to the young uniformed Home Guard, who attempted to scale the gate to rescue two dogs who were trapped inside. Finding this impossible, with the help of others the Home Guard broke the gate down, only to find one of the dogs, Jack, had died from suffocation, and the other, Nellie, was badly burnt but alive. Before the NFS was able to control the flames, most of the baled waste had been destroyed. After the incident, the Home Guard disappeared into the night. Is that 'young Home Guard' reading this account, over 60 years on?[235]

The Home Guard's Important Role for D-Day

By this late stage of the war, a large-scale invasion of Britain was improbable. However, GHQ Home Forces worried about German paratroop counter-attacks designed to wreck the Allies D-Day preparations. In reality, German paratroopers were bogged down fighting in Italy and elsewhere, never to be dropped again en masse after their mauling three years earlier in Crete.

One anti-invasion exercise occurred on 30 April 1944, when the 1st (North Leicester) Battalion took part in Exercise READY. A report noted 'Excellent shooting by "E" Company with Blacker [Bombard] at taxi [target] at 300 yards.'[236] The Home Guard's anti-gas training was also renewed, as the WO believed the Germans might use this form of warfare in one last desperate move.

On 6 May 1944 hundreds of parachutes were reported descending east of Leicester, around Scraptoft and Tilton.[237] But the Home Guard had nothing to worry about: these were US paratroops of the 82nd Airborne Division training for their biggest jump, just one month away.

Home Guards also helped on other slightly more menial, but nonetheless important, tasks, including the packing of invasion stores, such as at the No. 10 Royal Ordnance (fuses and detonators) factory near Queniborough. Elsewhere, former No. 1 (Glenfield) Platoon, 3rd (West Leicester) Battalion John Swan remembers:

'Parties were sent to the REME Old Dalby Ordnance Depot to pack material for D-Day. I remember we always seemed to be packing crosspieces for the tops of signal posts to attach wires to, like telegraph poles. We used to get one shilling and sixpence subsistence allowance for this.'[238]

And, of course, there was always the harvest to gather in that summer. A cynic may say the Home Guard grabbed these jobs with relish as they had little else to do. This aside, no one can deny the Home Guard played their part in preparing for D-Day.

Leicestershire Home Guard Help Train Special Forces

Unbeknown to most Home Guards, several battalions engaged in two joint exercises, the importance of which many may never have discovered. Records stored in the National Archives, Kew, reveal some Home Guards took part in the secret training of Special Forces for their coming role behind the lines in occupied France.

Exercise CURB: This was in two parts, starting at 20.30 hrs on 11 May 1944 and finishing at 07.00 hrs next day. 'D' (Billesdon) Company of the 7th (Market Harborough) Battalion took part in an exercise against 'paratroop demolition parties at night'. Then, at 20.30 hrs on 13 May until 12.00 hrs the following day, one company from the 6th (Quorn) and the 7th (Market Harborough) battalions and a mobile column of the 12th (Motor Reconnaissance) battalion acted in a mobile role against these 'paratroop demolition parties'.

On both nights, the 'paratroop demolition parties' were composed of 'a complete force of 60 officers and NCOs of an Allied Commando Establishment'. They were identifiable as 'wearing a new form of steel helmet worn by Airborne Forces'. Parachute supply drops to the Special Forces were made the night before both exercises, the first drop ¼ mile south-west of Lyddington, Rutland and the second ¾ mile south of Somerby. The Home Guard were specifically ordered not to interfere with either drop. On the second night, the Special Forces would drive east from Welham to Medbourne, then head north to Hallaton.

The exact identity of this particular 60-man Special Forces unit is unknown. However, it may have been the 2nd SAS, some of whom are known to have been based locally at this date. Captain Michael Marsh MC, of 1 Troop, 2nd SAS Regiment, lived at Gartree, Sandy Lane, Melton Mowbray. Earning his MC in the Western Desert, he was seconded to the SAS under Col. David Stirling and saw action behind the lines during the Battle of El Alamein. As Trevor Hickman explains:

'Early in 1944 Marsh was detailed to train his troop of nine men in subversive actions behind enemy lines by infiltrating a Midlands airfield, marking planes as destroyed on the runway and returning to base without being observed. It is thought the airfield was Cottesmore. Travelling by night and hiding during the day, they successfully "attacked" the airfield, much to the annoyance of the regiment guarding the base who said this could not be done.'

Shortly afterwards, 1 Troop parachuted into France in support of the D-Day landings. They carried out daring missions with the Resistance, blowing up railways. After France was liberated, Marsh parachuted into Germany, again carrying out many dangerous operations until Germany was defeated. Tragically, Marsh died in a house fire at Burton Lazars in 1983.[239]

Exercise LASH: Three weeks later, on the night of 3-4 June 1944, the Leicestershire Home Guard once again undertook manoeuvres with Special Forces, called Jedburgh teams, who were based at Milton Hall, Peterborough. This time the exercise took place across the Charnwood Forest area, and, as can be seen from the amount of Home Guards and Jedburgh forces involved, was a big operation, especially so late in the war.

Jedburgh teams were an elite unit composed mainly of British, American and French troops. Their task was to parachute in small, three-man teams deep behind enemy lines into occupied France, to train and supply local resistance fighters. Jedburgh forces were also used to co-ordinate, via wireless, the actions of the resistance with SOE HQ and Supreme HQ Allied Expeditionary Force, into the overall strategy of the Allied armies following D-Day. Jedburgh teams sped about the French countryside in jeeps and worked alongside the SAS.

For the exercise, the 'British' were several companies of the 9th (Loughborough) Battalion, the 10th (Charnwood) Battalion, the 3rd (West Leicester) Battalion and the 8th (Market Bosworth) Battalion, with a mobile force of two companies each from the 4th (Central Leicester) and 12th (Motor Reconnaissance) Battalions. The 'Germans' were 300 officers and men of 'an Allied Commando Establishment', which amounted to the entire Jedburgh force.[240]

Again the exercise was dual purpose: for the Home Guard it was re-training 'against a surprise attack at night against VP guards and mobile units,' and for the Jedburgh teams it was valuable last-minute training: they were to contact a 'resistance group' and use it to help attack 'enemy' rail communications and other targets indicated via radio. The exercises gave the Special Forces training in cross-country driving and they provided night training for the Home Guard.[241] The first Jedburgh teams parachuted into France only two days later on the night of D-Day. For 20 Jedburgh troops, Leicestershire would be one of the last English counties they saw, as they did not return alive.

The Home Guard's Last Birthday

Between 13 to 20 May 1944 Leicestershire and Rutland celebrated the joint occasion of the Home Guard's fourth birthday and the National Savings 'Salute the Soldier' week, the target of which was to raise £5 million (£1.5 billion) for the armed forces.

'1,000 Home Guard's in Leicester "Salute The Soldier" Parade'

On Saturday 13 May 1944 a military parade of 3,000 men and women marching six abreast, plus a variety of armoured vehicles, stretched for over a mile through the streets of Leicester for the city's War Savings "Salute the Soldier" parade. Large crowds lined the route, which started on London Road ending in Town Hall Square. 1,000 Leicester Home Guards, led by the band of the 1st Battalion, took part.

The parade were met at the saluting base at the Town Hall by a Guard of Honour, headed by the band of the Leicestershire Regiment. Gen. Sir Clive Liddell, Hon. Colonel of the Regiment, took the salute and inspection. He was accompanied by the Lord Mayor of Leicester Councillor C.E. Gillot, the Sub-District Commander Col. F.G. Troup, Col. H.W.H. Tyler of the Leicester Home Guard, Mr Percy Gee the Chairman of the Leicester War Savings Committee, a Major General of the Czechoslovak Forces and an officer of the US Army.'[242]

'Gallant' Home Guard Attempts to Rescue Display Pilot

Several thousand spectators watched a military display the following day at the Abbey Park Oval, Leicester, as part of the campaign. The main event was to have been a competition between the Home Guard and RAPC, which the 13th (GPO) Battalion team won.[243] But the competition was overshadowed by the tragic death of 45-year-old Alfred Wykes, head of Taylorcraft Ltd of Rearsby, makers of the Auster light spotter aircraft. Wykes had been display flying in an Auster when it crashed behind the railway embankment on Abbey Lane.

During the final stages of the RAPC and Home Guard's assault course competition, two Austers flew over. The aircraft dived and looped several times to show their manoeuvrability. A Typhoon fighter-bomber then raced over them to show the contrasting speeds.

Few people noticed Wykes's Auster until its proximity to the ground in such a vertical position caught their gaze. The assault course continued unaware of the crash until there was a murmuring from the crowd. Only when a spire of black smoke rose above the embankment did anyone realised there had been an accident. The announcer on the loudspeaker appealed 'Civilians, remain where you are, please'. Despite repeating his request, curiosity overcame much of the crowd, particularly small boys, who swarmed over to the crash scene. Soon the railway line had a silhouette of figures.

First on the scene was Home Guard J.S. Matts, who made a gallant attempt to rescue the pilot, but he was driven back by the flames. When the fire died down, the deceased was seen to be pinned down under a wing. Matts lifted the wing and two other men named Lee and Orton dragged Wykes clear. Wykes had been killed on impact. The police had great difficulty trying to control the large crowd that gathered near the crash. All that remained was the framework of the burnt-out tailplane reared into the air.

The inquest was told Wykes was a qualified test pilot who had considerable flying experience and he had not tried any reckless manoeuvres. The other Auster's pilot, Geoffrey Edwards, chief test pilot for Taylorcraft, explained both aircraft were flying at 800ft when Wykes's aircraft dived, then made a steep climbing turn. He appeared to stall at the top of this turn. There was insufficient height to recover and the machine nose-dived into the ground and burst into flames. Wykes's wife and mother saw the crash.

Alfred Wykes lived in Barrow-on-Soar and had been a pilot in the Royal Flying Corps in World War One. He had started an aircraft engineering company with his uncle Percy Wykes in 1938 and helped design the Auster aircraft, which was used by the army for artillery spotting. Wykes's funeral was held near his home.[244]

Home Guard Birthday Party Poopers

On a lighter note, on 14 May 1944 the Quorn Home Guard held their birthday display on the Cricket Field to assembled military dignitaries. Lt-Col. William E. Ekman, CO of the Quorn-based 505th Parachute Infantry Regiment of the US 82nd Airborne, was invited but politely declined – unbeknown to his hosts, D-Day was just over three weeks away.[245]

Meanwhile, 'D' (Groby) Company of the 3rd (West Leicester) Battalion must have thanked their CO, who helped them 'celebrate' their anniversary by making them take a 14-mile ceremonial march through their company area, including Anstey, Newtown Linford and Groby. How celebratory these Home Guards must have been by the end of the march![246]

A month later, over 4,000 spectators witnessed a 'Home Guard Through the Ages' tattoo at the Brown's Lane ground, Loughborough. Over 500 performers demonstrated 1,000 years of home defence, from the Viking threat through to the present.[247]

Souvenir programme for the No.13 (Quorn) Platoon, 10th (Charnwood) Battalion's 'Home Guard Sunday' event, Sunday 14 May 1944, commemorating the fourth anniversary of the founding of the Home Guard.
(Quorn Home Guard Archive)

D-Day: 'Battle's Commenced!'

Although it had been long expected, the invasion of Europe came suddenly to the people of Britain. For the first time in years, the Home Guard once again prepared to stand to and looked to the skies for German paratroopers, as Major P.S. Wakefield recorded:

'Tuesday 6:6:44
"Battle's Commenced!" As I arrived in the Brush this morning I heard General Eisenhowers broadcast telling the world that Allied forces had landed in France...The Home Guard are wondering whether they will be called out tonight to stand against suicide interference raids by German paratroops. This, by the way, is called "D"-Day, whatever the initial stands for.'[248]

Fortunately, the counter-attack never came: the Germans had their hands full attempting to fend off the Allied invasion. The boot was now well and truly on the other foot. D-Day was also a significant date for the Home Guard, as it marked the last time they had to worry about any German attack on this country.

Young Home Guard Absentees 'Fail to do Their Duty at a Critical Time'

Perhaps due to the general belief that there was now no chance of a German invasion, in May and June 1944 seven cases of absenteeism were heard in court. In each case the magistrates dealt harsh fines to the offenders, who were once again mainly young miners. Home Guard chiefs pressed for strict fines because the force had once again gone on to the alert.

A 20-year-old miner from Breedon-on-the-Hill was charged with being absent from Home Guard parades. In his defence he said he had not been issued with any boots. Lt White said the defendant had not collected them and had only attended one parade in 12 months. He said the defendant and 'other young chaps seemed to think they could just show defiance towards the Home Guard'. Chairman of the Bench, Col. G. German, said the miner had 'failed to do his duty at a critical time' and fined him £3 and 13s 6d (£100) costs.[249]

Perhaps the biggest fine was handed down to a 19-year-old van driver, who was a member of the Hinckley Home Guard. He was summonsed on six different charges for failing to perform Home Guard duties without reasonable excuse. He was fined £3 on each charge and 5s costs, a total of £18 5s (£750). When he told the magistrate he could not afford to pay, he was told 'Married men with children are out there fighting for a mere pittance compared with what you are getting. You will have to pay or go to prison.'[250]

Sad Fatality Due to the Detritus of War

An inquest was held at the end of June 1944 into the death of Leonard Pearson, 36, a railway platelayer from School Lane, Scalford, who was killed by a Home Guard (possibly a No. 69) hand grenade in a railway cabin on the LNER railway at Scalford. He had suffered multiple injuries and burn marks to his face. Another man had found the grenade on the permanent way and placed it in the cabin. The following day, Pearson was found dead in the cabin by his brother, who also worked on the railway. The Melton coroner, Mr A.P. Marsh, who was also a Home Guard officer, said Pearson might have caused the grenade to explode by simply turning it.[251]

The wedding of LCpl Jim and Dorothy Tailby at the Methodist Chapel, Main Street, Dunton Bassett, 1 July 1944. The guard of honour is made up of Dunton Bassett Home Guards. (Jim Tailby)

Tragic Suicide of Troubled Home Guard Officer

On 19 July 1944 Leicester Corporation Transport Inspector and Home Guard Lieutenant Ronald Carlisle, 44, of Belgrave Road, Leicester, was found shot dead in a sand pit at Beaumont Leys Lane, used by the Home Guard for arms training. He had failed to turn up for work and his body was discovered by the police. He had a single bullet wound to the head and a service revolver was found by his body, filled with five cartridges and one empty one.

At the inquest it was revealed he had been involved in an accident in March 1943 while on Home Guard duties and suffered head injuries, a broken jaw and concussion of the brain. (This may possibly be the tragic Wanlip exercise where Lt Moffat was killed.) Apart from discomfort and sleeplessness, his wife believed he had made a full recovery. That morning he had seemed fine and had gone out to check on Home Guard ammunition, as he was the officer responsible. The coroner returned a verdict of 'suicide, while the balance of his mind was disturbed'.[252]

Marching to a Different Beat

'Holidays at Home Saturday' was on 12 August 1944. Three thousand CD, army, RAF, cadets, ex-servicemen and contingents from five Home Guard battalions marched down London Road and along Charles Street to the Town Hall, where a salute was taken by the Leicester Sub-District Commander, the Lord Mayor Councillor C.E. Gillot and other civic dignitaries. The Home Guard provided the guard of honour. The parade then marched to Abbey Park for dispersal. During the procession, at least seven different marching bands took part, including those of the Royal Horse Guards, the Leicestershire Regiment, the RA, the Home Guard, the RAPC Club, Leicester Imperial and Sea Cadets. Amusingly, the CO of the 101st Home Guard AA Rocket Battery noted:

'Captain R. Mawby led 100 Officers, NCOs and men of this battery in perhaps the largest parade Leicester has ever seen during the present war. The marching was almost perfect despite the fact the contingent had a band on their heels, keeping a different time from the one in front.'[253]

The End is Nigh

The invasion of Europe was now in full progress, beating the Germans back on all fronts. The Home Guard still exercised, as on 27 August 1944 when they held a District Spigot Mortar competition,[254] but this was more of a sporting competition rather than military training. There was a palpable feeling the good news on the continent meant the Home Guard's days were numbered.

There was much speculation among Home Guards about the force's future. The men were beginning to become disgruntled with the lack of information and the government's indecisiveness. They felt they were being treated shabbily and held in limbo. So, although the news must have been greeted with mixed emotion, it came as some relief when, on 6 September 1944, Mr P.J. Grigg, the Secretary of State for War, announced all Home Guard duties would cease forthwith. All training stopped a few days later, and it was later announced in October that the Home Guard would be stood down on 31 December 1944. Locally, training parades became voluntary from 11 September 1944.[255] However, many Home Guards continued attending and the force started to resemble a leisure club.

Final Moving Memories

John Bevis, then an 18-year-old in the Loughborough College Platoon, remembers his final Home Guard camp that summer:

'Shortly before the Home Guard was disbanded I was promoted to lance corporal and we had a weekend camp at Shepshed, sleeping in bell tents. Nobody took it very seriously, as there was no fear of invasion. So, it was a party, a lot of beer was consumed and I was sick in the tent. I didn't enjoy it and I have never been drunk since. One of the boys had a motorbike, which he wanted to sell. He offered it to me and I said I would think it over. When I returned he had offered it to another chap. I was for tossing a coin but the other chap fancied a shoot-out on the range. I agreed as I knew I was a good shot. Captain

Choate agreed to let us use the range and gave us .22 ammunition. I scored the highest and won the bike!'[256]

Maurice Woodward, formerly a private in the Snibston Colliery Platoon of 11th (Ashby-de-la-Zouch) Battalion, later recalled:

'D-Day came and went, our training still went on, but it was autumn of that year that I remember one particular day, which will be with me always.

Day: Sunday [17 September 1944], destination: unknown, orders: firing practice. As we were bussed to this firing range on the other side of the Six Hills crossroads, we realised it was no ordinary one. It consisted of 24 targets, the largest we'd been on. Our orders for a start were to occupy the butts and record scoring for those firing, and it was here we discovered the difference from those ranges we'd previously been on. It turned out to be an American range and as we went up and down the targets, their names, their towns, their states, were all cut on the wooden beams and posts, all relating to the American 82nd Airborne Division: just another name to us then, but history now shows it was one of their crack divisions.

Our spell in the butts over, we had a few rounds of rifle fire and then went on for a spell of machine-gun practice with the Bren gun. It was just after our platoon had finished firing and the cease fire whistle went. Everyone was surprised: surely they had not brought us all this way out just to call it off? We played football to wile away the time and then the reason why we had stopped firing became obvious: first it was just the noise of planes in the sky, then it became a crescendo. We stopped playing and sat on the grass and witnessed an incredible sight: Dakotas loaded with paratroops also towing gliders, from the airfields just beyond. They were flying so low they were only just missing the tree tops: it seemed you could pluck them out of the sky. I can only presume it was the 82nd Airborne, for wasn't we occupying their firing range? Whether it was them or the British Airborne Division, for them their training was over – for many, their lives. It now has a place in history – "A Bridge Too Far" [The Battle of Arnhem].'[257]

Stand Down – At Last?

As a signal from the government the war's end was now in sight, from October 1944 the blackout restrictions were relaxed. The Stand Down of the Home Guard was meant to be another such fillip, but when the official order took effect on 1 November 1944 it received a mixed reception. Bernard Spiers, a Home Guard signaller in the 12th (Motor Reconnaissance) Battalion, shares a recollection common among the interviewees: 'it just faded out, as if nothing had happened'.[258] The minutes of the Leicestershire and Rutland TA Association reflect this frustration,

'Straight away we would like to say the manner in which the problem of standing down the HG has been handled was regrettable, whether due to some political question or something did not function quite properly at the War Office cannot be said, but the method was peculiar and certainly not in accordance with military custom.'[259]

But for others, such as Jack Cox of the Belton Platoon, 10th (Charnwood) Battalion, Stand Down had not come too soon:

'I worked sixty hours a week and had to do two nights Home Guard duty. I was married with young kids, so I could spend more time with my family. But when it ended, I missed the camaraderie as I had made lots of friends.'[260]

Albert Purchase, of the LNER Braunstone Gate Goods Yard Platoon, also had mixed feelings – although he definitely felt cheated!

'We were all working fellas, so really, we were glad to see the back of it. However, I had been practising with my rifle for months and on the last Sunday I finally earned my marksman's badge. But on that same Sunday, I heard we were to be stood down, so I never got my badge!'[261]

SS and Luftwaffe POW's on the Loose in Leicestershire

Just when the Home Guard thought it was all over, some members were partially recalled for duty in an exciting muddy chase across a cold and dark Leicestershire,

'On 30 November 1944 a car stolen in Lichfield by four German POWs was found abandoned on the farm of Mr Stopps at Kibworth. The bonnet was still slightly warm. It was soon checked as missing. Then it was found Kibworth Golf Club House had been broken into. The lockers were opened and the floors of the dressing rooms literally carpeted with pullovers, flannel trousers and all other golfing apparel. In the clubroom, on the table, were laid a dozen empty grapefruit bottles, four empty jam pots and some sugar. Twenty packets of cigarettes and half a dozen boxes of matches were also missing.

The whole force of specials of the immediate neighbourhood were called out with regular policemen, and the Kibworth Home Guard was also summoned. Then started a midnight search of the fields and ditches. On the top of a strawstack not far from the golf club house, a motorcar rug and shirt were found. This pointed pretty clearly to the fact the prisoners had lain up on top of this half-cut stack to await an opportunity for breaking into the club house.

The hunt was really on after this and not only did the Home Guard join the police but half the villagers of Kibworth and farmers, plus British Military Police, men of the RAF and of the American Army Police. A moonlight night was a help, but it was a long and weary job over heavy country. Barns had to be searched, lorry drivers stopped and a stretch of railway line patrolled.

Then by 10 o'clock this morning came the news of the recapture of the prisoners. They had been located at East Norton, seven miles away as the crow flies. They were found not long after daylight by Sergeant Herbert, who was in company with PC Bradshaw, Mr G.R. Hector and some members of the special constabulary. Before they were captured, warning shots were fired by a police officer and Mr Hector, an RSM in the last war. The men had golf jackets over their uniforms. They stated they had lived on turnips from the fields.

Thus ended the biggest police force hunt ever organised in Leicestershire during the war. It was not confined to Leicestershire, the police of Leicester City, Rutland, Northampton and other adjoining counties were concerned.

"I'm going home now. I need about five dinners" said one special when the hunt was called off. Searchers carried either rifles or revolvers, were muddied up to their knees and looked a formidable search party. Later the prisoners were brought to county headquarters in Leicester for return to their camp. It is understood the prisoners' English was not good. At least one belonged to the Luftwaffe.'[262]

So, it seemed, the story ended there. However, in October 1981 the *Leicester Mercury* received a letter from Alfred Jean Schneider, of British Columbia, Canada, who revealed he was one of the POWs. The three other escapers were SS man Paul Haas, Helmut Luftsky and Karl Hans Gehricke. They had escaped from POW Camp 194 at Penkridge, between Stafford and Wolverhampton in Staffordshire. By strange coincidence, the POWs were all recaptured on Winston Churchill's birthday.[263]

But why had they escaped at this particular time? Penkridge was a notoriously harsh POW camp, housing mostly 'black' inmates, the name given to the most ardent Nazi prisoners.[264] As with other POW escapers, it is possible the men just wanted to escape the poor conditions and return to their families in Germany, hence their journey eastwards towards the coast. But there may also be another more sinister reason.

By late 1944 it was clear Germany was losing the war. Its armed forces were retreating on all fronts and many German troops were now POWs in Allied hands. It occurred to German High Command that, in effect, they had a large sitting army of around 250,000 men (equivalent to 48 divisions) languishing in British POW camps. British and American forces stationed in the UK numbered considerably less, as the majority of their forces were fighting overseas. If the POWs were to escape and cause havoc, they could weaken the British advance from the rear. So was born a wild and desperate plan centred on POW Camp 23 at Devizes, Wiltshire, where inmates planned to break out, seize weapons, tanks and aircraft from local bases, and march on London. This attack was planned to coincide with the German Ardennes offensive, The Battle of the Bulge, on 16 December 1944.

Fortunately, the British uncovered the plan at the last minute and stopped the breakout. However, several other POWs did escape – notably, on the assigned day, from Penkridge Camp. Thirteen POWs cut the wire in foggy conditions. Once free, they split up into small parties. But two were caught in Wolverhampton, two in Walsall, two in Derby, as well as four single-handedly by a police officer who tricked them into believing he was taking them to get a lift when their stolen car ran out of petrol, and two more in Liverpool. The 13th POW, who, it is thought, was heading for Liverpool to stowaway on a merchant ship, never returned to the camp and it is not known whether he successfully escaped.

Were the POWs captured in Leicestershire escaping as part of this march on London? One of the escapers was a member of the Luftwaffe, and it is known part of the plan was to capture Allied bombers and use them to bomb London. A crew of four may have been enough to pilot an Allied medium bomber. One of the other escapers, Paul Haas, was a member of the SS, the most fanatical wing of the Nazis. They unofficially ran the POW camps and were responsible for running the London plan: so was Haas the leader of this four man POW escape team?

However, the group escaped a full two weeks before the official breakout on the 16 December, so, alternatively, did these escapers just want to escape the harsh regime at Penkridge and co-incidentally made their escape near the same date?

Attempts to track the escapers again have proved unsuccessful, so we may never know. However, we do know that, despite being stood down, the Leicestershire Home Guard played a part in recapturing them. This dramatic episode appears to be the last active war duty of the Leicestershire Home Guard.

Programme of the National Home Guard farewell parade and Stand Down party in London, Sunday 3 December 1944.

STAND-DOWN PARTY
Royal Albert Hall
For members of the Home Guard only

Given by the following artists:—
TOMMY TRINDER
CICELY COURTNEIDGE
VERA LYNN
GEORGE ROBEY and
VIOLET LORAINE
BENNETT & WILLIAMS
JOSE FEARON and
CHARLES GILLESPIE
ELSIE & DORIS WATERS
ROB WILTON
AND
LOUIS LEVY with his Band of Fifty and a
Chorus of Thirty with MONIA LITER.

HOME GUARD
Farewell
PARADE
HYDE PARK
At 3 p.m.
AND
STAND-DOWN PARTY
ROYAL ALBERT HALL
At 6.30 p.m.
SUNDAY, 3rd DECEMBER, 1944.
PROGRAMME

The End: The Home Guard Stands Down
Leicestershire and Rutland Representatives Attend
the National Parade

Sunday 3 December 1944 was announced as the official day that would mark the Home Guard Stand Down. Nationally, there was a big farewell parade through Central London with over 7,000 Home Guards from each of the nation's battalions. Leicestershire and Rutland were represented by 45 men under Lt Frank Johnson. The men left on Saturday 2 December 1944, marching from Stanley Road, Stoneygate, to the London Road LMS Station. They were accommodated at barracks in London, where they were treated as guests of honour.[265]

The following day the men took part in the 90-minute parade with the King, as Colonel-in-Chief of the Home Guard, taking the salute at Hyde Park. Despite the rain, spectators stood 10 deep in places and the march gained front page news coverage. That night, famous stars of stage and screen including Vera Lynn, Tommy Trinder, Rob Wilton and Elsie and Doris Waters entertained many of the Home Guards at a Farewell Concert in the Albert Hall. Not unsurprisingly, Home Guard shortages continued right until the end: there were not enough seats, so lots had to be drawn. But it seems those Home Guards who were unable to gain entry did not lose out completely, as, by all accounts, they 'headed up West' and visited many London pubs and nightclubs where they were bought drinks and celebrated into the early hours! Ray Elgood, then a corporal in HQ Company, 1st (North Leicester) Battalion remembers:

'As we had all personally financed the furniture at our HQ, we sold it off and had a weekend in London. We had a 1934 Ford, which we had bought for Home Guard use. We had been getting in with fixed bayonets and bicycles, so you can tell what the inside was like, but we also sold that. With the money about 75 of us went in uniform down to London for two nights. We stayed in the Strand Palace Hotel and went to a show at Aldwych Corner House, where we had all the horseshoe balcony tables. Two of the boys objected to the chamber music, went downstairs and took over the instruments and everybody joined in!'[266]

In Leicester

In direct contrast, the Stand Down event in Leicester seems far from joyous. There was no big parade through the city, just a march past on Victoria Park. It was a drab, rainy day, perhaps reflecting the feelings of most of those taking part. Yet it was not all gloom: many Home Guards would leave the event with up to four and a half years of memories, coupled with a great sense of comradeship that would last long afterwards as friendship. The *Leicester Mercury* recorded:

'Leicester Sector Home Guard on its Stand Down parade in Victoria Park mustered a strength of nearly 5,000 and for this farewell there was a public attendance which reached a couple of thousand, a worthy compliment to the Home Guard this, remembering the conditions overhead and underfoot, and the lack of public transport.

Memories recalled

The parade ground of earlier times being in other use [it was now the site of the 101st Leicestershire Home Guard/RA AA Rocket Battery], the battalions formed up upon ground near Victoria Park Road. With the Lord Lieutenant came the Lord Mayor Alderman J. Minto and awaiting were Col. H.W.H. Tyler MC commanding the sector: Lt-Col. C.A.B. Elliott, second in command, with other officers of the Home Guard: Lt-Col. G.B. Stafford, Commander, and Capt. C. Sydenham (Leicester Sub-District); also the OCs of the RAOC and RAPC, and the OCs of the navy, army and air cadets.

Having inspected the guard of honour, the Lord Lieutenant, before reading the King's Message, addressed the parade through loudspeakers, saying "I have come here to thank you for and to congratulate you on work very well done." He thanked them for the enthusiasm that had been shown and for all the sound work done in what should have been their own spare time. He hoped that the comradeship which had grown up in years of Home Guard duty would continue through the days of peace.

Following the Royal Salute, the battalions formed six abreast and, through a lane which Police Messengers and Specials lined with markers, reached the path to the main gates.

At Saluting Base

Here on a platform halfway along the drive stood the Lord Lieutenant, the Lord Mayor, Col. Tyler and Lt-Col. Elliott. The band of the 1st Battalion Home Guard, under Bandmaster C.A. Anderson, was formed in on the other side of the path. The Regimental March of the Leicesters is good music. Then came the 1st Battalion's "Eyes right, eyes front" and out through the North Memorial gateway. As each commanding officer reached the saluting base at the head of his battalion, he wheeled out to take a place on the platform beside the Lord Lieutenant and see his men go by. Soon the little platform was filled with battalion commanders. Most who were there yesterday must have felt rather sad on that last parade, but they would be thankful to recall the time they took part in it.'[267]

Across the County

In Loughborough, over 1,200 Home Guards attended the Stand Down ceremony. The 9th (Loughborough) Battalion paraded on Brown's Lane ground, where the Sub-District Commander J.A.S. Hopkins DSO read the King's proclamation. Lt-Col. H.J. Stamper, CO of the 9th Battalion, thanked the men for contributing 'in no inconsiderable way, to winning the war'. He also urged them in the difficult years that lay ahead to help 'win the peace'.

The 10th (Charnwood) Battalion had planned to parade on Loughborough College Playing Fields, but, due to the wet weather, instead assembled in the Odeon Cinema, Loughborough. A service was conducted by their padre, Revd F.C. Hargreaves. After the King's Message had been read by Brigadier-General R.S. Abbott, Lt-Col. C.H. Martin, the CO of the 10th Battalion, addressed his men.

His speech was met with three cheers. Afterwards, both battalions marched past the saluting base in the Market Place to music provided by the Brush band. Members of the women's Home Guard

Lt Frank Johnson leads a parade of 45 Home Guards, containing representatives of all Leicestershire and Rutland's Battalions, to the LMS Station, London Road, Leicester, Saturday 2 December 1944. The men took part in the national Stand Down parade in London the following day.

Home Guards parade in the rain past the saluting base on Victoria Park car park, Leicester, Sunday 3 December 1944. Taking the salute, from left: Leicestershire's Lord Lieutenant Sir Arthur Hazlerigg; Sector Commander Col. H.W.H. Tyler MC (partially obscured); Leicester's Lord Mayor Alderman J. Minto and Leicester Sector Deputy Commander Lt-Col. C.A.B. Elliott.

Auxiliary also attended, but did not parade. From there, the various companies dispersed and marched through their respective villages.[268]

Elsewhere, over 1,000 officers and men from the Hinckley, Earl Shilton, Market Bosworth and Ibstock Home Guard paraded at Queen's Park, Hinckley, where they were inspected by Col. J.L. Griffiths DSO DL. Lt-Col. J.T.L. Baxter gave the final dismissal.[269]

In Market Harborough, Lt-Col. H.D. Belgrave, CO of the 7th (Market Harborough) Battalion, gave thanks for the services of not only the officers, NCOs and men of the battalion, but also the 'wives, mothers and others who have contributed so much to the success of the battalion by the work they have done behind the scenes.'

Home Guard companies from the Coalville and Ashby areas paraded at Coalville and then marched to the Regal Cinema, where, in the presence of members of the local urban council, Col. G. German DSO read the King's Message. Lt-Col. Statham, CO of the 11th (Ashby-de-la-Zouch) Battalion, read a message from General H.E. Franklyn, C-in-C. Home Forces. Lt-Col. Statham then said he was proud of the 11th Battalion, whose men had more proficiency badges than any other battalion in the North Midland District. The battalion then paraded in Marlborough Square and marched to the War Memorial, where Col. German took the salute.

Men of the 5th (Belvoir) and 6th (Quorn) Battalions took part in the Stand Down parade at Melton Mowbray. Buses from a wide area brought village Home Guards into the town, where they also attended a film show in the town's cinemas. Sub-District Commander Col. J.A.S. Hopkins DSO addressed the men and read the King's Message. Both battalion commanders, Lt-Col. H.J. Fellowes-Prynne of the 5th Battalion and Lt-Col. Sir Harold Nutting of the 6th Battalion, spoke appreciatively of the loyal service shown by the officers and men. On behalf of the officers of the 5th Battalion, Major Sir Arthur Curtis presented Lt-Col. Fellowes-Prynne with an illuminated address signed by every officer of the battalion. After the cinema show, the men marched through Melton to the saluting base outside the Modern Girls' School, where Col. Hopkins took the salute. The final dismissal was given on the Wilton Road car park. In the evening, the Melton Mowbray companies held a Stand Down supper at the Oddfellows' Hall.[270]

In Rutland

The *Lincoln, Rutland and Stamford Mercury* recorded:

'The Rutland Home Guard assembled for their "standing down" parade on Sunday morning [at Oakham]. The Rutland Battalion is a very scattered unit and each village and hamlet has had its own platoon or section. This, therefore, was a unique occasion, for it was the only opportunity the inhabitants of the county had of seeing its Home Guard parade as a battalion.

Signed 10th (Charnwood) Battalion Leicestershire Home Guard Stand Down dinner souvenir menu, Friday 29 December 1944. (Quorn Home Guard Archive)

The companies assembled in different parts of the town and marched to the battalion assembly point near the railway station under their company commanders. The battalion was then taken over by the Commanding Officer, Lieut-Col. H.E. Whaley, and headed by the Rutland Police Band and the Drums of Oakham School JTC marched past the saluting base at the County Cinema, where the salute was taken by the Lord Lieutenant of the County (The Earl of Ancaster, GCVO)…

On reaching the market place, the battalion was drawn up in close formation and was inspected by the Lord Lieutenant, who afterwards ascended a platform accompanied by his Deputy-Lieutenant (Major G.K.F. Ruddle), the first commanding officer (Lieut-Col. the Hon. C.H.D. Willoughby), Mr Billows (vice-chairman of the Oakham UDC), Mr Watchorn (chairman of the Oakham RDC), Capt. A.D. Potter and Mrs Street, WVS…

Colonel Whaley, in taking farewell of the battalion, read a letter from a former Commmanding Officer (Colonel Ogilvy-Dalgleish OBE) who was ill in hospital, but sent his best wishes to the men of

Officers of 'B' Company, 4th (Central Leicester) Battalion at their Stand Down dinner, Saturday 30 December 1944, the night before the Home Guard was officially stood down. From left: Lt J.H. Corah; Major J.W. Lancaster; 4th Battalion Commander Lt-Col. W. Nelson Dunn; mess president Lt W. Bentley and 'B' Company Commander Major O.B. Knight.

his old battalion. The companies then marched off separately to be dismissed for the last time by their company commanders.'[271]

Christmas 1944 was truly bleak, the bad weather made all the worse by a lack of food and gifts in the shops. And to cap any possible chance of the former 1,685,000 Home Guards forgetting by drowning their sorrows in New Year's celebrations, the force was officially stood down on 31 December 1944. [272] But the end was not all despondency. Most battalions also held farewell suppers and dances for the men and out of 808 Home Guards honoured by the king for their services to the force, seven were from Leicestershire and Rutland, the recipients receiving two OBEs, three MBEs and two BEMs (See Appendix E).

1945 and Beyond

'Another great value the Home Guard had [was that] it also built up a comradeship, which is a precious thing. Gentlemen, we must not let this pass, as I do feel this is what will help us in the post war years and I am certain we shall need every atom of comradeship to help us to overcome the many difficulties which will take place after the war.'

Stand Down dinner speech by Lt C.W. Thornton, CO 13th (Quorn) Platoon,
10th (Charnwood) Battalion, Leicestershire HG, 9 March 1945.

Some Thanks

At the start of the new year, those still serving at Stand Down began to receive certificates marking their service in the Home Guard. However, issue of these certificates was piecemeal. Ironically, those Home Guards who had left the force and were now serving their country overseas did not receive a service certificate, just the same as those Home Guards who had been dismissed from the force on disciplinary grounds. Many have never received a certificate to this day. Although discussed, a separate Home Guard service medal was never struck. Instead, those who had served in the force for a minimum of three years were entitled to the Defence Medal, but, again, issue was inconsistent, as former Ibstock Home Guard Albert Squires remembers:

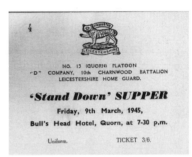

Ticket for the Stand Down supper of No.13 (Quorn) Platoon, 'D' Company, 10th (Charnwood) Battalion Leicestershire Home Guard, at the Bull's Head Hotel, Quorn, Friday 9 March 1945. (Quorn Home Guard archive)

'The one disappointment I have of those years is that I wasn't allowed to claim a Defence Medal as all the others in the unit did. I was told not to apply as I had joined underage and did not qualify. At this time, my mind didn't dwell on such things as medals. But as I have grown older I can see the injustice, as I did all that the others did and faced what others faced in the way of risk and danger.'[273]

To add insult to injury, the Home Guard were told they would have to return their uniforms. Not only were the men proud of their uniforms, but they had little else in way of a memento of their service. Their uniforms were also valuable in a time of clothes rationing: badges could be removed and hard-wearing battledress could be used for all sorts of domestic tasks. It was only once Churchill had personally intervened that this mean-spirited decision was overturned and they were allowed to keep them.

It is not difficult to see why the Home Guard felt they had been treated shabbily by the very authorities who had called upon them when they needed them in the first place.

The Defence Medal, awarded to some Home Guards.

The TA's Hard Work Continues

However, the 1944 Stand Down did not mark the end for the hard-pressed Leicestershire and Rutland TA Association. Home Guard work continued in abundance: processing final accounts

and paperwork, clearing and closing down offices and accounts, and collecting and checking stores and ammunition. The final statement regarding the Home Guard in the TA minutes relate:

'All equipment, clothing, arms and ammunition were withdrawn by HQ staff of the TA to Leicester and dealt with there:

Rifles: 11,758
Sten guns: 5,947
Light MGs: 399
Ammunition: 225 tons
Components of small arms and equipment: c.75 tons
Clothing and personal equipment: c.100 tons'

Clearing Up

As can be seen, in four and a half years the Home Guard had amassed a lot of ammunition. Ray Elgood, then a corporal in HQ Company, 1st (North Leicester) Battalion, had the highly-dangerous task of disposing of some of it.

'When it came to Stand Down, we had to clear out the armoury at Humberstone Lido. We got rid of the ammunition easily, but we had all these blasting powders and hundreds of '36 grenades. We were told to get rid of it all in Beaumont Leys pit. By this time the explosive was particularly unstable and leaking on the armoury floor. One of the sergeants got some nitro on his hand and it put him in hospital. He had colossal headaches and couldn't see anything.

For some reason they delivered us dozens of trailers. So I got the Ford and rigged up a towbar about ten feet long with a trailer on the end. We put amatol and nitro in and drove very gently up to this pit. We only went on the roads when there was no traffic. Once at the pit, I got quite adept at backing these trailers up to the edge. Somebody would then pull the tow pin out, I'd drop it in reverse, give it a nudge and then I'd go forward as fast as I could while the trailer went over and bang! None of them reached the bottom it was so unstable.

I also had a team with Mills grenades sitting on the side of the pit, putting a fuse in and chucking them over. But then we got complaints from the houses about the grenades' baseplugs landing on the roofs, so we thought "why are we putting them on anyway?" We found most of the grenades would go off without them. Some had two-second fuses, horrible things as used by the Special Forces. All sorts of things went in…whole cases of SIP bottles: plenty of those. It was like a war there for about a month.'[274]

For Maurice Woodward, formerly a Private in the Snibston Colliery Platoon of 11th (Ashby-de-la-Zouch) Battalion, the clear up was quite cathartic:

'When the weather picked up in the spring [1945], orders came that all live ammunition was to be destroyed. One Sunday morning, before dismantling the bombing bay, surplus hand grenades were primed and thrown for the last time. The Molotov Cocktails were taken out and lined up just like a shooting gallery and were destroyed with small arms fire – this also used up the Sten gun ammunition. There was a great amount to destroy, but magazine after magazine was emptied before the task was completed. Some fired in anger, some in relief, but all knowing a new life lay around the corner. Looking back, I was proud to do my bit "for King and Country". I was equally proud to serve with the men of Dad's Army, for the quality of man was not measured in the wallet, but in the man himself.'[275]

The Home Guard's Part in the VE Thanksgiving Celebrations

Within five months, the war drew to a close in Europe as Germany was finally defeated. On VE Day 8

May 1945, celebrating crowds thronged the streets of Leicester and danced around the Clocktower. However, as fighting was still occurring in the Far East, there was no victory procession through Leicester. Instead, on 13 May 1945, over 1,000 service personnel, including representatives of the Home Guard, attended a Thanksgiving Service in Leicester Cathedral, followed by a march past the Town Hall, but the event attracted little more than a few paragraphs in the local press and did not even make the front page. It would be over a year before full official victory celebrations occurred. Almost as an afterthought, the Home Guard were finally disbanded on 31 December 1945.

A representative honour guard of Home Guards march past Leicester town hall steps during the VE day Thanksgiving parade, Sunday 13 May 1945.

1946 Victory Day Celebrations: the Final Parades

However, the Home Guard's final ceremonial duties did not end there. On 7 June 1946 nine members of the Home Guard and the Leicestershire and Rutland TA Association, led by Major R.E. Cruickshank VC, left the LMS station to attend London's Victory Parade.[276]

On Saturday 8 June 1946, the same day as the London National Victory Parade, Leicester similarly held a large march past. Braving the grey skies, the parade marched down London Road to the centre of town. All the services, civil and military, were represented. However, the small Home Guard contingent that marched in the parade was merely token. A year and a half since the Home Guard had stood down, most men had moved on. Huge crowds, greater than at any of the wartime parades, lined the route, often up to eight deep. Among the dignitaries on the saluting base in Charles Street was Lt-Col. H.W.H. Tyler, former head of the Leicester Group Home Guard. However, most of the afternoon's outdoor events were cancelled due to a downpour. As the *Leicester Mercury* reported:

'The centre of Leicester had the appearance of Christmas Day rather than Victory Day. Streets were deserted and infrequent trams and buses operating a skeleton service carried few passengers.'[277]

In this way, Leicestershire's Home Guard made their last public appearance, ending the force's war with more of a damp squib than a triumphant blast.

Keeping the Home Guard Spirit Alive?
Home Guard OCAs and Rifle Clubs 1944–1970

The Home Guard Old Comrades Associations: 1944 Onwards

Lapel badge for the 1st (North Leicester) Battalion Home Guard Old Comrades Association.

On 11 September 1944, the day it was announced all Home Guard parades would become voluntary, the *Leicester Mercury* reported Home Guard commanders were putting out 'feelers'. One officer stated at least half his men wished to continue. It was proposed the Home Guard's spirit of comradeship could be continued into peacetime through the creation of Old Comrades Associations.

Perhaps the strongest of these associations was the 1st (North Leicester) HG OCA, who had their own badge. One sub-section, the Birstall HG Comrades Association, met at the White Horse Inn and had a membership card.

Some OCAs started a financial hardship fund for any of their members who had suffered misfortune. OCAs also raised funds for charity, such as the Leicestershire POW Fund or local causes, the funding of a 4th (Central Leicester) Battalion Home Guard Bed at the Leicester Royal Infirmary for example. On 5 May 1945 the battalion's chaplain, the Revd A.E. Harris, officiated a dedication service at the hospital, with the CO of the battalion, Lt-Col. Nelson Dunn, performing the unveiling ceremony. The battalion had raised £1,170 (£36,270) and the balance was spent on trophies for annual sports competitions.[278]

But although these OCAs started with high hopes and good intentions, it appears most Home Guard OCAs simply fizzled out within a few years of their formation. The reasons for this are not clear. Regular Army regimental OCAs thrived and continue to this day.

The key to their swift decline may be because, although there was a large amount of service veterans in the force, many of the Home Guards were, in reality, 'directed' into it through compulsion. There was a great feeling of 'start again' in 1945 and many had simply had enough of the war and wanted to move on. Many of the younger Home Guards were now in the armed forces or demobbed and looking for work, often outside the county.

As a rule, OCAs were mainly composed of older Home Guards, and it seems the associations simply died out with them. Ironically, the Home Guard Rifle Clubs that were formed as sub-sections of the OCAs appear to have outlived their parent associations.

Souvenir programme for Leicester City Transport Home Guard Supper, Friday 6 April 1945. (Kathy Heald)

The Home Guard Rifle Clubs: 1944 Onwards

Born as the sporting wing of the OCAs, many Home Guard Rifle Clubs were formed before Stand Down. They met official WO requirements and were affiliated to the National Rifle Association.

From the start, some, such as the 10th (Charnwood) Battalion, realised battalion-sized rifle clubs were not practical 'owing to the scattered nature of the battalion,' so smaller clubs were formed.[279] In some areas this worked, 'A' Company of the 10th Battalion formed a club, as did 50 Home Guards at Beaumanor Hall. Some thrived, with 10th Battalion members reaching the top 100 on the national Home Guard Rifle course.[280] Long before the days of firearm bans, platoon-size clubs must have had fervid fun, as records show not only were they issued with five .22 rifles and 10 .300 rifles, but also 10 Sten sub-machine guns!

The Home Guard was reformed in 1952 to meet the growing threat of the Soviet Union. However, it was a flop compared with the success of its wartime predecessor. An attempt was made to raise seven battalions in Leicestershire and Rutland but none of them reached more than platoon strength. In a time of nuclear weapons and instant mass destruction, a Home Guard seemed pointless to the populace. The government quietly ended the second-phase Home Guard in 1957.

Post-war 3rd (West Leicester) Battalion Home Guard/National Rifle Associaton rifle club blazer badge. (Roger Miles)

Just before they did, the existing battalions were given the opportunity of forming shooting clubs. At first 'great interest' was shown, but when the final Stand Down came, economic factors decided matters. As most battalion districts covered large rural areas, members would have to travel long distances to make the clubs viable. Without central funding, most decided this would be too difficult and only the 1st (Leicester City) Battalion kept its rifle club, to whom the Home Guard commanders left their brief parting words in the TA minutes: 'We wish them every success in their competition shooting within civilian leagues in the future.'[281]

Members from these post-war Home Guard Rifle Clubs may well have simply joined the few wartime OCA rifle clubs still in existence. Their stalwarts still met but it seems there was little fun to be had, as the Thurnby Home Guard Rifle Club logbook records, 'Club room very cold with few amenities. However, a few members valiantly formed a team and shot fairly regularly at the Leicester University rifle range once a week.' However, when the club secretary Bob Hakewell left Leicester, it acted as one of the final nails in the club's history, as the then acting secretary J.A. Cooke recorded 'Owing to lack of support, unable to form a team for the season's winter league.' The final forlorn entry records the club's last meeting was held at Leicester University in October 1970: 'Club would no longer carry on through lack of support and a gun dealer would value stock.'[282]

The Royal British Legion: 1944 to the Present

Left Out in the Cold

Ironically, the British Legion, who had done so much to help set up and support the LDV, now turned their back on the Home Guard. At a meeting of the Leicestershire and Rutland Council of the British Legion in November 1944, Mr A.S. Burdett of the Aylestone Branch forwarded a motion that Home Guard service should not constitute ordinary membership for the Legion and the use of Home Guard rank should be dispensed within Legion circles. The motion was carried unanimously.[283]

Traditionally, membership of the Legion had been open to all those who had seen active service in the armed forces, and this move may have been taken so as not to antagonise returning troops. Although former Home Guards could join the Legion as Honorary members – the same as the general public – they were refused the ordinary membership ex-services were entitled to. It appears very few Home Guards took up this halfway offer. Harry Gudger, formerly of the Birstall Platoon, 1st (North Leicester) Battalion, recalls 'We felt very let down. We felt the ex-services put themselves in a different class, implying they served and we hadn't.'[284]

This did seem rather heartless and reinforced the misbelief they were not 'proper' soldiers. With sound reason, it can be argued many Home Guards saw more action than a lot of Regular troops who served in support services at barracks or depots. Home Guards captured enemy airmen, rescued Allied airmen from crashed aircraft, manned AA defences and engaged enemy aircraft, provided defence for military installations and relieved Regular troops of more mundane sentry duties. Most poignantly, 1,206 Home Guards died serving their country. The war was fought in Britain too, and it was with good reason the term 'Home Front' was created. Under these terms, it is hard to see how the Home Guard served any less.

It was in this spirit, on 3 December 1944, the Lord Lieutenant of Leicestershire, Sir Arthur Hazlerigg, used his Stand Down speech in Victoria Park, Leicester, to say he hoped the Legion would 'rectify' their decision. But it made no difference. For this reason, separate Home Guard OCAs were formed.

The British Legion's 'no' decision was reinforced when, in May 1945, without debate, delegates at the national British Legion conference in London decided by an overwhelming majority against amending the charter to admit Home Guards as ordinary members.[285] However, as a slight concession, they allowed local branches to decide whether Home Guards could join. In some parts of the country, local Legion branches independently accepted the Home Guard straight away at Stand Down – most did not. As far as ordinary membership in Leicestershire and Rutland is concerned, it appears most Home Guards were left out in the cold.

A New Attitude: Local RBL 'Prepared to Fight' For Home Guards

Locally, it would seem the first seeds of change sprouted in August 1975, when Oadby Royal British Legion Club made a 'determined effort' to contact former members of the Home Guard, NFS and other CD services, because they 'never got the recognition they deserved'. Perhaps this interest was partly kindled by *Dad's Army*, which was then at the height of its popularity. The Oadby Club wanted to organise a special 'thank you' bank holiday musical night for them.

The *Leicester Mercury* reported attempts were being made at a national level to allow members of the former civilian services to join the Royal British Legion.[286] At the Leicestershire British Legion County quarterly conference, Oadby branch put forward a motion for the admission of Home Guards. It appears at a local level the RBL's attitude towards the Home Guard had mellowed somewhat. The branch had presented the motion five times and each time it had got through county level but had come to a 'dead end' at national level. Frank Jew, the branch's public relations officer, said when the motion reached the next national meeting the 'members were prepared for a fight'.[287]

However, it would take another six years of fighting before the RBL finally relented. Delegates at their 1981 Annual Conference voted to allow 'Men who served in the Home Guard for at least six months…or who were awarded the Defence Medal in respect of service in the Home Guard…' to become ordinary members, the same as other ex-services. This meant the ruling became RBL law nationally. While this could only have been welcomed, it came too late for thousands of Home Guards who had since passed on.

What was the reason for the RBL's late change of heart? Would it be cynical to say almost 40 years since the war, natural depletion had caused membership to fall, so allowing former Home Guards to join would boost this flagging membership? Yes it would, says George McGilvery, Head of the Secratariat at the RBL's London HQ. 'They became eligible for membership while the Legion was still a very healthy membership organisation just short of one million members.'[288]

This may have been the general case nationally, but at least one local branch was not so healthy. Oadby branch had tried to maintain a 60–40 ratio of Ordinary to Honorary membership, but at one stage ex-services were not coming forward anymore, so Honorary membership had to be closed for two years. At Oadby branch, it was not until 1984, a full three years after the national ruling, that former Home Guards were finally allowed to move from Honorary to Ordinary membership, three of whom took advantage of their new status and became full members.[289]

Today, the Royal British Legion's membership rules are all inclusive. According to the RBL website, 'We welcome men and women of all ages, whether they have served in the Armed Forces or not.'[290]

Perhaps a final marker of recognition can be dated to Remembrance Sunday in November 2002, when, for the first time, with the RBL's support, a small contingent of 15 former Home Guards, including *Dad's Army* creator Jimmy Perry, marched and laid a wreath in memory of their colleagues at the London Cenotaph service.[291]

To The Last Round: Home Guard Reunions

Despite the dissolution of the Home Guard OCAs and Rifle Clubs, some reunions did occur to rekindle a bit of the old Home Guard spirit. In May 1977 20 of the original 27 members of the No. 7 (Illston-on-the-Hill) Platoon, 7th (Market Harborough) Battalion, held a reunion at their local Fox and Goose

The last round? Nearly 20 former Home Guards of No.7 Platoon, 'B' (Wigston) Company, 2nd (South Leicester) Battalion went to a reunion at the Wigston Royal British Legion club on 20 November 1980. Raising a toast to the Home Guard from the left: William Tyler, Victor Williams, Tom Rainbow, Ted Williams, Joe Hopton, Albert Thompson, Cecil Richards, Bob Cross, Albert Vann and Harold Ward.

pub. The *Leicester Mercury* reported many happy stories were recalled for the first time in 33 years over 'jars of ale', which was organised by former Home Guard Private Clarence Jones.[292]

Although not yet full members, one platoon even held a reunion at their local RBL club.

'"Most Successful!" was the verdict of ex-Home Guards, who attended the reunion at Wigston Royal British Legion on 20 November 1980. It had been brought about by a Memory Lane Photograph in the *Oadby and Wigston News*. Nearly 20 members of No. 7 Platoon, "B" Company (Wigston Area) of the 2nd Leics Bn HG turned up. It was organised by Ted Williams, who was the head barman at Wigston British Legion. He had joined the Home Guard at the age of 15. His father was a lance corporal, C.P. Williams, also in the Home Guard. It was on the suggestion of Mr Stan Bunting of Loughborough.'[293]

It is not known how many other reunions took place – or even if there were any others – but for many Home Guards these happy social events over a pint really were 'the last round'.

CHAPTER 3:

THE MILITARY DEFENCE OF LEICESTERSHIRE AND RUTLAND 1940–1944

First Phase: Summer 1940-November 1941: 'Every Round a German'

LDV: Look But Don't Touch

As soon as the LDV achieved some basic semblance of organisation, they took their first tentative steps to defend the two counties. Due to their limitations, their chief role was to report parachutists, not to engage the invader. Thirty-five observation posts were set up on high ground in Rutland, including on Glaston tunnel hill and Whissendine Windmill.[294] A surviving LDV map shows the OPs plotted throughout Charnwood.[295]

As arms began to appear, where they could the LDV were to 'attack and harass the enemy'. Defence Posts were situated throughout the countryside 'to attack enemy airborne troops…and prevent them from coalescing…' Because of double summer time, there was now an early dawn, and it was feared the enemy might take advantage. Correspondingly, dawn patrols were made across high ground between Oakham and Uppingham. A night patrol was provided for the Rutland half of the Welland Railway Viaduct with the Northamptonshire LDV, until Army Home Defence detachments succeeded in October 1940.

However, the most vulnerable points were the RAF airfields. Even though the LDV were unable to provide any meaningful defence, surviving plans of an LDV defence exercise on Braunstone aerodrome[296] and Col. Ogilvy-Dalgleish both underline this.

'The chief danger spot in Rutland at that time was Luffenham air station, then under construction. The control tower was partially finished…but the fine airfield was complete and the enemy could have landed large numbers of men by troop carriers, right in the heart of the country, on any suitable night or early morning. Application was made for regular infantry to guard the airfield, but no troops were available and none of the local RAF Commands seemed responsible for seeing the airfield was blocked, as was done elsewhere in similar circumstances.

After some circumlocation I got in touch with the Air Ministry Civil Dept. responsible and had the airfield blocked with old motor buses, tree trunks, lorries, etc, leaving a space clear for light aircraft to land at the top end. This did not give complete security, of course, but would cause some delay…Three Air Stations in a comparatively small area were a heavy liability and we accordingly received a generous allotment of weapons, as these became available…'[297]

First Defence Plans

The first serious attempt at defending Leicestershire and Rutland occurred at the beginning of June, when troops began returning from Dunkirk. 'The Rutland LDV were now included, for first time, in a military sector i.e. a geographical sub-division in which all troops were under the operational command of a designated sector commander. This was the Southern Sub-Section Sector X, of 1st Corps, under command of Lt-Col. J. Dawson DSO of 4th Cheshires at Burley. It included the following:

"A" Company 4th Cheshires, E Company 4th Cheshires, HQ Company 4th Cheshires, 50th Royal Scots Fusiliers at Melton Mowbray, 50th Seaforth Highlanders at Somerby, RE Searchlight Company at

Ashwell Camp, Cypriot Company, RASC at Ashwell Camp and the Rutland LDV.

The 4th Cheshires were to form the main defence of Oakham, assisted by Oakham and district LDV; the support of these battle-tried troops in the defence of the county town was very welcome.'[298]

In Leicestershire, returning Leicestershire Regiment troops were also available. About this time, the first temporary roadblocks were erected. Around Leicester, concrete sewer pipes filled with

An earth mover on a transporter, heading for Croft Quarry, negotiates one of the first improvised roadblocks, seen outside 71 Lutterworth Road, Blaby. It was made from sections of concrete sewer pipes filled with sandbags and five old cars from Tommy Simpson's scrapyard, weighted down with boulders from Croft Quarry. Hilda Sanders, wife of village policeman Bll Sanders, stands on the left. (Norman Sanders)

sandbags, plus old cars and rubble, were used to partially block main roads. In Syston, 'The Authorities decided to have a roadblock on the Leicester Road which consisted of a couple of 12-ton steam rollers, one of which could be moved by a winch to shut the gap if it became necessary, a brilliant idea this and something even a heavy tank would look at twice.'[299] In Ratby, '…near to Robin Hill (last house on the right of Desford Lane), a large tree trunk was attached to a cart wheel and hinged, so it could be swung out across the road to act as a barrier.'[300]

The other great fear was of landings by troop-carrying gliders and instructions were issued for the obstruction of all potential landing grounds. Golf courses were viewed as particularly vulnerable and obstructions for the Leicester Golf Course were finalised as '26 coal carts from Pingle Wharf, a car body

Regular troops of the Leicestershire Regiment, armed with a Bren machine gun, man the emergency roadblock at the junction of Loughborough Road and Greengate Lane, Birstall, summer 1940.

and one lorry'.[301] Major H.E. Inglesant, CO of 'C' (Keyham area) Company, 6th (Quorn) Battalion, later recalled the naïve enthusiasm with which these defences were built:

'…in those early days we expected to see a Bosche around every haystack and chasing down every lane, with no less enthusiasm did we look forward to a flotilla of planes bumping into our wooden posts, and excitedly anticipated armoured fighting vehicles to be held up by roadblocks consisting of ancient hay-wains, old motor cars, to say nothing of a two-foot deep trench, all of which we were quite certain were going to hold up with effect the Prussian military machine. Truly has it been said the English never know when they are beaten and equally true is it they always win the last battle. Certainly in those days we could never have won the first.'[302]

Just a Line On a Map

The Commander-in-Chief of Home Forces, General Ironside, had the most unenviable job of 1940: to defend the defenceless.

With a lack of mobile armoured might, Ironside reverted to the static defence strategy of World War One. A 'Coastal Crust' of pillboxes and obstructions were built along the beaches. Behind this, he planned a series of 'stop lines' to frustrate any enemy advances until his limited mobile reserves could intercept them. As a last ditch stand, he planned the GHQ Line, a spinal defence that ran down the eastern half of Britain to protect the industrial Midlands, looping round to protect London and finishing near Bristol. The GHQ Line followed natural obstructions such as rivers and was backed with pillboxes. It passed just east of Rutland, up through Lincolnshire, almost grazing Leicestershire's north-eastern tip. It was only to be manned if the invader reached this far inland. Once the Germans had penetrated this final line, as Ironside said, the enemy 'would be free to rip the guts out of the country' and there would be little hope left.

On 30 June 1940 the order was given in 44th Infantry Division Operational Instruction No. 3 to construct the GHQ Line from Lincolnshire to Yorkshire, but, a week later, it was rescinded. Materials were needed more in the south, where invasion was most likely. From Lincolnshire northwards, the GHQ Line seems to have got little further than a suggested line on the map.

There was a stop line along the Leicestershire-Derbyshire border, following the River Trent, but the concrete defences were on the Derbyshire side, protecting only that county. At this date, there is no evidence of stop lines running through Leicestershire or Rutland.

The central reserve force, based at Guilsborough House in Northamptonshire, was also very weak. It was composed of around 180 light tanks armed only with machine guns and the 43rd Infantry Division with minimal artillery support. It was the sole mobile reaction force, designed to meet any main invading force wherever they landed or penetrated the GHQ Line.[303]

All in all, this means there was no GHQ Line or internal stop lines to protect the two counties. The military defence of Leicestershire and Rutland throughout the summer of 1940 was woefully inadequate.

Type FW3/22 pillbox on the A47 near Morcott, overlooking Welland Valley. It is built into the hedgerow for camouflage.

Consolidation Behind Concrete

Without armour, General Ironside looked to concrete. He replaced the temporary roadblocks with stronger concrete blocks and, in lieu of tanks, built concrete pillboxes. These blunt, squat buildings can still be seen occasionally throughout Leicestershire and Rutland. At first glance, plotted on a map, the vast majority appear to be in a buffer zone running behind the GHQ Line, giving the appearance of defence in depth.

However, research shows this is merely an illusion. In actual fact, all of the pillboxes in the two counties were for the defence of vulnerable points or searchlight sites. In July 1940 AA Brigade HQ issued a directive that all searchlight sites must be 'wired and dug in for all-round defence,' and a pillbox must be built at each site. This explains the location of single pillboxes seen on high ground in both counties. The searchlights were usually placed in belts of up to six lights. Four single pillboxes remain representing the six searchlight sites that stretched from Gotham in Nottinghamshire over to Stathern in Leicestershire, with a further five pillboxes in a line from Launde in Leicestershire via Ketton in Rutland, over the border to the east of Stamford. Four more pillboxes form an arc north of Melton Mowbray.[304] In Rutland, these pillboxes would have been manned by 400 Coy, 50th AA (TA) Bn, spread over 14 searchlight sites with their HQ at Ashwell Camp.[305] Other point defence pillboxes include those surrounding airfields, or by the Burley Road bridge over the former canal, defending Ashwell military camp (now Ashwell Prison), Rutland. As there were no stop lines, there are no bands of mutually supporting pillboxes, as seen in other counties.

An example of Leicestershire and Rutland's most common type of pillbox, the FW3/22, seen on Welby Lane, Melton Mowbray, overlooking the old Asfordby works. It has double pistol embrasures above the entrance and the brick shuttering is now eroding to reveal the concrete core.

In June 1940 WO Branch FW3 (Directorate of Fortifications and Works 3) issued a series of standard pillbox designs, known today as 'Types'. Seven main Types are known, ranging from Type 22 to Type 28.

Nearly all surviving examples in Leicestershire and Rutland are an adaptation of the most common pillbox design, Type 22, although confusingly they have a pistol loophole either side of the entrance, partially giving them the appearance of the Type 24. Instead of the standard internal Y-shaped anti-ricochet wall, there is only a central supporting pillar, thereby allowing dangerous shoot-throughs.

The only known exceptions are two of a seemingly indigenous type, with wide embrasures, along the canal south-west of Hinckley and two square prefabricated Type 26 pillboxes on the southern corners of the former Air Transport Auxiliary airfield at Ratcliffe. It is believed there were many more pillboxes originally.

Type FW3/22 pillbox near Castle Hill, Oakham Road, Withcote. In the background is Whatborough Hill Iron Age Hillfort.

Nearly all these pillboxes were built by local contractors and share the same construction: external London Brick Company brick shuttering infilled with concrete, giving the false external impression they are only built of bricks. Internally, the pillboxes have rounded concrete firing shelves below each embrasure.

Examples of Anti-Invasion Defences:
Leicestershire
Type 22 Pillbox: SK 444264 between Castle Donington and East Midlands Airport
Local Type Pillbox: SP 409929 next to canal, Nutts Lane, Hinckley
Type 22 Pillbox: SK 809404 Home Farm, Normanton (RAF Bottesford)
Type 26 prefabricated pillbox: SK 623154 Ratcliffe-on-the-Wreake (RAF Ratcliffe)
Type 26 prefabricated pillbox: SK 628151 Ratcliffe-on-the-Wreake (RAF Ratcliffe)
Type 22 pillbox: SK 722215 Welby Lane, Asfordby
Type 22 pillbox: SK 767206 Melton Spinney Road, Waltham on the Wolds
Type 22 pillbox: SK 819300 Croxton Lodge Farm, Croxton Kerrial
Type 22 pillbox: SK 775305 Stathern-Eastwell Road, Stathern Hill
Type 22 pillbox: SK 718308 Hose Lodge Farm, Hose
Type 22 pillbox: SK 790355 by Grantham Canal, Redmile

The inside of a Type FW3/22 pillbox on Castle Hill, Oakham Road, Withcote. There are concrete firing shelves below each embrasure. Wartime pencilled graffiti also remains on the walls.

Type 22 pillbox: SK 789057 Castle Hill, Withcote
Type 22 pillbox: SK 792154 Brickfield Farm, Little Dalby
Type 22 pillbox: SK 740249 Landyke Lane Farm, Holwell
Anti-tank cubes: SK 724218 Welby Lane, Asfordby
Anti-tank cylinders: SK 796042 stream bank by Launde Abbey, Launde

Rutland
Truncated Type 22: SK 899146 built onto a barn wall at Warren Farm (RAF Cottesmore)
Type 22 pillbox with AA platform: SK 900147 north of Warren Farm (RAF Cottesmore)
Type 22 pillbox: SK 017109 north of Ryhall Road, Tolethorpe
Type 22 pillbox: SK 836147 north-east of Manor Farm, Whissendine
Type 22 pillbox: SK 866111 by Burley Road bridge over the canal (Ashwell Camp)
Type 22 pillbox: SK 993059 Steadfold Lane, Ketton
Type 22 pillbox: SK 918003 south of Morcott services, on the A47
Type 22 pillbox: SK 960011 west of Shire Oaks, on the A47
Type 22 pillbox: SK 852200 east of Garthorpe Lodge, Wymondham (destroyed)
Type 22 pillbox: SK 943151 between B668/Greetham Wood Near (RAF Cottesmore)
Type 22 pillbox: SK 842053 north of Braunston-Brooke Road, Brooke
Type 22 pillbox: SK 919103 south-west of Exton
Type 22 pillbox: SK 896052 Manton-Edith Weston Road, Lyndon
Type 22 pillbox: SK 940055 south of Edith Weston-Ketton Road (RAF North Luffenham)
Type 22 pillbox on stilts: SK 934046 attached to firing range (RAF North Luffenham)

In northern France, permanent roadblocks had actually slowed Allied troops. The front page of the *Leicester Mercury* on 31 July 1940 declared 'Road Barriers to be Removed – Our Troops Need Freest Passage' – 'the GOC Northern Command, acting in collaboration with the North Midland Regional

Commissioner, is adopting a policy of removing all except single roadblocks, and where possible these single roadblocks will be cut back'.[306] Col. Ogilvy-Dalgleish records Northern Command ordered the County Surveyor to construct six concrete roadblocks under the direction of REs on the main roads leading out of Oakham; however, 'these were sited rather far out' and were also cancelled in August 1940.[307] Dumped by the side of the road, halfway up Welby Lane, just north of the former Asfordby Mine, are six concrete anti-tank cubes, 3ft by 3ft, with a steel rail running through the centre. Presumably they blocked the approach to Asfordby Mine, an important vulnerable point. Crowds of fleeing French refugees had also blocked the Allies, so instructions were issued to British civilians to 'stay put'.

The First Defence Schemes

The responsibility for the defence of the two counties was transferred from the army to the Home Guard at an early date, when most of the Regular Forces were moved to the coast where invasion was expected most. Now the first tentative defence schemes were drawn up. Leicester's draft defence scheme survives on a typed sheet of yellowed paper:

A rare example of a prefabricated Type FW3/26 square pillbox on the A46, just north of Ratcliffe College. The pillbox guarded the northern approach to Leicester and the southern end of RAF Ratcliffe airfield.

Five concrete anti-tank blocks, with protruding RSJs lie beside Welby Lane, Melton Mowbray. They once blocked the northern approach to Asfordby Mine.

'General Defence Scheme Of Leicester Group
22 August 1940

1. LEICESTER will be defended on its perimeter which will be formed approximately by a line joining the OUTER or MAIN ROAD BLOCKS, 26 in number. The area within the perimeter thus formed will be held by means of:-
a) ROAD BLOCKS with forward observation positions.
b) Previously reconnoitred, and, if necessary, prepared positions to cover ground between ROAD BLOCKS. Posts on various open spaces, in many cases some distance inside the perimeter.
2. INNER DEFENCE OF CITY on which more information is required. A suggested scheme of Road Blocks along an inner circle of railways and canals has been received from Colonel Somerville.
3. AREA outside LEICESTER perimeter will be prepared, village by village, on the lines laid down by the Area Commander to Battalion Commanders which will:-
a) Take toll of the enemy.
b) Deflect the enemy.
c) Form rallying points in the event of troops outside being driven back.
Note. While defence is spoken of in the forgoing, it must not be forgotten observation, and speedy and accurate reports are of paramount importance.'[308]

Loopholed wall outside Chestnuts, Leicester Road, Uppingham, guarding the main appoach into Uppingham from Leicester.

Pencilled notes by Major C.A.B. Elliott, Leicester's Assistant Group Commander, suggest the city's main defence would be a long, static perimeter:

'[The scheme's aim is] to deny access to our group area, and to take toll if they enter it. To do this, we must have the whole perimeter of Leicester held by troops both for observation and fighting purposes.'[309]

Dick Elliott remembers accompanying his father as he planned Leicester's defences. 'Although he had seen some tank warfare, as with most retired First World War veterans, he was probably not up to date with more recent mechanical warfare or air power, but he had a good eye for the country.

I went out with him when he was studying places to site concrete pillbox gun emplacements and noting where destroyed bridges might help to make river and canal crossings more difficult obstacles against tanks and armoured cars.

I also helped him place tree trunks across Oadby Golf Course to stop enemy gliders landing! I also remember in about 1941 or 1942, he went up in an RAF Handley Page Hampden to get an aerial view of the problems involved in the defence of Leicester.'[310]

An idea of how the counties' towns were defended in summer 1940 can be gained from Col. Ogilvy-Dalgleish:

'…The defence of Oakham became the sole responsibility of the Home Guard. I went round the town with Cahusac and the Officers of 'C' Company and a defence plan was made based on the slender resources then available.

I requisitioned timber from the Agricultural Show stands to build fire steps for bombers and riflemen behind the high Catmose wall on the Stamford Road and the garden wall of Yule House. Tank traps were planned further out at such places as Barnsdale Hill and the stream by the flooded fields on the Stamford Road; there was a dump of telegraph poles near the stream bridge half-a-mile out of Oakham on the Burley Road and A. Dawson, Burley Village Commander, devised an ingenious method of rapidly blocking the road with these poles. All obstacles had to be covered by fire from carefully chosen positions and many slit trenches were dug. The roadblocks would have stopped road transport and armoured cars from rushing the town, but we could not expect to improvise anything that would stop a tank…'[311]

'Every Round a German'

Leslie Furnival, formerly a corporal in No. 14 (Croft) Platoon, 3rd (West Leicester) Battalion, remembers being told to lay 'a row of dinner plates across the road so German tanks would think it was mined.'[312]

Airfield Battle HQ: this concrete cupola allowed the Local Defence Officer 360° viewing. He was also provided with an emergency exit and hatch which still exists, as seen at RAF Market Harborough, Leicestershire.

Such was the desperation of the hour. The Home Guard were also encouraged to 'make every shot count'. 'The meagre ammunition ration could soon have been shot away and the importance of strict fire discipline and control was more than ever impressed on all Ranks; it was a matter of holding fire, until ordered, and then, if possible, every round a German, should action come…All ammunition was to be removed from casualties.'[313]

Threadbare Airfield Defence?

By late 1940 most pillbox building had virtually ceased. The only exception was at RAF airfields, which were still viewed as highly vulnerable to paratroop attack. In late September 1940 the Air Ministry's Taylor Report graded airfields to three classes of defence. Most airfields in the two counties, namely Bottesford, Saltby, Cottesmore, North Luffenham and Woolfox Lodge, were graded Class II, meaning they were supposed to be defended by 20 pillboxes.

However, there is little evidence today to show anything like this amount were built. Either there was an efficient programme of demolition at the war's end or, more likely, concrete shortages and the general veering away from pillbox-based defence meant they were never built.

At earlier airfields further east, such as Rutland's RAF Cottesmore and North Luffenham, pillboxes remain, but there are very few further west into Leicestershire. Warren Farm, next to RAF Cottesmore, has been fortified, creating a Defended Locality. A half-hexagonal pillbox has been built onto the exterior of a farm building, and there is also a hexagonal pillbox with an open annexe that contained an AA machine gun.

Airfield defence was further tightened in 1941. Often mistaken for pillboxes, semi-sunken Battle Headquarters, of an official Air Ministry pattern No. 11008/41, were built at several local airfields. In the event of attack, the Local Defence Officer would co-ordinate the airfield's defences from a concrete viewing cupola, passing orders down to a PBX (Private Branch Exchange switchboard) room or messengers. Such Battle HQs survive at North Luffenham, Bruntingthorpe, Wymeswold and Market Harborough airfields.

At the latter site, there is no evidence of pillbox construction. Work started on this airfield in mid-1942, finishing a year later. By this date, concrete was even scarcer and pillbox construction had virtually ceased. However, there are several open-topped, brick blast shelters around the perimeter. It is possible these shelters doubled as defence posts and were linked to the Battle HQ via field telephone. Alternatively, as the threat of invasion had receded, the defences were never finished. A lack of fittings in this Battle HQ also reinforces this idea.

Second Phase: November 1941–August 1942: The First Proper Defence Schemes

Deep in the National Archives, Kew, lie four aged, buff card files holding several dozen yellowing sheets of typed foolscap. The files are tied shut with ribbon and are marked 'SECRET'. These are the sector defence schemes for Leicestershire and Rutland.

Their existence is remarkable: not all counties' defence schemes have survived. Once stored under lock and key, their former secrets now provide us with a valuable understanding of how the two counties were to be defended to the last round – there would be no surrender and no withdrawal. Listed are the locations of all the military units, roadblocks and supply dumps, together with instructions during invasion, plus a set of coded warnings.

By late 1941 the Home Guard provided the main defence of Leicestershire and Rutland, backed up by a few scattered detachments of Regulars and administrative or service personnel that happened to be stationed locally. In mid-1941 Northamptonshire left the Sub-Area, leaving just Leicestershire and Rutland. For defence purposes, the two counties were further divided into three military sectors, namely: No. 1 (Oakham-Melton) Sector, No. 2 (Bosworth) Sector and No. 3 (Leicester) Sector. Regular Army officers commanded No. 2 and 3 Sectors; however, Col. Ogilvy-Dalgleish commanded No. 1 (Oakham-Melton) Sector.

Although over a year after the main invasion threat, it seems it was not until late 1941 when the first proper countywide sector defence schemes were drafted. These sector defence schemes were carefully thought out, making full use of all available men and resources, and were based upon the latest military thinking, namely defence in depth. Col. Ogilvy-Dalgleish recalls 'Major H. Wing, of the Sherwood Foresters, was appointed to my HQ as Sector Staff Officer and between us we produced comprehensive operational instructions for the sector as a whole; it seems a formidable dossier as I look at it today, about 15 pages, but it was not really so. I was not joining in the paper war.'[314]

Today, out of the first round of 1941 sector defence schemes, only the defence scheme for No. 3 (Leicester) Sector survives. Fortunately it provides us with a valuable insight into the first proper defence plans for the city. First, it analyses the nature of the threat at that stage of the war.

'Types of Enemy Action to be Expected:

a) Landings by parachute troops and airborne units over wide areas, the capture of aerodromes, suitable landing grounds and seizure of ground of strategic importance.

b) Attacks on VPs [Vulnerable Points] by airborne units and/or saboteurs.

c) Seizure of road junctions etc, to open up communications with enemy detachments landed elsewhere.

d) The cutting of telephone wires etc, to disorganise communications, and general menacing of the rear of troops holding East Coast defences.'

Although Sector Command may have been unsure about the enemy's precise form of attack, they were definite about their defence policy. 'All ranks in this Sector will defend their allotted post to the last man and the last round. THERE WILL BE NO WITHDRAWAL FROM POSITIONS WHICH THEY HAVE BEEN ORDERED TO HOLD…'

Unlike the bravado-led ideas of 1940, which suggested panzers could be defeated with crowbars, these plans were realistic. Until the widespread issue of anti-tank weapons, the plans accepted the Home Guard were unlikely to be able to destroy tanks, but nonetheless had a valuable part to play.

1941: The Consolidated Defence of Leicester

Leicester's first defence scheme of August 1940 was flawed from the start. Changing little from mediaeval defence strategies of 700 years previously, it relied on a single static perimeter defence, which, as had so overwhelmingly been proven in France, was frail and easily penetrated by German Blitzkrieg tactics. The defence of Leicester's periphery would have relied on a limited number of poorly-armed Home Guards thinly stretched along a 26-mile perimeter.

Nonetheless, even at this early date it was realised a further level of defence was needed to stop any attackers running wild if the perimeter was breached. Colonel Somerville had suggested an 'inner circle' of roadblocks that followed the line of the central canals and railways, which would provide protection for the city's vital core. By November 1941 this inner roadblock line had been put in place. Leicester was now 'divided into two cordons known as the Outer and Inner Perimeters'.

The Outer Perimeter followed the general line of the 25 roadblocks on the suburban outskirts, as well as some rail blocks and a river block, obstructing the main approaches to Leicester. The Inner Perimeter consisted of a ring of roadblocks guarding the city's core, forming a last-ditch defensive keep. It would be here that the final bloody battles for Leicester would be fought.

This double perimeter appears to have been the standard defensive layout for most large Midland cities and was mirrored in Derby, Nottingham and Northampton.

Defending the Vulnerable Points

Most of Leicestershire's Vulnerable Points were located in Leicester, although there were also some in the county's towns. Due to its lack of conurbations, apart from airfields, Rutland had very few VPs (See Appendix B for a list of the Vulnerable Points).

Home Guard Ray Elgood worked at Parmeko Ltd on Percy Road, Aylestone Park, Leicester. The factory was engaged on vital war work for the Ministry of Aircraft Production and Ministry of Supply. His recollections provide a valuable insight into the security and importance of a Vulnerable Point.

'In 1940 I was 20 and working as a Senior Designer. We were always making specialist wound components such as transformers, plus audio equipment and radar parts. We made propaganda broadcast speaker vans in Humber ambulances that went to Libya.

Things tightened up at the outbreak of war. There were sandbags around critical parts such as the inspection and test areas. Security tightened after we were photographed from the air. On aerial photographs we stood out like a sore thumb. So they sent over camouflage specialists who painted zig-zag lines all over the works and it was photographed again. But it had an 80-foot chimney, which was difficult to hide!

I had wanted to join the army but they wouldn't let me as I was in a reserved occupation. So instead I joined the Home Guard, as my certificate says on 6 July 1940. I took my air rifle. It was a bit light, so we put a bit of gas pipe on it to give it some weight like a proper rifle. We were then issued with Ross rifles, which came in boxes of 12 and set in grease. We got the thick off with rags and we then used the big degreasing tanks at the factory. There was no armoury so all the weapons were kept in the Managing Director's office. We only had five rounds each, which we used to exchange at the end of our guard duty.

At the back of the factory was a yard, which we used for parading. We had to have ID cards which had a coloured bar across the bottom, which denoted levels of authorisation. I was entitled entry in any area of the factory, but most people were only entitled to go in the area of their card colour. Anybody found out of their area would get instant dismissal.'[315]

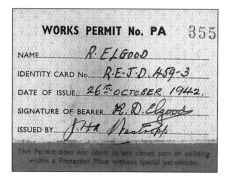

Raymond Elgood's work security pass at Parmeko, Aylestone. The bottom is coloured orange, indicating which parts of the factory Elgood was allowed in.

Improved roadblocks

From October 1940[316] the summer's temporary roadblocks were replaced with a sturdier, more permanent standard design, later detailed in Northern Command's August 1941 pamphlet *Notes for the Home Guard on Road Blocks and Check Points*.

Roadblocks now comprised of two large concrete cubes either side of the road, the remaining gap being blocked with a removable obstruction of upright metal rails and concrete cylinders. This formed an improved, but not infallible, obstruction that would slow down attacking tanks and allow Home Guard anti-tank weapons a better chance of success. Forty-four of these cylinders can still be seen strengthening a stream bank at Launde Abbey, Leicestershire. The pamphlet suggested 21 cylinders per block grouped in threes, but due to the concrete shortage, photos reveal sometimes the original concrete sewer pipe sections were retained. Aneurin Owen remembers, around Market Harborough, rubble-filled oil drums were also used.[317]

Initially the Home Guard were tested to see how quickly they could close the roadblock. Often the older sections manning them found it difficult to shift the heavy RSJs and cylinders, so it was decided roadblocks would be closed partially at 'stand to', leaving a small single-file gap for traffic that could be closed on 'action stations'. Former No. 1 (Glenfield) Platoon, 3rd (West Leicester) Battalion Home Guard John Swan, remembers:

'I joined Glenfield Home Guard at 16. I was working at D. Byford hosiery on Blackbird Road, Leicester. I left at 10pm and cycled to Glenfield, put on my uniform, and went to the HQ which was close by. Village defences were minimal. Everything seemed to be at the Kirby Muxloe side. The old water mill on this side of the village was fortified with sandbags and was used until the roof collapsed! A concrete pillbox stood in the field close by. I remember during our training, a roadblock entry to the village on Kirby Lane. A row of holes was set in the road and we were supposed to insert upright tram or rail sections, cut into about six foot lengths, into them. A spare section of line was available

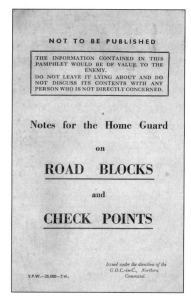

Northern Command manual instructing Home Guards on roadblocks and check points, dated July 1941.

and we were told to ram this in the track of an enemy tank! I don't recall anything else to defend the village, and we village lads knew where anything was.'[318]

Leicester's system of perimeter roadblocks with a central keep was mirrored on a smaller scale in the county's towns. Nationally, these fortified towns were called 'nodal points' or 'anti-tank islands' (or 'tank keeps' in Rutland). Generally, 'defended localities' were small, squad positions with all-round defence, mainly sited at road junctions. However, Col. Ogilvy-Dalgleish refers to whole 'groups of villages' as defended localities.[319] Quorn had up to four defended localities within its perimeter (See Appendix C).

Some houses overlooking roadblocks were also fortified, such as by the roadblock at Kilby Bridge, Leicestershire.

The strategy of obstructive defence using fortified cities, anti-tank islands and defended localities was designed to gradually slow and wear down the invader. The policy had been formalised nationally by General Brooke after June 1941 and was based on Russian defence against the German invasion.[320]

In addition, the River Soar/Grand Union Canal, though not a fortified stop line, was viewed as a 'Line Vital to the Defence'. This line bisected both the city and the county and was to be 'held to prevent penetration from the North and North-East'.[321] The Leicester Sub-Area Commander Col. M.A. Studd DSO MC noted 'we could, unaided, only hope to hold the enemy for 24 or possibly 48 hours on the flanks of…Leicester, but this delay might be invaluable to our striking forces operating against the enemy'.[322] The numerous canal bridges across the Soar were also to be obstructed with upright rails.

However, the Home Guard's defences were not purely static. Mobile units were created to nip out of the defended places, harrass, attack and destroy smaller groups of invaders, and then scurry back. In addition, as another last ditch measure, it was proposed to 'make use of anti-aircraft defences within the area for ground defence, when they can no longer carry out their primary role.'

Although there was a greater mobile element to the improved defences of late 1941, the continuing reliance on fortified perimeters of roadblocks bore shades of the 1940 static stop-line mentality. By now, pillboxes were well and truly out of the defence equation. Eric Smith of Oakham Home Guard remembers using one, outside Oakham on the Brooke Road, but only to shelter from the rain as he stood on lonely sentry duty at a roadblock.[323]

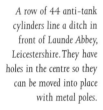

A row of 44 anti-tank cylinders line a ditch in front of Launde Abbey, Leicestershire. They have holes in the centre so they can be moved into place with metal poles.

1942: Militarisation of the Populace

The spring invasion season was again approaching. It was genuinely believed once Russia was beaten, the Germans would again turn their attention to Britain.

Previously, the populace had been told to 'stay put'. In official circles, the public were largely viewed as a hindrance that would get in the way. By 1942, using lessons from Russia, it was realised the populace were actually an untapped resource. The population were now told to 'stand firm' and were organised by the largely forgotten, but one of the most interesting, aspects of wartime home defence, Invasion Committees.

Invasion Committees

In March 1942 Sir John Anderson announced the formation of Invasion Committees, with the *Leicester Mercury* reporting 'CIVILIANS WILL KNOW THEIR TASKS IF THE HUN COMES'. The Invasion Committees were to survey their locality and consider the defensive needs if fighting should reach their district, ensuring smooth liaison between the civil and military authorities.

Defence of Loughborough 'Tank Island Town', November 1941

Defence of Loughborough 'Tank Island Town'

● Roadblock
● Checkpoint

'There are countless ways in which the help of civilians will be needed – in cooking and distributing food, filling craters and shell holes to enable military vehicles to pass, digging trenches, providing billets for troops or for neighbours bombed or shelled out.

In a village or small town the Invasion Committees will be able to allot specific jobs to particular individuals, and most of the able-bodied inhabitants will know in advance what their role will be. There are three broad principles which we should all bear in mind:

1. All of our people must do everything they can to help each other.
2. No one must do anything which would be of the slightest help to the enemy.
3. All have the right and duty to do everything they usefully can under responsible direction to defend their hearth and homes and their native land.'[324]

Breaking the Rules

But official encouragement went further. In this desperate time of total war, the technicalities of the Geneva Convention were overshadowed as civilians were encouraged to 'have a go':

'Point 97: Sir John Anderson said "The first essential is that, except under definite orders, everyone should stand firm so as to avoid those refugee movements which proved so disastrous in the fall of France. That does not mean the civil population are expected to adopt a purely passive role. *On the contrary, the Government has always expected the people of the islands will offer a united opposition to an invader and every citizen will regard it as his duty to hinder and frustrate the enemy and help our own forces by every means ingenuity can devise and common sense suggest.*"'[325]

The instructions went further:

'Point 100: If stray enemy marauders or small parties of enemy soldiers are moving about in an area not in the effective occupation of the enemy, *the government expects every stout-hearted citizen will use all his powers to overcome them.*'[326]

Had civilians engaged the invader there would have been widespread reprisals, as seen in Europe, but this was how desperate home defence had become.

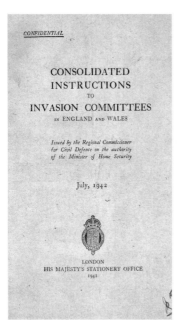

CONFIDENTIAL

CONSOLIDATED INSTRUCTIONS TO INVASION COMMITTEES
IN ENGLAND AND WALES

Issued by the Regional Commissioner for Civil Defence on the authority of the Minister of Home Security

July, 1942

LONDON
HIS MAJESTY'S STATIONERY OFFICE
1942

All towns and nearly every village had an Invasion Committee. All local committees were overseen by a central Invasion Committee.

In Leicester, the Leicester City Invasion Committee was composed of the Emergency Committee, the Civil Defence Controller, the Food Executive Officer, the Chief Constable, the Medical Officer of Health, the Feeding Officer, the Water Engineer, the City Surveyor, the Area Fire Force Commander, the Home Guard Commander and the Sub-Area Military Commander. The committee also had to plan the reception of up to 22,000 refugees from Great Yarmouth, Lowestoft and Colchester during an invasion.[327]

In the county, the members of the Leicestershire County Invasion Committee were Lt-Col. Sir Robert Martin CMG, Mr V.R. Pochin and Mr J.B. Galloway.

Loughborough Borough: Mr G. Hill JP, Mr G.H. Bowler JP, Mr A.E. Armstrong JP.

Melton Mowbray Urban District: Mr O. Brotherhood JP, Mr T.R. Stockdale, Mr P.D. Prior JP, Mr A.L. Sleath.

Hinckley Urban District: Mr F. Burton JP, Mr F. Hall, Mr W.C. Rigby.

Ashby-de-la-Zouch Urban District: Mr A.G. Atkinson, Mr J.J. Staley, Mr L.M. Darlow.

Market Harborough Urban District: Mr H.H. Pickering JP, Mr W.R. Reynolds, Mr R.K. Gardiner, Mr A. Cowling JP, Mr A.W. Briggs.

Lutterworth: Mr E.E. Benford, Mr G. Taite, Mr G.W.W. Morris.

Coalville Urban District: Mr C.W.H. Gutteridge JP, Mr J.D. Smith, Mr R. Blower JP.[328]

Although the local Invasion Committee's role was to assist the military, they were not privy to all Home Guard plans:

'Invasion Committees…were in no circumstances executive bodies and there were confidential matters that could not be disclosed to them…In the event of military operations in the neighbourhood, the military Comdr. would assume control…'[329]

Local Defence Schemes

It was the role of the Invasion Committees to draw up the local defence scheme. Some, such as the Kibworth defence scheme, were not actually finished until January 1943[330] and Quorn's was not updated until June 1944, well after the threat of invasion. However, surviving 'secret' defence schemes for Quorn,[331] Rothley,[332] Ibstock,[333] Kibworth,[334] Croft,[335] Houghton-on-the-Hill[336] and Uppingham[337] reveal they were all written to a standard script. The scheme was split in two parts, civil and military (Home Guard). The two main objects of the civil part were:

'a) To ensure co-ordinated action by the various civilian interests in the event of invasion, especially in case the area is cut off from outside assistance.

b) To secure appropriate co-ordinated action within the community in response to any call from the military for civil assistance.'

There were four levels of planned reaction, starting with operations in the event of bombing prior to invasion, right through to the final stage 'when the enemy is in temporary occupation of the neighbourhood' and it will be noted that 'as long as there is any armed resistance, the Invasion Committee will assist it'. Two interesting points are that there was to be no surrender, not even to prevent further casualties: as long as there was 'any armed resistance', defensive operations would continue. Secondly, the phrase 'in temporary occupation' is striking: defeat was not considered.

As well as a central Food Store, food stocks of all shops would be requisitioned and distributed by rationing. Shops would become 'Food Distribution Stores'. Under this system of food rationing, it was estimated Ibstock would be able to feed 5,000 people for two weeks. Self-sufficiency was key, as Col. Ogilvy-Dalgleish noted:

'The "Tank Keep" role of Oakham and Uppingham involved many things besides the actual defence, for example, water, if the water works were destroyed. A survey and map was made of wells in Oakham, which would, of course, have required chlorination, and I was surprised at the great number of wells there were still in existence, if not in use, all over the town.'[338]

Bathing and flushing of toilets would be forbidden to save water, which would also be rationed, as in Ibstock's case, by 'Water Police'. Official edicts would be posted on noticeboards outside places such as the police house and official records would be broadcast from speaker vans.

The military side of the scheme makes desperate reading and is perhaps one of the reasons why it was kept secret from the civilians on the Invasion Committees (see Quorn's Military Defence Scheme in Appendix C). As the Houghton-on-the-Hill defence scheme states, 'stand firm' was the chief aim.

'The police will do their utmost to enforce the Government Policy under this heading, in particular, roads must be kept clear for the passage of military reinforcements. The Police may have to evacuate the civil population from certain houses to provide defence posts and to clear fields of fire under the local Military Defence Scheme. Billets will be found for such people by the local Billeting Officer. The homeless will not be allowed to become refugees, but will be directed by the Police and Wardens to the Rest Centres.'

In short, civilians would be herded as the military required. Their bleak status was further reinforced in the Rothley defence scheme:

'The military must be free to move, at all times, to attack and destroy the enemy. Civilian needs, and, if necessary, lives, at such times, must be regarded as of lesser importance. Military requirements, under invasion conditions, must be regarded as of paramount importance.'

There were bound to be casualties, especially as the population was to be confined within the boundaries. Areas for mass graves were planned, as in Ibstock:

'a) The Committee has collaborated with the Medical Officer and the following sites have been selected…

1.) Three acres of land adjacent to the Pretoria Road Cemetery, at present occupied by Mr J.A. Dawson.

2.) Land adjacent to the Parish Council Burial Ground.

b) The Parish has no official mortuary, but the Committee has earmarked Mr W. Newman's Coach House and Messrs. Harratt's Paint Shop as a mortuary, and have appointed a mortuary attendant.

c) Burials will be carried out as quickly as possible, during the hours of darkness whenever possible. The following gravediggers have been appointed: Mr G.S. Bancroft, Copson Street; Mr W. Baines, Copson Street and Mr Godfrey, Pretoria Road.

d) The Committee propose to arrange for graves to be constructed by digging long trenches, separating the bodies by a 6in earth wall. Each body to bear a metal identification disc, and each grave numbered. A separate record, in duplicate for safety's sake, is to be kept, enabling each body to be identified at a later date. In order to facilitate dis-interment the Committee propose shallow graves, but the Medical Officer suggests a minimum depth of 4' 0".'

The Houghton-on-the-Hill scheme added one final proviso: 'In the event of fatalities the Church will be used as a Mortuary and the dead will be interred in the field on the East side of the Church. Our own in separate graves and the enemy in communal graves.'

The local defence schemes are surprisingly ancient in style: their detail is reminiscent of the 1086 Domesday Book, listing all chattels from each car down to numbers of spades and even numbers of teaspoons in the Auxiliary Rest Centre (village hall).

The schemes list available manpower, including civil and military personnel, as well as those civilians who would be available to assist in manual work such as the digging of slit trenches or the erection of obstructions. The schemes make it clear every able-bodied citizen had a role to play, including children as messengers.

The pinnacle of the village defence scheme was the Invasion Committee, composed of what in times past were the 'village elders', but were now parish councillors and heads of local organisations, who would implement the scheme. The village's military representative, namely the Home Guard platoon commander, was ultimately in charge in the event of invasion.

No different to the Saxon burgh, the village would become an isolated and autonomous defended centre of resistance, sheltering the population from attack while also attempting to hinder the invaders. These defence schemes may have been forgotten for 60 years but they provide an alarming record of how our recent predecessors intended to fight to the bitter end.

Third Phase: The Defences Reassessed: August 1942–December 1943
Fatal Flaws

The most important question for the defenders was 'how effective would these defences have been?' Apart from actual invasion, the nearest answer was gained from the results of the annual countywide exercises. Following Exercise LEICESTER in July 1942, major faults were noticed in the Leicester Sector defence scheme and, for a third time, the schemes were amended. In August 1942, following a local military conference, Major C.A.B. Elliott noted:

'A i) The Inner Perimeter line: which the 4th Battalion was primarily responsible. The greater part of the Inner Perimeter was in built up areas, with little field of fire and troops manning it would not be called on to fight until the enemy were within the city.

ii) The Outer Perimeter Line: tended either to become a thin extended line, lacking in depth, or when depth was attained there was a tendency to push forward too far and indefinitely and so weaken the main points of resistance.

B) These weaknesses will be overcome as under:

   i) The Inner Perimeter line as hitherto known will cease to exist. The 4th Battalion will hold all road and rail crossings over the Soar…Within it the 4th Battalion will hold the bulk of their strength ready to go out as striking forces wherever needed.

   ii) Outside the square…will be the Fighting Zone of the 1st, 2nd and 3rd Battalions with a clearly defined forward and backward limit, which will be held by a series of DLs sited in depth and covering with fire the maximum amount of ground, particularly the approaches to the City. Patrols will be sent out from these localities with a view to breaking up enemy formations before they approach the main resistance of DLs within the fighting zones. Hanworths and fougasses will do the same thing. Personnel engaged in the above will return to their DLs when their work is done along previous determined lines of approach.

   iii) a) Certain villages outside the fighting zone will be selected where the garrison is not less than 37 and their functions will be hitherto i.e. take toll, deflect, no retreat.
   b) Where the garrison of the village is under 37…the garrison will…strengthen one of the neighbouring villages in iii) a).

Under Phase A authorized zones will be laid down into which HG units may go out and shoot up airborne troops without higher authority being given. Under Phase B DLs must not be denuded in order to deal with airborne troops…'[339]

In short, the 1941 scheme was fatally flawed because it only allowed the Germans to be fully engaged once they reached the city centre keep (Inner Perimeter). The ensuing battle would have caused tremendous damage to the city centre and would have made it easier for the invaders to capture Leicester.

The new theory was not to defend the city using a series of perimeters, but by fighting zones. Instead, the invader would be harried and broken up in the surrounding countryside or Outer Zone. Those invaders who made it through to the city would be engaged and finally destroyed in the suburban Middle or Fighting Zone. The old Inner Zone would be used as a Sector Reserve for the now mobile 4th Battalion, from where they would rush out and counter-attack where needed most.[340]

This more outwardly aggressive and offensive scheme allowed for greater defence in depth, meaning the enemy would hopefully be ground down before they reached central Leicester.

Wishful Defence Thinking?

This attempt to move from static to mobile defence was still more an ideal than reality. As Major C.A.B. Elliott frankly noted, 'Garrisons of villages where Home Guard personnel was less than say 37 could not be expected to do an effective job of work [and] would have been mopped up one by one.'

In blunt terms, the platoons manning these defended localities would have been cannon fodder to slow down the invaders while Regular Forces arrived. But in France in 1940, Rommel's panzers had simply driven round these 'hedgehogs', as they were termed, and headed for their main targets. The 'hedgehogs' were only cleared afterwards, but by then the battle's outcome had been decided. This system of village defence or defended localities was also flawed.

Despite the Home Guard's desire for mobility, they did not have enough vehicles. It was the Home Guard's local knowledge, planned defences and anti-tank ambush weapons that meant, despite their limitations, they were better suited to manning defended localities and other static defences.

Additional Measures

As the war progressed, the likelihood of a full invasion lessened. The view was that more surreptitious warfare would take its place, so the Home Guard were also on the look out for spies and saboteurs. Col. Ogilvy-Dalgleish describes the main anti-Fifth Column measure:

'During the winter of 1942 we were ordered to practice manning check points at the two Coy areas involved; these were not ordinary roadblocks but secret points selected by higher authority, in accordance with a general plan, where all traffic, of whatever nature, could be effectively stopped at short notice when ordered. The checkpoint, with a moveable obstacle, was covered by 12 HG riflemen, suitably distributed under an NCO having a sub-machine gun, with whom was a civil police officer.

Home Guard hold-up! Men of the 3rd (West Leicester) Battalion Leicestershire Home Guard help local policeman Herbert Timson check the identity card of a driver of a passing horse and cart at this rather rickety-looking check point by Elm Tree Farm, Kirby Road, Glenfield, during Exercise LEICESTER, Sunday 5 July 1942. Note the roadblock RSJ and socket cover, bottom right.

Twenty-four men were required, 12 on duty at a time, and a detention park was ear-marked nearby. The object of the checkpoints was primarily to collect enemy agents, in vehicles or otherwise, and also to prevent the movement of unauthorised vehicles at "Stand To" or just prior to action stations being ordered...'[341]

In 1942 Ken Allsopp, then a 17-year-old Blaby Home Guard, remembers being challenged from an unexpected quarter while manning a check point:

'One night, Reg Greasley, the village coal merchant, and I were on point duty on top of Grove Road. The village policeman, PC Saunders, came over and asked me if he could borrow my rifle. So me, being as he were a policeman, I gave it him. He said "How would you like to get shot with your own rifle?" So I said "You'll have a bloody job because the bullets are still in my pocket!"'[342]

Plans were also made for the partial destruction of Vulnerable Points so they could not be used to aid the German war effort. This involved the destruction or removal of key parts so machinery would not function.[343] Instructions were issued in September 1942 for the destruction of the secret BBC 'H' Transmitter at the Swain Street Institution (workhouse), Leicester. This was a low power transmitter which normally broadcast the Home Service, but could be used for emergency broadcasting in an invasion by BBC officials, the Regional Commissioner, Chief Constable or ARP Controller. It was stated it would take two hours for BBC staff to immobilise the transmitter, although others could do this quicker if need be![344] There was another 'H' transmitter at Leicester University.

As a further anti-invasion precaution, because they were well inland, Rutland Home Guard kept copies of the Sussex Home Guard's records.[345]

The Final Defence Schemes: June–December 1943
As the tide of war gradually swung in the Allies favour, the invasion threat also changed.
'Types of Enemy Action Expected:
i)   Sabotage of VPs and Key Points of supplies or communications by fifth columnists and paratroops.
ii) Landings by paratroops and airborne troops whose role may be to capture and hold airfields and points of strategic importance, cut communications and menace the rear of our troops holding the East Coast.

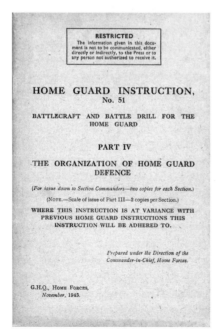

Home Guard instruction No.51 Part IV: The Organization of Home Guard Defence.

iii) Chemical and bacteriological attacks e.g. water supplies, centres of population etc.
iv) Attack from seaborne troops after penetration of coastal defences.'

From mid-1943 the three sectors were redrawn and renamed:

Leisec was responsible for the defence of the Leicester and district and was manned by the 1st, 2nd, 3rd and 4th Battalions.

Cottesec was manned by the 6th (Quorn) and 7th (Market Harborough) Battalions.

Charnsec was manned by the 8th (Market Bosworth), 10th (Charnwood) and 11th (Ashby-de-la-Zouch) Battalions.

The new defence schemes also incorporated the updated defence strategy for Leicester. Believing in 'the best form of defence is attack,' the planners also demanded a new level of aggression from the Home Guard:

a)   The enemy will be ruthlessly destroyed immediately on arrival in the sector. Every stage, if any, of his progress will be harassed, his AFVs will be destroyed.

b) All VPs, aerodromes and other resources will be denied to the enemy.

c) Each man will fight to the last round. There will be NO withdrawal from defended localities.

d) Attack and counter-attack until success is gained.

e) Active patrolling will take place between all defended localities, communications will be maintained with all adjoining units and sub-units.

f) The enemy will be exterminated from whichever direction he may come.

'REMEMBER in all your actions you are dealing with desperate men WHO EXPECT TO DIE and who will stop at nothing once they have set foot in this country'

'Fight to the Last':

Although the defence schemes still strived for the ideal of mobility, nonetheless they were more realistic about the Home Guard's capabilities. Almost back-pedalling, importance was once again placed on static defence. 'It is of the utmost importance that it is clearly understood that the whole basis of Home Guard tactics is an Area one, consisted of a series of defended localities where the Home Guard and regular troops are prepared to fight it out to the last without thought of surrender or dispersal. The cumulative effect of these tactics on an invading enemy will be very considerable.'[346]

Airfield Defence

By now there were 19 military airfields in the two counties. Next to industrial war production, they were key to the local war effort and were the most important vulnerable points. For this reason, from mid-1943 local airfield defence policy was updated.

Airfields would no longer be defended with single static perimeters, but by three concentric levels with a mobile element, creating defence in depth.

The furthest level of defence, called the Observation Line, started two to three miles out and was manned by the Home Guard. They would provide warning of any approaching threat.

The next level was the Outer Defence, one to two miles out, again composed of Home Guards and Air Defence of Great Britain personnel (i.e. searchlight and AA sites) who would disrupt any attack.

The final and innermost defence was the Perimeter Defence of the airfield, under the command of the Station Commander. This consisted of at least four defended localities, sited to cover runways. Each DL was constructed of small slit trenches and surrounded by triple dannert barbed wire and double apron fence. They were manned by infantry or RAF personnel and were in direct communication with the Battlefield HQ. There would also be a mobile reserve platoon of infantry or a flight of RAF within the perimeter.

In the Charnsec Sector there were two Mobile Relief forces, the first a detachment of RAPC at Kirby Mallory (SK 456007) and the second the 8th Battalion RAOC (Derby), who would assemble at Garendon Hall (SK 503198). Both were under the command of 8th (Market Bosworth) Battalion Home Guard.

The scheme notes, 'Existing posts which do not conform to the above will be filled in or utilised as "Dummy Positions"': this means the pillboxes of 1940 were well and truly redundant by this date, viewed as static deathtraps from which troops could not escape.[347]

The Threat Evaporates

With the ever-decreasing threat of invasion, some defences could now be relaxed. Directional street signs had started to reappear in Loughborough in November 1942,[348] and from June 1943 church bells – the former portents of a paratroop invasion – could be tolled freely. From August 1943 instructions were issued stating that all flame fougasses were to be removed from the Sub-Area[349] and, the following month, anti-glider obstructions could also be taken down.[350] By now roadblock cylinders and rails lay partially overgrown in verges, a mere memory of more dangerous times. Any major threat to Britain was largely dismissed in the evaluation of the Sub-Area's last defence scheme in November 1943.

Leicester Sector Defences
1940–1944

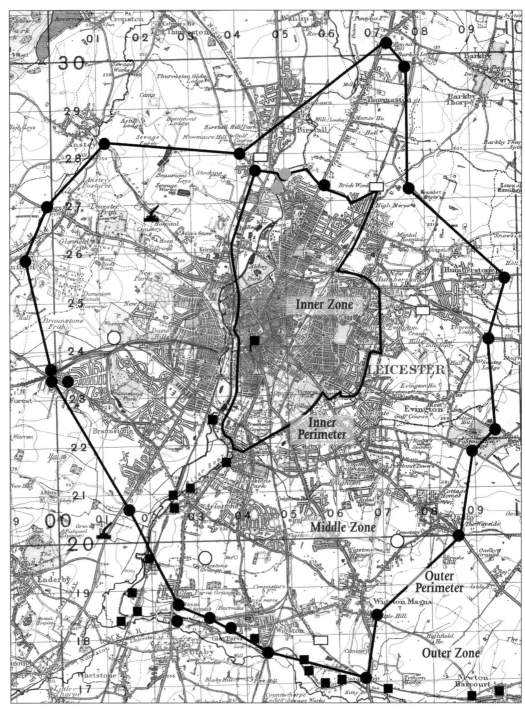

Leicester Sector Defences 1940–1944

Different emphasis put on various perimeters & zones by successive defence schemes

● Permanent roadblock	● River block	Anti-Aircraft battery *(can be used for ground defence in invasion)*
■ River/canal crossing block	■ Leicester Sector HQ	
▢ Rail block	○ Searchlight site	

'The present degree of risk, apart from air attacks, is appreciated as:

a) Invasion of UK: Not probable at present.

b) Raids: Major seaborne raids – unlikely, and if attempted there would be time for special measures to be taken in this sector.

c) Commando Raids: Possible between the Wash and Lands End, but unlikely on East Coast north of the Wash.

d) Airborne Raids: Unlikely, except in conjunction with commando raids.

e) Sabotage: Attempts by individuals domicile in UK or small parties landed by parachute are an ever-present danger to be guarded against.'

From June 1943, North Midland Command stated that US troops stationed in the sub-district could be used by the local officer in charge for defence purposes. The majority of US personnel in Leicestershire at this time were black service corps personnel.[351] From February 1944 the county defences were further boosted by paratroops of the elite US 82nd Airborne Division, based at Braunstone Park and Oadby Racecourse in Leicester and also at Quorn, and Ashwell Camp in Rutland, bringing the total US troops in both counties to 12,000 men. Also, there were Poles, Commonwealth troops, service units and RAF personnel stationed locally.

By early 1944 the Home Guard were better equipped and numbered more than ever before. They were finally beginning to achieve proper mobility, culminating in the formation of 2079 (Leicester) Motor Transport Company in February 1944, whose role was to intercept any paratroops that landed in the Sub-Area.

There had never been so many military personnel in Leicestershire and Rutland as there was in the run up to D-Day. Apart from a minor alert in mid-1944, when it was feared the Germans may attempt a counter-attack against the D-Day forces assembled in the Sub-Area, the next time Home Guard forces assembled was for Stand Down in December 1944.

Conclusion

In conclusion, although carefully planned and resourceful, the wartime defence of Leicestershire and Rutland can be summed up by the following irony. The defences were formed too late: the Home Guard and their sector schemes were weakest when the threat was greatest and at the point they were strongest, both had been made redundant by the course of the war.

CHAPTER 4:

WHO WERE THE HOME GUARD?

The Home Guard was mainly composed of men who can be broadly divided into three categories. The first and eventually the largest of the groups were 17–18, awaiting call up, although some lads either lied about their age or an official 'blind eye' was turned, as Home Guard Albert Squires recalled:

'I left school and went to work at Ibstock Brick and Tile Works. The works had a Home Guard platoon and I used to tag along at parades and weapon training until, one day, I was asked by the Officer in Charge if I would like to join. Can you imagine the excitement of a 14-year-old? I was given a Sten sub-machine gun as the rifles issued to the Home Guard were as tall as I was at the time!'[352]

The excitement factor also attracted Ken Allsopp to the Blaby Home Guard.

'Me and a friend joined the ARP as Messengers but there was no bombing, so we didn't do anything. This wasn't exciting enough, so we asked if we could join the Home Guard. We were only 16 but they accepted us. We trained at Ibstock range. They had a big trench and fired bullets over us which was quite scary, but we were young and daft and thought it was the bee's knees – we thought we were men.'[353]

The next group were men in reserved occupations, who were not eligible for call up or medically unsuitable but either volunteered or, after 1942, were conscripted into the Home Guard. The final group were men over 55 and beyond call-up age. The majority were World War One veterans and brought valuable experience. Former 12th (Motor Reconnaissance) Battalion Home Guard Bernard Spiers adds:

'The older men had "strong backbone". They would not have run if the Germans had come. That said, some of these gents were very old and the way they walked was very comical! Towards the end, there was not many young men in our platoon.'[354]

Former Wigston Home Guard Arthur Kirkpatrick remembers when some of the older men in his platoon lay down to fire at targets, 'you had to help them up afterwards!'[355]

Officers

In February 1941 the Home Guard were given commissions

    Zone and Group Commander: Colonel
    Battalion Commander: Lieutenant-Colonel
    Company Commander: Major or Captain
    Company 2nd i/c: Captain
    Platoon Commander: Lieutenant
    Platoon Officer: 2nd Lieutenant

Social and class boundaries were much more prominent in 1940s Britain, none more so than in the British Army and, by connection, the Home Guard. Officers were generally over 50, had served in World War One, or even previous conflicts, and were upper or upper-middle classes. Senior officers were well connected, of the archetypal huntin', shootin' and fishin' county set. They were usually managing directors of large businesses.

An example of a senior officer's background can be seen in the life of Major (later Lieutenant-Colonel) Charles Aubrey Babington Elliott, the Assistant Group Commander of the Leicester Home Guard. Born on 9 September 1894 at Winterbourne, Gloucestershire, Elliott was educated at Clifton College, Bristol, then Kings College, Cambridge. At the outbreak of World War One, Elliott joined the 8th Battalion Leicestershire Regiment and became a captain. He was wounded in 1916 during the Battle of the Somme and reported as killed in action. He was wounded again in October 1917 during the Battle of Ypres and finished the war with the rank of major. In 1920 Elliott moved to Leicester and became

Director of Coal Merchants Joseph Ellis and Sons. He moved to The Orchards, High Street, Oadby. He was a member of the Oadby Urban District Council, a local magistrate, was involved with the church and became the Chairman of the Leicestershire District Nursing Association.

Six months before World War Two he applied for the Army Officer's Emergency Reserve. During the Phoney War he manned an air raid siren opposite his home. He joined the LDV in May 1940 and became Assistant Group Commander of the Leicester Home Guard, second-in-command to the Leicester Group Commander Colonel H.W.H. Tyler MC. As his son Dick Elliott states: 'I think the fact our family had been friends of the Tylers for many years probably helped'. On Home Guard duty, he was based in his office at the Magazine, Leicester. By 1943 he was promoted to Lieutenant-Colonel, a rank he honorarily held after the war. Between 1943 and 1945 he was President of the Coal Merchants Federation of Great Britain and travelled to London to advise the government. He became Chairman of the Braunstone South Conservative Association and was awarded an OBE in 1955. He died on 26 November 1971.[356]

Major Charles A.B. Elliott, Assistant Group Commander, Leicester Home Guard, September 1940. He wears the locally-produced LDV armlet on his right arm and carries a .455 revolver in a holster.

There was no shortage of gallantry awards among the officers of the Leicestershire and Rutland Home Guard, with no less than 46 awards for bravery. These included one Meritorious Service Medal, six Military Medals, two Distinguished Conduct Medals, 25 Military Crosses, 10 Distinguished Service Orders and two Victoria Crosses, the highest award for gallantry.[357]

The first Leicestershire Home Guard officer recipient of the Victoria Cross was Lt-Col. William John Symons, CO of 12th (Motor Reconnaissance) Battalion between 1940–1943. Born in Australia, during World War One he served as a Lieutenant in the 7th Battalion, Australian Imperial Force. On the 9 August 1915 Lt Symons led a charge and captured some Turkish trenches. He was awarded the Victoria Cross for showing great coolness and determination in the face of the enemy. He died aged 50 on 24 June 1948.[358]

The second recipient of the Victoria Cross was Major Robert Edward Cruickshank, Company Commander of 'C' (Blaby and Whetstone) Company, 2nd (South Leicester) Battalion. Born in Canada, during World War One Cruickshank was a Private in the 2/14th (County of London Battalion) London Regiment (London Scottish). On 1 May 1918, while east of Jordan, he volunteered to take a message to HQ from his platoon who were trapped by the enemy at the bottom of a wadi. He was repeatedly wounded but 'displayed great endurance and was uncomplaining throughout'. He died aged 73 on 30 August 1961 and is buried at Gilroes Cemetery, Leicester.[359]

Junior officers were largely middle class and, while I have tried to veer away from the *Dad's Army* stereotypes, I have to admit half of Melton Mowbray's six platoon commanders were bank managers!

NCOs and Privates

Next in the pecking order were the NCOs. 'The backbone of the HG were the sergeants – the fellows who very soon knew all the answers. Many dared not tell their wives how much their soldiering called from their own pockets. There was the 1914–18 sergeant or WO who could not forget the trenches of Flanders.'[360]

Included among the NCOs was the only known black Home Guard in the two counties, Corporal 'Lol' Miller, of 'C'

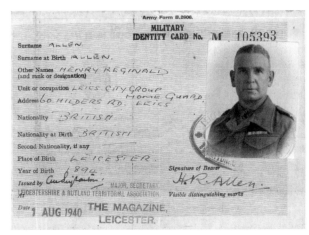

Officer's Home Guard military identity card for Captain Henry Allen, August 1940. (Captain Bob Allen)

Sir David Attenborough as a Home Guard.

Private James F. Mitchell, October 1941. He was a former England and Leicester City goalkeeper and represented Britain as a high jumper in the 1920 Olympics.

(Shepshed and Hathern) Company, 9th (Loughborough) Battalion. The NCOs and privates were mostly working class or lower-middle class, from landworkers in rural areas through to factory workers in urban battalions.

The vast majority of Home Guards were Volunteers (retitled 'Privates' in May 1942). Among this 'PBI' were some famous Leicester sons, including world-renowned naturalist Sir David Attenborough, who, as a 19-year-old, is believed to have been a Private in No. 1 (Leicester University) Platoon, 'A' (Oadby and City) Company, 2nd (South Leicester) Battalion, before he joined the Royal Navy. Sir David remembers taking part in exercises around the university, involving 'climbing walls and so forth'.[361]

Sporting star Private James Frederick Mitchell, of the 1st (North Leicester) Battalion, was a famous 1920s international goalkeeper and Olympian. Born in 1897 he played for Blackpool, Preston North End (appearing for them in the 1922 FA Cup Final) and Manchester City, before joining Leicester City in 1926. He played for England in 1925 and is believed to be the only goalkeeper to wear spectacles in League games. He also represented Britain in the 1920 Olympic high jump. Mitchell died in 1975.[362]

However, not all of the local Home Guard were fully able-bodied.

'Is he the only blind HG? Victor Higgens, 49, of Waltham, near Melton Mowbray, is believed to be the only blind active member of the Home Guard in the country. As he possesses a remarkably retentive memory, keen hearing and a first-rate knowledge of Morse, the Home Guard authority gave way to his enthusiasm when he volunteered to do his bit. He now does most things the Home Guard do and goes regularly on route marches, without the aid of a stick. His uncanny sense of direction has amazed his fellow Home Guard members, to many of whom he has passed on his knowledge of Morse. Mr Higgens is also a poultry farmer and does his own correspondence on a typewriter. When workmen put a new weather vane to the spire of the local church, Victor went alone to the top – a climb of 127 feet – and swung the vanes round to make sure it was working properly. He has been blind since the age of 12.'[363]

In Rutland, Col. Ogilvy-Dalgleish wrote 'In June, 1943…Sergt. A. Dawson of Burley was promoted to Lieut. i/c of No. 9 Platoon in 'C' Coy. [He]…like so many others, too numerous to mention, [was] valued and experienced veteran of World War One and still fighting fit. Dawson had lost a leg below the knee in the 1914–18 War but no one would have known it, he was as active as most men with two complete legs.'[364]

'Parsons were eligible for enrolment as combatants and we had two members of the Church militant, the Rev. D.W.G. Bartlett, Rector of Market Overton, who left the district in 1940, and the Rev. C.B. Wheeldon, Rector of Stretton. The latter was very keen and later commanded No. 3 Platoon in "A" Coy for some time until the Church authorities decided that parsons must not be combatant: so he became C.Q.M.S. as the next best thing.'[365]

Likewise, the Revd C.M.K. Parsons was second in command of No. 3 (Breedon and Coleorton) Company, 11th (Ashby-de-la-Zouch) Battalion.

The Reason Why

Practically all the Home Guards interviewed said they joined the force for two main reasons: to 'do their bit' and for patriotism.

The Structure of the Leicestershire and Rutland Home Guard

Apart from its professionalism, the British Army is world-renowned for its high level of military organisation and bureaucracy. What the Home Guard lacked, it more than made up for in bureaucracy. For the first three years the organisation was in a constant state of evolution, with frequently changing

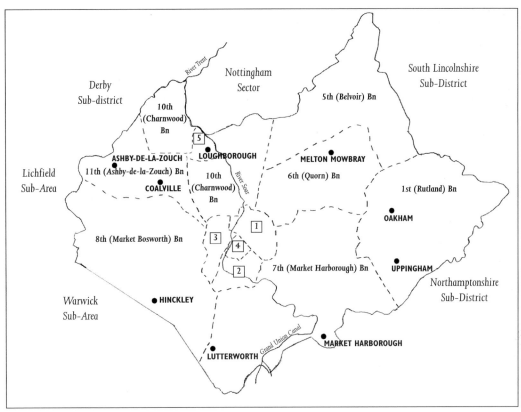

Leicester Sub-District
1943 - Showing Battalion
boundaries

1   1st (North Leic) Bn
2   2nd (South Leic) Bn
3   3rd (West Leic) Bn
4   4th (Central Leic) Bn
5   9th (Loughborough) Bn

Plus:
12th (Motor Reconnaissance) Bn
13th (25 G.P.O.) Bn
Both cover Sub-District area

units and areas. These contained an equally fluid membership, as Home Guards were either called-up, retired, or moved due to war work. Not surprisingly, this constant restructuring confused many, and attempting to understand the organisation today can prove equally testing.

Britain was divided into seven Commands: South-Eastern, Southern, London District, Eastern, Western (including Northern Ireland), Scottish and Northern Command (the largest). These were sub-divided into Areas (later Districts).

Leicestershire and Rutland formed their own Sub-Area (later Sub-District). This was part of the North Midland Area (later District), which also contained two other Sub-Areas/Districts: Derby and Nottingham. The North Midland Area (later District) was part of Northern Command, e.g:

Pre-Summer 1942
Northern Command
North Midland Area
Leicestershire, Rutland and Northants Sub-Area
(minus Northants after 1941)
Leicestershire Zone and Rutland Zone
Leicester, Bosworth, Melton/Oakham Groups

Post June 1942
Northern Command
North Midland District
Leicestershire Sub-Area/District*
(including Rutland)
—
Leisec, Charnsec, Cottesec
Sectors

Battalion Areas/Sub-Sectors
* '25 May 1943: Leicester Sub Area to be known henceforth as Leicester Sub-District'[366]

Battalion Areas/Sub-Sectors

Manpower

Date	Ceiling	Actual
November 1940	23,000	22,737

November 1942   –   21,180
November 1943   24,094   22,773[367]

The Leicestershire and Rutland Home Guard reached a peak of 22,773 in 1943. But how many men and women served in the local force in total? In his Stand Down speech, CO of the 10th (Charnwood) Battalion Lt-Col. C.H. Martin stated 2,800 men of all ranks had passed through the battalion, representing more than double the battalion strength at any one time.[368] If this is taken as a battalion average, then around 50,000 men and women served in the two counties' Home Guard.

General Service Battalions

The Home Guard mirrored the existing infrastructure of its older brother, the British Army. With some notable exceptions, nearly all of the battalions in Leicestershire and Rutland were General Service (infantry) battalions dedicated to the defence of their immediate area. Those battalions in urban areas mainly guarded industry, whereas their rural counterparts covered airfields and defended localities. Leicestershire had 11 GS battalions, 1st to 11th Battalions, and two extra-zone units 12th (Motor Reconnaissance) Battalion and 13th (GPO) Battalion, which operated across the Sub-Area. Rutland, exemplifying the fact it is the smallest county in England, had only one battalion, 1st Rutland Battalion, although it covered an area of 287 square miles, including two towns and 45 villages.[369]

Battalion strength and composition varied depending on the size of the area and manpower available, with battalion areas larger in sparser rural parts. Generally, however, the battalions were divided thus:

  1 Battalion contains six Companies (1,000–1,200 men)
  1 Company contains five to six platoons (200–240 men)
  1 Platoon contains 4 sections (35–40 men)
  1 Section contains (8–10 men)

(For a full list of the battalions, companies and platoons in Leicestershire and Rutland see Appendix A.) Some units acted uniquely in the defence of important vulnerable points:

4th (Central Leicester) Battalion

Leicester, as the county capital, with its large population and important centre, was made into a Group (later Sector) containing four battalions: the 1st (North Leicester), the 2nd (South Leicester), the 3rd (West Leicester) and the 4th (Central Leicester), totalling 10,000 men.[370] Later the Leicester Group was enlarged to include the 12th (Motor Reconnaissance) Battalion and the 13th (25th GPO) Battalion. This raised the total to 12,000 men.[371] From the start, Col. H.W.H. Tyler MC was Group Commander, with Lieutenant-Colonel C.A.B. Elliott second in command.

Leicester was traditionally a hosiery and textiles capital but most companies switched to war work, divided up between the Admiralty, Ministry of Aircraft Production and the Ministry of Supply (for a full list of factories engaged on war work, see the Vulnerable Points List in Appendix B).

From the LDV's inception, several keener factories started their own 'private armies'. Recognising the importance of the city centre, and at the same time controlling the homogeneous growth of these semi-independent works units, a 4th (Central Leicester) Battalion was formed on 9 August 1940. At first, the various works raised 'detachments', but by 1941 they were renamed platoons. The CO was Lt-Col. A.S. Whitehead, who was replaced in November 1942 by Lt-Colonel W.N. Dunn.[372]

The first three Leicester battalions guarded the suburbs and drew members from their geographical areas. However, there was little residency within the 4th Battalion's central location, so it drew its members from the city's workforce, irrespective of where they lived.

4th (Central Leicester) Battalion Platoon Examples:
No. 2 Detachment (LNER (Great Northern) Railway, Belgrave Road Passenger Station)

Leicester was the central point at which all the county's railways converged. A London main line also ran through it. Road transport was minimal due to petrol shortages, so Leicestershire's railway network became vital to the war effort. Many ammunition and troop trains also used the network, so the defence of the railways was a vital Home Guard priority, as Horace Gamble remembers.

Horace, then 18, joined the Home Guard (although it was still locally known as the LDV) at Charles Street police station on 31 July 1940. A few days later, he reported to the LNER (Great Northern) Railway Detachment, which was perfect for him as he was fascinated by trains.

'Imagine my surprise and delight when I was notified my presence was required at the former Great Northern Railway station in Belgrave Road, Leicester...

Horace Gamble stands easy, in the uniform of the 4th (Central Leicester) Battalion Leicestershire Home Guard. (Horace Gamble)

On the first Sunday morning an assorted collection of citizens assembled in the concourse where sufficient ancient rifles were produced to initiate some very awkward, and disjointed, arms drill. "Square bashing" was practised on the long platforms, which were ideal for the purpose, especially when it rained, being under cover of the cavernous roof. The platoon was divided into six "sections" which carried out guard duties on the premises every night, clad in khaki denim blouse and trousers worn over normal clothing. A tin hat, civilian gas mask and LDV armband completed the ensemble.

As there were no train movements during the night, guard duties commenced at 9.00pm – shortly after the last goods train had left the yard – until 5.00am next morning, with each patrol consisting of two men on an allotted beat. Patrols lasted two hours, after which one was allowed to sleep on a camp bed in the Guard Room, in reality the General Waiting Room.

Night watches could be extremely tedious but if one happened to be posted at the gates of the goods yard in Catherine Street there was enough to do to relieve any boredom. Every lorry which arrived at the yard had to be searched for infiltrators (!) and each driver's identity papers checked. However, my regular partner and I seemed to be the guardians of Catherine Street viaduct against the force of the enemy although what good we might have been, armed to the teeth with ammunition-less rifles, we could never quite comprehend.

Our most popular post, undoubtedly, was the goods shed where one member could kip down on a bale of straw for half an hour's shut-eye while his companion stayed ever on the alert, although I doubt whether you would have been shot at dawn for sleeping on duty in the LDV.'

As we shall see later, Horace transferred to a different platoon in the 4th Battalion. However, that was not the last of his Home Guard dealings with the railways, as nearly two years later he took part in exercises at the LNER yards.

'On Palm Sunday 29 March, a cryptic but more meaningful entry in my diary proclaimed "Home Guard parade 10.30 hours. We attack LNER shed and capture it."

The assembled platoon was briefed that the morning's exercise was to capture the LNER (Great Central) locomotive shed [south of Upperton Road] from the defending railway platoon. There were several avenues of approach because the shed was situated at an angle to the main running lines, one mile south of the station and it backed onto the towpath of the Grand Union Canal. Between the shed yard and the nearest road was a large area of allotment gardens alongside the canal. Spies in civilian clothing, posing as gardeners armed with spades not rifles, were strategically posted to ascertain the deployment of the defenders. Our section was to make a frontal attack while others approached from the rear. We climbed a fence beneath Upperton Road viaduct, where it passed over Western Road, to gain a foothold in enemy territory. As if by prior arrangement a much needed piece of cover presented itself in the shape of the B16 4–6–0 No. 2378, slowly hauling an up freight and coming to a stand south of the bridge. Upon recognising that an engine change was about to take place the experts pointed out to the sergeant our patrol could easily secrete itself on the footplate, travel right into the garrison (like an iron horse of Troy) and capture our objective to the applause of the umpires for being so resourceful.

Was our NCO impressed by our cunning strategy? Not on your life. He was determined to do it the proper way and sent a man ahead on a reccy to liase with the spies. There was nothing more to do than stay hidden by the wagons awaiting further orders. One member of the patrol, who probably had had a late night, propped himself up against the solebar of a van totally oblivious of the relief locomotive which had attached itself to take the train southwards. Upon getting a clear road the driver was eager to go and opened up the regulator purposefully causing the wagons to leap forward abruptly. Our dozy colleague, rudely awakened from his reverie, somehow only just managed to avoid committing the heinous crime of dropping his rifle on the ground!

The patrol moved stealthily on towards South Goods signal box in the engine yard unchallenged, for it seemed the defenders had not contemplated a daring attack from that quarter. Victoriously we informed the occupants of the office the game was up…'[373]

No. 13 (Leicester County Council Offices) Platoon, 'B' Company

After serving two months in the LNER Platoon, Horace Gamble transferred to another city platoon responsible for guarding the Leicester County Council Offices on Grey Friars. This was an important Vulnerable Point because it not only housed the council's main administrative offices, but also the control room of the county ARP HQ.

'With winter approaching I viewed the prospect of foggy and frosty nights at Forest Road crossing with some gloom, but a saviour was at hand. My brother, who worked at the County Council Offices, joined a platoon which guarded the control room of the County ARP HQ on the premises, where my father also worked. It did not take long to effect a transfer to this more cushy billet.

Once the entrance gates had been closed at 10pm the night guard took up position inside the entrance foyer. Another Home Guard stood guard at the gate of the car park on Friar Lane. The password always began with the first letter of that day, but from August 1942 they stopped using passwords.

There is one "special" occasion, well remembered…The Minister for Education, Rt Hon. R.A. ("RAB") Butler MP made a visit to the County Education department. It was suggested the two most efficient Home Guard Privates should mount guard outside that evening. My brother and I were chosen and I well remember challenging "Halt who goes there?" to Mr Butler. I also recall the times when we

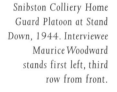

Snibston Colliery Home Guard Platoon at Stand Down, 1944. Interviewee Maurice Woodward stands first left, third row from front.

stopped Lt-Col. Sir Robert Martin, the Lord Lieutenant and Major Brockington, Director of Education, during our guard duties.

We also had lighter moments. Being young we always found a lot of ways to lark around. We had a cycle section. One day I was ordered to cycle to HQ, so I decided to wear my gas mask – the alarmed faces of the people in Leicester High Street! During the summer we used to stand on the roof and use a stirrup pump to spray people below in the street. They used to look up and wonder where the rain was coming from!

My own call up into the armed forces was deferred so I spent nearly three years as a Home Guard Private before I donned navy blue uniform and served on minesweepers.'[374]

In September 1942 works' units were subject to 'drastic changes', which attacked their 'private armies'. They were forced to provide cover for their surrounding neighbourhood. Changes to the Leicester Sector Defence Scheme in August 1942 envisaged a mobile role for the 4th Battalion, as a striking force anywhere in the city limits.

There was also a shake-up among the commanders. New orders stated 'Many executives…who are Home Guard officers more by virtue of their positions in the factory than by their soldiering ability will have to go.'[375] Once again, this transferred more power from local commanders to top brass.

Other battalions outside the Leicester Sector also guarded specialised sites.

The Defence of the Collieries

Maurice Woodward, formerly a Private in the Snibston Colliery Platoon of 11th (Ashby-de-la-Zouch) Battalion, recalled:

'As a 16-year-old, I worked down the pit at Snibston Colliery, Coalville, and joined its LDV unit. We marched and countermarched around the pit yard in our own civvy clothes with a four-foot wooden pole.

It was a few months afterwards we were eventually fitted out with uniforms and the American .300 rifle, along with a few bayonets, but no ammunition. It became a bore! We were relieved one day when the CO informed us that he'd actually got hold of some.

For a start we stood guard at the pit gate on a rota system from 12 noon Saturday until Sunday 10pm. There was no official guard during the week as the risk of sabotage was minimised by the presence of workmen and officials involved in their round-the-clock routine pit activities.

When the Americans entered the war, weapons and ammunition began to filter through more quickly…but friends of mine became disenchanted, and asked if I would go with them to volunteer for one of the services. I explained under the Essential Works Order it was impossible – this was our life until the end of the war. Some did go to the nearest recruiting office in Leicester, to test it. They answered "Name", "Address" – but when it got to the third question "Occupation" and they replied "Coal miner", they were shown the door in no uncertain terms – so it was to be.'[376]

Beaumanor Hall 'Y'-Station: No. 21 (Independent) Platoon, 10th (Charnwood) Battalion

The most important Home Guard platoon in Leicestershire – and arguably one of the most important in Britain – was No. 21 (Independent) Platoon, 10th (Charnwood) Battalion. From October 1941 they were based at the most vulnerable point in the two counties, MI8's Y- (Wireless) Intercept Station at Beaumanor Hall, Woodhouse, south of Loughborough, and were responsible for its point defence.

Beaumanor Hall was the army's main wireless intercept station. The Army Y-Service were the 'ears' that intercepted all of the German army's (Wehrmacht) radio traffic and passed this intelligence to Bletchley Park for decryption. Their work was vital to the war effort and, as Skillen states, since much of the intercepted material indicated the plans of German High Command it is not unfair to argue that many of the key military decisions taken by the British 'began their life in the huts scattered around Beaumanor's grounds'.[377] Often forgotten and overshadowed by the fame of 'Station X' at Bletchley Park, without Beaumanor Hall and the handful of other Y-Stations there would have been no Bletchley Park.

Beaumanor's Home Guard originated at the Y-Service's original station at Fort Bridgewoods, Chatham, Kent. Due to the threat of invasion and bombing, the station moved to Chicksands Priory, Bedfordshire. However, due to limited space, it was decided to split the Y-Service: RAF operators would remain while the army would move to Beaumanor Hall. The large mansion had 300 acres of land including woodland, which provided cover from the air. It had been occupied by the WO's No. 6 Intelligence School early in the war. Although radio reception was not ideal, Beaumanor's central location was well away from the invasion-vulnerable coast.

The increasing amount of German radio traffic at the start of the war meant there was a shortfall of radio interceptors, so women were drawn from the ATS, WRNS and WAAF. They were called Special Wireless Assistants (SWAs). Male civilians, many drawn from amateur radio enthusiast groups, were also recruited.[378] They were called Experimental Wireless Assistants (EWAs).

Beaumanor Hall intercepted the Wehrmacht's enigma coded traffic for the Government Codes and Cipher School at Bletchley Park. The work was mainly done by 900 ATS SWAs and EWAs in camouflaged huts around the grounds. Kay Staddon, a SWA, remembers the wireless operators also practised morse in the surrounding fields in the event of Beaumanor Hall being captured.[379]

All civilians, even EWAs, had to do some form of additional war service. About 45 EWAs composed Beaumanor's Home Guard platoon. Lieutenant (later Captain) Dick Whitford was the CO, assisted by Lt Harry Dix. Their immediate superior was the station commander, retired naval officer Lt-Commander M.J.W. Ellingworth.

Due to the site's high importance, the platoon was 'independent': it did not receive commands from the local 10th Battalion but operated wholly independently, solely in defence of Beaumanor and would not leave Beaumanor's immediate area to engage the enemy. For this reason, the platoon was better equipped than any other platoon in Leicestershire, in fact it was over-armed. It was equipped with all the standard Home Guard weaponry, but had extras. As well as Sten guns, it had Thompson sub-machine guns as well as Lewis guns, a Hotchkiss medium machine gun, a Northover Projector and four spigot mortars, a two-pounder anti-tank gun complete with 15cwt Bedford towing truck. Most of these weapons were stored in the Hall's cellars or outhouses. Peter James, an 18-year-old Royal Signals wireless interceptor, served in the Beaumanor platoon:

'I was one of the sergeants and was responsible for the spigot mortar section. We used to fire it at improvised targets on Buddon Hill. We also had a two-pounder anti-tank gun that came along at the end, but I don't think we ever fired it: we didn't have any shells, except a single wooden practice shell! We had a tommy gun – an awful thing that was so heavy – and we took it to an unofficial range up at Hangingstone Quarry. One chap had a particularly short fuse. He was supposed to be firing this tommy gun at these targets, when one of the officers said something which annoyed him and he turned around with his finger on the trigger and suddenly everybody was diving for cover because there were bullets flying everywhere! It was a bit horrific at the time and the nearest I came to death!'

Security at Beaumanor proved to be a problem. As Nicholls points out, 'it had to be effective but not obvious. If the place was heavily guarded, it would have attracted gossip and attention that was not wanted.'[380] A public footpath ran through the grounds through which 'a child could have come in'.[381] Indeed 'a few teenage boys climbed into the grounds from the footpath that led from the Loughborough Road. They were very quickly found and removed.'[382] Peter James recalls:

'I think Beaumanor's defences were negligible, almost non-existent really. We were guarded by Royal Corps of Military Police, who manned a blockhouse at the gate. Most of them were anything but young and capable, but were helped by well-trained Alsatians, which were quite ferocious. Even so, any enemy attack would have made short work of them. Lt-Col. Ellingworth used to issue directives because the base's personnel often used to take a short cut across the lawn and a path began to form, which would indicate to German aerial reconnaissance large numbers of personnel were stationed there.'

The intercept staff went on duty together and were locked in once work started. They were also warned not to tell anybody of their top secret work and their silence was tested by agent provocateurs. It was said one ATS SWA got drunk at a Loughborough dance and told one of these undercover overseers about her work. By the next morning her bed was empty and her bags packed and gone. The rumour was spread among the staff she had been sent to the Tower of London. Despite these precautions, before teleprinters were installed the valuable secret intercepts were sent each night in the blackout direct to Bletchley Park by a lone motorcycle despatch rider down the A6! Peter James continues:

'If you had just finished Home Guard parade, you could wear your uniform for wireless work in the hut. It was an arduous job at Beaumanor – it really was – and most of us had to give up our own spare time training: we took it that seriously.'[383]

Despite the platoon's vitally-important role, in her book on Beaumanor former SWA Joan Nicholls says 'The Beaumanor unit was always seen as boys playing soldiers and no one ever took them seriously.'[384] Peter James responded:

'I thought Joan Nicholls was very dismissive of our efforts and the amount of work we had to put in, much more than most HG units, but to her we were apparently figures of fun. We were there to defend the ATS girls at Garats Hay as well as Beaumanor. Given an attack by well-trained enemy troops, I doubt we would have lasted long, but who knows?'

Because the EWAs were generally young men, locals did not believe they were really Home Guard, thinking their uniform was a cover for some Special Forces unit.

'They used to say "You're not really Home Guard, are you?" Perhaps one can understand their curiosity as we were always smartly turned out and we went everywhere by army transport, whereas other platoons had to use whatever they could.'[385]

As we shall see, unknown to nearly all the Beaumanor Hall platoon there was an elite undercover Home Guard unit, whose task was also to defend Beaumanor (see page 143).

Extra-Zone Units
12th (Motor Reconnaissance) Battalion

As the majority of Leicestershire and Rutland is rural, a mobile striking force was needed to meet the invader wherever he landed. As a result, the 12th (Motor Reconnaissance) Battalion was formed. The battalion initially comprised of two motorised companies with their HQ at Leicester Stadium on Blackbird Road and from 1941 in Canning Street, Leicester. It was raised and commanded by Lt-Col. W.J. Symons VC, and from July 1943 by Lt-Col. R. Taylor. At first, transport was loaned by members. It is believed Fred (Bob) Gerard, who ran a garage on Abbey Lane, was part of the battalion:

'He used his fleet of vehicles to transport his platoon. Even the oldest trucks were brought into action. A 1924 Albion saloon, which had to be crank-started, could often be seen motoring along crowded with eight men or more, the taller ones sticking through the sunroof. This mobility enabled them to venture out as an attacking force and test other platoon's defences. One such occasion involved an attack on Desford aerodrome on a Sunday morning.

We had great fun going across the field. One of our chaps found a whole load of milk bottles, which we flung at the brick walls sheltering the "enemy". That soon shifted the opposition' said Mr Gerard, who drew on his experience as a motor-racing and pre-war touring driver to pass on his knowledge of map reading to his men.[386]

Bill Stevenson joined the 12th Battalion:

'I was about 16 and lived in Newfoundpool. There was a chap in the same street who had been a corporal in World War One and he was in this Home Guard unit. I had wanted to do my part as I had three brothers in the forces, so I joined at Canning Place, St. Margaret's. The 12th's main HQ was at the Stadium on Blackbird Road. We had a guard on the entrance because we were told there was ammunition buried in the centre of the ground. We slept in the old ticket offices at the back when not on duty.

We were a mobile "emergency" unit that could respond to any area if paratroopers dropped in a certain place, we'd dash off in the vans. Most of the transport was provided by local haulage contractors, such as Fred Edlin Haulage and Cooper Furniture Removals.

We used to go for a lot of field training in Abbey Park and practised throwing dummy grenades in the Stadium. There was always great banter and humour when the men got in the back of the trucks.

On 30 November 1942 we went up to Ratcliffe airfield at Six Hills, where we were transferred for the day to the Sherwood Foresters on defence duty. We dug in at a spinney opposite. Another time, we went for a training camp at Whitwick Monastery and were well fed with legs of pork, which was amazing for wartime.'[387]

Alan Clare, then in the 12th Battalion's Medical Section, recalls transport gradually evolved from taxis and vans, through to buses loaned by Leicester City Transport until finally army trucks.

Once the main county defence schemes were drawn up at the end of 1941, the 12th Battalion played a key role as back-up to the three sectors. By this date, with a lot of young men waiting to go into the forces, the 12th Battalion became a truly mobile and responsive fighting force.

In February 1944 2079 (Leicester) Motor Transport Company was created under the command of Major L.H. Cox as one of six new MT Companies forming the North Midland Home Guard Transport Column, who covered Nottinghamshire, Derbyshire, Lincolnshire and Leicestershire, although they could be sent anywhere in Britain. The Column HQ was in Nottingham.[388]

13th (25th GPO) Post Office Battalion

Post offices and telephone exchanges were viewed as key targets for paratroopers, who could throw defensive operations into chaos if they sabotaged the communications system. In those days the GPO was responsible for the telephone system, and a surprising amount of Home Guard and military communication relied on civilian landlines. The protection of GPO buildings and telephone systems became a key priority for the Home Guard.

Initially, post office sub-units were attached to their local battalion. However, in late 1940 GPO sub-units were formed into their own extra-zone GPO Battalions. In the Leicestershire Sub-Area, all GPO sub-units were formed into the new 13th Battalion, commanded by Lt-Col. A. Wells, with two company HQ's: 'A' Company: Head Post Office, Leicester and 'B' Company: 66 London Road, Leicester. There were also platoons and sections at Hinckley, Loughborough, Oakham, Melton Mowbray and Stamford Head Post Offices.

The county designation only reflected where the battalion HQ was located, which was Leicestershire. However, as the units were also part of the national GPO Home Guard, they were subtitled the 25th GPO Battalion, explaining the double designation: 13th (25th GPO) Battalion. But the GPO's operational area was much broader, stretching well beyond the immediate county boundaries, so a strange situation arose where Home Guards well outside Leicestershire wore 'LEI 13' shoulder titles.

This caused some resentment, further kindling inter-county rivalry. In neighbouring Northamptonshire, the Home Guard Zone Commander, grandly-named Sir Hereward Wake, wrote to the East Midlands Commander stating '…a Post Office battalion at Leicester is very far from convenient, and against the interests of the men, nor do they desire it. They would be cut off from training facilities and supervision by HG officers.'[389] But the strange extra-zone organisation continued, as on 20 September 1942, when a Kettering platoon of 13th (GPO) Battalion Leicestershire Home Guard fought alongside the 4th (Kettering) and 5th (Kettering District) Battalions of the Northamptonshire Home Guard, during a defence exercise in Kettering – a good seven miles from the nearest part of Leicestershire.[390]

Staffordshire's Burton-upon-Trent GPO platoon also wore the 'LEI 13' flash with the tiger cap badge of the Leicestershire Regiment, but were all Staffordshire men. 'In the event of a general muster, however, the platoon would have come under the command of the local military commander, and it was therefore attached to the 8th (Burton) Staffs. Battalion Home Guard for operational purposes.'[391]

Far Sentinel of the Leicestershire GPO Home Guard Killed Doing His Duty
Perhaps one of the farthest members of the 13th Leicestershire Battalion was Volunteer Stanley Boyce, a GPO worker of Wisbech, Cambridgeshire – almost 40 miles from Leicestershire – who was the only person killed when the town was bombed on 17 July 1941.[392]

Three GPO Home Guards were on night sentry duty at the rear of Wisbech post office. A lone Nazi aircraft dropped a stick of bombs across the town. Two 13th Battalion Home Guards, Bertie Barwick, 38, and Stanley Pye, 33, were wounded. Sadly, Volunteer Boyce, 44, died from his injuries. Eleven people were injured in the raid, but Volunteer Boyce was the only fatality.[393]

Volunteer Boyce was married with three children. During World War One, he had 'raised' his age so he could join the army and was subsequently badly wounded. His funeral was held five days later at St Augustine's Church, Wisbech. Members of the 13th Battalion formed a guard of honour as his coffin, draped in the Union Jack and bearing his steel helmet, belt, bayonet and World War One medals, was carried in. After the service, the Home Guard led the cortege to Mount Pleasant Road Cemetery, Wisbech.[394]

By 1941 three types of GPO Home Guard existed:
a) Mobile specialists engaged on essential defence communications (telephones).
b) Mobile specialists engaged on essential postal service works.
c) Static HGs engaged on military duties, chiefly the defence of GPO buildings and installations. They were not to be used in the general defence of the locality unless as a last resort.

The mobile specialists wore distinguishing blue and white diamond signals shoulder designations,

Staff Platoon, HQ Company, 1st (North Leicester) Battalion Home Guard photographed at Humberstone Lido, Leicester, Stand Down, November 1944. Interviewee Raymond Elgood is third from left, middle row. (Raymond Elgood)

A mobile 'enemy' column wait for the order to attack Loughborough during Exercise PARTRIDGE, Sunday 11 October 1942.

indicating their important role. During invasion, Home Guard operators would operate all manned exchanges in areas affected by enemy action.

By 1941 the 13th Battalion had 37 GPO Vulnerable Points to guard within the Sub-Area.[395] Frank Cooke worked at Loughborough's Sparrow Hill Head Post Office and joined his GPO LDV sub-unit:

'I lived at Cobden Street, Loughborough. I joined the GPO in 1936 and was a sorting clerk and telegraphist. At 20, I joined the LDV in 1940. The 14–18 men became the NCOs and the rest of us the ORs. Dennis Ford was a GPO Overseer, so he was made sergeant but the officer in charge was the manager of the telecoms department.

There was an automatic telephone exchange upstairs with the post office downstairs, so that's why it was a vulnerable point. We were a unit designed essentially to protect the post office and so we spent most of the time in the forecourt training and drilling. Our rifles were stored in our GPO HQ room. We all did sentry duty on the main gate. All the post office staff were automatically regarded as troops in the event of attack. Because I was in the GPO, when I was called-up I went straight into the Royal Corps of Signals.'[396]

Battalion Sub-Units:
Headquarters Companies
All battalions had a HQ company who performed a service role to the rest of the battalion. In early 1941 Ray Elgood transferred to the HQ company, 1st (North Leicester) Battalion.

'I was lecturing at Leicester Polytechnic and there was a chap called Jack Moffat, who was in the 1st Battalion [see below]. He said "Why don't you come and join us and play with the big boys?" I didn't fancy standing guard on the factory roof for the rest of the war and these people were actually doing something, so I joined them and became a corporal.

Our HQ was at the old Humberstone Lido and we had stores there, including explosives. We couldn't get all the equipment we needed, so we used to "borrow" some of it, mainly from the American camp at Scraptoft. They had enormous stores and didn't know what they had and didn't care either, so we used to go on midnight raids and help ourselves to coils of ropes etc, but not the arms, they were locked up. We took a few radio sets, but they were useless: they spent days stored on the floor, so were bound not to work.

Instead, I had a Canadian CR100 radio from a Wellington bomber, which was much better. One day though, I was using it and someone got a direction finder on it. Because there was so many harmonics from these old sets, it was upsetting Stoughton airfield!'[397]

Pioneers
Hardly any records survive about these units, but it appears that, from around 1942, some battalions formed small pioneer units, often a sub-section of the HQ company. Similar to the Royal Engineers, they performed a wide range of manual tasks, including the construction of Home Guard assault courses. Lt Jack Moffat was CO of the Pioneer unit attached to the 1st (North Leicester) Battalion's HQ company. He was tragically killed in a training accident in March 1943 (see page 58)

Guides/Intelligence Sections

One of the Home Guard's chief strengths was its local knowledge. The Home Guard had to be able to direct reinforcements, so Home Guard Guides (later called Intelligence Sections) were created. Each Guide had to know his area intimately. Col. Ogilvy-Dalgleish attributed his local knowledge to riding with the Cottesmore Hunt. Guides proved more useful in predominantly rural areas such as Rutland, as Col. Ogilvy-Dalgleish explains:

'In January 1942, Sterndale Bennett became Bn Intelligence Officer and Chief Guide with the rank of Captain; Guides were already functioning in Coy areas and they now came under Sterndale Bennett's control and received further training.

It was essential that Guides should be quick witted, know their own countryside thoroughly and be capable of reading maps easily, gridded or otherwise [especially as their were no road signs in wartime]…

[Sterndale Bennett] amassed a mine of information of every kind, all of great potential value. He set himself one particular exciting task in producing a map showing the known name of every field in Rutland. As countrymen know, all fields have their own individual names, sometimes dating back for centuries, and to collect these much research was required among tenants, workers, owner-farmers, landlords, agents etc.

Sterndale Bennett's idea was that, in an agricultural district, the best, most accurate and quickest way of reporting the presence of the enemy would be by giving the names of the field, or fields, in which they had been seen. Sterndale Bennett's map remains as a monument to his infinite capacity for taking pains. The map has historical interest through its record of field names in Rutland; it is now in [Oakham Museum].'[398]

Mobile Units

Rather than waiting for the enemy to attack, offensive mobile units were formed, usually from the youngest and fittest, leaving the older men to man static defences. Col. Ogilvy-Dalgleish explains:

'In Oakham a mobile fighting patrol of 20 men with machine guns had been trained under S.S. Watson, No. 9 Platoon Commdr. with Sergt. R. Atton as driver of the ear-marked vehicle, all of whom were likely to be available at short notice; parachute troops were vulnerable for a time after their drop in strange country and the patrol might have done some very useful work at such a time. The patrol was frequently exercised and, under Watson's continued leadership…it was extremely keen and efficient. Mobile fighting patrols were later ordered by higher authority and, in 1942, the whole of No. 11 (Braunston and Brooke) Platoon became mobile.'[399]

Strangely, despite the two counties' boast of having the most famous fox hunts in Britain, unlike other areas such as Exmoor, Dartmoor and the New Forest, no records have been found to indicate either Leicestershire or Rutland's hunts formed mounted patrols to combat a more threatening prey.

Signals Sections

Communications were vital to the Home Guard. A communications breakdown could cause the network of Home Guard defence to collapse. From May 1941 each battalion set up signals sections, under a Signals Officer. At first, Signals Officers taught their sections locally, but later men were sent on courses at the North Midlands District Home Guard Training School at Bestwood Lodge, Arnold, Nottingham. Once qualified, Home Guard signallers wore the distinguishing crossed flags signals flash on their lower left sleeve. There were five branches of signals Home Guard:

Messengers/Runners: Initially, no signalling equipment was available for the Home Guard, so messages were written and sent via messengers/runners. Young lads had always been interested in the Home Guard and this unarmed role suited them perfectly, especially as they were more spritely. They were officially accepted at 16, but were often unofficially accepted younger. David Salmon was a messenger for the Market Bosworth Home Guard. 'I was about 11 years old and at Dixie Grammar

Home Guard despatch riders of the 1st (North Leicester) Battalion at Abbey Park, Leicester, October 1941. The line of motorcycles reads like a history of British motorcycle manufacturing – from left: Triumph, BSA, Panther, Velocette with Royal Enfield and Aerial behind.

School. My father was commanding officer of the Market Bosworth Home Guard and I became a messenger runner for them that way. There were about three of us boys with bicycles. I remember during one exercise, a Tiger Moth from nearby RAF Desford was used. I felt great excitement when it dropped a message in a little sandbag about troop movements. We then had to get the message to Home Guard HQ, which entailed cycling a couple of miles to the Red Lion in Market Bosworth!'[400]

Despatch Riders: Runners were obviously limited to how far they could deliver messages, so motorcycle despatch riders were employed, about one or two per platoon. They had to be able to ride in all weathers and terrains. Although supplied with maps, they had to know their locality inside out. An example of their skill was exhibited at Abbey Park, Leicester, during the 1944 Salute the Soldier display, where they performed 'stunt riding'. They also played an important part in all the countywide exercises.

Despatch riders were armed with Sten sub-machine guns, usually only issued to NCOs, reflecting their important role. The Sten gun was more manageable than the long, heavy P17 rifle and was more useful if ambushed. They wore standard army despatch rider dress, namely a leather jerkin, high-domed crash helmet and blue and white signals armlets on both arms. Jim Tailby was the Dunton Bassett platoon's despatch rider.

'I was born and brought up in Dunton Bassett. I was 25 and worked at BSA, Abbey Meadow Mills, Leicester. I rode to work on my motorbike. I felt it was my duty to join the Home Guard as I was in reserved occupation. I joined about 1940 and became a despatch rider. I had a Panther motorbike and still remember the registration "EXU 501". There was only one DR in our platoon, because motorbikes were scarce.

My job was to deliver messages mainly because they didn't have any radios. I stuck to the roads although I could off-road if needed, but there wasn't much of that because there wasn't much petrol, so I mainly trained with the troops on foot. I was issued with a drop extra, but it wasn't used much so I conserved it for private use if I could.

I had to swap my rifle for a Sten gun. They were very utility. I was warned to be very careful and not to drop it, because it would just keep firing until the magazine was empty! Like all despatch riders, I carried the Sten slung over my back and the joke was you could always tell a despatch rider because he only had one ear!'[401]

Pigeons: One small but important cog in the signalling organisation were the pigeon sections. Wigston Boy Scout Duncan Lucas helped his local Home Guard pigeon section.

A rather amusing message sent during Exercise PARTRIDGE, Sunday 11 October 1942. It appears that Home Guards of No.13 (Quorn) Platoon ambushed an 'enemy' mobile column of 12 army Bren gun carriers in Castldyn [sic] Avenue, Quorn. However, it appears the army did not want to be 'dead' and refused to be 'destroyed'! (Quorn Home Guard Archive)

'I worked as a bicycle messenger for the Home Guard. There were manoeuvres and several of us Boy Scouts were given some training with carrier pigeons by Mr Middleton of Welford Road. We were shown how to write the message and place it in a little capsule which was then attached to the pigeon's leg.

The day was wet and we wore our bike capes. We were ordered by the Home Guard officer, Mr Payne of Wigston Fields, to remove them. They were brilliant yellow and of course were seen for miles! Suddenly, advancing up the fields were several lines of soldiers with rifles held in front. They came up the fields at a steady march and made quite an imposing sight. At the footbridge ("Rally Bridge" to those who knew it well), another group became active, we were told to find out what was happening so we could send our message. The message duly written we lads said was wrong. Instead of the words "Enemy advancing in large numbers", we felt we should state the exact number, but we were soon told to obey orders and use the "official jargon".

We sent the pigeon off, forgetting in our excitement to check for overhead wires that were there, fortunately the pigeon missed. We then went down to the bridge to see what was happening. Throwing discretion to the winds, we walked across and saw a large machine gun being mounted on a tripod. Fire-crackers started to go off, all hell broke loose. One of the local Home Guards who had got some blanks and had been itching to fire these off all day, slipped the first one "up the spout" of his rifle and banged away happily. Men appeared all around. A soldier wearing a white arm band with "umpire" on it and an agitated expression was shouting, "You bloody fools, you're shooting at your own side." Thank goodness it was only a practice!'[402]

The greatest distance travelled by a pigeon in the Sub-Area must have been flown by Rutland Home Guard signal section's pigeons: '…messages by pigeon had already been exchanged between Oakham and Leicester Sub-Area HQ [24 miles] with the help of H. Benham, of Oakham, an old soldier of long service, who was a pigeon fancier.'[403]

Semaphore Flags and Heliographs: Semaphore flags and heliograph mirrors were used for visual communication. Arthur Mitchell, a former Oadby Home Guard, remembered his platoon used heliographs on flat-roofed houses to communicate with the neighbouring Wigston Home Guard.[404]

Wireless Equipment/Radios: From 1942 proper army wireless equipment began to filter down to signal sections, including man-portable, chest-mounted short-range No. 38 radios, larger back pack No. 18 radios and the morse-tapper Fullerphone. Field telephones were also used and trunk lines were laid between important points within battalion areas, such as in March 1944 when the 1st (North Leicester) Battalion laid a trunk line to RAF Leicester East (Stoughton Aerodrome).[405] Dennis Underwood was in 'C' Company, 6th (Quorn) Battalion's Signal Section.

'I was 16 and lived in Rearsby. I joined the ATC, who paraded at Roundhill School, Thurmaston, but in 1941 I joined the Home Guard because we thought it would be more fun as they had guns! I joined the signals section, under Battalion Signals Officer Arthur Chandler. There were about 18 in the section. We used to train at the old hall in Keyham, close to the Dog and Gun pub. At first we just used semaphore flags. We didn't use naval semaphore, but morse. We then built field telephones. There was

The signal section of the Keyham Home Guard. Interviewee Dennis Underwood stands first left; Jack Twiss stands fifth from left. The officer standing is Arthur Chandler, Peter Hooper stands second from right, while first from right is Duncan Miller. Three of the men hold rolled up semaphore signal flags, while a field telephone lies on the floor.
(Dennis Underwood)

a searchlight where Thurmaston Shopping Centre is. After they moved away, they left a lot of cable in the hedgerows and we spent hours rolling it up, and used it with our field telephones. Just before I left to join the services, we started to receive proper radios. We had the No. 38 set. We had quite effective radios – on a hill you could get quite good transmission up to six miles. We passed messages to officers on exercise.'[406]

Medical Sections

When the LDV was formed, most effort had been put into fighting skills with little thought to what would happen to the wounded. In the event of casualties, the Home Guard were to use ARP First Aid Parties, but these FAPs were limited or altogether lacking in rural areas, where much of the fighting would occur. Although basic provisions were made, it was almost a full year before a Home Guard medical organisation was raised in April 1941. As Col. Ogilvy-Dalgleish stated somewhat obviously:

'It is bad for morale if men think that the wounded will be left to die. First aid and the use of field dressings had been taught from the start and, with the appointment of a Medical Officer, stretcher bearers were trained in each platoon and casualty exercises were carried out.'[407]

The Home Guard Medical organisation consisted of:

Home Guard stretcher bearer section at Wigston Magna station. A stretcher and first aid kit bag can be seen in the foreground. Half the section are wearing 'SB' (stretcher bearer) armlets.
(Duncan Lucas)

i) A Battalion Medical Officer, a Major.

ii) Stretcher-Bearer squads and Medical Orderlies. Officially, four Stretcher-Bearers per platoon (two stretchers). They wore standard Home Guard battledress but also a white armlet marked 'SB', while Medical Orderlies wore a white armlet with a red cross. Their job was to apply basic first aid before the wounded were taken to Regimental Aid Posts. Although Home Guard medical personnel were unarmed, official instruction stated they could still be called upon to fight in an emergency. Alan Clare was in the 12th (Motor Reconnaissance) Battalion's medical section:

'I lived on Narborough Road, Leicester. I was 16 in 1942, but I told the enlisting sergeant at Canning Place I was 17. He must have believed us as they put me in the medical section. There were about ten of us. I wore a white armband with "HG" and a red cross. I was not issued with a weapon. A sergeant taught us first aid. Somebody lay on the stretcher and we learned where the pressure points were, how to put bandages on, how to stop bleeding etc. We used to go for exercises on Abbey Park where we practised carrying people on the stretcher, bandaging them up or putting on splints.'[408]

Home Guard Brass Bands

There appears to have been few Home Guard bands in the two counties. The main one was the 1st (North Leicester) Battalion Band, based at Humberstone Lido. Private C.A. Anderson was made Band Sgt Major in February 1942.[409] On 8 August 1943 the band broadcast on the radio. This was the first of a new series of BBC band concerts and was 'an honour greatly appreciated by the bandsmen.'[410] At the war's end, they became the Leicestershire Constabulary Band, then the Leicester Foresters Band, and, as they are today, Foresters Friendly Society Brass.[411] Henry Shipley played in the band:

'I lived on Tournament Road, Glenfield. I used to play for the North Evington Working Men's Club brass band. One Sunday morning, a senior member of the Home Guard came down to the band room and asked if we were prepared to join the Home Guard and become the 1st Battalion's official band. We all agreed. I said I was only 15, but he said I looked older so could join! We wore a brass harp band badge on our left shoulder and later a white lanyard.

My brother had given me a post horn for my 15th birthday. Leicester City Football Club asked the Home Guard band to play on match days at Filbert Street. Of course, the post horn gallop was their signature tune, so I played it when the players came out. We also entertained the crowd at half time. I played every home match, from the founding of the Home Guard band through to 1957.

Other times, an army lorry would pick us up and take us to Home Guard manoeuvres. We would stand at the side of the road and play as they marched by. Then we would get in the van, get to the finishing point, get out and play for them again!

We were unarmed. Some of the band acted as stretcher bearers and others acted as pigeoneers. Once we had a large parade from Victoria Park down to Abbey Park, with the big bass drummer playing at the rear. All of a sudden he went quiet and the brass band were playing on their own. It turned out he

The brass band of the 1st (North Leicester) Battalion. Standing fifth from right, back row, is Henry Shipley, who played the post horn gallop at the beginning of the Leicester City football matches. Sidney Guest stands first right, back row. Band Sgt Major C.A. Anderson stands on the left and the band's mace bearer Norman Clark stands on the right. Taken at the Humberstone Lido. (Sidney Guest)

was only very small, with this big drum blocking his view. He had turned left down Belvoir Street while the rest of us marched on to the Clock Tower! The next moment he was running as best he could with his big drum, trying to catch us up!

We also played at Oakham several times and once travelled to record at the BBC in Birmingham. I was called-up as a Bevin Boy in 1944, at Cresswell Colliery, Derbyshire, but I travelled back to play in the Home Guard band.'[412]

The 7th (Market Harborough) Battalion also had a brass band. On 17 May 1944, 400 spectators saw 'E' (Westcotes) Company, 3rd (West Leicester) Battalion, at a 'Salute the Soldier' parade in Town Hall Square. The battalion's corps of drums beat the retreat to a changing of the guard under Captain J. Harris.[413]

Home Guard Women Auxiliaries

Although the Home Guard is regarded as an all-male preserve, unofficially many women helped behind the scenes. Labour MP Dr Edith Summerskill campaigned for women to play a more active role than making tea and sandwiches, but the WO had always refused.

However, with the growing manpower shortages and ever-increasing administrative work, the WO finally relented. In June 1943 women were officially allowed to join, but were never simply called Home Guards. First they were called 'Nominated Women' and then, from July 1944, 'Home Guard Auxiliaries'.[414] Those women who thought they would finally be coming to grips with weaponry were, with few exceptions, sorely disappointed. In reality, their new title simply formalised what they had been doing all along.

Reflective of their lukewarm welcome by the WO, they were not issued with uniform, but a simple plastic brooch labelled 'HG', surrounded by what looked like a funeral wreath. Few women joined this rather unwelcoming force: by Stand Down, only 32,000 women had joined, as opposed to 404,000 women in the CD services.[415]

Auxiliaries were employed in both Leicestershire and Rutland, mainly in office work. However, a 1944 inventory of the 10th (Charnwood) Battalion lists 11 Auxiliaries in a signals section of the HQ

Home Guard 'B' (Central) Company, 1st (Rutland) Battalion Home Guard. Sitting centre, front row with the stick is Major H.E. Whaley. Next to him sits his secretary, Home Guard auxiliary Miss E.M. Evans. (E.M. Eayrs)

company. This use of Auxiliaries was uncommon.

With the Auxiliaries' mainly indoor role, it is small wonder that out of 50 male Home Guard interviewees, only one knew of their existence. Although 1943 service ceiling figures allowed a maximum of 1,000 women in the two counties' Home Guard, it seems likely the true membership was no more than a third of that figure.[416] Out of 1,100 Home Guards in the Rutland Battalion, only five were Auxiliaries.

```
Subject:- Employees.                          RA/16229

To:-      Mrs. E.C. Bracegirdle (A)
          Miss E.M. Evans        (B)
          Miss V.C. Henderson    (C)
          Miss K.M. Dickins      (D)
          Mrs E.  Atkins         (D)
From:-    1st Bn Rutland H.G.
----------------------------------------------------
          Leicestershire & Rutland Territorial Association
has informed this Headquarters that your services will not
be required after 30th December, 1944.
          Will you please, therefore, accept this letter
as notice to terminate your employment by the above named
Association.


Drill Hall,
Oakham.                                    Capt.Adjt
24 Nov 44.                            1st Bn Rutland H.G
JFM.
```

Stand Down notice to Rutland Home Guard's Women Auxiliaries, 24 November 1944. (E.M. Eayrs)

With little archival material surviving to show Auxiliaries even existed, it is not surprising the women's role in the Home Guard was soon forgotten. As early as 1951, Mrs B. Whaley, wife of Lt-Col. H.E. Whaley, final Commander of Rutland Home Guard, wrote to the *Daily Mail* to clarify the matter:

'In our little Rutland, there were five of us officially recognised by the War Office and called "Camp Followers". When we objected we became "Nominated Women". I ask you! Could anything be more insulting? We worked as drivers, clerks, telephonists – whatever was wanted at the time – besides running our own homes.'[417]

Edith M. Eayrs (née Evans) served as an Auxiliary to Major H.E. Whaley throughout the war:[418]

'I was 25 in 1940. I lived in Oakham and cycled to Major Whaley's house everyday at Ashwell. Major Whaley was an ex-army officer and I worked before the war as his secretary. He had a big poultry farm. When war came, I carried on the farm business, coupled with Home Guard work. The office was really his study. I used to type and send out the correspondence to all the platoons in the area. There was quite a bit of typing to do. I occasionally accompanied him. I remember we once went in his car to the North Road [A1] and watched British paratroopers parachuting on to RAF Woolfox Lodge. When the Home Guard finished I never received an official Stand Down certificate, just a few words on a typed letter of thanks to say my services "would no longer be required". Perhaps I should write in for my certificate now! I was a little cog in the wheel and I'm glad I played my part in the Home Guard.'[419]

The Women's Voluntary Service (WVS) also helped the Home Guard, supplying food and tea during exercises.

Tired of waiting, in December 1941 Dr Edith Summerskill set up her own unofficial Home Guard, Women's Home Defence. It is not known whether a WHD unit existed in either county, but a reference in the *Leicester Mercury* in December 1942 suggested there may have been: 'Mrs Preece, of Leicester, was second in the Women's Home Defence championship rifle shoot in London, her score being 98, against 99, scored by Miss Dodds, of Edinburgh, the cup winner.'[420]

Home Guard Cadets

The Home Guard's activities often attracted small bands of onlooking boys. Some boys lied about their age to join the force, so, from around early 1941, a countywide Home Guard cadet force was formed, composed of boys aged 14–16, referred to in the local press as the 'Junior Home Guard'.[421] They acted in an unarmed role, mainly as messengers. Bill Tollington lived in Hathern:

'I was only about 15, just left school. I wanted to join the army, so, to get to know the weapons in the meantime, I joined Hathern Home Guard in 1942. The officer took me and this other lad on as cadets, although he couldn't get us a proper uniform, he got us denims and a forage cap. We did everything alongside the other men. We were Home Guard cadets not army cadets. At 16, they took us on proper into the Home Guard.'[422]

The 1943 Home Guard ceiling figures reveals a maximum of 450 'boys' were allowed in the two counties' 'Junior Home Guard', but by then the Army Cadet Force was in full swing and only a few boys stayed on as messengers.[423] On 2 November 1941, 15-year-old Leicester Home Guard Cadet Kenneth Burnard collapsed and died on exercise.

Civil Defence Training: Although Home Guards often helped out at air raid incidents, from early 1941 and the introduction of the Fire Precaution (Business Premises) Order, a degree of compulsion was forced onto the Home Guard, much to their disquiet, as P.S. Wakefield noted:

'Thursday 9:1:41. General Eastwood, Director General of the Home Guard, addressed a meeting of Loughborough Group officers at the Town Hall today…He made it quite clear that if a HG did fire duty he did it as a civilian and must leave it at once if called out to military duties. A Home Guard enlisted as a soldier for military duties and could not be turned at will into an ARP man…So that's the end of that little conspiracy!'[424]

For some, the Director General's pronouncement made little difference. Three days later, Home Guard Frederick Hanley, 21, of Cambridge Street, Leicester, died while on firewatch duty at the Spalding Street works of Dallow Lambert and Co. Ltd, where he worked as an apprentice sheet metalworker. Firewatchers in a neighbouring premise turned on the main gas valve to boil water to make tea, causing gas to leak from the cooking stove in the mess room where Hanley and another firewatcher were sleeping. Hanley died but the other firewatcher, William Siddell, survived.[425]

In view of the receding invasion threat, it was thought the Home Guard would be more useful as a back up to the CD services. From October 1942 the Regional Commissioner for North Midlands Area issued instructions to train the Home Guard in various CD duties.[426] Furthermore, in August 1944, with the emergence of the German V-weapons, 200 Leicester Home Guards were trained in light rescue work.[427] But this passive role did not appeal to the Home Guard whose *raison d'être* was armed combat. Replying to the initial proposals, the CO of the 2nd (South Leicester) Battalion noted begrudgingly '…will go along with, but…bearing in mind our role is primarily Home Guard… [this] should not take up HG evening training. It would be necessary for the HG to be definitely released from the routine firewatcher's lectures.'[428]

This standoffishness was mutual: the CD were not enthused about having the HG encroaching on their role. However, in Rutland, where manpower was limited, both forces valued each other and liaison worked.[429] But in Leicestershire, where the organisations were two large beasts treading the same territory, there appears to have been quiet rivalry. The fact heavy retaliatory air raids never materialised meant the two services never really bonded and, although they participated in countywide exercises, this was the extent of their co-operation. Allan Hopcraft, of Quorn Home Guard, remembers some unofficial CD work:

'One night we had been to a dance at Barrow. The Germans used to jettison their load to get more speed and they dropped a load of incendiary bombs all across The Slabs. These incendiaries would light up the place and then the Germans would realise there was a railway down there and bomb it, so we had to put these incendiaries out as quickly as we could. The only thing we had was, er…cow dung [chuckles]. And it worked!'[430]

Associated Services:

Armed CD Wardens and Police: In February 1942, Minister of Home Security Herbert Morrison announced some members of the CD services would supplement the Home Guard where the force had been depleted through call up. These CD workers would only be called upon for military duty in the event of invasion and fighting in their immediate neighbourhood. This would also apply to part-time NFS members.[431] But the scheme was not widely implemented, partly due to inter-service rivalry and because most men wanted to stay in the service they had volunteered for.

From October 1942 Leicestershire Home Guard gave the local CD weapons training.[432] An example of the CD taking up arms was seen in October 1942 during Exercise PARTRIDGE, when the *Loughborough Monitor* described an attack on the town by Leicester Home Guards.

'It was obvious pressure was being applied by a strong force on all sides of the Town and the position became so difficult that by 11.30am on Sunday morning the whole of the Town's civil organisation had been given instructions to join the nearest Home Guard units to defend the Town to the last. At one stage in the exercise when there was a threatened break in, the Warden's Service were requested to take up arms.'[433]

By 1943 there was an allowed ceiling of 200 CD personnel in the two counties' Home Guard, but it is unknown if this was ever attained. Walter Hall, then an air raid warden in 'G' (West Leicester) Division, recalls in 1943 he and his fellow wardens formed a small bore rifle club:

'It went on to produce some of finest shots in the county – winning many medals and cups.' The wardens drilled on the old Co-op Dairy ground on Glenfield Road, first with dummy rifles, then with real ones, shooting against the Home Guard on an adjacent outdoor range. 'We had a lot of lads who were Messengers…whom I instructed to handle rifles at Granby Halls Range.'[434]

During the invasion threat in 1940 the local police were also armed, mainly with revolvers, in case they apprehended spies, saboteurs or Nazi airmen. Mr Hall remembers 'a lone policeman stood outside Hinckley Road School with a gun'.[435] Dennis Underwood worked as a civilian clerk at the old police station in Melton Mowbray. He remembers the police there were issued with revolvers, which were new to some officers. This resulted in a dented radiator![436]

The arming of the civil side of the defence structure, in breach of the Geneva Convention, would have immediately made all CD services targets, but their militarisation was a reflection of the new total war.

Army Cadet Force

The Army Cadet Force, created in 1942, was open to boys 14–17, providing pre-entry training before army or Home Guard service. Cadets trained to attain the army qualification Certificate 'A'. They had no combat role in the event of invasion. The Home Guard was inextricably linked with the ACF from the start, as the *Loughborough Monitor* explained, 'The [ACF's] attachment to the local Home Guard will mean in the initial stages instructors will be provided, and later it is anticipated the cadets, when trained, will be a useful help in Home Guard activities.'[437]

By March 1942 the Leicestershire and Rutland Cadet Committee ran four ACF companies, each affiliated to their local Home Guard battalion and the Leicestershire Regiment.[438] Each company consisted of 100 cadets and could not exceed 1,200.[439] The President was Lord Lieutenant of Leicestershire, Sir Arthur Hazlerigg, with Lt-Col. A. Halkyard the County Commandant and Major J.F.A Pitcairn the Acting Secretary. All were local TA officials and provided the link with the WO.

The Home Guard also ran the initial recruitment drives. The ACF was popular from the start and if anything was too successful. Initially, there were no uniforms and Sir Lindsay Everard warned 'uniforms were essential otherwise the movement would fail'.[440] Sir Arthur Hazlerigg wrote to Viscount Bridgeman also calling for uniforms. This top level petitioning seems to have worked and soon the ACF were supplied with standard army battledress. By late 1942, the ACF was thriving well in both counties.

Norman Bazeley was a founder member of the Countesthorpe ACF, part of the 3rd (City of Leicester and District) Battalion, under the command of Lt-Col. Whowell, based at the Magazine, Leicester:

'The Countesthorpe detachment was formed in April 1942 by Captain J. Cole of the Home Guard. We used to meet at the village institute, forerunner to Countesthorpe village hall. Later, we expanded to include boys from Wigston and Blaby and met in a

Leicester army cadets' physical training exercises at Bitteswell Camp, August 1943. (Norman Bazeley)

large aircraft container, where the Blaby Social centre is. At the start there were about 30 boys, all from Countesthorpe. There was also about six orphaned lads from Countesthorpe Cottage Homes. I felt a bit sorry for them, as the home was very strict. They had to all walk together looking down and not talk to the rest of us. They were very strict about who they allowed to join the cadets. These lads really loved the ACF because it was the only time they were allowed out. They never messed about because they feared they would be kicked out and sent back to the home.

We wore the Leicestershire Regiment badge on our forage caps. On our epaulettes, we just had a khaki title that said "Leicestershire". We didn't have a badge saying "Cadet Force".

Our training was based on regular infantry training: map reading, fieldcraft, vehicle training, signalling, weapon training and naturally square-bashing. We had .22 Mosberg rifles and used the indoor range at Glen Parva barracks. We then went onto the SMLE rifle and did some firing at Kibworth range. In the end we also trained with Sten guns. We were shown how grenades worked but never used them. I also went to Bestwood Lodge in Nottingham. They had a mock-up town, and I did map reading and infantry training alongside Regular troops.

On 8 August 1943, about 1,000 cadets went on a week-long summer camp at Bitteswell Park, now part of Lutterworth Town FC's ground. We were joined by cadets from Oundle Public Boys School in Northamptonshire. We called them "Oundle Hounds" as they thought they were a bit superior to us village lads, so we just took the mickey out of them! Their presence created instense rivalry as they wore the Northamptonshire Regiment's badge, but it was a good-spirited camp. The commandant was Major C. Burton. We all slept on straw-filled palliasses in army eight-man bell tents. When we went on manoeuvres, we used wooden dummy rifles. There was also a bit of fun – filmshows, sing-songs, and a final sports day where the Leicestershire Regiment's band played.

I was a cadet sergeant when I took War Certificate "A" in June 1943. I was made 2nd Lieutenant and became the first cadet ever commissioned. I then went to No. 1 Young Soldiers Training Centre at Markeaton Park, Derby, for basic training. I was a lot more advanced compared to the other recruits. I ended up in Burma with the 2nd Battalion Nigeria Regiment. The war ended and I was recalled to the Regimental Depot at Glen Parva where I took over as depot company quartermaster and was demobbed in 1948.

The Army Cadet Force gave you something to do and away from home, which was the first time for most boys. The discipline prepared you for the army. Most cadets went into the forces. It brought you up to be good citizens.'[441]

The ACF exists today as a voluntary organisation for boys and girls 12 to 18 with the same military training, but with additional activities such as the Duke of Edinburgh's Award.

Home Guard Anti-Aircraft Units

227 (M) (101st Leicestershire Home Guard) ('Z') Anti-Aircraft Rocket Battery

'Although no action has been seen, the battery kept up a high state of efficiency and any enemy airman who might have ventured over Leicester would have had a warm and accurate reception. The great regret of the battery has been that they couldn't "have a go" at the Hun.'

Captain C. South RA,
Battery Commander,
101st (Leicestershire) Home Guard AA Rocket Battery

The Luftwaffe's Spectre

After Germany turned its attentions to Russia, Britain took the opportunity to gradually move onto the offensive. In autumn 1941 the WO decided to transfer up to 50,000 Regular AA troops overseas. However, the 1942 Baedeker Raids proved the Luftwaffe still had bite. General Sir Frederick Pile, C-in-C AA Command, suggested the manpower deficit should be made up by the Home Guard. This made sense, as the invasion threat was diminishing daily. Churchill agreed and the Home Guard began to man AA sites from 1942.

Leicester's industry was now working full stretch towards the war effort. Any repeat of the 1940 Blitz would prove disastrous to output, so it was decided Leicester should be provided with further heavy AA defence.

Many of Britain's standard 3.7in heavy AA guns were now being sent abroad and so a new alternative was needed for home defence. The answer was the 3in Unrotating rocket Projectile (UP), which was launched from a projector rather than a gun. They were easier and cheaper to manufacture and simpler to operate, making them perfect for Home Guard service. The Home Guard operated 93 AA rocket batteries nationwide. For Leicester's defence, one rocket battery was built on Victoria Park.

Fortunately, the unpublished history of Leicester's AA Rocket Battery is one of only a handful to survive. This short typed document was produced by the battery's commander, Captain C.A. South RA at Stand Down. In July 1945 a copy was sent by Major F.C. Pitcairn, Secretary of the Leicestershire and Rutland TA, to the WO Library, London. It was then held under the 30-year rule at the National Archives, Kew, but declassified early and much of the following detail is derived from it.[442]

The Battery's Formation

On 13 January 1943 a notice appeared in the *Leicester Mercury* appealing for volunteers to man a new AA battery. Due to wartime censorship, scant detail was included. However, the location's secrecy was somewhat compromised by the fact volunteers were told to report to the Old Horse Hotel's Clubroom, Old Horse Yard, London Road, which was opposite the battery site on Victoria Park, now the Old Horse pub's games room.

Worried that local battalions would be denuded as Home Guards jumped at the chance to hit back at the enemy, the advert stated 'Transfers from existing HG units will not be permitted.'[443] But there was no rush. The city's workforce was now working longer than ever and had little time for additional war duties. Over 1,000 men were needed to man the site, but by the end of February only 267 had come forward. As a result, transfers from local battalions and compulsory labour direction, including of boys aged 16 and 17, commenced in March 1943.

Some local battalions 'thought it was a good method of getting rid of their unwanted personnel,' but the National Service Officer 'gave every help… sending only the type of man the battery required'. Full strength was only attained in June 1944 via the compulsory transfer of 230 Home Guards by the Ministry of Labour.

Organisation and Administration

The battery was manned during the day by the men and women (ATS) of the 227 (M) [Mixed i.e. with ATS] AA Regt RA, and at night by the men of the new 101st Battalion Leicestershire Home Guard,

No.6 Relief of 101st Leicestershire Home Guard 'Z' Anti-Aircraft Rocket Battery at Stand Down, Victoria Park, Leicester, 1944. Walter Killingley stands back row, sixth from left. It is thought that the officer sitting centre front row is Captain C.A. Browne. The No.4 nine-barrelled rocket projector can clearly be seen behind the men as well as the various corrugated crew and ammunition shelters. (Roger Killingley)

hence the joint title '227 (M) (101st Leicestershire Home Guard) "Z" AA Battery'. 'Z' was used as a cover letter to denote a rocket battery before the apparatus was publicly declassified in May 1944. The battery's title was then changed to the 101st Leicestershire Home Guard Anti-Aircraft Rocket Battery.

The RA troops were commanded by Major P. Clubb RA until October 1944, when Major L. Bubb RA assumed command. The Home Guard component was initially temporarily commanded by Major H.H. Horley, from the 12th (Motor Reconnaissance) Battalion. On his resignation, Major D. Christy assumed permanent command in May 1943, with Captain C. South RA replacing Captain Lynch RA as Administrative Officer.

The Leicester AA Rocket Battery was a junior battery (fewer rocket projectors) with two senior (full strength) batteries, the 195 (101st Northamptonshire Home Guard) Rocket Battery at Peterborough and the 126 (101st Cambridgeshire Home Guard) Rocket Battery at Cambridge.[444] All three were part of the 16th 'Z' AA Regiment, commanded by Lt-Col. E.B. Morison TD RA.

The Battery HQ Office was set up at 148a London Road, Leicester, in February 1943, under 2nd Lieutenant Doore. Miss Hebb and Miss Freer were the civilian staff. The Old Horse Hotel's Clubroom (skittle alley) became the Battery Stores, run by Storesman/Battery Quartermaster Sergeant Gelder.

The men were divided into eight nightly duty Reliefs. This rotating system relieved pressure on the RA contingent but required eight times as many men to operate the site. Major Christy stated 'never at any moment did a projector remained unmanned'. This was almost correct, as former AA Home Guard Derrick Malyon explains:

'I recall an incident, which was rather serious. I was guard commander during one of the nights we manned the site. We changed guard every two hours…that is until 2am when the whole guard slept through until 6am! I was woken by one of the cooks – the affair was all hushed up – but we had a good laugh about it later!'[445]

In April 1944, Leicester, Peterborough and Cambridge batteries were regimented as the 10th Home Guard AA Regiment, with their HQ at Peterborough. The CO was Lt-Col. Bromige, who often visited the Leicester Battery.

Training

Training started in February 1943 at premises in Friday Street, Leicester, and consisted of foot drill and elementary No. 2 projector (U2P) training. Lieutenant Palmer RA was the original Training Officer, but was soon succeeded by Lieutenant R.C. Martin RA. Battle training on the Victoria Park site commenced in June 1943 and 'enthusiasm was increased by the use of fireworks, which made it almost like the real thing'.

The late Walter Killingley, then aged 45, of Evesham Road, Leicester, was a Gunner in No. 6 Relief. He remembered the tough training: 'Sometimes we had to run around the park with a 56-pound rocket on outstretched arms. We were proud to wear our bow and arrow [AA Command] flash.'[446] Indeed, the AA Command insignia was only granted once the wearer had been to firing camp and was fully trained.

Men also went on exchange visits to the Cambridge and Northampton batteries. Monthly relief competitions were held until June 1944, when it was felt they were no longer needed.

Live Firing Camp at Heacham, Norfolk

Live firing took place well away from built-up areas on a firing range at Heacham, south of Hunstanton, on the north-west Norfolk coast overlooking the Wash. Nine practice firings were carried out, the first on 30 May 1943. The battery paraded at 06.45 hours in a rainstorm, and of 162 Officers and ORs, there were only three absentees. 'Despite the fact it poured with rain all day, every man fired live projectile rounds and enthusiasm was very marked.' The last firing occurred on 2 July 1944.

Walter Killingley recalled manning a Saturday relief in Leicester, then travelling the following day to Heacham. There 'we received a ration of two slices of bread and a meat chop. I hesitate to think what animal it came from. The day's final exercise was firing 50 rounds from a Sten gun at a target in the sea.'[447] Robert Reay, then 18, also went:

'The coast there was heavily defended with masses of barbed wire and concrete blocks. We trained with Sten guns and shot at silhouette targets in the dunes. We then went to watch the rockets fired. We loaded them in and were told to run back and jump in a slit trench and keep our heads down as the rockets were fired. Well, being young and curious, I wanted to see what happened and I stuck my head above the trench. There was a big "whoosh" followed by a big explosion a hell of a long way off over the sea. But the result of my curiosity was that I got a load of grit in my face and my eyebrows were burnt off!'[448]

It could have been a lot worse. On 14 November 1943 Private Joseph Keeling, 35, of 102nd Derbyshire AA Home Guard, was killed and four others wounded when one of the rockets exploded during practice at Heacham.[449]

Derrick Malyon, promoted to lance corporal in No. 7 Relief, recalls 'Watching the rockets being fired was quite an experience – they made a noise like an express train going through a tunnel and left all the ground burnt on firing. I always felt sorry for the elderly members struggling to load the rockets. Once we had a misfire and the loaders refused to come forward and remove the offending missile! The situation was resolved by the camp's S/Major, who lifted the rocket off and marched with it down the beach and calmly defused it!'[450]

Officer Training

RA Battery officers were sent for training at the Regimental School (later 32nd AA Brigade School) at Chesterton, Cambridgeshire, with Leicester supplying more officers and NCOs than any other battery.

In April 1944 it was decided the Home Guard were capable of taking over the training without RA supervision and 2nd Lt W.H. Kirk was appointed the first Home Guard Training Officer. 2nd Lt H.A. Underwood was appointed W/T Officer after attending a course at Catterick barracks, North Yorkshire. 2nd Lt A.E. Cadwallader, Officer-in-charge of A/G (Anti-Gas) Training, attended training at the Army School of Chemical Warfare, Winterbourne Gunner, Wiltshire. Major

Stand Down photograph of officers and NCOs from the 101st Leicestershire Home Guard 'Z' Anti-Aircraft Rocket Battery at Victoria Park, Leicester, 1944. Standing centre rear is Edward Needles. A Nissen crew hut, two nine-barrelled No.4 rocket projectors and the War Memorial arch can be seen in the background. (Derek Needles)

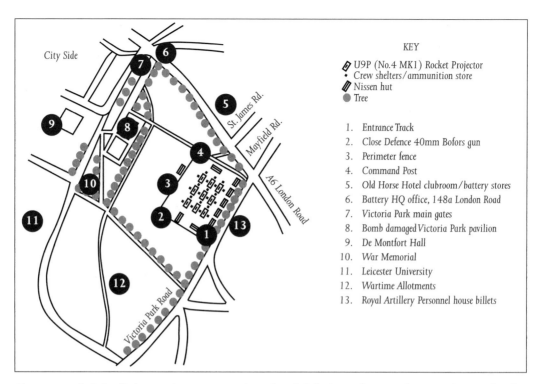

227 (M)/101st Leics. 'Z' Rocket Anti-Aircraft battery, Victoria Park, Leicester, March 1944.

KEY
U9P (No.4 MK1) Rocket Projector
• Crew shelters/ammunition store
Nissen hut
Tree

1. Entrance Track
2. Close Defence 40mm Bofors gun
3. Perimeter fence
4. Command Post
5. Old Horse Hotel clubroom/battery stores
6. Battery HQ office, 148a London Road
7. Victoria Park main gates
8. Bomb damaged Victoria Park pavilion
9. De Montfort Hall
10. War Memorial
11. Leicester University
12. Wartime Allotments
13. Royal Artillery Personnel house billets

Christy noted Cadwallader was 'never more pleased with life than when inside a gas chamber'! After intensive training, each Relief had a Plotting Officer. Lt W.R. Elliott qualified as a Plotting Officer after attending a course at the RA Range at Manorbier, on the Pembrokeshire coast, Wales. These officers trained other instructors who taught their own Reliefs.

The Victoria Park Site
'Z1', as the battery was designated, occupied a quarter of the main playing field, in the corner nearest the present Mayfield Road roundabout. Standard 16ft Nissen huts were situated around the edge of the site, with a vehicle entrance off Victoria Park Road. At first there was no security fencing, as Robert Reay remembers:

'Because of the blackout, at night the site was very dark, quiet and creepy. One night, I was sent out on my own on sentry. I had no rifle, just a pickaxe handle. There was no moon and every noise raised the hairs on the back of my neck! While walking around the site perimeter, feeling quite nervy, I almost had a heart attack: I felt two "hands" from behind me, slap down on either shoulder with heavy breathing! Was this a Nazi saboteur or assassin? I gathered courage to turn round and, much to my relief, found it was a large friendly dog, whom I believe belonged to the head of the university, Mr Attenborough. I almost passed out!'[451]

From July 1943 targets were detected by a single on-site Mk II radar, transferred from the HAA gun site at Anstey.[452] It could detect raiders up to 30 miles away. However, by Stand Down it been replaced by a Mk 1 No. 1 radar powered by 15 kva generators,[453] which only had a range of 17 miles.[454] As it was a built-up area, radar coverage must have been limited. It is believed the radar plots were processed in a combined command post and plotting room, in a Nissen hut along the perimeter nearest London Road. From here the targets' range and bearings were sent by field telephone to the projectors.

From October 1943 a 40mm Bofors gun was emplaced in the corner of the site nearest the centre of the park, for close defence against raiders flying below the projectors' range. It was only manned by the RA, during daylight hours.[455] On 16 August 1944 eight rounds were test fired – presumably blank rounds![456]

After Stand Down, ATS personnel continued to live on site. Questions were raised in Parliament because rats bit the women as they slept in the cold and draughty huts. The site was only finally cleared in June 1950.

Operational Manning

The battery became operational on 22 July 1943, when 'A' Troop of No. 6 Relief manned the first relief 'The battery felt it was able to take its part in the defence of the City of Leicester. The "101" were a fighting unit at last.'

At first, the battery appears to have been armed with three standard No. 2 Mk 1 Projectors (U2P), which fired two rockets mounted side-by-side.[457] The projectors stood on a concrete hardstanding and had a two-man crew, one standing to the left of the weapon operating the traverse, the other standing on the right controlling elevation with a handwheel.

The 3-inch rocket was known as an 'Unrotated Projectile' or 'UP' to disguise its secret status. It was 6ft 4in long, with a 22lb warhead, equivalent to a 3.7-inch AA shell. It was solid-fuelled and could be armed with several fuses. The rockets were fired electrically, reaching a maximum velocity of 1,500ft per second. They were stored between the projectors in Anderson shelters, which had breezeblock-reinforced sides. A total of 48 rockets could be stored in each shelter.[458]

The rockets were unguided ballistic projectiles that worked on a scattergun principle, similar to a shotgun. The rockets could not achieve pinpoint accuracy so were fired in one simultaneous cluster. They exploded at around 20,000ft in a thunderous roar, which rocked the area below.[459] As one author states, they created 'a lethal giant firework display, which bracketed a large expanse of sky with the brilliant red of detonating shells and unseen shards of potentially-withering shrapnel'.[460]

On 26 June 1944 the battery's armament was upgraded to new, nine-rocket No. 4 Mk 1 Projectors (U9P). The U9P was the scarcest type of rocket apparatus, with only 100 projectors ever manufactured, forming eight batteries nationwide.[461] The standard U9P battery consisted of 12 projectors, but due to the Leicester site's limited space held only nine. Nonetheless, these multi-barrelled weapons produced a greater density of fire, and the battery was capable of firing 81 rockets in a single salvo. The projector was far larger than the U2P and needed a crew of seven. The weapon was mounted on a mobile truck chassis, derived from a World War One 3-inch AA gun mounting. A cover sketch on Captain C.A. South's history shows how the chassis had the roadwheels removed and the stabilising legs lowered in use. There were two armoured firing cabins, either side of the projector. The left-hand cabin held two men, one of whom received the orders from the Command Post via headphones and shouted them to the rest of the crew, while the other man controlled elevation. The man in the right-hand cabin operated traverse. Four loaders stood behind the projector, and after they had loaded all nine launch rails they took cover at the double to the shelters on order of 'target'. The nine rockets were mounted in two vertical rows. Both crewmen had to press their foot pedal to launch the rockets, which ripple fired in four 0.75 second salvos.

In August and September 1944, the U9P projectors were sent in pairs by train to Messrs Bruce Peebles Engineering Works Ltd, Edinburgh, for upgrading to electromagnetic fusing. The projectors returned within eight days.[462] So the battery was never underarmed, two projectors were sent from the Cambridge battery, meaning, by Stand Down, Victoria Park was actually home to 11 projectors.[463]

It has been stated the rockets were eventually 'replaced by wooden imitations'.[464] This is highly unlikely as the battery was active until Stand Down and the source may be confused with training rounds. When Stand Down was announced, three complete troops were manning nine U9P weapons nightly.

Stand Down

Despite the Stand Easy, each relief continued to send at least one team on its regular manning night to relieve the Regular personnel who would otherwise be confined to the site due to the disbandment of the Home Guard contingent.

The battery became non-operational on 1 November 1944.[465] At the beginning of December, 10 U9P projectors were withdrawn from the site and sent to the Receiving Station at Morpeth Dock, Birkenhead. From there they were sent via the Great Western Railway to the AA Equipment Park, Arrowe Park, Woodchurch, Cheshire. On 4 December the site's 40mm AA gun and radar followed suit. On 22 December eight U2Ps were also sent from the site to Cheshire.[466] It would appear the site had become a temporary storage depot for projectors from surrounding sites: U2P projectors can be seen stored together in the background of photographs.

How Effective Would the Battery Have Been?

Leicester's AA rocket site was strangely positioned. Located in the corner of a playing field, the battery's fire was instantly limited by the tall surrounding trees and houses. The projectors were kept facing eastwards over London Road as this was the direction the enemy was most likely to approach from. Ironically, the battery's firepower was a problem in itself, as Derrick Malyon explains:

'The principle of our type of gun battery was to create a "box" of 81 exploding projectiles over Leicester. Yet the experience of doing this in London showed the ensuing damage to the area below could prove more destructive than enemy action. Consequently, certain compass bearings were blanked out in the firing cabin. The only area over which we could directly fire was if raiders approached the City from the direction of Oadby – which in those days was far less built up.'[467]

However, the rockets' sheer noise and flash caused the Luftwaffe to dub the weapon 'Pilot's Terror.' But, as this name suggests, the rockets' bark was generally worse than its bite. Because of the time it took to reload the entire battery, the enemy had often flown over and out of range, meaning it was too late to fire a second salvo. As one Luftwaffe pilot stated, 'We have established the "reloading" of the "ghostly cannon" takes about five minutes. So we wait for the next shot and then go in.'[468]

However, an army report stated the rocket's 'Deterrent effect is considerable,' even if its actual performance in destroying enemy aircraft was less so. 'Enemy aircrews have been able to see the majority of rocket salvos fired at them in sufficient time for effective avoiding action to be taken. The characteristic response was a sharp "jink" away from the target as soon as the flash was seen… discouraging accurate bombing.'[469] It was for this 'jinking' reason Leicester's rocket battery was located as close to the city centre as possible. Also, the weapon was equally impressive to friend and foe alike, making it good for civilian morale.

Social and Welfare

In June 1943 a Battery Entertainments Committee was formed under the Welfare Officer Captain J.P. Hings. 'The Committee arranged dances, concerts, sports etc, and enthused into the battery a real "esprit de corps".' The Committee also provided financial support for sick members of the battery and their

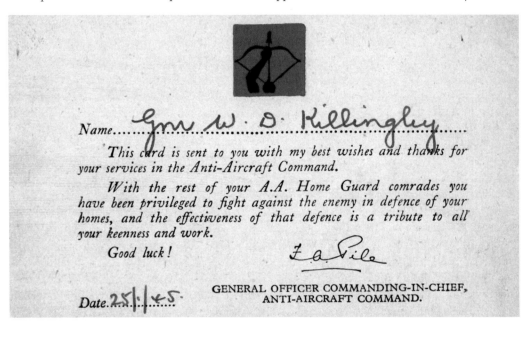

Anti-Aircraft Command Stand Down certificate to Walter Killingley of 101st Leicestershire Home Guard 'Z' Anti-Aircraft Rocket Battery. (Roger Killingley)

Name... *Gnr W. O. Killingley*...

'*This card is sent to you with my best wishes and thanks for your services in the Anti-Aircraft Command.*

With the rest of your A.A. Home Guard comrades you have been privileged to fight against the enemy in defence of your homes, and the effectiveness of that defence is a tribute to all your keenness and work.

Good luck!

Date. 25:1:45.

GENERAL OFFICER COMMANDING-IN-CHIEF, ANTI-AIRCRAFT COMMAND.

families. £50 (£1,550) was raised for the RA POW Fund, and £10 (£310) was sent to the Leicestershire Regiment POW Fund.

Each Relief had its own Committee that organised events, including dinner parties and 'real old-fashioned smoking concerts with sandwiches and beer. These efforts were of great value in keeping members in touch with each other and many were happy evenings.'

A NAAFI opened on site in April 1944 and concerts were held on Monday evenings. Walter Killingley remembered the NAAFI food was very good for wartime: 'Stew was the main course with spotted dick pudding for after.' The high-energy food was aimed at setting the men up for the demanding training that followed.

Old Comrades Association
Following a meeting on 1 October 1944, an Old Comrades Association was formed under Chairman Captain J.P. Hings with Major Christy as President. It is not known how long this OCA lasted, but it probably merged with a larger OCA.

Conclusion
Enemy aircraft were last seen over Leicester in 1942, almost a year and a half before the 'Z' Battery was installed on Victoria Park. Although Leicester had 15 siren alerts in 1943 and 1944 as enemy aircraft passed over the county, the battery never fired a single rocket in anger. As the battery's CO, Major D. Christy records:

'Many have been disappointed no action has taken place, but there is the satisfaction of knowing that, as a result of our service, a fairly large number of soldiers have been released for duty elsewhere and we were at times left in sole defence of Leicester against air attack.

I should like to pay my tribute to the wonderful keenness and hard work that has been put in by all ranks. The battery has a very fine record for regular attendance, the percentage of absence being less than one percent for many weeks. That this record has been kept up after a long day's work in civilian occupations reflects great credit on all concerned.

We believe we have been a successful battery, we certainly have been a happy one and I sincerely hope the spirit of friendship and helpfulness one to another that has been so evident during the past years will be kept up in the difficult years that will lie ahead. If we are able to make this place a better world for all to live in, especially for those who have fought for us, this same spirit will be needed more than ever in the future.'

Regular and Home Guard Battery Officers, 1944

227 (M) AA Rocket Battery RA Staff:
Major L. Bubb RA
Captain L. Russell RA
Lieutenant R. Martin RA
Lieutenant P. Heading RA
Subaltern MacMurray ATS
101st Leicestershire Home Guard AA Rocket Battery Staff:
Major D. Christy: Officer Commanding
Captain C. South RA: Administrative Officer
Captain R.A. Knight: Training and Foot Drill Officer
Captain J.P. Hings: Welfare Officer and acting Administrative Officer
Major G. Waring-Taylor: Medical Officer
2nd/Lt Doore: i/c HQ Office Staff
2nd/Lt H.A. Underwood: W/T Training Officer and Sten Gun Officer

2nd/Lt A.E. Cadwallader: Anti-Gas Training Officer

No. 1 Relief: Captain R. Mawby, Lieutenant E.E. Wells, 2nd Lts R.A. Haigh and R.C. Branson

No. 2 Relief: Captain T.J. Mumford MC, Lts J.H. Pentney and W.R. Elliott, 2nd Lts J.A.H. Savage and T.D. Laker

No. 3 Relief: Captain J.E. Portsmouth, 2nd Lts A. Clayton, H. Bowles, H.A. Underwood, J.H. Sibley, H.E. Doore (At Battery HQ) and F.G. Ashton

No. 4 Relief: Captain H.P. Tyler, Lt F.W. Hemming, 2nd Lts E.A. Hartshorn, D.B. Jephcott and F.M. Birch

No. 5 Relief: Captain J.P. Hings, Lts A. Manley, J.A. Uttley, 2nd Lieutenant L.T. Williams

No. 6 Relief: Captain C.A. Browne, 2nd Lts R. Simpson, A. Ludbrooke, F.O. Huntroode and A. Dodd.

No. 7 Relief: Captain C.J. Shackleton, 2nd Lts S.J. Wingrove, H.M. Goddard, K.G. Kennard and A.R. Hardwick

No. 8 Relief: Captain R.A. Knight, Lt W.H. Kirk, 2nd Lts A.A. King, C.H. Brompton, R.N. Brookhouse and G. Powell (At Battery HQ)

At Stand Easy, the battery strength was 1,065 Home Guards, including 45 Officers, 56 Sergeants, 117 Corporals and Lance Corporals and 825 ORs. Over 1,770 men served in the life of the battery, including 555 volunteers, 991 directed men and 320 transferred from GS battalions. There were 150 men called-up, 207 medical discharges and 37 transferred to GS battalions.

Home Guard Light Anti-Aircraft Factory Units

Several of Leicester's more important Vulnerable Points had machine guns manned by their own Home Guard platoons against low-flying raiders. Examples included twin Browning light machine guns on British Thomson-Houston, Melton Road,[470] and similar weaponry on Jones and Shipman, Narborough Road. Queniborough Home Guards manned Vickers 'K' light machine guns in the Light AA defence of Rearsby Aerodrome, while 7th (Market Harborough) Battalion Home Guards were instructed by RA personnel in the use of 40mm Bofors AA guns at RAF Husbands Bosworth.[471]

Although the Luftwaffe were unable to repeat the Blitzes of 1940–41, they tried to maintain the pressure by sending fast, low-flying, radar-avoiding fighter bombers on missions, mainly against industrial targets. These raiders caused a disproportionate amount of damage. In response, from November 1943 the WO created 237 Home Guard LAA units. Unlike the separate Home Guard HAA battalions, these units were part of their local battalion.

They were mainly equipped with surplus 20mm aircraft cannons fitted to ground mountings.[472] Each unit, or Troop, was trained by a PSI, normally a Regular RA Sergeant and a RA fitter who maintained the weapons. The Home Guard crews would receive early warning from either the Regular Army gun operations room or the factory's roof spotters, immediately down tools and run out to man the cannon, only returning to work at the all clear. Initially, the guns were only manned during daylight hours, but eventually all hours. Although the threat of invasion had all but vanished, the cannon could also be turned earthwards and used in a ground defence role. From April 1944 there were two Home Guard LAA Troops in Leicestershire:

Home Guards manning a 20mm Oerlikon Anti-Aircraft gun, as used to defend British United Shoe Machinery factory.

530 'A' 1st (North Leicester) Battalion LAA Troop at British United Shoe Machinery Co. Ltd, Leicester

Ron W. Lambell was a Home Guard in 530 'A' (1st Battalion) LAA Troop, which defended BUSM Co. Ltd on Ross Walk, Belgrave Road, Leicester. At 17, Ron joined BUSM in 1940 as an apprentice engineer. The works were of vital importance and security was tight, with Ross Walk fenced off to the public.

'I was in the B.U. Home Guard. We were equipped with nine single 20mm Oerlikon cannons as ack-ack defence of the factory, which was producing vital parts for Rolls Royce, Armstrong Whitworth, plus other war work.

At certain points, there were four-

Section of British United Shoe Machinery Home Guard, 1943. Ron Lambell stands first left, back row. Sgt Liddiard sits centre, front row. Note the triangular metal factory identity badges that all BUSM workers had to wear to gain access to the factory. (Ron Lambell)

storey high blocks jutting out the main building, containing the stairwells and toilets. Their flat roof was accessed via steps and a trapdoor. On top of these blocks were mounted the 20mm cannon, surrounded by duckboards covering the gun base: all this on a roof about ten feet square with no surrounding safety wall – a long way down if you missed your footing!

Sgt Liddiard was in charge of the gun crews. Each crew consisted of a gunner and loader. The gunner stood to the left side of the gun and controlled it by two handles, one in front and operated by his left hand, and the other behind, operating the trigger with his right hand. The loader stood on the right. The 60-round magazines were about a foot in diameter and clipped on top of the breech. Training was quite thorough and was carried out on a training gun in the factory grounds. When not in use, the guns were covered by tarpaulins. We had a guardroom with uncomfortable beds.

On one occasion we were "attacked" by a Hurricane, piloted by a Canadian. This gave us plenty of practice swinging the gun to keep the plane within the sights – and to avoid falling off the roof! Not an easy job when the plane is diving at you around 200 plus mph!'

Mr J. Follows also manned the cannon, 'Practice for us was on Sunday mornings, after which almost everyone retreated to the "Balmoral" on Belgrave Road for liquid refreshment. Being under age I had to go home! I believe some BUSM personnel were temporarily detached to Hunstanton to help combat the V1 flying bomb menace, but this may just have been a rumour at the time.'[173]

532 'B' 2nd (South Leicester) Battalion LAA Troop at Power Jets Ltd, Whetstone

John Bennett-Powell was a 20-year-old graduate engineer working on Frank Whittle's secret jet engine at Power Jets Foundry at Ladywood Works, Leicester Road, Lutterworth. He joined the works' Home Guard, who manned a single Marlin machine gun mounted on the roof of the engine assembly block for AA defence of this highly-important site. Those working an overnight shift were expected to man the weapon during air raids.

In 1942 Power Jets moved to a new, larger, purpose-built site at Cambridge Road, Whetstone. Some of the men from the Lutterworth Power Jets platoon were incorporated into their local platoon, while a new platoon was formed at the Whetstone site. Although John Bennett-Powell went on to work at the Whetstone site, because he lived in Lutterworth he was transferred to the local Lutterworth platoon, where he became the commanding Lieutenant.

By July 1943 'C' Company of 458/138 LAA Troop manned nine 20mm Oerlikon AA cannons at the Whetstone site.[474] They were replaced by 456 Independent LAA Bty, who, in February 1944, moved to Thrapston Camp and were themselves replaced by 475/134 LAA Battery.[475] In April 1944 Home Guards from the Power Jets platoon formed the 532 'B' 2nd (South Leicester) Battalion LAA Troop and took over the defences.[476]

With the Stand Easy, from 11 September 1944 manning of the LAA defences at both sites became voluntary.[477] Leicestershire's LAA Home Guard had a very short service span of just five months. Like the Home Guard's HAA unit on Victoria Park, it appears these LAA units also never fired their guns in anger.

However, had they the opportunity, their multiple quick-firing 20mm cannon, capable of firing 480 shells per minute, would have been able to greet any low-flying raider with a devastating crossfire.

The Specialists Units

Home Guard Auxiliary Bomb Disposal Squads

Britain's war factories were key Luftwaffe targets. There were always more UXBs than disposal squads and the delay in their defusal could seriously disrupt war production. The MAP asked the WO if they could form squads of skilled workers who would locate, report and prepare sites for the arrival of the BDUs. The WO consented and new sections named Auxiliary Bomb Disposal Squads were formed. Despite their independent formation, from September 1942 the WO decided all ABDSs would become sub-units of their local Home Guard battalion, not always to the ABDS's pleasure. ABDS sub-units now also had a secondary role as GS infantry if the enemy attacked their area.

Due to Leicestershire's large industrial base, from late 1942 four Home Guard ABDS sub-sections were formed, at British Thomson-Houston Co. Ltd, Melton Road, Leicester; at Brush Electrical Engineering Co. Ltd, Loughborough, under J.A. Houghton; at Imperial Typewriter Co. Ltd, East Park Road, Leicester, under R.H. Williams and at Jones and Shipman Ltd, East Park Road, Leicester, under H.H. Oakley.[478] Three more sub-sections were subsequently formed, making a total of seven Leicestershire ABDS in November 1943.

	No. of Men	Battalion
British Thomson-Houston Co. Ltd, Melton Road, Leicester	20	1st
Brush Electrical Engineering Co. Ltd, Loughborough	21	9th
Jones and Shipman Ltd, East Park Road, Leicester	18	4th
Imperial Typewriter Co. Ltd, East Park Road, Leicester	15	4th
Partridge, Wilson and Co. Ltd, Evington Valley Road, Leicester	Unknown	4th
Power Jets Ltd, Whetstone	Unknown	2nd
GPO, Campbell Street, Leicester	Unknown	13th [479]

Three categories of ABDS existed, from Category C, units still under training, up to Category A, 'units authorised to work on bombs, including the discharging and removal of certain types of fuses without RE supervision'. By March 1944 all Leicestershire's ABDS were Category B, 'units able to work on bombs and remove some fuses, but only under RE supervision'.[480] Their technical adviser was Captain P.E. Sawle, of the British Thomson-Houston Sub-Section.[481] All ABDS received training from No. 3 Bomb Disposal Company, RE,[482] but it is believed none of Leicestershire's ABDS ever had to go into operation on their own premises.

However, at least one county ABDS did see some action. In September 1944 the *Loughborough Monitor* reported the 'Brush Home Guard Bomb Squad' (*sic*) had been 'in action' on the East Coast under its commanding officer Lieutenant J.A. Houghton,[483] perhaps indicating the unit had been on the highly

Jones and Shipman's Auxiliary Bomb Disposal Squad.

dangerous and lonely job of beach mine clearance. Despite the approach of the Home Guard's Stand Down, Lt Houghton stated his unit would 'continue at full strength until the end of the war,' probably because there were so many mines still to dispose of. This may indicate the unit continued even after Stand Down.

To their lasting credit, the ABDS carried out possibly the most dangerous work of all Home Guard units.

The Secret Units: Post-Invasion Resistance Organisations in Leicestershire

Home Guard Shock Sections

'He said "You're only amateurs, you won't last very long. Everyone you take…it's for the good"…This was the idea: if our troops had left, we were supposed to just make a bloody nuisance of ourselves: how severe depended on you.'

Allan Hopcraft, Lance Corporal, Quorn Home Guard Shock Section

I only discovered one of Leicestershire's most secret and unique World War Two organisations by accident, when an unintentionally ambiguous question led an interviewee to reveal he had been a member of a Home Guard Shock Section, a unit that had lain secret for 60 years.

Former Quorn Home Guard Shock Section Lance Corporal Allan Hopcraft, 2006.

Research into this unit proved frustrating: military experts had never heard of it and there were no related records. I met with a wall of silence from the only other member of the unit, who did not want to talk and hung up the phone. With only one man's testimony, no leads, and continued secrecy, I could not prove the organisation even existed. I started to wonder whether I was chasing shadows due to some big misunderstanding.

Then, while flicking through a stack of yellowed papers relating to the Quorn Home Guard, a typed sentence, crossed out in Xs, caught my eye. Scanned and enlarged, the obscured text became clear 'No. 3 Squad (Shock)'. This one line proved Shock Sections, or Shock Squads as they became, did exist. Had correction fluid existed in 1943, this proof would have been lost forever!

Secret Recruitment

Fortunately, now 60 years had elapsed, Allan Hopcraft, a former lance corporal in the Quorn Home Guard Shock Section, was willing to talk. In 1940 he lived on Wood Lane, Quorn, and worked in the village as a wages clerk at M. Wright and Sons' Mill.

'Our factory was making webbing side packs, straps and backpacks for the Forces. I had volunteered to join the RAF, but because our firm was on important war work, I had a deferment order for two years. While I was waiting, I joined the LDV.

About late summer '41, somebody called Lieutenant Whitford called us in to have a chat about joining a "special section". He explained he was in charge of Beaumanor Hall's defences. We didn't know what was going off at Beaumanor then. He said "We don't want it spread around, but we are looking for some young, active men." He did not tell us what it was about until we got into it. He said he wanted to form a "Shock Section" in "dirty tricks". They wanted a silent section: if the Jerries had come, we'd have gone about in civilian clothes trying to raise havoc.

He wanted about a dozen young lads, between 17 and 20. Old men are all right guarding a bridge, but if it comes to going out and doing damage, he needed younger men. We just had normal Home Guard uniforms, nothing to tell us apart, except we used to carry knives in a belt.'

The Right Type of Man

Allan Hopcraft was perfect for the Shock Section. 'I think the English are very slow to anger, but I come from Scotland and they tend to be more direct. The English are willing to compromise – I'm not: in

Scotland, we don't know the meaning of the word. They used to call me "Stroppy 'Oppy" at work. My family came down in 1938, looking for work. I was born and brought up near Aberfeldy, in Perthshire, where the Black Watch was raised. My father taught me to shoot. In those days, most lads used to have a shot at something and you knew the area. I had carried a knife with me since I was about five. In the Highlands, you got your rabbits and skinned them, stuff like that.'

'Dirty Tricks'

'About a dozen of us joined the section. Someone would say, "there's a special meeting tonight, we want to see you, you and you". We'd go to Beaumanor and Whitford would be there. He'd have some new dastardly methods or some inside information.

Being an ex-Palestine policeman, Whitford knew all about dirty tricks and was willing to teach us youngsters. We then used to give demonstrations at Rothley and Barrow, because they'd just started up their Shock Sections.

We were taught to climb, get over walls etc. He told us how to use steel knitting needles. He said in Palestine, the criminals used to keep knitting needles down the sides of their pockets. They'd go behind a bloke and push it right up behind the ear. Within ten seconds, he's dead, and it only leaves a tiny hole with no blood. Whitford said if one German saw a dead German lying there, first thing he'd look for is bullet wounds. Well there wouldn't be any. So it would cause confusion and panic: they'd ask "how did he die?"

He also told us how to use a wire or rope garrotte. And, oh yes, the old knuckleduster. You hit them on the side of the head, at the temples, the jaw. We also made coshes: you made whatever you wanted.

We were all taught how to use knives: never attack over arm but in front of you so you do not leave yourself open to attack. I made my own single-sided knife. We were taught how to approach German sentries silently and take them out. The German helmet had a leather strap, which you could use to break their neck.

Whitford taught us a lot of Jui-Jitsu and commando-type actions. We used to put inch and a half thick planks against the wall. He taught us how to break those and then break your fall, by running and putting your feet back, so if it was a man, you'd break his back. There was no sentimentality. He was very callous…a hard nut.'

Guerrilla Training

'We had a small book on guerrilla tactics, and I think it was written by Whitford. We used to read it and "inwardly digest".

We had rifles and Sten guns, some had Tommy guns. The only time we went out of this area for training, was when we went to Six Hills Range or Belvoir Castle for .303 shooting. The only .22s we had were privately owned. We used to train with them in the village for marksmanship. We did not have a sniper in the section, but we knew who our good shots were.

We had sticky bombs in a metal case. You were supposed to crawl up via a trench at the side of the road, undo the cover which would fly off and stick this thing to the side of the tank. Then you got about seven seconds to get away. We were also taught to climb on to the tank's parapet and put a grenade in the top – if you could get near – but that would have been a short life and a merry one.

We were taught demolition on dud grenades up at Mountsorrel quarry. One possible target was the Great Central Railway because of German troop trains. We were taught to get a block of TNT and how to put it each side of the railway line, with a bit of safety fuse in it, which would give you 15 minutes to get away and it would blow the line.'

Operational Role

'When invasion came, we'd carry on at work until we got the message from our sergeant or officer. We'd then all go and do whatever we were supposed to do. There was talk about secret message holes but it never really got down to that. I don't think we had a radio, it was all word of mouth. We'd go on operations in civilian clothes. At night, you had your face blacked, that was all. We knew it was against the Geneva Convention, but we weren't worried [chuckles].

You'd know where to get a rifle and what to do. We had stashes here and there. We knew various houses in Quorn where you could get ammunition or supplies. I suppose those people must have taken quite a risk as well, had the Germans found they were hiding ammunition for the Shock Section. Whitford said if you killed a German, take his weapon and ammunition. We might have taken prisoners, but the idea was to kill 'em. That was the main thing. Because there was only ten of us, we weren't meant to get in a big battle, 'cos we wouldn't have stood a chance.

In a copse at Bull-in-the-Hollow Farm, I think, was an underground base. You'd go through a lot of little pathways to find it. You'd pull the hatch down and cover everything up. It wasn't a doorway, just a hatchway down. Inside were bunks, explosives, ammunition and medical equipment. I don't know for certain, but I believe there was a number of them all over the place. They were special places for people just to fade away. Once you'd blown up the railway or whatever, you'd probably escape there or try to get home, maybe get rid of your weapons. We also had one position on top of Buddon Wood. There was a trench dug there already for defence or for hiding. If you had been in trouble, you could have gone up there and held people off.

If there had been a change of plan and they said "Defend Quorn at all costs", then we'd have all just gone out in our Home Guard uniform and joined the rest.'

If the Germans had occupied the area, the Shock Section would have become a resistance organisation. Survival would have been paramount and all obstacles would have been eliminated.

'Traitors in the village? [Quietly smiles] I thought we would have collaborators in this country: spivs and wide boys out on the make. Whitford told us to give 'em the chop. [Grinning, Allan silently draws a finger across his throat.] You had to, because we'd soon be eliminated if they got hold of someone who talked: it would be like a chain, a brick wall collapsing…and we'd all be shot. Even living in a small community, any unease about it never entered our minds to be honest – it was as serious as that.'

Whitford was blunt about the Shock Sections' life expectancy,

'He said "You're only amateurs, you won't last very long. Everyone you take…it's for the good," sort of thing. But you didn't worry about things like that. You were just taught: if you can make yourself a nuisance, make yourself a nuisance. How severe depended on you, I suppose: how brash you were or how foolish. We were a back-up: if our troops had left, I reckon we would have taken a toll of Germans.

I was not worried about repercussions on my family: my old man had served in World War One and was very anti-German [chuckles] he was all for it. In fact, when I joined the RAF he said "I'll take your place," and he joined the Quorn Home Guard.'

Operational Training

'[Around Winter 1941] Whitford said "I've told Beaumanor they're going to be attacked by a Home Guard unit and they've got to be on the lookout. I'll tell you when to attack". One night we got the call. There were about ten of us. It was a flaming cold night. We were blacked up and as it was snowing, we had white sheets on to blend in.

One of the reasons they wanted young people was Beaumanor had a six-foot wire fence around it. Two men would hold a rifle, another would jump onto it and you'd throw him over and he'd roll over on the other side. There wasn't anything as sophisticated as electronic surveillance. I can't remember any searchlights but they had guards. So we got over the fence and attacked.

We didn't have any guns, just grenades and chalk bombs. We made dummy grenades, which were like three-six grenades, but without explosive, just black powder to make a bang. We knew where the guardhouse was and got within striking distance. Somebody threw a stone at the door, and a squaddie came out and had a look around, and while the door was open, we lobbed in one of these grenades, and "bang": "right you're out!" [chuckles]. The language from the sergeant in charge of the guard was horrible…I never heard such language! When the grenade went off, it made all the others come running to that one spot, while we dispersed and went our ways, 'cos we knew Beaumanor grounds.

We then went round the various places taking them out. We knew where the generators were and placed little bags of chalk on them to say they'd been attacked.

After the operation, we had to make our escape, and I think we reported back at Quorn station. It might not have come off: we might not have got over the fence if it had been a nice moonlight night. But I don't think we had any "casualties", we were all young and enthusiastic.

We were attacking Beaumanor to find the weakness of their defences, and as Whitford was in charge, he got all the write-ups about it after. We also used to attack the searchlight unit at Woodhouse Eaves.'

Who Was Behind the Shock Sections?
Without records, it is impossible to say for certain who ran the Shock Sections. The Shock Sections' role and methodology seems remarkably similar to the national Auxiliary Unit resistance organisation: secrecy, small teams of hand-picked men, underground bases, specialised training, sabotage, 'dirty tricks', assassination and a continued post-invasion resistance role. The Auxiliary Units had been formed by MI (R) (Military Intelligence Research) and were later governed by GHQ Home Forces. Yet Allan claims never to have heard of 'Auxiliary Units', nor trained at their HQ at Coleshill House, Highworth, Wiltshire.

Instead, it seems Shock Sections trained and operated on a purely local basis. But their organisation, authority and role (including the construction of underground operational bases) seems to have been above the jurisdiction of a local Home Guard commander.

The clue to the Shock Sections' origin and purpose lies in their proximity to the important secret wireless interception Y-Station at Beaumanor Hall. It is also notable that Lt Whitford, who commanded Beaumanor's Home Guard, recruited and trained members from other platoons into the Shock Sections.

Allan believed the exercise where his Shock Section broke in and sabotaged Beaumanor was to test the Y-Station's defences. However, in a similar role to the Auxiliary Units, it could equally have been to train the Shock Section to sabotage Beaumanor had it been occupied by the Germans, who may well have used the large hall as an HQ. The other Shock Sections at Rothley and Barrow-on-Soar that Allan mentioned were also within striking distance of Beaumanor. Bull-in-the-Hollow Farm, where Quorn Shock Section's underground base is said to have been located, was then part of the Beaumanor Hall estate. The Shock Sections were a second-line back-up to Beaumanor's Home Guard platoon.

Possible evidence to support this theory can be found in Worcestershire. There was an underground operational base one mile north-west of the BBC Y-Station at Wood Norton Hall, Worcestershire.[484] This is the same distance as the Quorn Shock Section was to the Beaumanor Hall Y-Station. Although the Worcestershire operational base was part of the Auxiliary Unit organisation, not a Home Guard Shock Section, and the members of this patrol claimed their main target was nearby RAF Pershore, this unit would also have been within striking distance of a Y-Station. A very thin and uninformative document exists in the National Archives entitled 'Defence of Y-Stations, January 1942 – January 1943'.[485] Although the brief document does not explain exactly what form the defence took, it lists Beaumanor Hall and the title dates approximately correspond with the known life of the Shock Sections. The document's existence in itself also suggests there may have been a specialised form of defence provided for Y-Stations.

There is, however, solid evidence of non-Auxiliary Unit, Home Guard Shock Section-type resistance organisations in Worcestershire,[486] Kent[487] and around Stirling, Scotland.[488]

So who was the mysterious Lt Dick Whitford? Fortunately, Lt Whitford's son, Fred, still lives locally and remembers his father's service. Born in 1899, Lieutenant, later Captain, Richard (Dick) H. Whitford had a long military career. He first served in the Merchant Navy as Third Officer on SS *Shirley* during World War One. In the 1920s he was a member of the Palestine Police Force. This was a tough job, and Whitford saw much action: once he was besieged in his police station by insurgents and had to shoot his way out. It was here he learned much about counter-insurgency and guerrilla warfare. In the late 1930s Whitford joined the wireless interception service at Chatham, Kent. In October 1941 he moved with the Y-Service to Beaumanor Hall, where he served jointly as a wireless interception Watch Officer and head of the Y-Station's Home Guard (see page 117). He also became recruiting officer and instructor to the Quorn Home Guard Shock Section. In the Auxiliary Units, Lieutenants were generally Group Leaders of several AU patrols. It may have been the case that Lt Whitford was equivalent to a Group Leader of the Shock Sections. Home Guard officers nicknamed him 'Two Guns Whitford', as on one hip he carried his Regular service revolver in a cut-down holster and a German Luger in a webbing holster on the other. This was an unusual trait in Home Guard circles, but was practised by some AU officers so they could also use captured German ammunition. Peter James, a wireless intercept operator at Beaumanor, remembered Whitford. 'He knew what he was doing and commanded quite a bit of respect.'[489] After the war, Whitford taught local army cadets and died after an illness in 1952.[490]

Captain Dick Whitford, of the 10th (Charnwood) Battalion, believed to have been the group leader of the Charnwood area Home Guard Shock Section. (Quorn Home Guard Archive)

The scant, partially-deleted reference to the Shock Section in the Quorn Home Guard archive mentions their immediate superior was a 2nd Lt Howard Leavesley. 2nd Lt Leavesley's daughter Norma Deeming also still lives locally and remembers her father's service. Born in 1900, 2nd Lt, later Lieutenant, (James) Howard Leavesley was a Fleet Air Arm pilot during World War One. His aircraft once ditched in the Mediterranean and he swam eight miles to land. His logbook is now in the RAF Museum, Hendon. Between the wars, he jointly founded luxury coachmakers Willowbrook in Loughborough. During the war, the company switched to making aircraft parts. At first, Leavesley was a Sergeant in Quorn Home Guard. In the Auxiliary Units, Sergeants were generally AU Patrol Leaders and it may be at one stage Sgt Leavesley was Patrol Leader of the Quorn Shock Section. Norma says her father's involvement with the Shock Section 'would make sense', as 'he kept mentioning Bull-in-the-Hollow farm and training on the railway beside it. After his forays there he often came home muddy. As a family of daughters, we used to tease our Daddy for "playing soldiers", little realising the seriousness of his Home Guard work.' Leavesley died in 1954.[491]

Lt Howard Leavesley of the 10th (Charnwood) Battalion is believed to have been the patrol leader of the Quorn Home Guard Shock Section. (Quorn Home Guard Archive)

Both fathers died shortly after the war, and never told their children about their service with the Shock Sections, so, after 60 years, it came as a revelation. However, they both were able to add further detail.

But were there other Shock Sections throughout Leicestershire and Rutland? Wendy Warren, the wife of 2nd/Lt John Warren, Platoon Leader of Dunton Bassett Home Guard, recalled:

'He never talked about it a lot, but he said within Ullesthorpe, Claybrooke, Ashby Parva and Dunton Bassett, there were some "first class" men whose fieldcraft was "magic". They formed a special group whose expertise was deployed in finding their way across open farmland at night under adverse conditions.'[492]

2nd/Lt Warren's slightly cryptic hint may suggest there were Shock Sections in south Leicestershire, as this particular area contained the main A426 road into Leicester, plus a railway line. However, there is no evidence to confirm this. Alternatively, he may have been referring to Home Guard Guides who also knew the land well. Col. Ogilvy-Dalgleish hints he may have known about Shock Sections, but did not approve and they did not exist in Rutland:

'Our intention was to train good irregular soldiers not dubious guerrilla bands; individuality would, of course, be important, but it would be of little use in a crisis without discipline. We did not wish to rely entirely on guerrilla tactics, not being guerrillas.'[493]

So Shock Sections may only have been located around Beaumanor Hall.

What Became of the Shock Sections?

Allan Hopcraft only served in Quorn Shock Section for around six months as he was called-up into the RAF in early 1942, so what became of Shock Sections? It is a distinct possibility they just faded away. The success of European partisans fired an interest in guerrilla warfare among the frustrated Home

Guard, who prepared for an invasion that had not come. A rash of commercially-produced training pamphlets reflected this interest. The new, younger Director General of the Home Guard, Lord Bridgeman, actually encouraged the move towards irregular warfare, stating in January 1942,

'Don't let us forget it is a cad's war. There are no rules, except to kill any German who lands in this country by any means; and the more lowbrow the battle is, the greater the likelihood of achieving the essential ingredient of victory, namely surprise...'[494]

This horrified the WO, who strongly disapproved of this radical new direction, fearing it would interfere with Regular operations. Unofficially, their objection was also a continuance of the long-running power struggle fought between the WO and the Home Guard. Lt-General Sir Bernard Paget, later C-in-C Home Forces, was irritated Lord Bridgeman had spoken out on operational matters. The WO and GHQ Home Forces had overall jurisdiction on military policy, not Lord Bridgeman. In November 1942 GHQ Home Forces practically banned the Home Guard's guerrilla role altogether.

Did this end the Shock Sections? Some Home Guard guerrilla units continued on regardless.[495] With their specialised role in the defence of Beaumanor Y-Station and their possible direction by an authority above the Home Guard, Shock Sections may have continued.

The Quorn Home Guard defence scheme, from late 1943, mentions that on general alert the Shock Section would muster the same as all other Quorn Home Guard sections. Their particular mustering point was at Quorn cricket pavilion. This may signify that by this date, with the almost complete disappearance of the invasion threat, the Shock Sections were now just used as a mobile battle platoon. A 1944 inventory book of the 10th (Charnwood) Battalion also lists '2/Lt J.H. Leavesley of Rawdon, Leicester Rd, Loughborough' as commander of a 'Mob.' (Mobile) unit. Alternatively, the fact the entry in the defence scheme was crossed through may signify the Shock Section was disbanded altogether.

Conclusion

The discovery of Home Guard Shock Sections and the piercing of 60 years of secrecy poses as many questions as it answers. There is much we do not know about: who governed the sections, how widespread were they and what precisely was their role?

But apart from confirming their existence, there is much we can answer. The Shock Sections' secrecy, advanced training and underground bases clearly indicate they were not just regular Home Guards. We know they were a specialised and possibly unique secret force, similar to Auxiliary Units.

These factors also suggest their creation was probably above the jurisdiction of the local Home Guard, from an authority with a knowledge of how the Auxiliary Units were organised and operated. Indeed, the similarities between the two organisations may indicate they were both run by the same authority, possibly GHQ Home Forces. There is also an indication a wider civilian support network may have existed, providing observation, supplies and communications.

The Shock Sections were strictly unconventional; they taught, in British Army Officer parlance, 'thuggery' and clearly operated outside the Geneva Convention. Not that the Germans would have cared anyway: had any of the Section been captured, torture and a firing squad were a certainty. Whitford was unequivocal about this and, as Allan Hopcraft wryly noted, a member's life would be a 'short and merry one'.

Home Guard Shock Sections also had a continuing role as resistance parties after occupation. From Nazi methods on the continent, we know any sabotage would have brought harsh and disproportionate reprisals: one possible scenario may have been the levelling of Quorn and execution of part, or even all, of its population.

However, this form of semi-suicidal defence reflected the desperation of the hour and the determined bravery of the men involved.

The author would appreciate any further information about this organisation.

The Charnwood Forest Resistance

Anne Cooper of Redcar wrote to me saying her father, Samuel Hall of Ellistown, was 'instructed in the case of invasion to form an underground resistance group in Charnwood Forest'. Hall had been a miner but joined the Leicestershire Regiment in 1932 and was sent to the North West Frontier. The Regiment returned to England at the outbreak of war and Hall, now a Sergeant, was posted to Glen Parva ITC. In 1940, aged 29, Hall was told in the event of German invasion to form an 'underground resistance group,' based in the caves of Charnwood Forest and using Mount St Bernard's Abbey as a 'contact point' to collect orders. This resistance organisation resembles the Army's Auxiliary Unit 'stay-behind' Scout Sections.

Lt Samuel Hall in 1942. *(Anne Cooper)*

Anne Cooper believes her father was chosen to head this resistance group because of his local knowledge. Before the war he had been a groom to Colonel Graham of Coleorton Hall. It appears that although this resistance unit was also located in Charnwood and based only six miles from the Quorn Shock Section, they were two totally separate organisations. The Charnwood Forest resistance group also appear to have a much wider operational area. They placed charges under the metal footbridge alongside Trent Bridge in Nottingham and were told to detonate them in the event of invasion. It was only in 1947 while the footbridge was being repainted that the explosive charges were discovered, forgotten for two years after the war had ended! In 1942 Hall was commissioned as a 2nd Lt into the 4th Prince of Wales's Own Ghurka Rifles and sent to India. Samuel Hall died in 1988.[496]

Again, the author would appreciate any further information about this organisation.

Industrial 'Sabotage Key Holders'

If industrial works were about to be captured, management had plans to disable, but not completely destroy, machinery *before* the plant fell into German hands. However, a mysterious fleeting reference in a 1960s *Leicester Mercury* article suggests there was an organisation of 'sabotage key holders,' whose specialist purpose was to sabotage war production *after* the Germans had occupied the county.

'There was, for example, a shoe machinery works [possibly the British United Shoe Machinery Co. Ltd off Belgrave Road, Leicester] doing research and experimental work of a highly secret nature. So secretive in fact that at a time when we were a high invasion risk, certain Leicester people were given "sabotage" keys. These would give them access to works where war research and classified weapons were being produced. The job of the sabotage key holders was to put the plant beyond the use of the enemy.'[497]

Who exactly organised these 'sabotage key holders' is unknown. Their role and existence seems to have remained a secret, with practically no information regarding these saboteurs existing in the public domain. This may be because the organisation was run by MI5, who are not compelled to release any records. However, recent research by Lowry and Wilks about 'Individual Urban Saboteurs' in neighbouring Birmingham may reveal a little about these 'sabotage key holders'.[498]

'Individual Urban Saboteurs' were recruited from an industrial background and told they would be working for 'X Branch'. They went on specialist training courses, mainly in the making and usage of explosives. They were also trained in the use of booby traps and 'dirty fighting'. These saboteurs were trained to operate alone, their only contact being their controlling officer. Most training was carried out alone at night, walking through the blacked-out city streets. This training allowed them to develop better night vision and operate stealthily, while developing a geographical knowledge of the city in darkness, hiding in doorways and moving silently with rubber-soled shoes. These saboteurs dressed as civilians, putting themselves outside the Geneva Convention but allowing them greater cover in an urban environment. Unusually they were not issued with official equipment, perhaps to give the impression if captured they were working alone. They made their own fighting knife, which was kept hidden discreetly in their trouser leg, plus other equipment such as a garrotte. The only official item they were supplied with were clockwork demolition fuses.

In Leicester's case, it appears the saboteurs were given keys to specific factories they were to sabotage. Nonetheless, with practically all Leicester's factories on war production, targets would have been plentiful, also suggesting several saboteurs may have operated.

Once the Nazis occupied a country, they channelled its industrial output into their overall war production, with individual factories making specific components. Had these Key Holders managed to destroy specific factories, they could have seriously disrupted part of the German war effort.

However, their effectiveness would have been purely down to how long they could operate: with a curfew and German troops patrolling Leicester's empty streets, movement would have been difficult. If a saboteur was caught carrying a knife and prepared charges, torture and a firing squad would have been inevitable.

The author would appreciate any further information about this organisation.

CHAPTER 5:
TRAINING

'A Rookie's Grouse'

'What is the use of a rifle,
If a fellow can't have a good shot?
That is my grouse – and it has been,
Since I joined this adjective lot.

Me and my pals, we've paraded,
Since the birth of the old LDV
Our drills we count up unaided,
But a Target we still have to see.

So out to the Ranges let us away,
Give us some bullets and guns,
Teach us to feel that we'll be O.K.
If we have to face up with the Huns.

That is the end of my grumble,
And I hope you won't think none the worse,
Of the Rookie who took an advantage,
And wrote of his grouses in verse.'

'Knightthorpe'
'B' Company, 9th (Loughborough) Battalion,
Leicestershire Home Guard
January 1941.[499]

Training was vitally important, as Keyham Home Guard Rowles Harrison remembers, 'There was no doubt that our commanding officers took a very serious view of our training and we were taken on various manoeuvres at night as well as day. Our training was very thorough and we were confidentially informed an invasion by the Germans was a distinct possibility. I remember Lieutenant Lee saying "If each of you kill at least one German the invasion cannot succeed." I think after that at least some of us realised the importance of the Home Guard and what might be expected of us.'[500]

Theory and Practice

Most Home Guards met twice a week. The first attendance was usually a midweek parade with theory training on a Wednesday evening at the platoon HQ, usually the local hall. Here they would watch lectures and some training films. However, the main day was Sunday, when theory was put into practice. Occasionally the day would start with a morning church parade, usually ending at a pub for lunchbreak, although this appears more often to have been a liquid meal! Field manoeuvres would then occupy the rest of the afternoon. Former Quorn Home Guard Allan Hopcraft remembers:

'If the Germans had invaded, they'd only need to come to the "Manor House" by Quorn station. Every Sunday was 12 o'clock opening and there was a row of rifles stacked outside against the wall [chuckles]. We always managed to get back to the pub for opening time, no matter what kind of manoeuvres were on. For youngsters, it was a laugh.'[501]

It is worth remembering that due to war production, many workers worked a six day week, so the only day they had to themselves, for resting or socialising, was occupied with Home Guard training.

'Something of a Joke'

Many LDVs had served in World War One. But that was 20 years ago and much of their military knowledge was outmoded, as Major H.E. Inglesant, CO of 'C' (Keyham area), 6th (Quorn) Battalion recalled:

'You will all remember how in those lovely hot early summer days of May, 1940, when [we] formed ourselves into groups of fire-eating soldiery, many of us with no more knowledge of modern warfare than when we had left off and resumed our bowler hats after 1918.

Training in those days was, to say the least of it, something of a joke, and we must all agree that, had the Bosche known just how very much we were underarmed with shotguns, ancient pistols and no ammunition, heavy walking sticks and anything else which came to hand, he would probably have risked it and invaded us at that time.

As time went on, however, we gradually learnt the wisdom of the modern army, and began to realise there were such things as defence in depth, airplane attacks, and a multitude of other tricks for which we had to account in modern warfare.'[502]

Training the Trainers

During summer 1940 Permanent Staff Instructors (PSIs) were authorised to train the Home Guard. However, there were only six allocated for the whole East Midlands area, three in Leicester and three in Northampton![503] This was clearly inadequate, so once platoon and company commanders had been chosen, some were selected to go to national Home Guard Training Schools. The Leicestershire and Rutland TA record:

Official Home Guard publications.

Commercially-produced
Home Guard manuals.

'Two schools of instruction have been opened for officers and Platoon Commanders:

i) War Office Home Guard School: originally opened at Osterley Park, but has since moved to Denbies, near Dorking [Surrey]. Here the course consists of three days intensive training and we have been allotted six vacancies during November [1940] for Platoon Leaders.

ii) Northern Command Weapon Training School at Catterick Camp [North Yorkshire]. Here the course lasts for four days and we have been allotted six vacancies during November [1940] for Platoon Leaders.'[504]

Wendy Warren recalls her late husband, 2/Lt John Warren, Platoon Leader of the Dunton Bassett Home Guard, was one of the six who travelled to the Denbies School. When he returned he was made Bombing Officer for South Leicestershire.[505]

There is no evidence of local Home Guard training schools in Leicestershire or Rutland, but Home Guards attended Glen Parva ITC or went on two-day patrol, street fighting and WT courses at the North Midland District Home Guard Training School at Bestwood Lodge, Arnold, Nottingham.[506] In 1944, Hoby Platoon received training from NCOs of the locally-based British Airborne Division, shortly before their fateful mission to Arnhem.[507] Battle training was also conducted in Bradgate Park.[508]

Attaining Proficiency
From April 1941 a national standard of proficiency was introduced for all Home Guards, eventually including all NCOs. On passing, each man attained a certificate and red cloth diamond badge, to be worn on their battledress sleeve. The influx of raw directed men from 1942 meant a special training programme was required. The Rutland battalion devised a comprehensive eight-week course, later adopted throughout the North Midland District.[509]

Paper Tigers
From summer 1941 training films were shown in village halls and cinemas, particularly during the winter months. Initially, the films were army hand-me-downs, then, from 1942, up-to-date training programmes.[510] Officers used maps and sand models to conduct TEWTs.

Despite the paper shortage, the Home Guard were never short of bureaucracy and its associated paperwork. Printed Home Guard instructions, information circulars, training pamphlets, amendments, together with typed district, Sub-Area, sector, battalion, company and platoon orders, all had to be

Home Guard proficiency certificate of Sgt J.H. Lee, 'C' Company, 1st Rutland Battalion, signed by Lt-Col. Whaley, CO of 1st Rutland Battalion. (Maureen Walker)

A.F.W. 4026.

Certificate of Proficiency
HOME GUARD

On arrival at the Training Establishment, Primary Training Centre or Recruit Training Centre, the holder must produce this Certificate at once for the officer commanding, together with Certificate A if gained in the Junior Training Corps or Army Cadet Force.

PART I. I hereby certify that (Rank)......SGT..(Name and initials)......LEE..J.H.........................
of .....C...... *Battery* ......1st. RUTLAND......*Regiment* HOME GUARD, has qualified
Company Battalion
in the Proficiency Badge tests as laid down in the pamphlet "Qualifications for, and Conditions governing the Award of the Home Guard Proficiency Badges and Certificates" for the following subjects:—

	Subject				*Date*	*Initials*
1.	General knowledge (all candidates)	..	..	..	19.3.44	
2.	Rifle .. ✓ ✓ ✓	..	..	..	19.III.44	
3.	36 M Grenade	..	..	..	19.III.44	
*4.	(a) Other weapon STEN CARBINE			..	19.3.44	
	(b) Signalling ..					
*5.	(a) Battlecraft, (b) Coast Artillery, (c) Heavy A.A. Bty. work, (d) "Z" A.A. Battery work, (e) Bomb Disposal, (f) Watermanship, (g) M.T.	..	..	..	19.3.44	
*6.	(a) Map Reading, (b) Field works, (c) First Aid	..	..	..	19/3/44	

Date.......19 Mar..194**4**.   Signature....Cartwright...MAJOR.
                                                 President or Member of the Board.

Date.......................194....   Signature............................
                                                 President or Member of the Board.

Date.......................194....   Signature............................
                                                 President or Member of the Board.

Date.......................194....   Signature............................
                                                 President or Member of the Board.

Date.......................194....   Signature............................
                                                 President or Member of the Board.

PART II. I certify that (Rank).....SGT..........(Name and initials)...LEE.J.H....................
of ...C... *Battery* ......1st. RUTLAND...*Regiment* HOME GUARD, having duly passed
Company Battalion
the Proficiency tests in the subjects detailed above in accordance with the pamphlet and is hereby authorized to wear the Proficiency Badge as laid down in Regulations for the Home Guard, Vol. 1, 1942, para 41d.

Date.......20 – 3 – 194**4**   Signature....N. Whaley...LT. COL.

                                                 Commanding 1st. Bn. Rutland H.G.

PART III. If the holder joins H.M. Forces, his Company or equivalent Commander will record below any particulars which he considers useful in assessing the man's value on arrival at the T.E., P.T.C., R.T.C., e.g., service, rank, duties on which employed, power of leadership, etc.

Date.......................194....   Signature............................
* Delete where not applicable.   O.C.

Syston and Queniborough Home Guard at Bitteswell Camp, summer 1943. Seated centre wearing the peaked cap is Lt Swain MC. Seated to the left with glasses is 2/Lt Carryer. Seated to Swain's right is the Revd Stanton, vicar of Queniborough. He was the padre for the whole of the 6th (Quorn) Battalion. The young lad sitting second from right, front row, would be dead within a year of appearing in this photograph. Able Seaman Robert Wright, aged 18, was killed three days after D-Day when his vehicle landing barge was hit by a German shell. He is now buried in France. (Dennis Booth)

distributed and digested by the force, which had few administrative staff. On top of this, numerous commercially-published booklets, of varying quality, were available for individuals to purchase.

Despite the risk that Home Guard offices could become overwhelmed by this blizzard of paperwork, Col. Ogilvy-Dalgleish believed 'The numerous War Office HG Training Instructions were, in my humble opinion, excellent.'[511] The WO helped, in 1943, with the publication of two volumes of Home Guard Regulations, which collated many previous rulings, cheering the overworked TA staff. However, their joy was short-lived.

The method of distributing these important instructions was varied, to say the least, and security could have been tighter. Anstey Platoon's orders arrived from Leicester with the village's newspapers and a platoon runner fetched them from the newsagent![512] Because of this, whereas previously the publications had been sent direct to the battalion HQs for distribution, from 1943 the TA had to distribute them to company level, entailing 'the sending of 95 packages as against 15 for most publications'.[513]

On Exercise

Field exercises were not supposed to be just a jolly boys' outing, as portrayed in *Dad's Army*. However, they often had lighter moments, as former Husbands Bosworth Platoon, 7th (Market Harborough) Battalion Home Guard John Greaves, explains:

Home Guards of 'A' (Campbell Street, Leicester) Company, 13th (25th GPO) Battalion cook in the field during a summer camp. Note the cook's cigarette dangling above the bowl!

'I remember mock battles on Leicester Racecourse with blanks and crackers on a string attached to your rifle and trigger. Some took the exercise very seriously and it almost came to blows, because no one would admit they had been "shot" first! Anyhow, we got separated and found ourselves on the Bypass – so we slipped into Oadby for a couple of pints.'[514]

Even night alerts had moments of hilarity, as former Ibstock resident W. Ruth Smith explained, 'Little Sergeant Sam Ottey always slept with his uniform beside his bed, braces attached to the trousers in readiness for quick dressing. One night they were called out on exercise. Sam dressed and ran. Later on in the night, having a call of nature, he could be heard cursing – his flies were at the back!'[515]

Modern Home Guard battledrill and battlecraft was introduced from mid-1942 and encapsulated all the army had learnt in recent campaigns. This tough battle drill was designed for Regular soldiers in their 20s – not men in their 40s, 50s or above. Nine Leicestershire Home Guard deaths were exercise-related.

Weapons Training

Rifle training usually occurred on a Sunday and entailed travelling by lorry to outdoor rifle ranges such as at Kibworth, Six Hills, Glen Parva Barracks and Beaumont Leys, or alternatively to indoor .22 ranges,

Dummy weighted Home Guard No.36 Mills training grenade, made at Fred Pollard Engineering works, St Saviours Road, Leicester. (Ron Bodicoat)

1940-dated No.36 MK1 Mills hand grenade base plugs found at the Home Guard grenade throwing range, Martinshaw Woods, Ratby. (Jim Briggs)

several of which existed in and around Leicester, as at the railwayman's working men's club on Highcross Street, Leicester.[516]

Grenades

Perhaps the most poignant memory is of grenade training. Several sites around Leicestershire, such as the sandpit at Beaumont Leys or the old quarry at Station Park, Glenfield,[517] were ready-made training areas. Alternatively, purpose-built ranges were used, as in Martinshaw Woods, Ratby, where a grenade throwing building, with observation blockhouse, tower and throwing pit, were constructed. Leslie Furnival, formerly a corporal in No. 14 (Croft) Platoon, 3rd (West Leicester) Battalion, remembers:

'There were two bays and you would stand in one bay on your own and remove the pin and throw the grenade. You were told to throw it straight ahead. There were large areas of burnt grass where the grenades had exploded. But to the right was a large pool of water. If you chucked it right, it would explode in the pool, making a big splash and covering all the observers with dirty, stagnant pond water!'[518]

Although it is now buried under the M1 motorway, Mills Bomb base plugs are still found in the surrounding woodland.[519]

Col. Ogilvy-Dalgleish recalls accustoming the men to grenades was an important part of training and, fortunately, there were no associated injuries in the Rutland battalion. 'A range near Peterborough was used under regular instructors, but this involved unnecessary transport and throwing bays were built locally by REs; disused ironstone workings were also used…The men…showed remarkable accuracy and range, probably a natural product of village cricket.'[520]

However, the same thing could not be said in Leicestershire. 'Near misses' were common. Former Ibstock Brick and Tile Works underage Home Guard Albert Squires almost lost his head while watching grenade throwing 30 yards away, 'By some freak the base cap of the grenade came flying back and actually cut through the shoulder strap of my uniform. Then it buried itself in the ground. The Gods certainly smiled on me that day!'[521]

Corporal Ray Elgood, of HQ company, 1st (North Leicester) Battalion, also had a heart-stopping moment as an instructor:

White painted Home Guard No.36 Mills training grenade.

'On the Humberstone parade ground we had some white-painted dummy grenades. After learning the rudiments, you'd practise tossing them. Everybody had to sit this course and then they had to throw one live. For this, we went up to a farm at Houghton-on-the-Hill. About 20 yards behind this wood, we tipped one of the trailers on its side. I was on duty and they were sending the men in one at a time to throw them over. How he got through I don't know, but one chap's arm locked in the vertical and his grenade went straight up in the air and straight down again, landing just the other side of the trailer. I grabbed him and dived down. There was a bloody great bang and it shattered the trailer. The other chap wasn't injured, but I took a couple of bits of wood in my leg and some grenade shrapnel hit my steel helmet. They would have given me a new helmet but I kept it – show some damage! They said they learned more swear words after I had a go at everybody concerned: I even had a go at the high ranks when they got it wrong!'[522]

Wendy Warren, the wife of 2nd/Lt John Warren, Platoon Leader of Dunton Bassett Home Guard, recalled her late husband's close shave:

'John and his platoon were doing grenade practice at the bombing range at Gumley. They lobbed one over the top and it didn't explode. John knew from his training you wait five minutes and then somebody – in his case it was him – carefully walked towards the grenade listening. Once there, you lit a charge next to the grenade. You then had twenty seconds to walk briskly away and then throw yourself down with your tin-hatted head facing the grenade.

Well, John walked very cautiously towards it, got the box of matches, knelt down and struck a match. However, the match broke. But suddenly, he heard the grenade's striker fall. He didn't have the twenty seconds to get away, so John sprinted for five seconds, threw himself down with his head towards it and the grenade exploded.

But he said the funniest thing was as soon as the men watching from the trench saw him run, they knew something had gone wrong and ducked below the sandbag parapet of the trench. As John turned around to get up, he saw this row of heads rising up over the parapet to see what had happened – there was just a line of eyes and tin hats over the sandbags, a bit like a row of Chads (of the 'Wot No...' fame)!

If it hadn't been for that match head breaking, he would have lit the fuse and slowly walked away, in which case he may not have heard the striker fall and he would have received shrapnel in his back – or worse.'[523]

It is surprising that there were not more casualties, especially with the advice one member of the Illston-on-the-Hill Platoon, of 7th (Market Harborough) Battalion, apparently gave his comrades, 'if a grenade should land in front of you, the best thing to do was to cover it with your tin hat and stand on it'![524]

Other Training

Anti-Gas
The effectiveness of poison gas had horribly been proven during World War One. With this in mind, the Home Guard undertook anti-gas training. P.S. Wakefield had been mustard gassed in 1917. It affected him for the rest of his life, eventually invaliding him out of the Home Guard in 1942. The training brought back bad memories:

'Monday 21:10:40. Saw an aerial gas demonstration yesterday. A low flying monoplane sprayed liquid over detachments of the K.O.Y.L.I. and us onlookers of the Home Guard. Most unpleasant if it had been the real stuff. The liquid could be felt on all our faces, splashed motor car windscreens and discoloured the special "training purposes" gas detectors.'[525]

Harry Gudger, on the other hand, then a young Home Guard in the Birstall Platoon, 1st (North Leicester) Battalion, had not experienced gas warfare before and consequently did not view the training so seriously:

'At Leicester, we went to a type of brick gas chamber and they let off tear gas. They then told us to take off our gas masks for a few seconds so we could experience the gas. We had to get our noses to the floor and quickly crawl through to the exit. The tear gas perishing well hurt, but it was funny to see 20 other lads crying at the same time!'[526]

Bloody Bayonets
Bayonet training was generally taught by the World War One veterans, often with some glee. At times the training was gruesomely realistic, perhaps courtesy of the local abattoir, as a Loughborough Officer later recalled:

'One remembers with pleasure the clever gadgets beautifully made with sound effects attached to imitate tommy guns and machine guns. These exhibited with great pride by their creators and handled rather sheepishly by the operators. And then there was the bayonet fighting, sacks suspended from frames, which seemed to even contain Aryan blood.'[527]

They don't like it up 'em!
Leicester Home Guard
practise on the bayonet
fighting course which they
built themselves, Thursday 5
September 1940. It is
thought the location is the
sand pit at Beaumont Leys.

Dunton Bassett Home
Guard c.1942. 2nd/Lt
John Warren sits middle row,
third from left. Cpl Wally
Clare sits middle row, fifth
from left. (Wendy Warren)

Wendy Warren, the wife of 2nd/Lt John Warren, Platoon Leader of Dunton Bassett Home Guard, recalled one of her husband's lectures:

Cartoon of No.25 (Leicester City Transport) Platoon, 'E' Company, 1st (North Leicester) Battalion Leicestershire Home Guard by Charles Herbert, shown at their 'Smoker' evening, held at Hotel Belgrave, Leicester on Tuesday 7 December 1943. The cartoon shows various characters and their represented roles within the platoon.

'John and another member of the unit, Wally Clare, the local publican, used to run an unarmed combat course. Wally was a very fat man but exceptionally nimble. The usual practice was for Wally to lie on the floor as the unarmed combatant and for John to attack him with a fixed bayonet. Wally would demonstrate in slow motion so that nobody got hurt and he would indicate when he was ready for John to attack.

On this particular night, John thought Wally had given the signal and he suddenly charged at Wally, who was lying on the floor, to bayonet him through the chest. Wally wasn't ready, but in that split second he had to use the technique for real, which was to knock the bayonet aside with your forearm so it stuck in the ground and then, because the attacker was still holding onto it, the defendant kicked the attacker in an arc through the air, straight over his head backwards.

Wally had no option but to do that to John – with some force. The bayonet stuck in the village hall's wooden floor and John went straight out through the door! If Wally hadn't been so quick, John would have bayoneted him through the chest. Nobody else watching that night could be persuaded to try it! Occasionally you got a clever clogs who thought they would manage to nail Wally, but of course they always went sailing out through the door too and the harder they came the harder they fell!'[528]

Members of the Keyham Home Guard platoon enjoy a drink and a light-hearted moment at their headquarters.

CHAPTER 6:

SPORT AND LEISURE

Sport

Various inter-unit sporting activities took place including cricket, boxing, athletics and darts.

Perhaps the most successful of these clubs was the Shepshed Home Guard Football Club, under Home Guard Cyril Mee. They played in the local Alliance League, Loughborough Lions League and for the Cobbin Trophy.

In February 1941, Shepshed Home Guard FC won their first victory in the Loughborough Alliance League, when they beat Notmanco 4–3 at Loughborough. Their victory was 'well deserved,' especially as they had lost their right-half P. Everett with a leg injury after only a few minutes play, but they 'stuck manfully to their task'.[529]

In August 1941 their first annual meeting was well attended at the Black Swan Hotel. Lt Hallam paid tribute to the management and players. It was stated expenses would increase considerably as Shepshed Town FC, who had previously paid part of the ground rent, had decided not to run a team that year, so Shepshed Home Guard FC would 'keep football alive in Shepshed'.[530]

In November 1942, Shepshed Home Guard FC thrashed 320 Company (army) 8–1 in the Alliance League.[531] They went on to reach the local Finals of the Cobbin Trophy in 1943, but, due to the call up of players, had to use local servicemen, including the league's first-ever black player Georgie Coggins. After the war, the team became Shepshed Albion FC and exist to this day as Shepshed Dynamo FC.

Leisure

The Home Guard's comradely nature was maintained through many leisure events, such as dinners, dances, smoking evenings, cinema outings and whist drives, all more often than not ending up at, or based at, the pub! At first, any profits generated were ploughed back into platoon funds, but as supplies to the force improved, various charitable causes, most notably the Leicestershire POW Comforts Fund, became recipients.

In May 1942 Major P.S. Wakefield and the men of 'D' Company, 9th (Loughborough) Battalion, handed over a cheque for £214 12s and 6d (£6,640) at Loughborough Town Hall to the Leicestershire POW Comforts Fund. It was stated the money would be used 'to send out a monthly parcel of tobacco and cigarettes, value 10s, addressed personally to each of the 821 Leicestershire POWs, as well as looking after their relatives'.[532]

Comrades in Arms

Maurice Woodward, formerly a Private in the Snibston Colliery Platoon, 5th (Belvoir) Battalion, later recalled, 'For entertainment in those days, you always captured the nearest pub with a piano, such as the Angel at Coleorton, Robin Hood and Station Inn at Swannington or the Waggon and Horses at Coalville, and a good old-fashioned sing-song was sure to follow. I might add that wherever we went, the locals were always very friendly. After a good night, and in spite of everything, everyone went home happy.'[533]

CHAPTER 7:

UNIFORMS, INSIGNIA AND EQUIPMENT

The Home Guards' appearance changed drastically in the space of four years. Starting with nothing but the civvy clothes they first paraded in, the Home Guard gradually developed into a fully-uniformed force with its own kit and insignia. A good idea of the local chronology and the scale of uniform and insignia issued can be gathered from the records of the 1st (North Leicester) Battalion.[534]

Uniform

Although Eden announced in his inaugural speech LDVs 'will receive a uniform', he did not say when. Uniforms were needed for more than just prestige: Nazi radio announced anyone resisting the German army out of uniform would be treated as *franc-tireurs* and summarily executed. It was announced as a stopgap that volunteers would receive an 'LDV' armlet, but, again, not when. In Leicestershire, as a stopgap for the stopgap armlet, locally designed and produced printed 'LDV' armlets were issued. It was not until 7 July 1940 that the official printed 'LDV' armlets arrived.[535]

Locally-produced Leicester pattern 'LDV' armlet.

Horace Gamble's official LDV armlet. (Horace Gamble)

Records suggest the first, if very limited, items of uniform to arrive locally were '4 suits of denim', which reached the 1st (LDV) Battalion in early June 1940.[536] These two-piece khaki denim suits had originally been issued to the army as overalls for dirty work. In LDV service, they became first-line uniforms worn over civilian clothes and were a temporary expediency. They were too thin for winter wear and it was joked they only came in 'too' sizes – 'too large or too small',[537] as an article recalled in the December 1940 issue of *Stand-Easy*, the magazine of 'B' Company, 9th (Loughborough) Battalion:

'Do you remember it? June 3rd and the subsequent days when our brand new platoons commenced on their tours of duty. Remember assembling at the rear of the Town Hall, and descending beneath the stage to array ourselves in "uniforms". And what did we look like when we eventually emerged? A perfect fit – well, perhaps. Size six men in size three uniforms, and vice versa, and one particular late-comer, of about size two, found only a size eight uniform left. Was he daunted? Not he! With the aid of pieces of string to take up the slack in various parts of his anatomy – and a permanent turn-up about a foot deep in his trousers – he duly fell in for duty. How proudly we marched down the Market Place, to the accompaniment of loud and undisguised "raspberries" from small, and very rude, boys and heartfelt prayers from other members of the populace thanking heaven we still had a Navy.'[538]

On 9 August 1940 the battalion received its first limited issue of greatcoats.[539] These thick, woollen standard army 1939 pattern greatcoats were very warm, perfect for lonely sentry duty on a cold winter's night, although they became a deadweight when rain-soaked.

Further issue of greatcoats was curtailed, with all new stocks issued to the regenerating army. As yet another stopgap, a strange expedient was introduced: a sleeveless cape, similar to a poncho. The 1st Battalion received stocks on 8 January 1941.[540] Instantly unpopular, they were awkward and viewed as a poor second. The capes were only withdrawn when the supply of greatcoats improved.

Following the name change to 'Home Guard' at the end of July, it would be a full month before 'Home Guard' armlets were

Official Home Guard armlet.

Official Home Guard GPO armlet.

received on 20 August 1940.[541] Post Office platoons were also issued with this armlet, but with two, overprinted, red, circled 'GPO' logos.

It was not until 5 September 1940 that the battalion received its first issue of 1,400 pairs of 1938 pattern army boots. On 26 September 425 pairs of brown leather anklets followed. Officers were issued with khaki webbing anklets.

The following day, the battalion received its first issue of 156 battledress suits.[542] This initial issue was either first pattern standard battledress, known officially in army-speak as 'Blouse and Trousers, Battledress, Serge,' which had pocket flaps and covered brass buttons. The other issue was the improved 1940 pattern. From mid-1942, some Home Guards were issued with a cheaper austerity pattern battledress. Fortunately for their prestige and warmth, few sets were issued.

Officers could wear their pre-war service uniforms, which they considered smarter, but had to wear Home Guard insignia. Later in the war, most officers wore battledress, although some had them privately tailored. A Leicestershire platoon photo shows an officer wearing riding breeches (Bedford cord pantaloons) and riding boots, apparently to look more 'officerly'. However, one platoon member remembered 'he'd never been on a bloody 'orse in his life!'

The standard headgear worn by all ranks, including many officers, was the Field Service Cap, also known as a forage cap, with the county's cap badge worn on the front left. Senior officers wore Regular Army peaked service caps. The only exception to this rule seems to have been Home Guard bands, who, from late 1943, wore 'flat hats' (peaked service caps)[543] with a white lanyard around their left shoulder.

Steel helmets do not appear to have reached either county in any great number until 1941. These Mk IIc helmets were of an inferior grade, rejected as sub-standard for Regular use but suitable for the Home Guard!

Due to material shortages, when young Home Guards were called-up, several recall they had to report to their reception stations in their Home Guard uniforms, as former Oakham Home Guard Eric Smith remembers:

'When I joined the RASC in 1943, I was told to report to Maryhill Barracks, Glasgow. I was told to take my Home Guard uniform, respirator and tin hat. When I got there, all I did was take off my Home Guard badges and replace them with RASC badges.'[544]

Cloth Insignia

The first attempt at some sort of shoulder title was in late 1940, when a rectangular 'Home Guard' patch was worn on the right arm of the greatcoat. A later photograph from March 1941 shows a Leicester Home Guard wearing commercially-available slip-on 'HG' shoulder titles on his shoulder straps. However, it would take over a year before the Home Guard received their first official shoulder titles. Major P.S. Wakefield records:

'Thursday 9:1:41. General Eastwood, Director General of the Home Guard, addressed a meeting of Loughborough Group officers at the Town Hall today. He was passing through the country and we were lucky to get a few words on equipment, training and duties from the very highest authority. A minor but very well received piece of news was that our Home Guard armlets, an outward and very visible sign of our irregular status, are to be withdrawn, he didn't say how soon, and we are to wear shoulder badges "HOME GUARD" like those worn by the Grenadier Guards.'[545]

Home Guard slip-on shoulder strap title.

Local records show 'Home Guard' shoulder titles were finally introduced on 16 June 1941.[546] Battalion titles had been discussed in local TA discussions with the WO back in August 1940, but with no outcome.[547] The 1st Battalion received their 'LEI 1' county and battalion flashes on 29 August 1941,[548] and the 9th (Loughborough) Battalion a month later.[549] The title

'HOME GUARD' was printed in white, while the county and battalion titles were dark blue print, both on a khaki cloth background.

Printed shoulder insignia for the 1st (North Leicester) Leicestershire Home Guard, issued from July 1941 to December 1944.

It has been disputed for years by historians and collectors alike whether the Rutland Home Guard actually wore any county and battalion designations, as they had their own county cap badge. Col. Ogilvy-Dalgleish makes no mention, but WO orders from 1943 state Rutland were given the county designation 'RU', but this insignia has proved extremely elusive.[550] However, company photographs and local correspondence reveal that unlike Leicestershire, where the wearing of county titles was compulsory, not all Rutland Home Guards wore them. Photographs show generally that the titles 'RU 1' (which sounds like a question from a Dick Emery sketch!) were worn in Rutland – the '1' signifying the first (and only) battalion – worn below the 'RU' as standard. However, a snapshot also shows a Home Guard wearing them the other way round, with the '1' above 'RU'.

Rutland Home Guard shoulder insignia.

No evidence has been found suggesting any additional command, formation, county, zone, sector or unit signs were worn.

At first, the Home Guard were viewed by the WO as armed civilians rather than a branch of the army. In the meantime, a series of 'appointments' were made, with their own rank structure and insignia. The 1st (North Leicester) Battalion received these rank insignia on 2 November 1940. Senior rank markings consisted of thin blue cloth bars worn on both shoulder straps:

> Battalion Commander: 3 bars
> Company Commander: 2 bars (2 i/c half a bar less than his CO)
> Platoon Commander: 1 bar
> Section Commander: three chevrons (sergeant)
> Squad Commander: two chevrons (corporal) [551]
> Junior ranks (NCOs) wore Regular chevrons on their left upper arm.

Standard army rank insignia was introduced to the force with the first appointment of officers and NCOs in February 1941.

From April 1941, Home Guards had to meet a level of military skill, for which they were awarded a Proficiency badge. This was a small red cloth diamond, worn on the lower-right battledress forearm, introduced locally from September 1941.

As a mark of service, from February 1944 the Home Guard and CD services were awarded service chevrons. For each year of service, a small red chevron was worn on the lower-right arm. This positioning clashed with the proficiency badge, and so the latter was moved to the lower-left arm.

Other insignia observed on local Home Guards in photographs include:

From 1941, post office workers in the mobile part of the 13th (GPO) Battalion wore a half-white/half-blue diamond badge on their upper arms, below the 'LE1 13' titles. These were the colours of the Royal Corps of Signals. Signal sections wore a blue and white crossed flags badge on the left forearm of their battledress.

Nationally, from August 1943 Auxiliary Bomb Disposal Squads wore a circular red badge with a pair of yellow crossed German bombs, on their right forearm. However, it has not been possible to observe this badge on existing photographs of Leicestershire ABDS.

Printed insignia of the Home Guard Auxiliary Bomb Disposal Squads. (Roger Miles)

Both Leicester's Light and Heavy Anti-Aircraft Units wore the first pattern AA Command sign on their shoulders. This was a convex black bow on a red square. This insignia also acted as an AA proficiency badge. LAA crews wore the badge below their local battalion title.

Leicestershire regiment cap badge.

Cap Badges

The Home Guard were affiliated to local regiments from 3 August 1940.[552] At first, the official WO list of October 1940 stated both the Leicestershire and Rutland Home Guard would wear the tiger cap badge of the Leicestershire Regiment.[553] However, for fiercely independent Rutland, wearing the county badge of its big neighbour was viewed almost as treachery, so they sought their own alternative, as Col. Ogilvy-Dalgleish explained:

'The Bn was, officially, the 1st Rutland Bn of the Rutland Home Guard (not the Leicestershire or any other HG) and had its own County Commandant…

I felt it was up to me to try and preserve intact Rutland's identity in its Home Guard, as it had been entrusted to me.

This matter of a badge may seem trivial, but such things can count for much, especially in a voluntary unpaid force: men take a pride in their county and its emblem and the men of Rutland were no exception to the rule.

Rutland Home Guard cap badge.

In the Military sphere the horse-shoe badge has long been recognised as the emblem of the county: the 58th Foot became the Rutlandshire Regiment in 1779 and wore the badge for over 100 years in the form of a horseshoe, points down, bearing the words "The Rutlandshire Regiment"… In the 1914–18 War, the Rutland Coy of the Home Defence Volunteers [sic] wore a horseshoe, points down, bearing the word "Rutland". One of these was given to me and I obtained permission from the Military Authority to use this badge as the Cap badge for the Rutland Bn HG.

The Leicestershire and Rutland Territorial Association, of which I was an ex-officio member, also gave unanimous approval at one of their meetings to my proposal that the Rutland Bn should use the county's badge…

There may be many of these badges about, retained by members of the 1940 Rutland Bn HG when it stood down in 1944; they have a certain interest through being, probably, the last appearance of the Rutland County badge in association with a Rutland Military Unit…'[554]

Home Guards were also authorised to wear regimental insignia on their steel helmets. A photograph taken at Glen Parva ITC in 1942 shows a Home Guard wearing a Tigers cap badge welded to his helmet. Two surviving steel helmets from Rutland bear gold transfers of the battalion's horseshoe insignia.

Women Home Guard Auxiliary's plastic badge.

From mid-1943 women Home Guard Auxiliaries were issued with a pin-backed lapel badge. Made of bronze-coloured plastic due to the metal shortage, the badge was a circular wreath surrounding the initials 'HG'. Auxiliaries were not officially issued with any uniform and this rather nondescript badge represents the Home Guard 'top brass' attitude towards women in the force.

The Shepshed LDV Club brass lapel badge was designed by Commander J. Nichol. It shows two crossed bayoneted rifles with a skull in a German helmet, impaled on a bayonet! This one is numbered '227' on the back.

Unofficial private purchase badges were also worn by some Leicestershire Home Guards. The earliest known badge, dating from summer 1940, is of the Shepshed LDV company. This lapel badge has the words 'Shepshed LDV Club', with a beheaded helmeted skull of a German soldier stuck on a bayonet: surely more a statement of warrior intent as opposed to any actuality! Badges were made by Usher of Birmingham and individually numbered on the back. Former Hathern Home Guard Bill Tollington recalls the origins of this badge:

'When the Home Guard started, it was the Hathern and Shepshed LDV. John Nichol, a Scotsman who wore a kilt, had a hosiery factory at Shepshed,

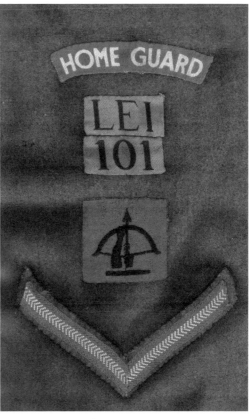

Far left: Shoulder insignia of Lt Noel H.S. Symington of 7th (Market Harborough) Battalion. (Roger Miles)

Left: Home Guard insignia of the 101st Battalion Leicester Anti-Aircraft Rocket Battery, which was based on Victoria Park, Leicester. Lance Corporal Derrick Malyon kept this battledress jacket sleeve as a souvenir.
(Derrick Malyon)

was the headman. He had special badges made from brass, because at first they had no uniform. It was worn on the ordinary suit in the buttonhole.'[555]

The second local lapel badge has the words 'Home Guard' on a blue enamel rectangle with a brass tiger of the Leicestershire Regiment above. This badge was probably distributed via the local TA to encourage *esprit de corps*.[556] Other county examples exist, so a version may have been made with the Rutland horseshoe on.

A private-purchase stirling silver lapel badge with the words '1st Leicester HG' and 'Hindoostan' also exists, as does a brass version. After Stand Down, another version with the initials 'O.C.A.' added to the scroll was issued to members of the battalion's Old Comrade's Association.

Far left: Commercially-produced Leicestershire Home Guard enamel lapel badge.

Middle: Enamel Home Guard lapel badge, worn by Quorn Home Guard Allan Hopcroft.

Left: Brass lapel badge of the 1st (North Leicester) Battalion Leicestershire Home Guard.

CHAPTER 8:

THE TIGERS' TEETH:
WEAPONS OF THE HOME GUARD

The Home Guard's armoury was largely second-hand, World War One vintage, Regular Army 'hand-me-downs' rejected for front-line use. However, by Stand Down the force had a large variety of weapons at its disposal.[557] Practically all Home Guard weapons had some sort of flaw, from design faults to quality defects. New weaponry continued to be issued even after the threat of invasion had receded, as much to appease the men and maintain their morale as for active usage. The following chapter only contains details of weapons *known* to have been issued to the Leicestershire and Rutland Home Guard: others may have been used, but have not been recorded.[558]

Small Arms

War Office issued single slug shotgun cartridge and shot.

12-bore Shotguns: From the start, 12-bore shotguns were used to supplement the LDV's lack of rifles. Former Home Guard Dick Tinsley remembered, in the beginning, Hoby Platoon just had 22 shotguns and two .22 sporting rifles. Their first task was to get the shotguns proved at the Birmingham Proof House to make sure they were safe to use with BB (Ball Bearing) shot or Ball shot. BB was the size of a small pea, with 15 in each cartridge, and normally used for shooting geese. Of the 22 guns submitted only one was good enough to use ball shot, the rest passed for BB.[559]

Conventional shot had a short killing range with little stopping power, so the WO issued a special cartridge only containing a single solid ball, to all intents, returning the shotgun to the days of the musket. Keyham Home Guard Rowles Harrison remembered the shot 'proved very powerful and when tested at thirty yards would penetrate a two-inch wooden plank'.[560] Col. Ogilvy-Dalgleish noted the shot 'would have been useful at short range or at night, the single ball having a drop of only about 6 inches from point of aim at 80 yards'.[561] This fearsome ammunition would have caused horrendous injuries; however, it was inaccurate and had a tendency to wear gun barrels quickly, but the LDV had no choice. In 1940 Jim Tailby was a Volunteer in Dunton Bassett platoon.

'We assembled at the HQ at Dunton and our sergeant said "Today, I'm going to take a squad and we are going to attack the HQ from the south and it's up to you to defend it." I was issued with a shotgun. We had shotgun blanks, but none for the rifles. The sergeant set off with his men and we went to the top field knowing they would attack from there. This person came through the hedge and didn't see me. I was only about 10 yards away from him and I put my gun up and shot. The wad hit him in the chest and he grabbed his chest and was frightened and so was I – I thought I'd fired a real one. He wasn't hurt too bad, but I learned my lesson.'[562]

Sporting rifles: In addition to shotguns, a request was made to the public for sporting weapons that would now be pitted against an altogether different type of 'game' that could fight back.

.303 P14 / .300 P17 Rifles: The .300 M1917 or P17, made by the Springfield, Remington and Eddystone companies, was the standard World War One US Army rifle. Stored in grease and crated between the wars, in the desperate summer of 1940 the US sold 615,000 P17s to Britain, with a further shipment of 119,000 in 1941, together with a supply of 138 million rounds of .300 ammunition.[563] Confusingly, before the war the Americans had also supplied the British with stocks of a .303 version of the rifle called the P14. The minutes of the Leicestershire and Rutland TA recorded:

Home Guards of the 2nd (South Leicester) Battalion, armed with P17 rifles, storm a farmyard, possibly during Exercise LEICESTER, Sunday 5 July 1942.

'The arrival of large numbers of the new American rifles presented some difficulties. They came, in most cases, full of grease which had to be cleaned out before issue. There were differences in construction and working from our service rifles which had to be explained and taught. To help with this, on 16 September [1940] a Mobile Armourer's Unit under the charge of Armourer Sergeant Fenwick was attached to us for one month...The unit went all around the country and carried out their duties with zeal and efficiency. After visits to Northamptonshire and Rutland, they are coming back to us for another month.'[564]

Due to the differences in size between the .300 and .303 cartridge, it was important to use the correct cartridge otherwise it could result in a misfire and injure the firer, so a distinguishing red band was painted on the P17,[565] although, as Col. Ogilvy-Dalgleish noted, 'The bands had to be frequently renewed to avoid accidents.'[566]

In Rutland, the first quota of 135 P14s arrived at Oakham Police Station 'towards the end of May' [1940],[567] later consolidated by 85 Canadian Ross rifles and 30 12-bore shotguns with ball ammunition. In November 1940 Rutland's Ross rifles were withdrawn and replaced by 610 P17 American Springfield rifles with bayonets.[568] Heavy, cumbersome and poorly balanced, the P14 and P17 were inferior to the .303 SMLE Lee-Enfield, but their solid accuracy made them good for sniping and accurate shooting. The P17 became the standard Home Guard rifle.

Home Guards generally took their rifles home with them. On patrol they were only issued a clip of five rounds. As Dunton Bassett Home Guard Jim Tailby noted wryly, 'There obviously wasn't going to be many Germans'![569]

.303 Canadian Ross Rifle: The Rutland Home Guard were issued with 85 Canadian Ross rifles. However, they only lasted six months before being replaced by P17s. The already confusing difference in P14/P17 ammunition was further complicated by the arrival of the Ross, which fired a different cartridge to either the British .303 or the US .300. The Ross rifle had been withdrawn during World War One due to its design faults. It was not popular as its mechanism tended to jam easily and could be damaged by dirt.

Bayonets: Bayonets were issued in September 1940, almost a month after the Home Guard received their rifles.[570] They were of the large World War One sword type. To distinguish the different fitting P17 bayonet from the P14 type, a double groove was etched in the wooden handle. Bayonet fighting was an integral part of Home Guard training. Wisely, bayonets were generally not used on manoeuvres.

.32/.38/.455 Revolvers: Home Guard officers were issued with service revolvers as a sidearm. At first, they were issued with the large .455 Webley Service revolver. This used a Victorian calibre bullet that had hideous stopping power. The cumbersome .455 had such a powerful kick, few firers could obtain accuracy. It was issued with its World War One brown leather holster and Sam Browne belt.[571] The .455 was superseded by the smaller, army .38 Webley and .32 Colt pistols, which, though more manageable, had less stopping power. They were issued with a webbing belt and holster.

Pikes: Despite the mythological status of this infamous Home Guard weapon, no records have been found indicating its issue to local Home Guards, no doubt much to their relief.

Captain H.R. Allen, Leicester Sector Home Guard Weapon Training officer, firing Leicestershire's first Thompson sub-machine gun at Kibworth Range, winter 1940. (Captain Bob Allen)

A corporal of the 3rd (West Leicester) Battalion Leicestershire Home Guard, armed with a Mk II Sten gun, takes cover during the attack on Leicester during Exercise LEICESTER, Sunday 5 July 1942.

A corporal of the Leicestershire Home Guard aims a stripped Lewis machine gun while his No.2/Loader directs the fire, summer 1941.

Sub, Light and Medium Machine Guns

.45 Thompson Sub-Machine Gun: The US M1928M1 Thompson was the first sub-machine gun to be issued to the Home Guard. Made infamous by 1930s US gangsters, Thompson SMGs arrived in late summer 1940, crated in grease. Captain Bob Allen, whose late father Captain Henry Allen was Leicester Sector Home Guard Weapon Training and Intelligence Officer, remembers as an eight-year-old sitting in his father's garage degreasing the county's first Thompsons. The Thompson was a very popular weapon with a large .45 cartridge and a rapid rate of fire of 650 rpm, meaning it could stop any attacker. Its large drum magazine could hold 100 rounds. While invasion threatened, issue was prioritised to the Home Guard who received limited numbers. Its effectiveness and the slackening of the invasion threat meant, with much regret, within a year Thompsons were given to the new Commando units.

9mm Sten Sub-Machine Gun: Much to the Home Guard's displeasure, the Thompson SMG was replaced by the cruder 9mm Sten machine carbine, better known as the Sten gun. Mass produced by various companies including the toy manufacturers Lines Brothers, for 30 shillings each, it consisted of only six components, making it easy to strip, clean and reassemble. Cheap and ugly looking, the Mark 1 had wooden grips and no safety catch: if dropped, it had a nasty tendency to fire off the full magazine. The Sten also had a short range, meaning its user had to engage the enemy at close quarters. Nonetheless, it had a rapid rate of fire and was useful for urban warfare. Its production ran into six different versions but the Leicestershire and Rutland Home Guard were only issued with the first three Marks, which were introduced locally from around 1942 onwards.[572] At the end of the war, the Leicestershire

and Rutland Home Guard returned 5,947 Sten guns.[573] Ibstock Home Guard Albert Squires recalls an unofficial use for the Sten gun:

'Later a scheme came into operation whereby ex-coal miners in the Forces could get a "Class B" release to go back in the mines, but only on condition they joined the local Home Guard units. One such return member of our Unit I remembers being issued with a Sten sub-machine gun. He promptly arranged with an army pal coming home on leave to bring ammunition with him which fitted the Sten gun. This pair then proceeded to go rabbit hunting! But the only result was that the poor rabbits were shot to pieces and so were quite uneatable!'[574]

.300/.303 Lewis Light Machine Gun: Many older Home Guards would have recognised the Lewis gun as a leftover from World War One. By the late 1930s it was regarded as obsolescent, but the lack of weaponry after Dunkirk gave it a new lease of life. It was issued to the Home Guard in two versions, the first being the standard heavier type, with a 47-round drum magazine and a full-length radiator jacket, giving the impression the weapon had a gaping muzzle. The second more widely-issued type, sometimes called the Savage, was the slimmer, stripped American .300 version, that had been used on aircraft in World War One.

Home Guards of the 3rd (West Leicester) Battalion armed with a Lewis machine gun 'on alert for approaching "enemy" planes' at Braunstone crossroads during Exercise LEICESTER, Sunday 5 July 1942.

It had a crude metal bipod, a 97-round drum magazine plus a spade grip. As with most of the Home Guard's first proper weaponry, most Lewis guns were shipped over from America. The .300 Lewis gun was issued locally from September 1940 and became the two counties' standard light machine gun.

Although some Home Guards were instructed in the use of the .303 Bren light machine gun, it also does not appear to have been issued locally – its efficiency making it a front line Regular Army weapon.

.300 M1918 Marlin Medium Machine Gun: The American Marlin machine gun was used during World War One in aircraft and tanks. It was reused in 1940 and some 17,000 sent across the Atlantic. However, they used the non-standard .300 cartridge, so were off-loaded on the Home Guard. Fed with a 250 round belt and mounted on an improvised mounting, the Marlin was issued in limited numbers making it practically forgotten today.

.303 Vickers 'K' Light Machine Gun: First used in pre-war biplanes, this light machine gun was similar in appearance to the stripped .300 Lewis light machine gun, as it also had a flat 96-round drum magazine and spade grip. With the wartime weapons shortage, it gained new life in the AA defence role. In Leicestershire, it is known to have been used by the Home Guard, mounted in pairs, to defend Rearsby Aerodrome's Taylorcraft aircraft factory.[575]

.303 Hotchkiss MLE Light Machine Gun: This antiquated French weapon is regarded as the first true light machine gun. Originally chambered for the French .65 round, during World War One it was rechambered to fire 30-round metal strips of .303 rounds in the first British tanks. Not one of the best light machine guns, it was quite a rarity among Home Guard units. However, a handful were issued with tripods to the 10th (Charnwood) Battalion, including Beaumanor Hall's Home Guard platoon.[576]

.303 Vickers Medium Machine Gun: Perhaps the most famous machine gun of World War One, the heavyweight, tripod-mounted, belt-fed and water-cooled .303 Vickers, with its corrugated barrel jacket, was a highly-efficient, devastating support weapon, able to lay down large amounts of fire for up to eight hours non-stop. Allan Hopcraft of Quorn Home Guard remembers his unit was issued with the Vickers.[577] Some units received training on the Vickers,[578] but very few units received it, as they were needed by the Regular Army.

.300 Browning Medium Machine Gun: Similar in appearance to the famous British Vickers medium machine gun, the M1917A1 Browning was an American sustained fire weapon, mounted on a tripod.

It had a heavy rate of fire, firing up to 520 rounds of belt-fed .300 ammunition per minute. Like the British Vickers, the gun was liquid-cooled with a water jacket around the barrel, fed by a hose from a can. This cooling system enabled the weapon to be fired for long periods. After Dunkirk, 10,000 Brownings arrived from America, starting to appear in Leicestershire Home Guard inventories from mid-1941.[579]

Hand Grenades:[580]

'Molotov Cocktail' (petrol bomb): The 'Molotov Cocktail' was the Home Guard's first desperate answer to the tank threat. Copied from the crude weapon used in the Spanish Civil War and the Russo-Finnish War, it was mockingly named after the Soviet Foreign Minister Vyacheslav Molotov. Col. Ogilvy-Dalgleish noted the crudity of the 'Molotoff' and, with help, improved the weapon.

'…there was a demonstration at the Remount Depot, Melton Mowbray, of methods of dealing with tanks by means of so called "Molotoff Cocktails." These were whisky-sized bottles filled with a mixture of Tar Naptha and Petrol (there were two formulae) to which was attached a fuse of inflammable material; this was lighted and the bottle thrown at the tank over which the liquid, if successfully ignited, would spread, being added to by further thrown bottles, thus rendering the tank untenable.

I took A.C. Cavell, Head of the Science Dept. at Uppingham School, to the demonstration, he was our chemistry and gas expert and he took endless trouble over these rather primitive weapons. Eight hundred empty bottles were collected in the county and taken to Uppingham where Cavell undertook the tedious job of filling them with the mixture as ordered, from Government issue. We carried out trials with these "Molotoff Cocktails" at Oakham and Uppingham, their weakest point was that the act of hurling the bottle violently through the air was apt to blow out a fuse soaked in petrol; once a bottle ignited itself on impact with a target, the fire could easily be fed by others. Dr Purdy solved this problem by soaking a fuse of his own design in ether, which, when lit, would not blow out in flight.'[581]

Despite these improvements, the Molotov Cocktail was still a crude weapon that could be more dangerous to the thrower than the target. An improved official version was developed called the No. 76 SIP Grenade (see below).

Sectioned Home Guard No.36 Mills training grenade. (Ron Bodicoat)

No. 36M Mills Bomb: Widely used in World War One, this distinctive 'pineapple' shaped grenade was the most common grenade in the Home Guard armoury. The bomb operated by pulling out the pin and throwing the grenade, which, in turn, freed the spring-loaded lever and striker, actuating a chemical fuse which detonated the high-explosive filling. There were four-second and seven-second fuses: rather sensibly, the local Home Guard were issued with the latter![582] The grenade had a greater killing range than many men were able to throw, meaning the thrower had to take cover immediately!

No. 68 Rifle Grenade: This flat-headed, fin-stabilised anti-tank grenade was fired from either the E-Y or Northover Projector. It was the first British weapon to use a shaped-charge. The head of the grenade contained a cone-shaped cavity which focused the explosive gases into a concentrated jet, giving greater armour penetration up to 30mm. This was sufficient against tanks in 1941; however, German armour outgrew the grenade's potency, which was limited by the width of the E-Y projector cup or the Northover's barrel. The impact fuse was also questionable, sometimes exploding prematurely or not at all. The grenade was declared obsolete by mid-1942, but remained in Home Guard service.

No. 69 Bakelite Grenade: This blast/shock grenade was mainly for house-clearing, to be followed by small arms fire. Due to its small, black, Bakelite barrel-shape, some were slow to realise it was not a toy but a dangerous grenade and it took a few fatal accidents to realise its lethality. Armed with a No. 247 all-ways percussion fuse, the thrower had to unscrew the cap, which revealed a length of weighted fabric tape, to be grasped as the grenade was thrown. Throwing the grenade pulled the safety pin from the fuse, leaving it free to detonate on landing. It was issued in limited quantities.

No. 73 Grenade ('Thermos' or 'Woolworths' Bomb): This anti-tank grenade, issued from 1941,[583] relied solely on its powerful explosive, so was of little use against well-armoured vehicles and was often used as a demolition charge instead. Dubbed the 'Thermos' grenade due to its cylindrical body and screw-top impact fuse, it was later nicknamed the 'Woolworth' grenade, as it was basically just a large can stuffed with explosive. At 9.5 inches and weighing a hefty 4lb, unless the thrower was strong this unaerodynamic grenade could only be tossed a short distance, endangering the thrower almost as much as the enemy. However, it did make a satisfyingly-loud bang.[584] Production ceased by 1943 and the grenade was consigned to storage.[585]

No. 74 ST (Sticky Type) Grenade ('Sticky Bomb'): This distinctive, toffee-apple shaped anti-tank grenade was issued locally from late 1941.[586] The head of the grenade was made of glass or bakelite and contained 20oz of jellified nitro-glycerine explosive. It was covered in a sticky birdlime adhesive woollen sock, protected when not in use by a hinged metal globe. When used, the safety pin was

White painted No.68 anti-tank training grenade.

Defending Home Guards crouch behind Coalville War Memorial during Exercise PARTRIDGE, Sunday 12 October 1942. The front two Home Guards are holding wooden dummy training versions of No.74ST 'Sticky bomb' anti-tank grenade.

removed from the throwing handle causing the firing lever to fly off and release the surrounding metal covers. The thrower then had five seconds to smash the glass globe against a tank, which would be held in position by the sticky coating – hopefully not to the thrower. The grenade had difficulty in sticking to muddy surfaces but it was powerful enough to penetrate thinner armour, although it often blasted the handle back at the thrower. The grenade was eventually rejected for Regular Army use as the nitro-glycerine filling became unstable, but it stayed in Home Guard service.

No. 75 Hawkins Anti-Tank Grenade/Mine: Looking more like a screw-top turps can, the No. 75 was really more of an anti-tank mine designed to blow off tank tracks than a grenade, although it could be thrown. It was mainly laid as a mine, often together with several others on a cord as a 'necklace' across roads. It operated with a crusher fuse and its 1kg charge was powerful enough to blow a track off any German tank up to Mk IV standard. In 1943 it was listed for use by local Home Guard Mobile Sections.[587]

No. 76 SIP (Self-Igniting Phosphorous) Grenade / AW (Albright and Wilson) Bomb: A slightly more advanced version of the Molotov Cocktail, this fragile glass grenade had to be handled carefully. Mass-produced by Albright and Wilson Ltd of Oldbury, it was called the A and W Bomb but was later renamed the No. 76 SIP grenade. Intended for use as an anti-tank or anti-personnel weapon, it resembled a clear continental beer bottle, filled with a highly inflammable mixture of phosphorous, naphtha or benzene, together with a slice of rubber to stick the contents to its target. The contents were sealed with a metal crown cap. Two versions were issued: a red-capped type for throwing and a green-capped type for launching from the Northover Projector. Col. Ogilvy-Dalgleish was impressed with the bomb's improvements over the Molotov Cocktail, particularly its fierce incendiary nature:

'A much better weapon, of the same type, the A.W. bomb was issued in August [1940]; this was a ready-filled bottle containing a mixture, including phosphorous, which ignited automatically when the bottle broke on the target and also made dense smoke; the tank could therefore be blinded as well as hotted up with the A.W…We tried these on the Oakham range and found them most effective, the fires they started could not be extinguished, but had to burn themselves out, in time.'[588]

As the phosphorous contents ignited on exposure to air, SIP grenades had to be stored carefully in crates. The Commander of Medbourne platoon, Mr Brooks, stored them submerged in his garden pond. At the war's end, it was found the crown caps had almost corroded away, leaving the grenades in a highly dangerous state.[589]

E-Y Projector/Cup Discharger: Invented in World War One and named 'E-Y' after its inventor Edgar Yule, (not 'EmergencY' as sometimes suggested),[590] this simple 2.5 inch calibre grenade launcher could be attached to any P14 or P17 rifle with the aid of an adapter. A special bulletless ballistite cartridge was used to fire the grenade. With the aid of a special sight, it could fire a No. 36 grenade with a baseplate or a No. 68 grenade up to a range of 200 yards. In Home Guard usage from 1941 onwards, the E-Y weapon was a useful adaptation, although it had an unpredictable nature, with fatalities in other counties when the grenade exploded prematurely in the discharger.

Home Guards of the 9th (Loughborough) Battalion defend a narrow lane on the outskirts of Loughborough, during Exercise PARTRIDGE, Sunday 11 October 1942. The Home Guard in the foreground is armed with a magazine-less Sten sub-machine gun, while his colleague standing to his right brandishes an E-Y grenade launcher.

Flame Weapons and Static Weapons

Surprisingly, in 1940 Britain still had large petroleum reserves. The Petroleum Warfare Department was set up to make use of them. The local Home Guard were issued with two of the PWD's inventions:

Harvey Flame-Thrower: Officially known in the broken English of army terminology as the 'Flame-Thrower, Transportable, No. 1 Mk 1', but more commonly the Home Guard or Harvey Flame-Thrower. Despite its transportable name, it could only be moved on a two-wheel frame, similar to a porter's barrow. It comprised a 45-gallon oil drum, a hand pump, 30ft of hose and a flame projector on a monopod. It would be set up at roadblocks, the crew manning the tank and pump behind cover, while the projector was hidden in the enemy's path. Fuel would be pumped down the hose and ignited by a SIP grenade or Very pistol.[591] Created in the desperate days of 1940, it was cumbersome and not greatly liked. Its effective range was only 15 yards and it only had enough fuel for 12 seconds fire, but it worked. Only 250 kits were made, Leicestershire being one of the few counties to receive it. The Harvey Flame-Thrower was demonstrated to the 1st (North Leicester) Battalion at Glen Parva in March 1941[592] but was withdrawn from local units six months later,[593] with the arrival of the slightly more manageable spigot mortar, and quietly put into storage until the end of the war.

Flame Fougasse: This devastating flame-trap weapon was the most powerful device in the Home Guard armoury. First used in the 18th century, it had changed little. The Flame Fougasse, or Petroleum Warfare Installation, as at least one local unit called it, was a set of six 45-gallon oil drums filled with a mixture of petrol and gas oil. This ambush weapon was buried in embankments alongside roads, where they narrowed or dipped to form a trap, or in front of roadblocks. Home Guard operators fired the fougasse by exploding a No. 76 SIP grenade on the front of the barrel. Later fougasses were fired electrically, as at Dunton Bassett, where 'a steel tube packed with gun cotton and an electrical detonator powered by a seven-volt battery was placed against each barrel. The cables from the detonators were taken back into the field. Drums could be exploded individually,'[594] spewing a huge ball of fire up to 30-yards, instantly engulfing and incinerating anything in their path. The flames burned for up to five minutes. Brutal in its efficacy, its use would have drawn an equally brutal response had the Germans captured the operators or any civilians unfortunate enough to be nearby. Fougasses were emplaced throughout Leicestershire, including:

- near the Grand Union Canal crossing by Kilby Bridge
- where the A6 crosses the LNER line, just south of Loughborough
- on the A6 Derby Road, just north of Hathern, after the King's Arms pub
- on the A6006, against the county bridge at Zouch
- on the Woodhouse Road, just west of Quorn LNER Station
- west of Sileby, where Mountsorrel Lane crosses the Grand Union Canal
- on the Loughborough Road, midway between Mountsorrel and Rothley
- at the A426/B581 junction at Dunton Bassett
- and by the bridge on the B4114 between Croft and Narborough, where former corporal in No. 14 (Croft) Platoon, 3rd (West Leicester) Battalion Leslie Furnival remembers admonishing two women hunting for firewood, who were prodding the fougasse barrels with a stick as they attempted to remove the wooden sleepers supporting the barrels.[595]

An instruction was issued in August 1943 for all fougasses to be removed from the Leicestershire area.[596]

Hanworth Torpedo: Several local defence schemes refer to 'Hanworth Torpedoes'. Despite much research and consultation of military experts, I was unable to discover what this mysterious weapon was. So I was surprised to read in *Loopholes*, the journal of the Pillbox Study Group, a passing mention of the 'Hanworth Anti-Tank Torpedo and Flying Mine'.

Further investigation revealed the weapon was originally designed in 1940 by a 24-year-old Lt in the 5th Field Company RE, Second Viscount David Hanworth of Camberley, Surrey. Lt Hanworth had previously studied mechanical sciences at Trinity College, Cambridge. As well as inventing several other weapons, Lt Hanworth also designed pillbox camouflage schemes with art dealer Horace Buttery.

Lt Hanworth designed the weapon bearing his name after he was evacuated from Dunkirk. However, the first trial of the weapon was not a success and he shelved it. In early 1941 Lt Hanworth was posted to HQ North Midland Command, Nottingham, as second in command of 213 Field Company RE. Promoted to captain, Hanworth advised

2nd/Lt Viscount David Hanworth, inventor of the Hanworth anti-tank torpedo. (Lady Rosamund Hanworth)

Plans of the Hanworth Torpedo, which carried four Mk IV anti-tank mines on possibly the world's first skateboard. (Lady Rosamund Hanworth)

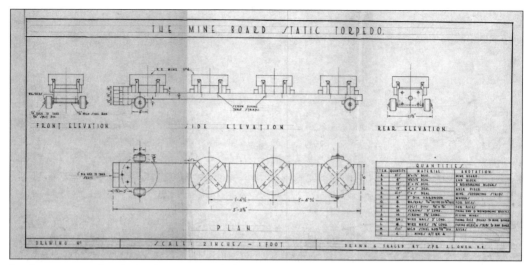

local Home Guard and Regular units on defence matters. During a chat, he told his superiors of his invention and the scheme was resurrected.

Captain Hanworth's invention was a roadside anti-tank ambush 'trap' weapon, the main operational part being a 'push-gun'. Its creation was heralded in the national press in June 1941 as 'Britain's secret anti-tank weapon,' although for security no details were given. GHQ Technical Notes indicate it entered army and Home Guard service in October 1941, although it seems the latter force made most use of it, perhaps because of the 'extreme simplicity' of the weapon's construction: a 3ft length by 1½in heavy gauge water pipe with a solid screw plug fitted at the base. This plug had a hole drilled to take the electrical leads that fired the ½oz gunpowder launching charge. The gun was fastened to its wooden base by three straps and the whole weapon was planted in the roadside. Sandbags and pickets were placed behind the weapon to absorb recoil.

The push gun fired two types of missile: a 'flying mine', basically a RE No.1 or a Mk IV anti-tank mine on a 2ft metal firing shaft and the second, an anti-tank 'torpedo' – it was this latter weapon that was employed in Leicestershire.

The 'torpedo' body was actually a wooden trolley – perhaps the world's first skateboard, complete with four small bevelled wooden wheels – carrying an anti-tank-mine, together with 10lb of explosive. A later, longer variation carried four anti-tank mines. The push gun's firing charge launched a 3ft by 1in metal firing shaft down the tube which struck a metal plate on the back of the 'torpedo's' trolley, projecting it across the road at about 45ft per second, the 'torpedo' detonating when the mine struck the tank's wheels. The 'torpedo' was only expected to travel 3ft, the distance between the roadside and the tank's wheels, although its maximum range on a smooth surface was 40ft. In tests against two 10ft lengths of 9in by 6in heavy tram rail hit from 20ft away, the rails were completely shattered, leaving a 3ft wide-crater and hurling a 4ft length of rail 40 yards and smaller lengths 80 yards!

The 'torpedoes' were emplaced in pairs at right angles. They were fired by a Home Guard about 150 yards directly behind the trap, with a tree or post in line on the other side of the road enabling the firer to align the tank with the 'torpedo'. He then pressed a battery-powered bell push button, just as the nose of the tank reached his line of sight.

The weapon was described as 'Deadly and invisible…almost childishly simple to make'. But the GHQ Technical notes warned when arming the anti-tank mine RE No. 1 'the lid must be correctly fitted…[or]…it may shear the striker mechanism, and thus detonate the mine' while still in the operator's hands. Also, because the simple wooden wheels on the 'torpedo's' trolley were not suspended, any bump in the road could cause the 'torpedo' to deviate. Home Guard operators were warned to flee after firing, as tests showed they were highly vulnerable once the enemy reacted.

Although blueprints were sent to other Commands, the Hanworth Torpedo was issued only to the Home Guard in the Northern Command, the area where Captain Hanworth was based. His widow, Lady Rosamund Hanworth, remembers 'My husband's letters to me during 1941 tell of his visits to various units to demonstrate it.'[597]

Hanworth's weapon was introduced at the same time as Lt-Col. Blacker's Spigot Mortar, and *Daily Telegraph* cuttings suggest there was competition between the two designs. Blacker's weapon was the favoured official design and, as a result, received greater funding, meaning it was better constructed and more capable than the Hanworth. However, as the newspaper stated:

'…an officer has invented a weapon for the same purpose. This, it is claimed, can be produced at half the cost of the official instrument [Blacker Bombard]. A demonstration of this unofficial weapon was recently attended by members of the Staff of Soviet Embassy and representatives of the Home Guard. It was learned at this demonstration that units of the Home Defence Force [sic] had favoured the unofficial weapon and had purchased it privately with a view to its adoption.'

Although authority was given for the manufacture of 30,000 Hanworths, the Blacker Bombard was issued in greater numbers, becoming the Home Guard's main anti-tank weapon. With Blacker's official backing and sheer weight of numbers, the Hanworth weapon eventually became overshadowed and, like the Flame Fougasse, was removed from local defence schemes by late 1943. Viscount Hanworth finished the war a major. Lady Hanworth remembers:

'David's name went forward for an MBE for inventing the thing, but he didn't get one. A civilian invented something similar after attending one of David's lectures and was awarded the MBE instead, although a letter from a patent agent acknowledges David's original concept. David was disappointed, but the government always encouraged civilians whereas the army were just "doing their job"!'[598]

Nonetheless, the existence of the Hanworth Anti-tank Torpedo and Flying Mine stands testimony to the ingenuity and hard work of a young Lieutenant who strove to provide the home forces with a viable anti-tank weapon at a time when there was little else.

Pipe Mine: Several villages had sub-surface, scaffold pipe mines, packed full of explosive. Similar to the Bangalore Torpedo, they were placed under approach roads to defended localities.[599] Elsewhere, in Essex, this weapon was called the McNaughton Torpedo or a 'Bosche Bump'.[600] However, the gelignite filling become unstable and by 1943 pipe mines were also removed.

Sub-Artillery / Special Weapons

Northover Projector: This grenade projector was privately designed by Home Guard Officer Major H. Northover, manufactured by the Bisley Clay Target and Selection Companies and locally under contract by the Leicester City Transport Department workshops. Feeble-looking, the Northover Projector resembled a length of drainpipe on legs and was also known as the 'Stove-pipe weapon'.[601] Issued from summer 1941 at one or two Northovers per platoon, it had a crew of three. It fired No. 36, 68 and 76 SIP grenades with the aid of a small firing cap and a black powder charge, up to 200yds. It was important not to mix up the green and red-capped SIP grenades, because the thinner latter type could shatter in the barrel on firing. Like all Home Guard weapons, it had its faults. Its tubular legs and cast-iron parts could crack if knocked and it gave off a

Leicester Home Guards man a Mk 1 Northover Projector while defending an obstructed bridge, 1941. The rather wilted camouflage appears to be more of a hindrance than help!

Home Guards of the 13th (25th GPO) Battalion train with a Spigot mortar, at Campbell Street Post Office, Leicester.

white cloud on firing, which obscured the target and gave away the projector's position.[602] John Greaves, then a Husbands Bosworth Home Guard, remembers the Northover Projector was considered 'more dangerous to the people using it. We never had the guts to fire it as we saw the potential hazards.'[603]

29mm Blacker Bombard/Spigot Mortar: From November 1941[604] local Home Guard units were issued with the mediaeval-sounding Blacker Bombard, named after its inventor Lieutenant-Colonel L.V.S. Blacker and made, among other places, under contract at the Leicester City Transport Department workshops.

Officially known in army-speak as 'Mortar, Spigot, 29mm, Mk 1', it was a close-range ambush weapon that lobbed a 20lb anti-tank projectile or a 14lb anti-personnel projectile. Non-explosive, concrete-headed practice bombs were also used. It had a firing crew of up to five men and was issued at one to two mortars per platoon.

Like all Home Guard sub-artillery, it had an eccentric appearance, resembling a large open paint can welded to bicycle handlebars with brakes (used for firing). Although in theory it could fire 15 rounds a minute, it was really a 'one shot' weapon, as for accurate use it had to let any attacking tank come within 100 yards. As a Home Guard Instruction conceded, 'While fairly easily camouflaged, it can be quickly spotted and neutralised once it has come into action.'[605] Although the large anti-tank bomb could disable a tank, it had such an insensitive fuse that it often passed through unarmoured vehicles such as lorries or hit the ground without exploding. When the bombs did explode, the remains of the tail fins often flew back towards the crew.[606] These factors, combined with the amount of smoke it produced on firing and the way the projectile slowly sailed through the air, meant the mortar crew would be lucky to fire more than a couple of shots before the hunters became the hunted.[607]

Fred Parr, formerly a sergeant in the Ab Kettleby Home Guard, remembers the temperamental fuses:

'We used to practise at Tilton-on-the-Hill. It was a hell of a way, but we needed the space. We used both dummy and live bombs. We fired one bomb and it failed to go off and we had to search the bushes to find it. The Sergeant-Major wouldn't let us within 100 yards of it and said "I'll sort it out." Then he defused it. It had hit a tree and was just lying there!'[608]

Ray Elgood was a corporal in HQ company, 1st (North Leicester) Battalion:

'We used to go for Blacker Bombard training at a quarry on Barkby Road, where the crisp factory is. Most of the Blacker's targets were static. It's easy enough to fire at something standing still, but in real life German tanks would be advancing, so we made a moving target. We rigged up a track from an old railway there and put an old water tank filled with bricks on the rails. It would trundle along and we would fire the Spigot mortar at it. I was quite good at hitting it but we used to miss a lot. The embankment had household refuse tipped down it and these mortar bombs used to go straight into it. We tried digging them

Home Guard Spigot mortar base with semi-sunken ammunition store, Rotherby. The mortar covered the high ground and main A607 Leicester–Melton Mowbray road.

Home Guard Spigot mortar mount at the junction of Main Street and Rearsby Lane, Gaddesby. It covered the approach to Rearsby Aerodrome and now has a new explanatory memorial plaque mounted on it.

An unsuspecting Ford Escort drives directly through the firing line of the Spigot mortar base position on the ramparts of Oakham Castle, overlooking the Burley Road and Station Road junction.

out, but sometimes they went so deep we couldn't retrieve them. Over 50 must be still there. In fact, I went to visit a factory built on top of it and told the man, who looked quite worried!'[609]

But it wasn't such a bad thing if the rounds failed to detonate, as Peter Wheeldon, formerly of Whitwick Home Guard, recalled, 'After practising with dummy bombs, we took it to Red Bank at Measham for live tests, where the bomb bounced onwards and finished up on the railway line, luckily without exploding.'[610]

In rural areas, the mortar was used in a mobile role.[611] Weighing 360lb and possessing a recoil of 20 tons per square inch, the mortar was issued with four heavy tubular legs, which were stabilised with four steel pickets hammered into the ground. John Greaves, formerly of the Husbands Bosworth Platoon, remembers 'the smallest man in the unit was given the job of carrying the heavy legs. He had great difficulty in getting them across hedgerows and walls!'[612]

However, it was found the mortar fired more accurately from a solid mounting, so was often mounted on a reinforced concrete pedestal. The mortar sat on a protruding stainless steel pivot and plate. The whole pedestal was sunk below ground level in a pit for extra cover. Several of these mountings still exist locally where they were positioned to defend Vulnerable Points, such as road junctions. The pedestal's stainless steel pivot is often still shiny and rustless, even after 60 years of exposure. Today, Spigot mortar mountings are the only solid archaeological reminder of the Home Guard's anti-tank role.

Examples in Leicestershire and Rutland:
- Spigot mortar mount: SK 687129 junction of Main Street/Rearsby Lane, Gaddesby
- Spigot mortar mount with ammo store: SK 682166 junction A607/Hoby Road
- Spigot mortar mount: SK 773192 B676 Saxby Road, Melton Mowbray
- Spigot mortar mount: SK 862090 Oakham Castle at Station Road/Burley Road junction[613]

3-inch Smith Gun: The 'Ordnance Smooth-bore, 3in. Mk 1' or simply the Smith Gun, is probably one of the most unusual 'artillery pieces' ever produced. Invented in 1940 by the chief engineer of the Trianco Toy Company, retired Major William H. Smith, not surprisingly it looked like a toy, with large solid wheels and a stubby barrel. Offered as an emergency gun for the Home Guard, at first the Ordnance Board rejected it, but Churchill intervened and overruled them. Production troubles delayed its issue, only entering Home Guard service in summer 1942.

Home Guard display on the fields at Wigston, probably summer 1943. This rare photograph shows two Spigot mortars and a Smith gun in the centre. Some of the Home Guards have camouflaged helmets.

It was operated by a crew of three. The gun and its separate 40-round ammunition trailer could be towed behind an ordinary car, though the tubeless solid wheels meant the driver had to drive slowly to prevent damaging the weapon. Unusually, in use, the gun had to be tipped onto the concave wheel which gave 360-degree traverse, while the upper convex wheel provided overhead cover for the crew. The weapon was fired with a lever and cable similar to a motorcycle brake. The gun had a very low muzzle velocity, was inaccurate and had an effective range of only 300 yards.

Possibly 'the most dangerously unstable item of ordnance ever produced in the UK',[614] there were several fatal backfiring accidents elsewhere,[615] with a West Country Home Guard officer stating the Smith gun had 'a terrifying reputation for killing its crew'. Fuses fitted to early batches of shells were so sensitive, even the official handbook was forced to admit they had 'a reputation for lack of safety'.[616] Bill Tollington, then in the Hathern Home Guard, remembers a near fatal incident:

'The accident involved Harry Baxter, who was with Hathern Brickyard platoon. It happened on a Saturday night at Mill Lane end, Sutton Bonington. One or two of us were taking a walk down to the river, when we heard a "bang". They had been towing this Smith gun and ammunition with an Opel car. What set the bombs off, I don't know, but the car was absolutely peppered at the back with shrapnel and Harry happened to be in the backseat. It didn't kill him, although he was injured.'[617]

In some areas the Smith gun was withdrawn as unsafe. Nonetheless, if it functioned correctly and the 6lb shell struck the target, it could pack quite a punch, being able to penetrate 80mm of armour plate or punch a 2ft hole in 9in reinforced concrete.[618]

Home Guards of the 4th (Central Leicester) and 'B' Company 2nd (South Leicester) Battalions are instructed on the two-pounder anti-tank gun at Newton Harcourt, around 1943.

Two-pounder Anti-Tank Gun: Although able to destroy German tanks at the start of the war, by the time the two-pounder anti-tank gun was issued in limited numbers to the Home Guard in 1943 it was obsolete, unable to penetrate the armour of the latest panzers. However, it would have proved useful in knocking out armoured cars and troop lorries. It required a crew of four.

.55 Boys Anti-Tank Rifle: One of the army's least-loved weapons, the long-barrelled, heavyweight, bolt-action Boys, sometimes mistakenly spelt Boyes, anti-tank rifle was known for its fearsome recoil. Its steel-cored bullet could penetrate 21mm of armour, but it was obsolete by 1941. It only reached a few local units by late 1943, in which time it was truly redundant, except perhaps against armoured cars. Former No. 1 (Glenfield) Platoon, 3rd (West Leicester) Battalion Home Guard John Swan remembers 'Unreassuringly, our anti-tank rifle could only be used to dent the rim of a Tiger tank turret, so it could not be traversed, as it was far too weak to penetrate the armour!'[619]

PIAT (Projector, Infantry, Anti-Tank): Approaching Stand Down, very limited numbers of PIATs were issued to the Home Guard. Originally called the 'Baby Bombard', Lieutenant-Colonel L.V.S. Blacker's next invention was basically a greatly improved, man-portable version of his Spigot mortar. It was versatile and up to date, capable of knocking out the latest German tanks with its shaped warhead. The PIAT's effectiveness meant the vast majority went to the Regular Army on the front line. Former No. 1 (Glenfield) Platoon 3rd (West Leicester) Battalion Home Guard John Swan remembers his platoon were issued with a PIAT, although it languished in the stores, only being brought out for lectures.[620] Likewise, No. 14 (Houghton-on-the-Hill) Platoon, 6th (Quorn) Battalion were also issued with a PIAT, which was stored at the home of their CO, Lt Geoffrey Lea.[621]

Home Guard Improvised Weapons

A few local Home Guards used their skills to improvise weapons to circumvent the shortage. Many seem to have worked better in theory than practice. In the early LDV days, P.S. Wakefield wrote:

'Tuesday 21:5:40. ...I have received the thanks of the Ministry of Supply – that's all. They don't want my Rifle Grenade invention.'[622]

Wakefield later recorded a more successful invention:

'Friday 17:4:42. Major Nichol MC came in on his way home and saw Popham's Grenade thrower at work. Thought it excellent and is to try it out with rapid firing at Bestwood School [Nottingham]. Popham is taking out a Provisional Patent for it.'[623]

Ray Elgood, a corporal in HQ company of 1st (North Leicester) Battalion, worked as a senior design engineer at Parmeko Ltd in Aylestone, Leicester.

'We were carrying this Northover Projector and I said "It's a pity we can't

The Home Guard ammunition store that stood in Home Field; to the right is Bloomhills Farm, Dunton Bassett. The store had a central dividing wall with a door at both ends. Bombs and ammunition were stored in one half and detonators and fuses in the other. The store was located in the middle of the field outside the village for safety reasons. It was finally demolished around 1998. The end wall of the wagon hovel in the background was used by the Home Guard for target rifle practice. (Wendy Warren)

put two of these together." The man I was with said "Why can't we put six together?" So we set to work. I made the multiple electrical firing mechanism and he got cracking at his factory and made the weapon up. When it was finished it had two Smith gun disc wheels and all these electrical triggers ganged up behind the two rows of three guns. The War Office came for a demonstration at Beaumont Leys pit. We didn't have any sights, just an engineer's protractor. This army officer said "13 degrees" and we said "30 degrees? Right". All six of these signal flares went right over the top of the quarry and lit up over Leicester then fell down. Suddenly all the city's air raid sirens went off causing everyone to run to the shelters! I've never seen a War Office man move so quick in my life! Everything was packed up and away! These Smith gun disc wheels were only meant to do a few mph but they sped off at about 50mph!'[624]

Some inventions appear to have been more successful. A censored *Leicester Mercury* report of July 1941 described a Home Guard exercise at Kilby Bridge, where 'a secret electrical device – the invention of a local Home Guardsman – enveloped a "tank" in flames and smoke and put it out of action...'[625]

However, one enterprise ended in tragedy. On 8 February 1942 Corporal William H. Williamson, 25, of 11th (Ashby-de-la-Zouch) Battalion, was killed demonstrating an improvised bomb at Measham.[626] A national ban at the end of 1941 forbade the Home Guard from making any more home-made devices, but for Corporal Williamson it was too late.[627]

Explosives

Some Home Guard battalions were issued with high explosives. Fortunately they did not distribute them too far, as Ray Elgood, then a corporal in HQ company, 1st (North Leicester) Battalion, explains:

'We used explosive charges during training. Once we attacked the farmhouse at Jacksons House Farm, just outside Houghton-on-the-Hill. We had to crawl in and put a banger on the doorstep and a 4oz charge in the manure heap. Only we got the two mixed up – and blew the front of the farmhouse down! The CO had to pay for the repairs at his own expense!'[628]

CONCLUSION

A Success Story Never to be Matched Again?

The Home Guard of 1940–1944 was the greatest and most important volunteer defence force the world has ever seen, representing the peak in the history of the British volunteer. The Nazi invader never came and so, like their predecessors in the Volunteers and Militias, the Home Guard were never fully tested, although they did capture the odd enemy airman.

Nor does it seem likely there will ever be a Home Guard again. Such large volunteer anti-invasion forces have become an anachronism in the nuclear age. Global terrorism has largely taken the place of the international confrontations of the last century. However, as history proves, volunteer defence forces are largely raised at the last minute, so who can tell what the future for the British volunteer tradition will be.

Vital to Victory

Without doubt, the Home Guard played an important role in Britain's war effort at several levels. They relieved Regular troops of comparatively mundane duties, such as the manning of roadblocks. In the long run, they helped the British Army to move on to the offensive.

Good Comradeship

On a psychological level, the force militarised the male populace, keeping them war-minded, which was essential in winning the war. In return, creating the force answered the men's call for arms, even if they were sub-standard. The Home Guard was also a great uniter of men of all classes. The good camaraderie and morale is fondly remembered to this day. Harry Gudger, then of Birstall Platoon, 1st (North Leicester) Battalion, recalls:

'The companionship in the Home Guard was great. There was a big friendship in the battalion and we all knew each other by first names. There was always a lot of jokes and we'd all go for a pint and a chat.'[629]

A Head Start

The Home Guard also provided useful training for those who were about to be called-up, as several former Home Guards testified, including Allan Hopcraft:

'It gave us an advantage the conscripts did not have: we could march, we knew a lot of rifle drill and we were disciplined. I know it helped me because when I went in I was made Section Leader. Being in the Home Guard Shock Section came in very useful in the rough and tumble of Forces life.'[630]

'Playtime Army'?

However, it must be stated that the Home Guard was far from perfect. It may have been the most successful volunteer defence force ever, but it is a sad fact that it was the only army in recorded history to have killed more of its own than the enemy: 1,206 Home Guards were killed – 18 from Leicestershire – and 557 injured in the line of duty, mainly through accidents.

The other great irony of the force was that it was weakest when it was needed most and strongest when the course of the war had made it redundant.

Jimmy Perry, creator of *Dad's Army* and a former Home Guard, said it had never been his intention to ridicule the Home Guard, just to show its comic side. This he successfully did, but unfortunately, ever since, the programme has been viewed as an accurate representation of the Home Guard. This perception had partially existed during the war. Writing in the magazine of No. 3 Section, No. 13 Platoon, 4th (Central Leicester) Battalion, Home Guard 'G.A.B.' protested:

'Have you ever paused to reflect on what a Home Guard really is, what a vital and unselfish part he is playing in our great war effort? The few "outsiders", usually the slackers, are apt to look down on our forces and remark about the "playtime army". A good example of this was noticed one day in the town; a group of young girls were standing on the pavement as a squad of Home Guards (young ones) approached. The maidens fluffed their feathers and bowed their lips, then one was heard to say, "Coo, they're only Home Guards," and they all turned away in disgust. Not that the said HGs noticed it, but there it was – ONLY HOME GUARDS.

Those thoughtless young lassies evidently do not realise those Home Guards are men who are giving up practically the whole of their spare time to form the great second line of defence of their country; some are men who fought in the Great War, others yet too young for active service; men in reserved occupations – munition workers, railway workers – vital to the life of the country, and workers in a hundred and one different jobs, without whom it would be impossible to carry on, and those unfit for active service.

When the wheels have stopped turning and the pens stopped writing, these men, within two hours, could mobilise into a potential fighting force of well over a million fully-equipped, fully-armed and fully-trained men. Think – an army of all ages mobilising every day – WORKERS BY DAY and SOLDIERS BY NIGHT. Every man an enthusiastic Volunteer – no slackers because slackers cannot stick it, they get out and join the few "outsiders".

A Sergeant-major of the Regular Army once said, "I should be proud to be a Home Guard, they are soldiers and workers, whereas we are only soldiers." So remember when walking down the street, whether as a soldier or a worker, throw out your chest and say to yourself, "I am proud to be a Home Guard: Here's to us! Who's like us? Damn few!"'[631]

Hard Work

'G.A.B.' was correct in stating 'WORKERS BY DAY and SOLDIERS BY NIGHT'. Robert Reay speaks for many:

'I wanted to join the RAF but I failed the medical because of a dodgy ear. So, at 18, I went on to munitions at British United Shoe. I worked in the fitting department, making parts for Oerlikon guns. After working 12 hours I would cycle up to man the AA site on Victoria Park for the rest of the night, during which I'd grab a few hours sleep and then work started all over again. Looking back, we worked damned hard – I don't know how we did it.'[632]

Perhaps the last word should be left to Winston Churchill, who stated the Home Guard were 'just as much soldiers as Grenadier Guards.'[633]

The Cost

Overwork, ageing years, poor diet and limited medicines meant many were not as healthy as they should have been during the war. Home Guard service was another drain. In November 1942 diarist Major P.S. Wakefield was suddenly hospitalised suffering from severe cystitis, caused by mustard gas poisoning he received during World War One. His doctor wrote:

'We consider his condition has been aggravated by his 2½ years service in the Home Guard – which he has done in addition to his responsible and urgent work at the Brush. We also consider he is absolutely unfit for Home Guard duties and should be invalided out at once.'[634]

Major Wakefield was invalided at the age of only 45. It was three months before he could return to work on restricted hours, and Home Guard service was out of the question. Wakefield recorded how, one by one, the senior officers began to leave due to stress and illness caused by combined work and Home Guard service.

'Monday 4:1:43. …Called at the Drill Hall to hand in my military identity card to the CO. He told me he too had been ordered out of the HG by his doctor and would be leaving soon. Its all wrong the pace should have become so heavy as to kill off the old LDVs like this.'[635]

Illness and stress caused by Home Guard service affected all ranks and, as we have seen, 18 Leicestershire Home Guards paid the ultimate price.

If the Invader Came…

It was stated as fact in several Stand Down speeches and unit histories that the Germans were dissuaded from invading because they knew Britain had a Home Guard. Unfortunately, this was not true. Not only did German propaganda mock the Home Guard, but nowhere in Operation Sealion, the invasion guidebook *Informationsheft GrossBritannien*, or German intelligence summaries were the Home Guard even mentioned. In fact, the Germans felt strong enough to invade Britain where defences were perceived to be the strongest. In short, while the Germans were winning, they disregarded the Home Guard.

However, as the war drew to a close, the Home Guard must have had the last laugh. As the Axis became desperate, the Germans formed their own Home Guard, the Volkssturm, and the Japanese formed civilian anti-invasion suicide squads.

The main enduring question remains: how would the Home Guard have fared had the Germans invaded? This is a difficult hypothetical question, but as far as Leicestershire and Rutland is concerned, had the invasion got this far inland the battle would have been all but lost. In the Home Guard's favour, they would be fighting on home ground and knew the area better than the invader. They would also have the added impetus of knowing they were now fighting for the very survival of their homes and families.

On reflection, all the Home Guards interviewed were both realistic and stoic. Albert Purchase of the LNER Braunstone Gate Goods Yard Platoon stated:

'Whether or not I could have shot anybody is a different matter. To take a rifle, point it at somebody and pull the trigger would take a lot of doing – unless he was shooting at you. It's surprising what you can do if you have to.' [636]

Bill Tollington considered his later army experience fighting the Germans:

'Well, the Germans were a well-trained lot, there's no doubt about that. We'd have taken one or two out, but I don't think we would have stood a great amount of chance. We'd have put up token resistance but we wouldn't have stopped 'em.' [637]

Aneurin Owen recalled:

'I don't think we would have been a lot of use: we would have just slowed them down. It would have been impossible to stop them with the equipment we had.' [638]

John Bevis adds:

'If they invaded England I would have done my damnedest to push them back into the sea. We would have fought with courage, but I believe we would have been slaughtered – we would not have stood a cat's chance in hell.' [639]

However, John Greaves was more positive:

'After a couple of years the Home Guard performed very well. We were fairly well trained and made a good account of ourselves. Most of us were quite keen and we had good morale.' [640]

In actual fact, they are all correct. The only situation in which the Home Guard would have been able to vanquish their enemy is if they had greatly outnumbered them, such as against limited paratroop landings or mopping up fifth columnists.

Sixty years on, in the sharp, piercing spotlight of history, it can be seen that the Home Guard were, in military terms, the cannon fodder that would be used to slow down the German invaders until the Regular Army arrived. And deep down, many knew this.

The cosy, parochial village image of *Dad's Army* would have vanished, as they became front-line fighters manning roadblocks against tanks and battling SS. To capture vital points, the Germans would have had to eliminate all Home Guard resistance and whole areas would have been cleared during their advance inland. The Germans had the fighting experience of capturing all Europe: the young and old Home Guards, although brimming full of defiant spirit, would have proved limited opposition to the heavily-armed and ruthless Wehrmacht.

When appraising the Home Guard, not only should the actual service they put in be acknowledged, but also the fact these men would have laid down their lives in defence of their fellow citizens.

Perhaps the most poignant and succinct answer to the question was given by Robert Beardsley, 'A very good question: in those days we were very determined and all united together. All I can say is we would have done our very best.'[641]

Which is the most anyone can do.

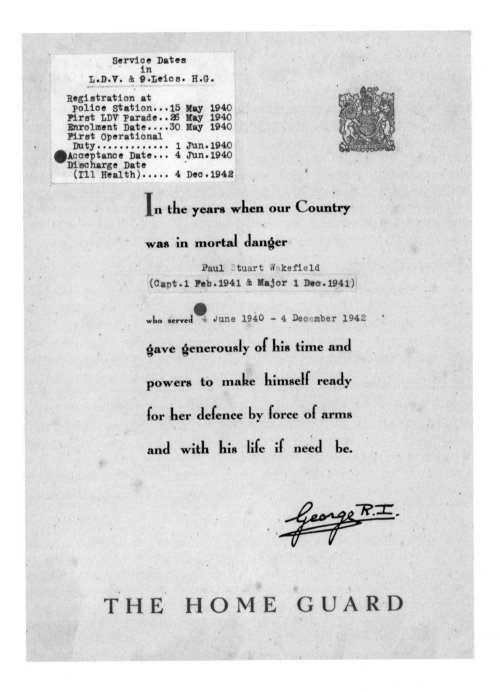

Service certificate of Major Paul S. Wakefield of 9th (Loughborough) Battalion, Leicestershire Home Guard.

LEICESTERSHIRE AND RUTLAND HOME GUARD ORDER OF BATTLE 1940–1944

The first part of this list shows the organisation of the Leicestershire and Rutland Home Guard while it was still in transition from the LDV. Several platoons have yet to be formed while others would later be reorganised and renamed. Nonetheless, this list, dating from September/October 1940, when the threat of invasion was highest, gives a valuable insight into the strength the local Home Guard would have had to meet the invader with, had he reached the two counties. The second part of the list shows the order of battle down to company level post-1941. No complete order of battle down to platoon level at Stand Down in 1944 is known to exist, and the author would be grateful for further platoon details.

PART 1:
LEICESTERSHIRE HOME GUARD – SEPTEMBER/OCTOBER 1940[642]

ZONE HEADQUARTERS: THE MAGAZINE, LEICESTER

Zone Headquarters Staff

Company Commandant and Zone Commander: Brigadier-General Sir Thomas Cope BT, CMG, DSO of Osbaston Hall, Market Bosworth
Staff Officer and Second in Command: Lieutenant-Colonel E.C. Packe DSO, OBE of Great Glen Hall, Great Glen
Leicester and Rutland Territorial Association Assistant Secretary: J. Mitchell MM

Leicester sector staff at Stand Down, at the Magazine, Leicester, 26 November 1944. Col. H.W.H. Tyler, Leicester Group Commander, sits centre.

Group Staff

Group Commander: Colonel H.W.H. Tyler MC, DL of Grey Roofs, The Broadway, Oadby
Assistant Group Commander: Major C.A.B. Elliott of The Orchards, Oadby
Staff Officer/Administrative Assistant: Captain J.W. Lancaster
Assistant Staff Officer: J.A.V. Boddy and A. Hall
Transport Officer: J.C. Vaughan-Harbourne
Training Liaison Officer: A.W. Richards
Musketry Officer: H.R. Allen
Bombing Officer: H.G. Wilson
Quartermaster: A. Hudson
Officer-in-charge Shotguns: H. Thompson
Medical Officer: Captain M.H. Barton MC
Headquarters Commander: J.H. Corah
Assistant Headquarters Commander: W.W. Noakes and C. Westby

NORTH BATTALION

Battalion Staff

Commanding Officer: F.B. Hitchings MC
Second in Command: Captain W.B. Jarvis OBE JP
Adjutant: J.R. Evans
Administrative Assistant: M.A. Crossen

Specialist Officers

Quartermaster: G.G. Grainger
Musketry Officer: F.J. Goldsworthy
Bombing Officer: F. Cayless
Transport Officer: W.J. Furber

'A' Company

Company HQ: Birstall Golf Club
Company Commander: A.N. Peach
Second in Command: W.L.E. Frisby

Platoon	Platoon HQ	Platoon Commanders
No. 1 Platoon:	Cropston Crossroads	P.A. Russell and K. Padmore
No. 2 Platoon:	Keeper's Lodge, Anstey Lane	W.J. Pyne
No. 3 Platoon:	Beaumont Lodge	D. Byford
No. 4 Platoon:	Blackbird Playing Fields	P.E. Daniels and A.J. Harrison
No. 5 Platoon:	Birstall Golf Club	J.D. Ward and F. Wain
No. 6 Platoon:	Belgrave Gasworks	F.H. Kelly and H. Jeyes

'B' Company

Company HQ: Rushey Fields
Company Commander: F.W. Briggs
Second in Command: F. Rains

Platoon	Platoon HQ	Platoon Commanders
No. 7 Platoon:	Gardener's Cottage, Wanlip Hall	H.W. Godwin and J.B. Moore
No. 8 Platoon:	The Grange, Birstall	R.G. Rogers and H.P. Lavender.
No. 9 Platoon:	Rushey Fields	H.G Boxall and W. Fillingham
No. 10 Platoon:	Ashwell and Nesbit, Barkby Lane	A.S. George and J.T.B. Swift
No. 11 Platoon:	Manor Farm	J.W.L. Carr and T. Browning

'C' Company

Company HQ: Leicester Golf Club
Company Commander: W.R. Harding
Second in Command: F.C. Flint

Platoon	Platoon HQ	Platoon Commanders
No. 12 Platoon:	Uplands Roadblock (7 Uppingham Road)	F.W. Harrison T.W. Allen
No. 13 Platoon:	Evington House	H. McCrory and T. Trevor Sawday
No. 14 Platoon:	Golf Club House, Stoughton Lane	N. Catlow and J.C. Condon
No. 15 Platoon:	CWS Farm/Jackson's House	F.C. Chapman and J. Lymburn
No. 16 Platoon:	Oadby Playing Fields/ Stoughton Waterworks	R.E. Williams and F.S. Harding

SOUTH BATTALION

Battalion Staff
Commanding Officer: Captain W.T. Pares MC
Second in Command/Adjutant: E. Smart MC
Specialist Officers
Quartermaster: M.A. Kent MBE, MC
Musketry Officer: R.S. Humphrey
Infantry Training Officer: L. Browning
Bombing Officer: H. Freer
Transport Officer: P. Ramsey

'A' Company: Oadby/City
Company HQ: Leicester University
Company Commander: Major H.A. Davy
Second in Command: Captain A.H. Day

Platoon	Platoon HQ	Platoon Commanders
No. 1 Platoon:	Leicester University	G.H. Shepherd and J.A. Barratt
No. 2 Platoon:	Gasworks	E.F. Lole and T. Crumbie
No. 3 Platoon:	Power Station	Captain P.A. Green and F.R. Mee MC
No. 4 Platoon:	British Legion, Sandy Lane	E. Armitage and O.V. Judkins
No. 5 Platoon:	Roadblock, 17 Narborough Road	H. Freer and R.G. Barker

'B' Company: Wigston
Company HQ: 139 Station Road, Wigston
Company Commander: W. Hylton Herrick
Second in Command: R. Meiklejohn/A.H. Hind MC

Platoon	Platoon HQ	Platoon Commanders
No. 1 Platoon:	Aylestone Lane	H. Tuckley MM and W.S. Papworth
No. 2 Platoon:	Newton Lane	A.D. Lippitt and C.P. Williams
No. 3 Platoon:	Kilby Bridge	A. Kimberley and A.A. Denton
No. 4 Platoon:	Countesthorpe	F. Skeffington and Captain D. Taylor
No. 5 Platoon:	Crowe Mills	H.P. Harper and W.F. Cranfield
No. 6 Platoon:	Station Sheds, Wigston Magna	S.A. Wells and A. Such

'C' Company: Blaby and Whetstone
Company HQ: 13 Cork Lane, Glenhills, Blaby
Company Commander: R.E. Cruickshank VC
Second in Command: E. Hannam

Platoon	Platoon HQ	Platoon Commanders
No. 1 Platoon:	Roadblock, Welford Road	E.A. Wood and R. Jones
No. 2 Platoon:	Roadblock, 16 Welford Road	W.E. Pickering and S. Johnson
No. 3 Platoon:	Enderby Road	W. Campbell and Mr Burns
No. 4 Platoon:	Whetstone Street	J.B. Backhouse and W.H. Taylor
No. 5 Platoon:	Whetstone Gorse Railway Viaduct	A.E. Day and A. Watson
No. 6 Platoon:	High Street, Whetstone	T. Loughland and H. Wale

CENTRAL LEICESTER BATTALION

Battalion Staff
Commanding Officer: A.S. Whitehead JP
Second in Command: Captain W. Nelson Dunn
Adjutant: Captain W. Whowell MC
Administrative Assistant: A. Clarke
Specialist Officers
Quartermaster: H.H. Pickin
Transport Officer: F. Bowles
Bombing officer: H.G. Wilson
Musketry Officer: W.E. Westhead

Detachments
No. 1 Detachment: London, Midland and Scottish Railway (LMS), LMS HQ
Detachment HQ: LMS Passenger Superintendent's Office, London Road
Detachment Commanders: Major D.S. Inman and Captain Hodkinson
No. 2 Detachment: London, North-East Railway (LNER), Great Northern Railway HQ
Detachment HQ: Great Northern Railway, Belgrave Road
Detachment Commanders: Major S.G. Evans MC, H.W. Breeze, B.C.S. Church and D.H. Hefford
No. 3 Detachment: London, North-East Railway (LNER), Great Central Railway HQ
Detachment HQ: Great Central Railway, Great Central Street
Detachment Commanders: F. Dickens, A. Hughes, C.F.W. Marshall, Whiting, Brookman-Flint, Webster, Hilton and Abbott
No. 4 Detachment: City Transport, Abbey Park Road and Blackbird Lane
Detachment HQ: Tram Sheds, Abbey Park Road
Detachment Commanders: C.H. Stafford and C.A. Herbert
No. 5 Detachment: City Sewage, City Sewage Disposal
Detachment HQ: Abbey Park Pumping Station
Detachment Commander: Watson
No. 6 Detachment: General Post Office Telephones, Free Lane Telephone Exchange
Detachment Commander: H. Bradley
No. 7 Detachment: Post Office, (General Post Office), Campbell Street Sorting Office
Detachment HQ: Post Office, Bishop Street
Detachment Commanders: A.H. Wells, J. Noton and W.F. Calwood
No. 8 Detachment: Prison, HM Prison, Welford Road
Detachment Commander: W.A. Richards
No. 9 Detachment: Petroleum Board, Shell Mex House, Catherine Street Depot
Detachment Commanders: Captain Crawford, J.D. Thorne, A.G.A. Barton, B. Silley, W. York and E.G.W. Ingram
No. 10 Detachment: John Bull Rubber Company, Works, Evington Valley Road
Detachment Commanders: T.T. Laker and H.N. Stroud
No. 11 Detachment: Standard Engineering Company, Works, Evington Valley Road
Detachment Commanders: H.W. Pochin and J. Way
No. 12 Detachment: Government Training Centre, Gipsy Lane
Detachment Commanders: R.H. Biggs
No. 13 Detachment: Leicester County ARP Control, Grey Friars
Detachment Commanders: Captain Fowler and W.E. Westhead

A rather stern-looking platoon of Leicester City Home Guards, possibly of the 4th (Central Leicester) Battalion, sometime after 1942. (Roger Capewell)

No. 14 Detachment: Parmeko Works, Percy Road, Aylestone
Detachment Commander: P.J. Toone
No. 15 Detachment: Wadkin Ltd, Green Lane Road
Detachment Commanders: M. Goddard, Billingham, Musson
No. 16 Detachment: F. Pollard Ltd Works, St Saviours Road
Detachment Commander: F. Pollard
No. 17 Detachment: Jones and Shipman Works, Gipsy Lane
Detachment Commanders: Houldsworth and R. Woolmer DCM
No. 18 Detachment: Partridge, Wilson and Co, Evington Valley Road
Detachment Commander: Wilson
No. 19 Detachment: Bentley Engineering Co, New Bridge Street
Detachment Commanders: Captain Beston and W. Bentley
No. 20 Detachment: Armstrong Siddeley Co, Walnut Street
Detachment Commanders: O.B. Knight and J.T. Hamps
No. 21 Detachment: Mellor Bromley Co, St Saviours Road
Detachment Commanders: P.H.P. Freeman and G. Murray
No. 22 Detachment: Taylor, Taylor and Hobson Works, Stoughton Street
Detachment Commanders: Captain Northover and E.A. Cook
No. 23 Detachment: British United Works, Belgrave Road
Detachment Commanders: A. Duncan and E. Smith
No. 24 Detachment: Charnwood Engineering Works, Abbey Lane
Detachment Commanders: A. Tolton and P. Dudolph
No. 25 Detachment: Gent and Co. Works, St Saviours Road
Detachment Commanders: H.K. Parsons and F.E. Fry
No. 26 Detachment: Leicester City Waterworks, Hallgates Service and Evington Service
Detachment HQ: Waterworks Office, Bowling Green Street
Detachment Commanders: T.S. Griffin and J. Hill
No. 27 Detachment: Cascelloid Works, Abbey Lane
Detachment Commanders: M. Mills and T.F. Stanley

Charnwood Engineering Company Platoon of the 4th (Central Leicester) Battalion, Abbey Lane, Leicester. Albert Marston is first right, back row. (Albert Marston)

LOUGHBOROUGH BATTALION

Group Headquarters: Drill Hall, Mountsorrel

Group Staff
Commanding Officer: Major C.H. Martin
Staff Officer: R. Dunn
Administrative Assistant: Captain A.E. Gray MBE, MC, MSM
Battalion HQ: Town Hall, Loughborough

Battalion Staff
Commanding Officer: S.K. Lewis
Second in Command: J.L. Ward MC
Adjutant: H.J. Stamper
Quartermaster: R. Monk
Administrative Assistant: Mrs R. Putsman

'A' Company: Shelthorpe, Nottingham Road and Viaduct
Company HQ: 59 Woodgate, Loughborough
Company Commander: J.C. Vidgen-Jenks
Second in Command: E.H. Thomas

Platoon	Platoon HQ	Platoon Commanders
No. 1 Platoon:	Company HQ	S. Moorhouse
No. 2 Platoon:	Shelthorpe	H. Lee MM
No. 3 Platoon:	Nottingham Road	J.H. Kidger
No. 4 Platoon:	Viaduct	A.S. North

'B' Company: Knighthorpe, Ashby Road and Nanpantan
Company HQ:
Company Commander: H. Chubb
Second in Command: S. Barson

Platoon	Platoon HQ	Platoon Commanders
No. 5 Platoon:	Knighthorpe	H.L. Murray
No. 6 Platoon:	Ashby Road	W.S. Yeates
No. 7 Platoon:	Nanpantan	A.A. Oliver

'C' Company: Shepshed and Hathern
Company HQ: 'The Haunted Castle', Belton Road, Shepshed
Company Commander: Captain J. Nichol MC
Second in Command: H.W. Bell MC

Platoon	Platoon HQ	Platoon Commanders
No. 8 Platoon:	Leicester Road, Shepshed	A.H. Brears
No. 9 Platoon:	Charnwood Road, Shepshed	W.H. Smith
No. 10 Platoon:	Belton Road, Shepshed	C. Short
No. 11 Platoon:	Hathern Road, Shepshed	E.A. Hallam
No. 12 Platoon:	Blackbrook	L. Boon
No. 13 Platoon:	Hathern	B. Fuller

'D' Company: Various Works
Company HQ: The Brush Works, Loughborough
Company Commander: L.G. Reid
Second in Command: P.S. Wakefield

Platoon	Platoon HQ	Platoon Commanders
No. 14 Platoon:	Brush Works, No. 1	R.C. Blunt
No. 15 Platoon:	Brush Works, No. 2	B.H. Mears
No. 16 Platoon:	Empress Works	J. Wright
No. 17 Platoon:	LMS and LNER Railway	J.S.H. Cope

'C' Company (Shepshed & Hathern), 9th (Loughborough) Battalion Leicestershire Home Guard. Commander J. Nichol sits centre front behind the big drum.

'E' Company: Various Works
Company HQ: Electricity Works, Loughborough
Company Commander: J.P. Tucker
Second in Command: L.P. Ingram

Platoon	Platoon HQ	Platoon Commanders
No. 18 Platoon:	Electricity Works	G. Smith
No. 19 Platoon:	Gasworks	L.P. Ingram
No. 20 Platoon:	Genatosan Works	Dr G.M. Dyson
No. 21 Platoon:	Clemerson's Works	T.W. Hawksworth MM

CHARNWOOD BATTALION

Battalion HQ: Drill Hall, Mountsorrel

Battalion Staff
Commanding Officer: Colonel W.S.N. Toller DSO, TD
Second in Command/Adjutant:
Administrative Assistant: Mrs D.I. Allen

Northern Company: Castle Donington, Belton and Long Whatton
Company HQ: Whatton Fields, Long Whatton
Company Commander: H.A. Swain MC
Second in Command: E.F. Windsor MC

Platoon	Platoon HQ	Platoon Commanders
Castle Donington Platoon	Castle Donington and Diseworth	A.T. Astle
Kegworth Platoon	Kegworth and Lockington	J. Harrison
Long Whatton Platoon	Long Whatton and Belton	A.F. Staniland

North-East Company: Wymeswold
Company HQ: The Old Parsonage, Hoton
Company Commander: W.J. Ironside
Second in Command: A.E. Start

Platoon	Platoon HQ	Platoon Commanders
Wymeswold Platoon	Wymeswold	F.F. Bailey
Hoton Platoon	Hoton and Cotes	R.J.M. Bailey
Burton-on-the-Wolds Platoon	Burton-on-the-Wolds and Walton	A.W. Panter

Eastern Company: Barrow-on-Soar
Company HQ: Strancliffe House, Barrow-on-Soar
Company Commander: E.H. Spalding
Second in Command: C.C. Tatham

Platoon	Platoon HQ	Platoon Commanders
No. 1 Platoon:	Sileby and Cossington	T.H. Stanley
No. 2 Platoon:	Barrow-on-Soar and Seagrave	A.L. Wykes

Western Company: Mountsorrel
Company HQ: The Grange, Quorn
Company Commander: S.F. Peshall MC
Second in Command: A.F.M. Wright

Platoon	Platoon HQ	Platoon Commanders
No. 1 Platoon:	Quorn	J.A. Belton
No. 2 Platoon:	Mountsorrel	R.H. Orton
No. 3 Platoon:	Rothley	W.S. Hancock
No. 4 Platoon:	M. Wright and Sons Factory, Quorn Mills	M. Wright

Forest Company: Charnwood Forest
Company HQ: Maplehurst, Maplewell Road, Woodhouse Eaves
Company Commander: J.R. Leeson
Second in Command: A.F.P. Wheeler

Platoon	Platoon HQ	Platoon Commanders
No. 1 Platoon:	Woodhouse Eaves and Woodhouse	W.A. Joels
No. 2 Platoon:	Swithland	G.F.L. Alexander
No. 3 Platoon:	Ulverscroft	C.Z.M. Booth
No. 4 Platoon:	Charley	J.B. Martin

MARKET HARBOROUGH BATTALION

Battalion HQ: 44 High Street, Market Harborough

Battalion Staff
Commanding Officer: Brigadier-General J.L. Jack DSO, ADC
Second in Command: R.G. Watson

Harborough Company: Market Harborough
Company HQ: Symington's Factory, Market Harborough
Company Commander: Major E.G. Gillilan DSO, DL
Second in Command: W.C. Gandy

Platoon	Platoon HQ	Platoon Commanders
No. 1 Platoon:	Market Harborough	C.F. Lea
No. 2 Platoon:	Market Harborough	G. Tranter
No. 3 Platoon:	Market Harborough	W.C.L. Smith
No. 4 Platoon:	Symington's Factory	L.B. Varney
Railway Platoon:	LMS Station	C.C. Harper
Great Bowden Platoon:	Great Bowden	W.E. Stokes

Officers of Lutterworth Company, 7th (Market Harborough) Battalion at Stand Down, in front of Lutterworth Grammar School pavilion, late 1944. Lt John Bennett-Powell stands first left. (Wendy Warren)

Lutterworth Company: Lutterworth etc.
Company HQ: Staging Camp, Lutterworth
Company Commander: Colonel H.D. Belgrave DSO

Platoon	Platoon HQ	Platoon Commanders
No. 1 Platoon:	Willoughby Waterleys etc.	C.F. Bray
No. 2 Platoon:	Broughton Astley etc.	J.W. Harrison
No. 3 Platoon:	Lutterworth etc.	Major Readman

Kibworth Company: Kibworth, Husbands Bosworth etc.
Company HQ: Grey House, Kibworth
Company Commander: Captain R. Turner
Second in Command: A.G. Briggs

Platoon	Platoon HQ	Platoon Commanders
No. 1 Platoon:	Kibworth	F. Stops
No. 2 Platoon:	The Langtons	Captain H.W. Simpson
No. 3 Platoon:	Lubenham	K.K. Homan
No. 4 Platoon:	Husbands Bosworth	J.C. Rowlands

East Norton Company: East Norton, Illston and Lowesby
Company HQ: Langton House, Tur Langton
Company Commander: Colonel H.O. Wiley MC
Second in Command: Captain F.W. Lee

Platoon	Platoon HQ	Platoon Commanders
No. 1 Platoon:	Tugby etc.	W.N.D. North
No. 2 Platoon:	Billesdon etc.	H. Barker
No. 3 Platoon:	Tilton-on-the Hill etc.	W.H. Walker
No. 4 Platoon:	Illston etc.	J.W. Hardwicke
No. 5 Platoon:	Lowesby	J. Crawford
Independent Section:		Mr Welford

Medbourne Company: Medbourne etc.
Company HQ: Barnsdale House, Great Easton, Market Harborough
Company Commander: Captain G.A. Champion de Crespigny

Platoon	Platoon HQ	Platoon Commanders
No. 1 Platoon:	Drayton etc.	T. Haddon
No. 2 Platoon:	Slawston etc.	G.M. Gibbs

MELTON MOWBRAY BATTALION
Battalion HQ: Remount Depot, Melton Mowbray

Battalion Staff
Commanding Officer: Colonel W.J. Lockett DSO
Administrative Assistant: Lieutenant-Colonel F.D. Alexander CBE

No. 1 Company: Belvoir
Company HQ: Estate Office, Belvoir
Company Commander: A.W. Groome

Platoon	Platoon HQ	Platoon Commanders
No. 1 Platoon:	Bottesford	W. Cook
No. 2 Platoon:	Redmile	A. Hempshaw
No. 3 Platoon:	Eaton	W.C. Carr
No. 4 Platoon:	Croxton Kerrial	H.C. Stannage and C.H. Roberts
No. 5 Platoon:	Belvoir	H.F. Jaggard

No. 2 Company: Waltham
Company HQ: Wymondham House, Melton Mowbray
Company Commander: A.J. Fellowes-Prynne
Second in Command: C.P. Smith

Platoon	Platoon HQ	Platoon Commanders
No. 1 Platoon:	Waltham	L.S. Elwell
No. 2 Platoon:	Buckminster	R.L. Black
No. 3 Platoon:	Wymondham	C.F. Saunders
No. 4 Platoon:	Freeby	A. Foyster

No. 3 Company: Long Clawson
Company HQ: Tiptree Cottage, Old Dalby
Company Commander: Lieutenant-Colonel C.C. Hickie

Platoon	Platoon HQ	Platoon Commanders
No. 1 Platoon:	Ab Kettleby	A.S. Platts
No. 2 Platoon:	Old Dalby	W. Sandford
No. 3 Platoon:	Scalford	K.N. Woods
No. 4 Platoon:	Long Clawson	W. Ison

No. 4 Company: Asfordby
Company HQ: Ragdale Hall, Melton Mowbray
Company Commander: Major W.P.C. Coutrell-Hubbersty OBE of Ragdale Hall
Second in Command: Captain J. Armitage

Platoon	Platoon HQ	Platoon Commanders
No. 1 Platoon:	Frisby	Captain F.M. Forsell
No. 2 Platoon:	Asfordby	W.A.J. Ewen
No. 3 Platoon:	Asfordby and Holwell Works	H.G. Barnes
No. 4 Platoon:	Saxelby	F. Coulson

No. 5 Company: Somerby
Company HQ: Burrough-on-the-Hill, Melton Mowbray
Company Commander: Lieutenant-Colonel F.D. Alexander OBE
Second in Command: C. Hilton-Greene

Platoon	Platoon HQ	Platoon Commanders
No. 1 Platoon:	Gaddesby	Captain G.S. Barrow
No. 2 Platoon:	Thorpe Satchville	Captain J.G. Leigh
No. 3 Platoon:	Burton Lazars	Captain J.M. Wilson
No. 4 Platoon:	Somerby	Captain H.J. Morton

No. 6 Company: Melton Mowbray
Company HQ: Bank Chambers, Melton Mowbray
Company Commander: Captain A.P. Marsh
Second in Command: M. Marsh

Platoon	Platoon HQ	Platoon Commanders
No. 1 Platoon:	Burton Hill	F. Warner
No. 2 Platoon:	Asfordby Road	R. Gates (Barclays Bank)
No. 3 Platoon:	Thorpe Road	W.G. Walker (Lloyds Bank)
No. 4 Platoon:	Saxby Road	G.H. Flint (Westminster Bank)
No. 5 Platoon:	LMS Railway Station	E. Powers
GPO Section:	Post Office, Melton Mowbray	E.E. Cutler

No. 7 Company: Syston
Company HQ: The Lodge, Thurnby
Company Commander: Captain Sir Harold Nutting BT
Second in Command: J.H. Lorrimer

Platoon	Platoon HQ	Platoon Commanders
No. 1 Platoon:	Queniborough	W.E. Rawlinson
No. 2 Platoon:	The Barricade, Humberstone	C.H. Cox
No. 3 Platoon:	Scraptoft	H.E. Inglesant
No. 4 Platoon:	Hungerton	L.C. Roberston
No. 5 Platoon:	The Barricade, Scraptoft Lane	N.R. Thompson

MARKET BOSWORTH BATTALION

Battalion HQ: Drill Hall, Hinckley

Battalion Staff
Commanding Officer: J.L. Griffiths DSO, TD
Second in Command: J.T.L. Baxter
Adjutant: S.C. Osborne

'A' Company: Hinckley etc
Company HQ: Conservative Club, Hinckley
Company Commander: R.A. Lumb MC
Second in Command: G.A. Palmer

Platoon	Platoon HQ	Platoon Commanders
No. 1 Platoon:	Burbage	A. Harding
No. 2 Platoon:	Hinckley, Stoke and Higham	F.H. Bromley MC
No. 3 Platoon:	Hinckley	G.W. Cholerton
No. 4 Platoon:	Hinckley	J.S. Reeve
No. A5 Platoon:	Sapcote, Stoney Stanton, Sharnford and Potters Marston	G.W.H. Moore
No. A6 Platoon:	Leics. and Warwickshire Electric Power Company	J.S. Smith

'B' Company: Market Bosworth
Company HQ: Sutton Cheney
Company Commander: B.A. Ryley
Second in Command: A.E. Hawley

Platoon	Platoon HQ	Platoon Commanders
No. 5 Platoon:	Market Bosworth	F.D. Salmon
No. 6 Platoon:	Sheepy Magna	J. Mayo
No. 7 Platoon:	Congerstone	Captain Griffiths
No. 8 Platoon:	Sutton Cheney	W.P. Jackson

'C' Company: Ibstock etc
Company HQ: 119 High Street, Ibstock
Company Commander: J.H. Harratt
Second in Command: H. Rutherford

Platoon	Platoon HQ	Platoon Commanders
No. 9 Platoon:	Ibstock	J.V. Measures
No. 10 Platoon:	Ibstock	E.L. Hunt
No. 11 Platoon:	Barlestone	S.A. Woodcock
No. 12 Platoon:	Bagworth	H.B. Wright
Colliery Platoon:	Ellistown Colliery	J. Harper

'D' Company: Barwell, Thurlaston and Newbold Verdon
Company HQ: 'Hollydene', Hinckley Road, Earl Shilton
Company Commander: J.T.L. Baxter
Second in Command: A.E. Ward

Platoon	Platoon HQ	Platoon Commanders
No. 13 Platoon:	Barwell etc.	L.W. Harvey
No. 14 Platoon:	Earl Shilton etc.	W.A. Wileman
No. 15 Platoon:	Thurlaston	S. Pegg
No. 16 Platoon:	Desford and Newbold Verdon	A.E. Wand
Aerodrome Platoon:	Desford Aerodrome and Factory	J.R. Brittain

ASHBY-DE-LA-ZOUCH BATTALION

Battalion HQ: Drill Hall, Ashby-de-la-Zouch

Battalion Staff
Commanding Officer: Major W.H. Sowter
Second in Command/Adjutant: Captain L.A. Statham
Administrative Assistants: Miss A. Spare and W. Beadsmore

No. 1 Company: Ashby-de-la-Zouch
Company HQ: Drill Hall, Ashby-de-la-Zouch
Company Commander: T.A. Woodcock
Second in Command: J. Stanleigh Turner

Platoon	Platoon HQ	Platoon Commanders
No. 1 Platoon:	Ashby	F. Tye
No. 2 Platoon:	Donisthorpe	S. Dowthwaite
No. 3 Platoon:	Measham	W. Metcalfe
No. 4 Platoon:	Moira	S. Tagg

No. 2 Company: Coalville
Company HQ: Drill Hall, Coalville
Company Commander: F.J. Simmons
Second in Command: R.O. Dalby

Platoon	Platoon HQ	Platoon Commanders
No. 1 Platoon:	Swannington	C.V. Lane
No. 2 Platoon:	Broom Leys and Greenhill	T. Wootton
No. 3 Platoon:	Ravenstone and Hugglescote	M.J. Wilson
No. 4 Platoon:	Bardon	F.J. Surman
No. 5 Platoon:	Whitwick	W. Bruce

Commercial Sections attached to No. 2 Company:
No. 1 Section: J. Burgess & Sons Ltd, Elastic Goods, Pioneer Works, Belvoir Road, Coalville.
Section Commander: Wollerton
No. 2 Section: Chutsom & Kemp, Elastic Web Goods, Highfields Factory, Coalville.
Section Commander: J. Kinsey
No. 3 Section: Leicestershire & Warwickshire Electric Power Co. Ltd, Mantle Lane, Coalville.
Section Commander: E. Foskett
No. 4 Section: London, Midland & Scottish (LMS) Railway Co, Coalville Station.
Section Commander: Curtis
No. 5 Section: Midland 'Red' Motor Services, Ashby Road Garage, Coalville.
Section Commander: Burder

No. 6 Section: Pegson Ltd Engineers, Mammoth Street and Mantle Lane, Coalville.
Section Commander: W.C. Perkins
No. 7 Section: Snibston Colliery Co. Ltd, Ashby Road, Coalville
Section Commander: H. Wortley
No. 8 Section: South Leicestershire Colliery Co. Ltd, South Street, Hugglescote
Section Commander: H. Woods
No. 9 Section: Whitwick Colliery Co. Ltd, Whitwick Road, Coalville.
Section Commander: Booth

No. 3 Company: Breedon and Coleorton
Company HQ: The Three Horseshoes, Breedon-on-the-Hill
Company Commander: J. Shields
Second in Command: The Revd C.M.K. Parsons

Platoon	Platoon HQ	Platoon Commanders
No. 1 Platoon:	Breedon-on-the-Hill	T.W. Thurley
No. 2 Platoon:	Worthington	C. Platts
No. 3 Platoon:	Griffydam	J. Ford
No. 4 Platoon:	Staunton Harold	The Earl Ferrers
No. 5 Platoon:	Osgathorpe	A. Millward
No. 6 Platoon:	Cole Orton	A. Walker
No. 7 Platoon:	New Lount Colliery Co.	F. Hodges

No. 4 Company: Snarestone etc
Company HQ: The Globe Inn, Snarestone
Company Commander: G.D. Lowe
Second in Command: D.E. Lewis-Jones

Platoon	Platoon HQ	Platoon Commanders
No. 1 Platoon:	Snarestone	H.R. Leddra
No. 2 Platoon:	Appleby Magna	D.E. Wileman
No. 3 Platoon:	Heather	H. Dronfield
No. 4 Platoon:	Packington	Dr. G.H. Lunge

Home Guards of the 12th (Motor Reconnaissance) Battalion outside their Canning Street headquarters, Leicester. Interviewee Alan Clare sits front row, sixth from left.

MOBILE UNIT

Battalion HQ: Leicester Stadium, Blackbird Road, Leicester

Battalion Staff
Commanding Officer: Captain W.J. Symons VC
Second in Command: P.W.G. Russell
Adjutant: J.G. Robertson
Administrative Assistant: F.L. Attenborough

'A' Company: East Midland
Company HQ: Leicester Stadium, Blackbird Road, Leicester
Company Commander: A.L. Bray
Second in Command: S.C. Castell

Platoon	Platoon Commanders
No. 1 Platoon:	F. Wale
No. 2 Platoon:	S.C. Castell
No. 3 Platoon:	J.W. Wilson
No. 4 Platoon:	G.V. Biscomt

Transport:
Two 8hp cars
Seven 10hp cars
12 12hp cars or over
Three motorcycles

'B' Company: East Midland
Company HQ: Leicester Stadium, Blackbird Road, Leicester
Company Commander: R. Taylor
Second in Command: S.H. Crace

Platoon	Platoon Commanders
No. 5 Platoon:	S.H. Crace
No. 6 Platoon:	T.L. Garner
No. 7 Platoon:	
No. 8 Platoon:	

Transport:
Two 8hp cars
Six 10hp cars
11 12hp cars or over
Six motorcycles

1st (Rutland) Battalion, Rutland Home Guard Order of Battle October 1940[643]

Zone Headquarters: Drill Hall, Penn Street, Oakham

Zone Headquarters Staff
Zone Commander: Wing Commander J.W. Ogilvy-Dalgleish OBE
Second in Command: Lieutenant-Colonel F.J. Cahusac DSO
Administrative Assistant: H. Cartwright

'A' Company: North-East
(Belmisthorpe, Casterton, Empingham, Essendine, Exton, Greetham, Pickworth, Ryhall and Whitwell)

Company Commander: V. Chaplin
Second in Command: E.G. Bolton

Platoon	Platoon Commanders
No. 1 Platoon:	W. Wakefield
No. 2 Platoon:	W. Cook
No. 3 Platoon:	J.C. Bell
No. 4 Platoon:	F.D. Little

No.6 Platoon, 'B' Company, 1st Rutland Battalion Home Guard, October 1944. (Maureen Walker)

'B' Company: Central

(Hambleton, Ketton, North and South Luffenham, Market Overton, Thistleton and [temporarily] Langham)

Company Commander: Major H.E. Whaley
Second in Command: Captain R.W. Wilson

Platoon	Platoon Commanders
No. 5 Platoon:	Captain J.A. Hornsby
No. 6 Platoon:	Captain C.C. Whadcoat
No. 7 Platoon:	W.G. Wakefield MC
No. 8 Platoon:	H.T. Lovell

'C' Company: Oakham and District

(Braunston, Brooke, Burley, Egleton, Lyndon, Manton, Oakham and [later] Langham)

Company Commander: Captain C.N. Newton MC
Second in Command: C. Stanley Johnson

Platoon	Platoon Commanders
No. 9 Platoon:	S.S. Watson
No. 10 Platoon:	C. Ball
No. 11 Platoon:	E. Palmer
No. 12 Platoon:	Lieutenant-Colonel Hon. D. Tollemache DSO

'D' Company: Uppingham and District

(Ayston, Belton, Bisbrooke, Caldecott, Glaston, Lyddington, Morcott, Preston, Ridlington, Seaton, Uppingham, Wardley and Wing)

Company Commander: V.T. Saunders
Second in Command: P.B. King TD

Platoon	Platoon Commanders
No. 13 Platoon:	W. Leatherbarrow
No. 14 Platoon:	D.J.J. Evans
No. 15 Platoon:	A. Turner MM
No. 16 Platoon:	A.H. Lewis

LEICESTERSHIRE AND RUTLAND HOME GUARD
ORDER OF BATTLE PART 2: FEBRUARY 1941–1944[644]

Sub Area Commander:		Col. M.A. Studd DSO MC
Zone Commanders:	Leicestershire:	Col. Sir Thomas G. Cope Bt
	Rutland:	Col. J.W. Ogilvy-Dalgleish CMG DSO
Sector Commanders:	Leicester:	Lt-Col. L. Sawyer DSO
	Melton-Oakham:	Col. J.W. Ogilvy-Dalgleish CMG DSO
	Bosworth:	Lt-Col. A.J. Trousdell DSO MC
Home Guard Group Commander:	Leicester:	Col. H.W.H. Tyler MC[645]

LEICESTER GROUP

	Battalion Commanders	From
	Lt-Colonel F.B. Hitchings MC	1.2.1941

1st (North Leicester) Battalion:
Battalion HQ: 25 De Montfort Street Leicester
'A' Company HQ: The Grange, Birstall
'B' Company HQ: Manor House, Thurmaston
'C' Company HQ: Leicester Golf Club
'D' Company HQ: Beaumont Leys
'E' Company HQ:

2nd (South Leicester) Battalion: Lt-Colonel W.T. Pares MC — 1.2.1941
Battalion HQ: The White Hotel, Oadby
'A' Company HQ: University College, Leicester
'B' Company HQ: Orson Wright's, Canal Street, South Wigston
'C' Company HQ: 42 Enderby Road, Blaby
'D' Company HQ: Midland Bank, London Road, Oadby

3rd (West Leicester) Battalion: Lt-Colonel T.B. Jones — 1.2.1941
Battalion HQ: 19 Magazine Square, Leicester
'A' Company HQ: Woodlands, Kirby Muxloe
'B' Company HQ: 410 Hinckley Road, Leicester
'C' Company HQ: The Institute, Enderby
'D' Company HQ: The Barn, Stamford Arms, Groby
'E' Company HQ: Westcotes Church School, Hinckley Road, Leicester
'F' Company HQ: Lockheed Brake Co, Narborough Road, Leicester

4th (Central Leicester) Battalion: Lt-Colonel W.N. Dunn — 10.8.1942
Battalion HQ: The Magazine, Leicester
HQ Company: Tramway Office, Belgrave Gate, Leicester
'A' Company HQ: Abbey Pumping Station, Corporation Road, Leicester
'B' Company HQ: 28 Great Central Street, Leicester
'C' Company HQ: Partridge Wilson & Co, Evington Valley Road, Leicester
'D' Company HQ: St Barnabas School, East Park Road, Leicester
'F' Company (Mobile) HQ: Wyggeston Girls' School, Regent Road, Leicester

MELTON MOWBRAY GROUP

5th (Belvoir) Battalion: Lt-Colonel A.J. Fellowes-Prynne — 1.2.1942
Battalion HQ: 31 Nottingham Street, Melton Mowbray
'A' Company HQ: Estate Offices, Belvoir Castle
'B' Company HQ:
'C' Company HQ: Sysonby Lodge

6th (Quorn) Battalion: Lt-Colonel Sir Harold Nutting BT   1.2.1941
Battalion HQ: Remount Depot, Melton Mowbray
'A' Company HQ: Dowson's, Main Street, Asfordby
'B' Company HQ: Twyford
'C' Company HQ: The Old Hall, Keyham
'D' Company HQ: Holwell Works, Asfordby
'E' Company HQ: Gartree, Sandy Lane, Melton Mowbray

MARKET HARBOROUGH/BOSWORTH GROUP

7th (Market Harborough) Battalion: Lt-Colonel H.D. Belgrave DSO   27.10.1943
Battalion HQ: 2 St Mary's Road, Market Harborough
'A' Company HQ: 33 St Mary's Road, Market Harborough
'B' Company HQ: Bray and Bray, Bank Street, Lutterworth
'C' Company HQ: The Paddocks, Tur Langton
'D' Company HQ: The White Heart, Billesdon
'E' Company HQ: Othorpe House, Slawston

8th (Market Bosworth) Battalion: Lt-Colonel J.T.L. Baxter MC   20.3.1943
Battalion HQ: Drill Hall, Station Road, Hinckley
HQ Company HQ: Old Cottages, Bond Street, Hinckley
'A' Company HQ: Conservative Club, Hinckley
'B' Company HQ: Old Vicarage, Sutton Cheney
'C' Company HQ: Toc H Rooms, Reform Road, Ibstock
'D' Company HQ: Hollydene, Hinckley Road, Earl Shilton
'F' Company HQ: R.A.F. Station, Desford

LOUGHBOROUGH GROUP

9th (Loughborough) Battalion: Lt-Colonel H.J. Stamper   30.12.1942
Battalion HQ: Drill Hall, Loughborough
HQ Company HQ: Granby Street, Loughborough
'A' Company HQ: Emmanuel Hall, Loughborough
'B' Company HQ: Granby Street, Loughborough
'C' Company HQ: Drill Hall, Shepshed
'D' Company HQ: Morris' South Works, Loughborough
'E' Company HQ: Corporation Gas Works, Loughborough

10th (Charnwood) Battalion: Lt-Colonel C.H. Martin OBE   1.2.1941
Battalion HQ: The Coppice, Rothley
'A' Company HQ: The Manor House, Kegworth
'B' Company HQ: The Old Parsonage, Hoton
'C' Company HQ: J. Ellis and Sons, Barrow-on-Soar
'D' Company HQ: The Temple, Rothley
'E' Company HQ: The Schools, Woodhouse Eaves

11th (Ashby-de-la-Zouch) Battalion: Lt-Colonel L.A. Statham   23.11.1942

Battalion HQ: Drill Hall, Ashby
'A' Company HQ: Donisthorpe Colliery
'B' Company HQ: 20 Wood Street, Ashby
'C' Company HQ: 'Wagon and Horses', Griffydam
'D' Company HQ: The Grammar School, Appleby Magna
'E' Company HQ: Tower Chambers, High Street, Coalville
'F' Company HQ: Owen Street, Coalville
'G' Company HQ: Drill Hall, Coalville

EXTRA-ZONE UNITS

12th (Motor Reconnaissance) Battalion: Lt-Colonel R. Taylor   1.10.1943

Battalion HQ: 51 Grafton Place, Leicester
13th (25th GPO) Battalion: Lt-Colonel A.H. Wells   26.7.1943
'A' Company HQ: Head Post Office, Leicester (Post)
'B' Company HQ: 66 London Road, Leicester (Telephones)
2079 (Leicester) Motor Transport Company: Major L.H. Cox   2.2.1944

HOME GUARD ANTI-AIRCRAFT UNITS

227 (101st Leicester Home Guard) AA Rocket Battery:
Victoria Park, Leicester
Battery Office HQ at 148a London Road, Leicester
530 'A' (1st Leicester Battalion) LAA Troop
British United Shoe Machinery Co. Ltd, Law Street, Belgrave, Leicester
532 'B' (2nd Leicester Battalion) LAA Troop
Power Jets Ltd, Cambridge Road, Whetstone

RUTLAND

1st (Rutland) Battalion: Colonel J.W. Ogilvy-Dalgleish OBE
Lieutenant-Colonel H.E. Whaley from 20.8.1943
Zone Headquarters: Drill Hall, Oakham

APPENDIX B
VULNERABLE POINTS LIST IN LEICESTERSHIRE
LIST OF VITAL FACTORIES 1941

(A) = Admiralty
(S) = Ministry of Supply
(P) = Ministry of Aircraft Production

Leicester Group

(S) Adcock & Shipley, Ash Street, Leicester

(P) Alvis Mechanisation Ltd, Castle Works, Mountsorrel

(P) Armstrong Siddeley Motors Ltd, Excel Works, Walnut Street, Leicester

(P) Asea Electric Ltd, Erith Road, near Aylestone, Leicester

(S + P) Automotive Products Ltd (Lockheed), Northfield, Narborough Road, Leicester

(P) Alvis Mechanisation Ltd at Bosworth & Wright Ltd, Empress Works, Hollow Road, Anstey

(S + P) Bentley Engineering Company, Comet Works, New Bridge Street, Leicester: Bofors guns

(P) Berridge I.L. & Co. Ltd, Sanvey Gate, Leicester

(A) Booton W.E. Ltd, Wanlip Street, Leicester

(P) B.T.H. [British Thomson Houston] Co. Ltd, Melton Road, Thurmaston

(P) B.T.H. Co. Ltd at Hall Erale [?], Blackbird Road, Leicester

(A) B.T.H. Co. Ltd at Hall & Pincus, Evington Valley Road, Leicester

(P) British United Shoe Machinery Co. Ltd, Union Works, Belgrave Road, Leicester: Spitfire parts

(S) BSA Guns Ltd, Agency Factory, Abbey Mills, Abbey Park Road, Leicester: A/T guns

(S) BSA Guns Ltd, Agency Factory, CWS, Knighton Fields Road, Leicester

(P) Canon & Stokes Ltd, 9 Orson Street Works, North Evington, Leicester

(P) Canon & Stokes Ltd, 80 Coleman Road, Leicester

(P) Castle Bromwich Aeroplane Factory, Old Skating Rink, Western Boulevard, Leicester

(P) Castle Bromwich Aeroplane Factory, late A.S. Yeats Ltd, Blackbird Road, Leicester

(P) Castle Bromwich Aeroplane Factory at Paton & Baldwins, Westbridge Works, Leicester

(P) Charnwood Engineering Co. Ltd, Abbey Lane, Leicester

(A + S) Coventry Gauge & Tool Co. Ltd, Filbert Street, Leicester

(P) Cascelloid Ltd, Abbey Lane, Leicester

(S) Coventry Gauge & Tool Co. Ltd, Two Steeples, South Wigston, near Leicester

(P) Daimler Co. Ltd, Braunstone House, Braunstone, Leicester

(P) Gent & Co. Ltd, Faraday Works, Leicester

(S) Grieve T. & Co. Ltd, Lancastria Works, French Road, Leicester

(S) Hinton D. Ltd, Star Works, Rothley, Leicester

(P) Jones A.A. & Shipman Ltd, East Park Road, PO Box 87, Leicester

(P) Jones A.A. & Shipman Ltd, Gypsy Lane, Leicester

(P) Lea Francis Engineering (1937) Ltd. at Vaughan & Harborne, Wellington Street, Leicester

(S) Lockheed Hydraulic Brake Co. Ltd (G. Gibbons Ltd), Aylestone Road, Leicester

(A + S) Mellor Bromley & Co. Ltd, Minotaur Works, St Saviours Road East, Leicester

(A + S) Parmeko Ltd, Percy Road, Aylestone Park, Leicester

(P) Pard F. Ltd, Corona Works, St Saviours Road, Leicester

(P) Premier Drum Co, Canal Street, South Wigston, Leicester

(P) Reid & Sigrist Ltd, Braunstone, Leicester

(P) Spencer & Co, 37a Victoria Road East, Leicester

(P) Standard Telephone & Cables at N. Corah, Leicester

(P) Standard Telephone & Cables at Chilprufe, Leicester

(P) Standard Telephone & Cables at Aylestone Dyeworks, Ranby Road, Aylestone, Leicester

(P) Standard Telephone & Cables Laboratories at T.G. Hirst, Abbey Park Road, Leicester

(S) Stibbe G. & Co, Maxim Works, Leicester

(S) S.S. Cars Ltd, premises of J.W. Black Ltd, at Central Eastern [?], near Leicester

(P) Taylorcraft Aeroplanes (England) Ltd, Colmore Road, Frog Island, Leicester

(P) Taylorcraft Aeroplanes (England) Ltd, En Tout Cas Ltd, Church Hill Road, Thurmaston, Leicester

(P) Taylorcraft Aeroplanes (England) Ltd at Britannia Works, Thurmaston, Leicester

(P) Taylor, Taylor & Hobson Ltd, Stoughton Street Works, Leicester

(P) Taylor, Taylor & Hobson Ltd, Glebe Street, Leicester

(P) Taylor, Taylor & Hobson Ltd, Avenue Road, Leicester

(S) Taylor, Taylor & Hobson Ltd, Byford Road, Leicester

(P) Turner Luke & Co, Deacon Street, Leicester

(P) Wadkin Ltd, Green Lane Works, Leicester

Loughborough Group

(P) Airwork & General Trading Co. at the Aerodrome, Dishley, Loughborough

(S) Brush Coachworks, Loughborough

(S + P) Bush Electrical Engineering Co. Ltd, Falcon Works, Loughborough

(S) William Cotton & Co. Ltd, Pinfold Gate, Loughborough

(P + S) Willowbrook Ltd, Derby Road, Loughborough

Charnwood Group

(P) Alvis Mechanisation Ltd, Castle Works, Mountsorrel

(P) Frigidaire Ltd, Boundary Road, Mountsorrel

(P) Slack & Parr, Kegworth

(P) Taylorcraft (Aeroplanes) Ltd, Leicester Road, Mountsorrel

(S) Wright M. & Sons, Quorn Mills, near Loughborough

Ashby-de-la-Zouch Group

(S) British Timpkin Ltd, East Works, Coalville

(P) Castle Bromwich Aeroplane Factory at Cascelloid Ltd, Owen Street, Coalville

(P) Dunlop Rim & Wheel Co, Coalville Mining & Technical College, Bridge Road, Coalville

(P) Dunlop Rim & Wheel Co. at Hutchbys Garage, Manor Road, Ashburton Road, Hugglescote, near Coalville

(P) Daimler Co. Ltd, Olsey Factory, Coalville

(S) Pegson Ltd, Coalville

(P) Rolls Royce Ltd, New Lount Pipeworks, Ashby-de-la-Zouch

Vulnerable Points in Leicester: 1941

Waterworks at Bowling Green Street, Leicester

Leicester Gas & Electricity Works

GPO Leicester

Co-op Telephone Exchange on Albion Street, South Wigston

Abbey Park Pumping Station, Abbey Park Road

Sub-pumping Station, Belgrave Road

LMS Station/LNER Station, Belgrave Road

LNER Station, Great Central Street

City Transport, Abbey Park Road

The Magazine, Newarkes

HM Prison, Welford Road

Petroleum Board, Parkhurst Street

Petroleum Board, Catherine Street

County ARP HQ, Friar Lane

Cropston Reservoir

Vulnerable Points in Loughborough:

Great Central

Central Electricity Board, Grid Sub-station

Gas Works, Green Close Lane

Gas Works, Britannia Street

Nanpantan Reservoir

Blackbrook Reservoir

Leicester to Derwent pipeline

LNER Railway Viaduct

LMS Railway cast metal bridge

Cotes Bridge

Zouch Bridge

Post Office Repeater Station

Hathern Post Office Telephone Exchange

Municipal Aerodrome

RAOC Workshops

Vulnerable Points in Charnwood

Swithland Reservoir

Service Reservoir

Mountsorrel Granite Company Ltd

Vulnerable Points in Ashby-de-la-Zouch

Coalville Waterworks

Pumping Station, Chilcote

J.E. Ison & Sons Ltd, Ashby-de-la-Zouch

J.E. Ison & Sons Ltd, Swannington

Appendix C
'QUORN MILITARY DEFENCE SCHEME, DECEMBER 1942 – SECRET[646]

a) Garrison Commander: Lieut. C.W. Thornton, No. 13 Platoon, 'D' Company, 10th (Charnwood) Battalion
Second in Command: 2nd Lieut. F. Astill

b) Troops Available:

	Officers	Sergeants	ORs
Home Guard	2 Platoon	6	76
	4 attached	2 attached	
Regular	Detachment R.A.O.C. at Tennis Pavilion, Manor House		

c) Weapons Held: 1 Blacker Bombard, 2 Lewis light machine guns, 2 Northovers, 7 Sten Carbines, 46 (P17) Rifles, 2 E.Y.

d) Transport held: 1 x 30 cwt lorry, 11 private cars (owned by members)

e) Location of Garrison HQ: "Sunnyside", Leicester Road, Quorn, 'phone: Quorn 149 – Ext. 17

f) Location of Ammunition Store: Home Farm outbuildings, opposite 34 Leicester Road, Quorn

g) I make my reports to: Major A.F.M. Wright, The Temple, Rothley 'phone: 115

h) Location of feeding centres: Company – The Temple, Rothley
Platoon – The Institute, Meeting Street, Quorn

i) Food supplies will be obtained from: Company HQ

j) Cooking utensils will be supplied by: Company and privately (WVS)

k) Cooking will be done by: WVS or platoon arrangements

l) Location of casualty collecting posts: Quorn House, 'phone Quorn 2

m) Church bells will be rung by: 1 member of the Home Guard

n) Keys of church kept at: The Vicarage, 1 by OC Platoon

o) Method of warning HG on receipt of ACTION STATIONS: DR and 'phone

p) Assembly points for HG on mustering: BHQ "Sunnyside"

q) Name and location of Chairman of Invasion Committee: Not appointed yet[647]

r) Name and location of Head Warden: J. Huntley, Loughborough Road, Quorn

s) Name and location of Police: PC Norman, 87 Leicester Road, Quorn

t) The following work will be carried out on Action Stations:
1) Completion of all trenches where sited
2) Partial establishment of 3 roadblocks where sited
3) Other work as detailed in platoon defence scheme

u) Labour for this work will be provided by: HG members and assistance from the Invasion Committee

v) Tools will be provided by: Company or local resources

Including:		
Picks	1	
Shovels	2	
Wire Cutters	1	
Wire Cutters gloves	1 pair	
Axes		
Sandbags		

These may be obtained on loan from Mr Frank Facer's Stable, Station Road (SK 562167)

Fell axe	1	
Cross cut saws	2	
Hand saws	4	
Wedges	6	
Spades	3	
Shovels	3	

Timber (all grades) from Facer's Yard, Meeting Street

Phase A Dispositions:

If attacks by paratroops or airborne troops is expected my troops will be disposed as follows:
"Sunnyside", Leicester Road; Quorn House Stables and the Cricket Pavilion.

Battle HQ: Porters' Room, Quorn LNER Station (SK 549162).

Defended localities at:
    1) O.P.15 (Highfields Farm) (SK 547159) 2 NCOs and 8 ORs
    2) R.V.17 (Loughborough Road) (SK 555169) 1 NCOs and 2 ORs

Check points will be manned at: Nil

OPs at (will be manned night/day):
    OP 15 (Highfields Farm) (SK 547159)
    Manned at night by 1 NCO and 4 ORs
    One hour before dawn until one hour after dusk
    by 2 NCOs and 8 ORs.

Roads (will be patrolled night/day): 3 patrols will cover all roads in platoon area, making contact with "C" Company at Barrow Bridge (SK 573174); 9th Battalion at Railway Bridge (SK 546182) and "E" Company along Woodhouse Road.

The area in which I am responsible for dealing with enemy paratroops without waiting for orders from higher authority is: [Quorn platoon area]

Method of communication will be: Telephone if available or DRs

Phase B Dispositions:

If attack by enemy mechanised troops is expected my dispositions will be:

"Sunnyside", Leicester Road; Quorn House Stables and the Cricket Pavilion

Battle HQ: Porters' Room, Quorn LNER Station (SK 549162)

Defended localities at:
    1) Quorn Station Bridge (SK 548162) 2 NCOs and ORs
    2) R.V. 17 (SK 555169) 2 NCOs and 8 ORs
    3) Leicester Road roadblock (SK 562165) 1 NCO and 2 ORs
    4) Soar Road roadblock (SK 567169) 1 NCO and 2 ORs

Flame Fougasse at: Woodhouse Road, Quorn (SK 548161)

Hanworth Torpedoes at: Leicester Road, Quorn (SK 563165)

Blacker Bombard at: Woodhouse Road, Quorn (SK 548162)

Northover Projector at: intend to keep these mobile with mobile section

Smith Guns at: (none)

Standing patrols to give warning of approach at: each post above

Method of communication will be: telephone if available or DRs'

Analysis

It will be noted that there were two different preparatory dispositions for varying forms of attack.

Phase A Dispositions, against airborne troops, involved the manning of only two defended localities, with the majority of the platoon in a mobile role ready to engage paratroopers wherever they landed in the platoon area. A 24-hour observation post was manned at Highfields Farm and three bicycle patrols would reconnoitre all the roads in the platoon area, a route that took 56 minutes.

Phase B Dispositions, against enemy mechanised troops and tanks, were more static, with four defended localities manned, including two rail roadblocks. A mobile section with Northover Projector(s) could be sent to reinforce any area. Weapon trenches were planned but were only to be dug on Action Stations, although some were built at O.P. 15. and the Defended Locality at R.V. 17. They appear not to have been dug deep enough, as one report later stated, 'slight building of the parapet would prevent heads appearing over the skyline'!

After an inspection of 'D' Company's defences by Major C. Burton on 6 December 1942, he stated that although the site chosen for Quorn Platoon's Blacker Bombard was 'OK', at this time there was no static mounting for it. However, he stated the 'defence scheme is quite the most comprehensive I have seen', unlike No. 14 (Mountsorrel) Platoon's defences, which were 'too spread out' with their Blacker Bombard 'sited in a flood area'. Likewise, No. 15 (Rothley) Platoon's Blacker Bombard by the Reservoir was 'in an impossible position 280 yards from the road' with the other 'Blacker position on Cossington Road much too far out of the platoon area. The Station Blacker not good. (These are all static mountings) and are not sited by the Company Commander who does not agree with them.'

A further inspection by Lt-Col. Harrison and Col. M.A. Studd the same month approved Quorn's defence scheme, with the exception of the Soar Road roadblock. They 'agreed…in every detail' with the defence of the bridge at Quorn Station, but disagreed 'slightly' with the positions at R.V. 17 and suggested alternatives. They left the ultimate decision to the Platoon Commander Lt C.W. Thornton, who promptly ignored their alternatives and 'therefore adopted the original positions'!

There were three versions of the Quorn defence scheme between December 1942 to February 1944, but changes were very minor, such as amounts of men and ammunition. The Hanworth Torpedoes and Flame Fougasses were removed by late-1943, to be replaced with one extra Blacker Bombard and Northover Projector, bringing the total to two each. By 1943 it appears the Shock Section may no longer have been a secret resistance unit, becoming instead a mobile section based at the Cricket Pavilion, and, by February 1944, it appears to have been removed from the scheme altogether. The scheme was wound down towards the end of 1944, with the slit trenches at O.P.15 (Highfields Farm) finally filled in on 22 October 1944.

Appendix D

LEICESTERSHIRE HOME GUARD ROLL OF HONOUR: THOSE WHO DIED WHILE IN THE SERVICE OF THE COUNTRY

'They shall grow not old, as we that are left grow old;
Age shall not weary them, nor the years condemn.
At the going down of the sun and in the morning
We will remember them.'

BOYCE, Volunteer Stanley, 44, of 13th (25th GPO) Battalion, killed while on duty during an air raid on Wisbech, Cambridgeshire, 17 July 1941

BRADBURY, Corporal Ernest, of 1st (North Leicester) Battalion, 31 August 1941*

BRANT, Volunteer Horace, 42, of 9th (Loughborough) Battalion, collapsed and died on exercise, 7 September 1941

BRISTOW, Sergeant Instructor James G., 39, of Leicester Home Guard, shot dead with own weapon, 11 August 1943

BURNARD, Cadet Kenneth, 15, of Leicester Home Guard Cadets, collapsed and died on exercise, 2 November 1941

CARLISLE, Lieutenant Ronald, 44, of Leicester Home Guard, committed suicide due to depression caused by previous Home Guard injury, 19 July 1944

GEORGE, Captain Arthur S., 47, of the 1st (North Leicester) Battalion, who died from illness, 23 December 1943

HALE, Volunteer Owen J., 19, of 9th (Loughborough) Battalion, accidentally shot dead while on duty, 26 February 1941

HAYWOOD, Volunteer Albert Charles, 55, of 8th (Market Bosworth) Battalion, 'developed a chill' and died, 3 October 1941

HENSON, Volunteer D.H., of the Leicester Home Guard, passed away in his sleep while on duty, 30 January 1942

MARTIN, Volunteer Bert, 42, of No. A6 Platoon (Leics. and Warwickshire Electric Power Co.), 8th (Market Bosworth) Battalion, accidentally died after fall while on duty, 19 October 1940

MARVIN, Private William Stanley, 43, of 8th (Market Bosworth) Battalion, who 'took ill while at exercise [and] died shortly afterwards', 14 June 1942

MOFFAT, Lieutenant Jack, 23, of 1st (North Leicester) Battalion, accidentally killed on exercise, 7 March 1943

MONK, Section Leader George T., of the Sutton Bonington Platoon, collapsed and died on exercise, 17 September 1940

PRATT, Private Albert S, 19, of the Leicester Home Guard, who died after accidentally shooting himself, 10 April 1943

WELSH, Private Ralph. S., 50, of 2nd (South Leicester) Battalion, died of an illness contracted while on duty, 14 March 1942

WILLIAMSON, Corporal William Hodson, 25, of 11th (Ashby-de-la-Zouch) Battalion, accidentally killed by a home-made bomb, 8 February 1942

YEATES, Captain William S, 43, of the 9th (Loughborough) Battalion, accidentally killed while on exercise, 28 March 1943

* The exact circumstances relating to the death of this Home Guard has not been fully determined. However, he died on a Sunday, the main day for Home Guard exercises, and his name is listed on the CWGC register, so it is assumed he died while on Home Guard duty. Any further information would be appreciated.
Note: The above list is composed only of those who died in circumstances relating to their Home Guard service. Ogilvy-Dalgleish records no Rutland Home Guards died while on Home Guard service. This list has been compiled through the use of as many different sources as possible, but unfortunately many official records are incomplete or inaccurate. If it is believed that an individual has been inadvertently missed out from this list and died of causes related to their Home Guard service, the author would be pleased to include their name in future editions of this book.

Appendix E
Home Guard Awards[648]

808 Home Guards were honoured for their services at the Stand Down in December 1944. Seven were from Leicestershire and Rutland:

OBE (Military)

Lieutenant-Colonel C.H. Martin, Commanding Officer of 10th (Charnwood) Battalion Leicestershire Home Guard, for 'inspiring leadership and efficient organisation'.

Major A.P. Marsh, Company Commander, Melton Mowbray Company, 6th (Quorn) Battalion (in 1943) for 'service to the defence corps'.[649]

MBE (Military)

Major E.G. Bolton, Company Commander, 'A' Company, 1st (Rutland) Battalion Rutland Home Guard.[650]

Major S.J. Fensome, Company Commander in the 5th (Belvoir) Battalion Leicestershire Home Guard, for 'raising the standard of efficiency and training in the battalion due to his interest and enthusiasm'.

Major H.L. Murray, Second in Command of 9th (Loughborough) Battalion Leicestershire Home Guard, for 'leadership and efficiency'.

BEM (Military)

Sergeant W.H. Mickleburgh, of the 6th (Quorn) Battalion Leicestershire Home Guard, for 'good work at the outset and for organising the local Home Guard in Houghton-on-the-Hill on the night it was bombed'.

Sergeant W. Scragg, of the 10th (Charnwood) Battalion Leicestershire HG, for 'great devotion to duty'.

Abbreviations

2 i/c: Second in Command
2/Lt: Second Lieutenant
AA: Anti-Aircraft
ABDS: Auxiliary Bomb Disposal (Sub) Section/Squad
ACF: Army Cadet Force
ADGB: Air Defence (of) Great Britain
ARP: Air Raid Precautions
ATS: Auxiliary Territorial Service (women)
AU: Auxiliary Units (British resistance organisation)
BL: British Legion (Royal British Legion from 1971)
Bn: Battalion
Capt.: Captain
CD: Civil Defence
C-in-C: Commander-in-Chief
Cmdr: Commander
CO: Commanding Officer
Coy: Company
Cpl: Corporal
CSM: Company Sergeant Major
DCM: Distinguished Conduct Medal
DL: Defended Locality
DR: Despatch Rider
DSO: Distinguished Service Order
E-Y: Edgar Yule (rifle grenade projector)
FS: Field Service
GCR: Great Central Railway
Gen.: General
GHQ: General Headquarters (the central army command in the UK)
GOC: General Officer Commanding
GPO: General Post Office
GS: General Service
HAA: Heavy Anti-Aircraft
HE: High Explosive
HG: Home Guard
HQ: Headquarters
ITC: Infantry Training Centre at Glen Parva, Leicester
KOYLI: King's Own Yorkshire Light Infantry
KP: Key Point
LAA: Light Anti-Aircraft
LCpl: Lance Corporal
LDV: Local Defence Volunteers
Leic.: Leicester
Leics.: Leicestershire
LMS: London Midland Scottish Railway
LO: Loughborough Record Office
LRO: The Record Office for Leicestershire, Leicester & Rutland at Wigston
Lt: Lieutenant
Lt-Col.: Lieutenant-Colonel

MAP: Ministry of Aircraft Production
MC: Military Cross
Mk: Mark
MM: Military Medal
MO: Medical Officer
MoS: Ministry of Supply
MSM: Meritous Service Medal
MT: Motor Transport
NA: National Archives (formerly the Public Record Office), Kew
NCO: Non-Commissioned Officer
NDC: National Defence Corps
NFS: National Fire Service
OC: Officer Commanding
OP: Observation Post
ORs: Other Ranks
P17: .300 Pattern 17 (rifle)
PBI: 'Poor Bloody Infantry'
PC: Police Constable
PIAT: Projector, Infantry, Anti-Tank
PSI: Permanent Staff Instructor
Pte: Private
PWD: Petroleum Warfare Department
QM: Quartermaster
RA: Royal Artillery
RAF: Royal Air Force
RAMC: Royal Army Medical Corps
RAOC: Royal Army Ordnance Corps
RAP: Regimental Aid Post
RAPC: Royal Army Pay Corps
RBL: Royal British Legion
RE: Royal Engineers
SAA: Small Arms Ammunition
SB: Stretcher Bearer
Sgt: Sergeant
SMG: Sub-machine Gun
SMLE: Short Magazine Lee Enfield .303 rifle
SOE: Special Operations Executive
TA: Territorial Army
TEWT: Tactical Exercise Without Troops
UP: Unrotated Projectile
US: United States
UXB: Unexploded Bomb
VC: Victoria Cross
Vol.: Volunteer
VP: Vulnerable Point
VTC: Volunteer Training Corps
WAAF: Women's Auxiliary Air Force
WHD: Women's Home Defence
WO: War Office or Warrant Officer
WRNS: Women's Royal Naval Service
W/T: Wireless Telegraphy
WVS: Women's Voluntary Service

Sources

Primary Sources
Leicestershire and Rutland Record Office, Long Street, Wigston:
DE 819: Minutes of the Leicestershire and Rutland Territorial Army Association 1940–1957
DE 1381: Rutland County Council Records 1908–1949
DE 1738: Records of Thurnby Home Guard Rifle Club 1943–1970
DE 2263: Home Guard papers of Major C.A.B. Elliott 1938–1946
DE 2932: Countesthorpe Home Guard records 1940–1944
DE 3548: Register of 'D' Coy, 2nd (South Leicester) Battalion
DE 3620: LDV/HG Records of R.E. Pochin 1939–1946
DE 4368: Croft Defence Scheme 1944
DE 4952: Records of Sgt F.N. Syer, 1st (North Leicester) Battalion
Misc 140: Records of 1st (North Leicester) Battalion
Misc 1361: OS Map of Charnwood LDV Observation Posts 1940
P 71: Order of Battle, Leicestershire Home Guard October 1940

Newspapers
Daily Mail 1951
Hinckley Times and Guardian 1941–44
Illustrated Leicester Chronicle 1940–44
Isle of Ely and Wisbech Advertiser 1941
Leicester Advertiser 1940–45
Leicester Mercury 1940–2005
Lincoln, Rutland and Stamford Mercury 1944
Loughborough Echo 1941
Loughborough Monitor 1940–45
Wisbech Standard 1941

Loughborough Library, Loughborough
LO: 355.35: *Stand Easy* Loughborough HG Magazines, 1941
LO: Rothley Invasion Committee Report

National Archives (formerly Public Record Office), Kew
HO 202/8: Postscript to Report No. 48
WO 166/1222: North Midlands Area HQ War Diary Sept 1940–Dec 1941
WO 166/1225: East Midlands Area HQ War Diary Aug 1940–Feb 1941
WO 166/1300: Leics. and Northants Sub-Area War Diary Nov 1941–Dec 1941
WO 166/6751: Leicester Sub-Area War Diary Jan–Dec 1942
WO 166/6820: North Midlands Area HQ War Diary Jan 1942–Dec 1942
WO 166/10871: North Midlands Area HQ War Diary Jan 1943–Dec 1943
WO 166/10974: Leicester Sub-Area War Diary Jan 1943–Dec 1943
WO 166/11206: 32nd AA Brigade War Diary Jan–Dec 1943
WO 166/14646: 32nd AA Brigade War Diary Jan–Dec 1944
WO 166/14427: North Midlands Area HQ War Diary Jan 1944–Dec 1944
WO 166/14516: Leicester Sub-Area War Diary Jan 1944–Oct 1944
WO 199/66: Defence of Y-Stations
WO 199/400: Auxiliary Bomb Disposal Sub-Units Aug 1942–Nov 1944
WO 199/1439: Operational Arrangements for Leicester No. 3 Sector Nov 1941
WO 199/1481: Home Guard Bomb Disposal Squads Sep 1942–Sep 1943
WO 199/1531: Operational Instructions for Charnwood Sector June 1943
WO 199/1532: Operational Instructions for Leicester Sector Nov/Dec 1943
WO 199/1533: Operational Arrangements for Cottesec Scheme July 1943
WO 199/3348: Review of the 101st (Leicestershire) AA Rocket Battery 1944

Quorn Home Guard Archive courtesy of *Quorndon Magazine*

Photograph Credits

Many photos do not state the copyright holders although we have endeavoured to find all. My apologies to those that have inadvertently been breached. Here are the ones we know of:
Leicester Mercury Group Limited and individuals

Secondary Sources

Ashworth, E.W. (5.1998): *Dad's Army Against the Panzers* in Military Illustrated, No. 120, p.42–47

Badcock, J.C. (1951): *Fleckney* Fleckney Parish Council, Leicestershire

Bell, D. (2001): *Those were the Days Leicestershire in the Forties, Fifties and Sixties* Countryside Books, Berkshire

Bishop, C. (Ed.) (1998): *WWII: The Directory of Weapons* Greenwich Editions, London

Boulter, D.C. (1988): *Wiggy's War* privately published, Wigston, Leicestershire

Boynton, Dr H.E. (2000): *The History of Victoria Park, Leicester* privately published, Leicester

Carswell, J. (Ed.) (1995): *At Home and Away* Coalville Publ. Co, Leicestershire

Cartwright, T. (2002): *Birds Eye Wartime Leicestershire 1939–1945* TCC Publ, Leics

Chamberlain P. and T. Gander (1975): *Mortars and Rockets* WW2 Fact File, Macdonald and Jane's, London

Churchill, W.S. (1952): *The Second World War: Volume V: Closing the Ring* Cassell and Co. Ltd, London

Crook, P. (1998): *Sussex Home Guard* Middleton Press, Sussex

Crook, P. (2000): *Surrey Home Guard* Middleton Press, Sussex

De Jong, L. (1956): *The German Fifth Column in World War Two* Routledge and Kegan Paul, London

Dobinson, C. (2001): *AA Command* Methuen, London

Erickson, Prof. J. (Ed.) (2000): *Invasion 1940: The Nazi Invasion Plan for Britain* St Ermin's Press, London

Finch, P. (1951): *Warmen Courageous: The History of the Essex Home Guard 1940–1945* Southend-on-Sea, Essex

Gander, T. (2000): *Allied Infantry Weapons of World War Two* The Crowood Press, Wiltshire

Goss, C. (2000): *The Luftwaffe Bombers' Battle of Britain: The Inside Story: July-October, 1940* Crecy Publishing, Lancashire

Gulvin, K.R. (1980): *Kent Home Guard* North Kent Books, Kent

Harrison, R. (1995): *A Foundry in a Garden: A Leicestershire Story* Sutton Publishing, Stroud

Hathern Local History Society (2003): *Hathern at War – A Leicestershire Village During WWII* Hathern Local History Society, Leicestershire

Harwood, D. (Ed.) (2004): *The History of Ratby Vol. 1* Ratby Local History Group, Leics

Hayward, J. (2003): *Myths and Legends of the Second World War* Sutton Publishing, Stroud

Hickman, T. (1998): *Melton Mowbray to Oakham* Britain In Old Photographs, Sutton Publishing, Stroud

Holloway, B.G. (1949): *The Northamptonshire Home Guard 1940–1945 – A History* Northamptonshire Home Guard, Northamptonshire

Lampe, D. (1968): *The Last Ditch* Cassell and Co. Ltd, London

Lewis, R.A. (1976): *Home Guard: Staffordshire Study Book 6* Staffordshire County Council, Staffs

Longmate, N. (1974): *The Real Dad's Army* Arrow Books, London

Lowry, B. and M. Wilks (2002): *The Mercian Marquis* Logaston Press, Hertfordshire

Lucas, D. (1993): *One Man's Wigston* Sutton Publishing, Gloucestershire

MacKenzie, S.P. (1995): *The Home Guard* Oxford University Press, Oxford

McCamley, N.J. (2004): *Disasters Underground* Pen and Sword, South Yorkshire

McDougall, J. (1979): *Civil Defence in Leicestershire 1939–1945* Privately Published, Leics

Mills, J. and T. Carney (2001): *In the Space of a Single Day* Warden's Publishing, London

Mills, J. (2003): *Home Guard List 1941: Northern Command* Savannah Publications, London

Nicholls, J. (2000): *England Needs You: The Story of Beaumanor Y Station* Surrey

Nicolson, N. (Ed.) (1967): *Harold Nicolson: Diaries and Letters 1939–45* Collins, London

Norman, B. (1993): *Luftwaffe Over the North* Leo Cooper, London

Ogilvy-Dalgleish, Col. J.W. (1955): *The Rutland Home Guard 1940–44* Oakham, Rutland

Osborne, Dr M. (2004): *20th Century Defences in Britain: The East Midlands* Concrete Publications, Lincolnshire

Perry, J. et al (Comp.) (1995): *Shepshed Wartime Memories* Shepshed Local History Society, Leics

Ramsey, W.G. (Ed.) (1988): *The Blitz: Then and Now: Vol. 2* After the Battle, Battle of Britain Publications, London

Rennison, J. (1980): *Wings Over Rutland* Spiegl Press, Stamford, Lincolnshire

Ruddy, A.J. (2003): *British Anti-Invasion Defences 1940–1945* Historic Military Press, Sussex

Shaw, F. and J. (1990): *We Remember the Home Guard* Hinckley

Skillen, H. (1993): *BSM – Four Years of War-Time Wit and Humour in the Royal Signals/ATS/Intelligence Corps* Middlesex

Spencer, W. (1997): *Records of the Militia and Volunteer Forces 1757–1945* PRO Readers' Guide No. 3, Surrey

Steppler, G.A. (1992): *Britons, To Arms!* Sutton Publishing, Stroud

Tedder, V. (1994): *The Pantry Under The Stair: Childhood Memories of World War II* Leicester City Council Living History Unit

Thompson, J. (1999): *War Behind Enemy Lines* Pan Books, London

Thornton Comm. Centre (1997): *Thornton Through the Years* Leicestershire

Turner, E.S. (1961): *The Phoney War on the Home Front* Michael Joseph, London

Warwicker, J. (2002): *With Britain in Mortal Danger* Cerebus Publishing, Bristol

Whiting, C. (1992): *The March on London* Leo Cooper, London

Whittaker, L.B. (1990): *Stand Down: Orders of Battle for the Units of the Home Guard of the United Kingdom, November 1944* Ray Westlake Military Books, Newport

Whittle, Sir F. (1957): *Jet* Pan Books, London

Wills, D. (1992): *Put On Your Boots and Parachutes!* Deryk Wills Publ, Leicester

(Various) (1946): *The Story of 'A' Sector Warwickshire Home Guard: 2nd and 7th Battalions* George Over Ltd, Rugby

Notes

1   Ironically, in the first series of *Dad's Army*, Corporal Jones is seen wearing the Tiger cap badge and shoulder titles of the Leicestershire Regiment. Indeed, the original working title of the sitcom was *The Fighting Tigers*.

2   *Loughborough Monitor*, 29.8.1940, p.7

3   Crook, 2000, p.6

4   Mills and Carney, p.1

5   De Jong, p.3

6   Hayward, p.16

7   *Leicester Mercury*, 29.5.1940, p.7

8   Contemporary financial values in the text are followed by approximate 2005 values in [brackets].

9   *Leicester Advertiser*, 8.6.1940, p.2

10   *Leicester Mercury*, 13.6.1940, p.5

11   De Jong, p.210

12   Major P.S. Wakefield's Diaries

13   MacKenzie, p.27

14   Quoted in Crook, 1998, p.11

15   Interview: Allan Hopcraft, 14.6.2003

16   Longmate, p.22

17   Lewis, p.11

18   MacKenzie, p.35

19   Steppler, p.149

20   Ogilvy-Dalgleish, p.5/6/14

21   *Leicester Mercury* 17.1.1940, p.12

22   Ibid, 24.5.1940, p.12

23   *Illustrated Leicester Chronicle*, 8.6.1940, p.11

24   LRO: DE 819/5

25   LRO: Leicestershire ARP Scheme Report, 30.5.1940

26   Crook, 1998, p.11

27   Major P.S. Wakefield's Diaries

28   Crook, 1998, p.16

29   Bell, p.7

30   *Leicester Mercury*, 11.5.1976

31   Thornton Community Centre, p.35

32   *Leicester Mercury*, 21.5.1940, p.13

33   Ibid, 22.5.1940, p.1

34   Holloway, p.25

35   Ogilvy-Dalgleish, p.8

36   *Leicester Mercury*, 24.5.1940, p.12

37   Quorn Home Guard Archive

38   *Loughborough Monitor*, 30.11.1944, p.1

39   Major P.S. Wakefield's Diaries

40   *Loughborough Monitor*, 4.7.1940, p.7

41   Major P.S. Wakefield's Diaries

42   Turner, p.269

43   MacKenzie, p.22

44   Tedder, p.11

45   LRO: DE 819/5

46   Interview: Allan Hopcraft, 14.6.2003

47   Ogilvy-Dalgleish, p.11

48   Nicolson, p.16

49   Ibid, p.90

50   Erickson, p.171

51   Adam Wakelin and Austin J. Ruddy, *Leicester Mercury*, 10.8.2001, p.11

52   Erickson, p.211

53   Ibid, , p.8

54   Ibid, p.76

55   Ibid, p.xxvii

56   Thornton Community Centre, p.35

57   Crook, 1998, p.8

58   *Loughborough Monitor*, 5.12.1940, p.6

59   *Illustrated Leicester Chronicle*, 22.6.1940, p.3 plus other local newspapers

60   *Leicester Advertiser*, 6.7.1940, p.3

61   Quoted in *Leicester Mercury*, 26.8.1975

62   *Illustrated Leicester Chronicle*, 22.6.1940, p.4

63   *Leicester Advertiser*, 6.7.1940, p.3

64   LRO: DE 819/5

65   Interview: Chris Long, 26.10.2003

66   Interview: Fred Parr, 14.1.2003

67   *Leicester Mercury*, 11.5.1976

68   Interview: Robert Beardsley, 13.1.2004

69   Interview: Frederick Gerrard, 18.12.2002

70   *Leicester Mercury*, 12.6.1940, p.5

71   LRO: DE 3620/29

72   *Loughborough Monitor*, 18.7.1940, p.2

73   *Leicester Mercury*, 20.7.1940, p.1

74   Boulter, p.16

75   Badcock, p.50

76   Major P.S. Wakefield's War Diaries

77   LRO: Misc 140/1

78   LRO: DE 3620/15

79   LRO: DE 3620/16

80   Ogilvy-Dalgleish, p.13

81   MacKenzie, p.43/LRO: DE 3620/17 Pochin

82   Mills and Carney, p.5

83   Holloway, p.68–69

84   MacKenzie, p.47

85   Eg. see *Annals of the Lynchburg Home Guard* by Charles Blackford (1891)

86   LRO: Misc 140/1

87   Steppler, p.149

88   Ogilvy-Dalgleish, p.13

89   MacKenzie, p.45

90   LRO: Misc 140/1

91   Ogilvy-Dalgleish, p.30

92   LRO: DE 819/5

93   Interview: Leslie Furnival, 19.8.2003

94   Interview: Robert Beardsley, 13.1.2003

95   *Leicester Advertiser*, 31.8.1940, p.3

96   NA: WO 166/1222

97   Major P.S. Wakefield's War Diaries

98 Ogilvy-Dalgleish, p.20
99 Interview: Tom Elliott, 8.12.2004
100 *Leicester Mercury*, 11.5.1976
101 NA: WO 166/1222
102 *Ibid*
103 Ramsey (Ed.), p.105–106
104 Major P.S. Wakefield's Diaries
105 LRO: Misc 140/1
106 *Leicester Mercury*, 2.5.1990
107 *Ibid* 23.5.1980
108 Perry et al, p.31
109 Interview: Aneurin Owen, 9.12.2002
110 *Leicester Mercury*, 9.8.1984
111 Sutton Bonington Local History Society, 'Sutton Bonington: A Patchwork', p.46
112 *Loughborough Monitor*, 26.9.1940, p.8
113 Ogilvy-Dalgleish, p.25
114 LRO: Misc 140/1
115 *Leicester Mercury*, 18.10.1940, p.12
116 *Ibid*, 26.10.1940, p.6
117 *Ibid* 21.10.1940, p.7 and *Leicester Advertiser*, 26.10.1940, p.4
118 Ed. Ramsey, p.274
119 *Loughborough Monitor*, 21.11.1940, p.1 and 5
120 For the full history of the air raids on Leicestershire and Rutland, see the author's forthcoming book.
121 McDougall, p.21
122 *Leicester Mercury*, 2.12.1940, p.1 and p.9
123 Steppler, p.150
124 Major P.S. Wakefield's Diaries
125 LO 355.35
126 *Leicester Mercury*, 27.2.1941, p.1
127 *Ibid* 1.3.1941, p6 and *Loughborough Monitor*, 6.3.1941, p.2
128 See www.cwgc.org/cwgcinternet/casualty_details.aspx?casualty=2692166
129 *Leicester Mercury* 20.3.1941, p.12
130 Mills, 2003, p.270–291
131 *Loughborough Echo*, 8.3.1941
132 Major P.S. Wakefield's Diaries
133 *Leicester Mercury*, 9.3.1979
134 Ramsey (Ed.), p.516–517. Another source states that the attacker may instead have been a Boulton and Paul Defiant night fighter flown by Sgt Allan Derek Wagner of 151 Squadron (see Goss, p.188). However, Stevens's combat report clearly matches the description of the combat and Kaufhold believes it was a 'Spitfire' [sic], a more similar looking aircraft to the Hurricane.
135 *Leicester Mercury*, 9.4.1941, p.1
136 *Ibid* 20.11.1973 et al
137 *Loughborough Echo*, 28.2.2003, p.22
138 Information via Judith Mileham
139 Goss, p.188–190
140 Ramsey (Ed.), p.518/519
141 Interview: Jim Bradley, 29.11.2003
142 Ramsey (Ed.), p.518/519
143 *Leicester Mercury*, 24.4.2003, p.14
144 Ogilvy-Dalgleish, p.32
145 NA: HO 202–8
146 *Leicester Mercury*, 26.5.1977
147 Interview: Jim Briggs, 26.8.2003
148 Ogilvy-Dalgleish, p.38/39
149 *Leicester Mercury*, 28.7.1941, p.6
150 Ogilvy-Dalgleish, p.43
151 LRO: Misc 140/1
152 *Leicester Mercury*, 9.9.1941, p.5. The CWGC records that on Sunday 31 August 1941, Corporal Ernest Bradbury, of 1st (North Leicester) Bn Home Guard, died while on duty. It has not been possible to find his exact cause of death, however, he died on a Sunday, the main day for Home Guard exercises, so he may be yet another victim of the strenuous training.
153 *Hinckley Times and Guardian*, 10.10.1941
154 *Leicester Mercury*, 3.11.1941, p.6
155 *Ibid* 20.7.1943, p.6
156 Whittle, p.219
157 Interview: John Bennett-Powell, 6.10.2004
158 *Ibid*
159 *Leicester Mercury*, 17.11.1941, p.1
160 Whittaker, p.19
161 *Leicester Mercury*, 30.1.1942, p.12
162 Longmate, p.76
163 *Leicester Mercury*, 12.2.1942, p.4
164 Ogilvy-Dalgleish, p.48
165 Major P.S. Wakefield's Diaries
166 Crook, 1998, p.51
167 Ogilvy-Dalgleish, p.37
168 *Leicester Mercury*, 14.4.1942, p.7
169 *Leicester Advertiser*, 25.4.1942, p.3
170 *Hinckley Times and Guardian*, 19.6.1942, p.2
171 *Leicester Mercury*, 24.6.1942, p.3
172 *Ibid* 4.7.1942, p.6 and *Leicester Advertiser*, 11.7.1942
173 *Leicester Mercury*, 6.7.1942, p.6
174 *Ibid* 13.7.1942, p.3
175 *Ibid*, 10.8.1942, p.5
176 *Ibid* 28.9.1942, p.7
177 *Ibid* 9.10.1942, p.6
178 *Ibid* 19.10.1942, p.3
179 Rennison, p.45
180 *Leicester Mercury*, 9.10.1942, p.3
181 LRO: DE 2263/8/2 and DE 2263/8/4
182 *Hinckley Times and Guardian*, 16.10.1942, p.5
183 *Leicester Mercury*, 12.10.1942, p.5
184 Interview: Arthur Kirkpatrick, 13.1.2003
185 Shaw, p.37
186 Quorn Home Guard Archive, letter 16.10.1942
187 Interview: Richard Tyler, 16.12.2004
188 Major P.S. Wakefield's Diaries
189 *Leicester Mercury*, 10.10.1942, p.4
190 *Ibid* 12.10.1942, p.1 and 15.10.1942, p.5
191 *Loughborough Monitor*, 26.11.1942, p.12
192 *Leicester Mercury*, 3.12.1942, p.6

193 Whittaker, p.19
194 *Leicester Advertiser*, 27.3.1943, p.3
195 *Leicester Mercury*, 22.2.1943, p.1
196 Information kindly via Steve Milnthorpe
197 LRO: Misc 140/1
198 *Leicester Mercury*, 8.3.1943, p.1
199 Interview: Ray Elgood, 14.12.2003
200 *Leicester Advertiser*, 13.3.1943, p.3 and *Leicester Mercury*, 9.3.1943, p.1
201 LRO: Misc 140/1
202 Interview: Judith Mileham, 2003
203 *Leicester Mercury*, 29.3.1943, p.3
204 Unknown Nottinghamshire newspaper cutting
205 Original manuscript via Jim Briggs with additional detail from Woodward, p.40
206 Interview: Bill Tollington, 16.12.2003
207 *Loughborough Monitor*, 8.4.1943, p.4
208 Interview: David Salmon, 22.1.2003
209 *Loughborough Monitor*, 1.4.1943, p.1
210 *Leicester Mercury*, 11.5.1976
211 *Ibid*, 17.5.1943, p.3
212 *Ibid* 17.11.1990
213 *Loughborough Monitor*, 27.5.1943, p.1
214 Quorn Home Guard Archive
215 Ogilvy-Dalgleish, p.59
216 *Leicester Mercury*, 3.8.1943, p.5
217 Interview: Arthur Kirkpatrick, 13.1.2003
218 *Leicester Mercury*, 16.8.1943, p.3
219 *Ibid* 11.8.1943, p.1 and 13.8.1943, p.8
220 Ogilvy-Dalgleish, p.60/61
221 *Loughborough Monitor*, 7.10.1943, p.1
222 LRO: DE 819/5 and DE 819/6
223 *Leicester Mercury*, 6.10.1943, p.6
224 *Loughborough Monitor*, 23.12.1943, p.1
225 Churchill, 1952, p.599/600
226 *Leicester Advertiser*, 1.1.1944, p.2
227 *Leicester Mercury*, 15.4.1944, p.1 and 3
228 *Ibid* 23.2.1944, p.3
229 *Leicester Mercury*, 12.2.1944, p.3
230 *Ibid* 4.10.1975
231 Original manuscript by the late Albert Squires, via his wife, Mavis Squires.
232 Major P.S. Wakefield's Diaries
233 Interview: Ray Elgood, 14.6.2003
234 *Illustrated Leicester Chronicle*, 1.4.1944, p.7
235 *Leicester Mercury*, 19.4.1944, p.6
236 LRO: Misc 140/1
237 Wills, p.53
238 Letter: John Swan, 17.6.2003
239 Hickman, p.34
240 Thompson, p.301
241 NA: WO 166/14516
242 *Leicester Mercury*, 13.5.1944, p.6
243 *Ibid* 15.5.1944, p.6
244 *Ibid*, 15.5.1944, p.3 and *Leicester Advertiser*, 20.5.1944, p.3
245 Quorn Home Guard Archive
246 *Leicester Mercury*, 15.4.1944, p.6
247 *Leicester Advertiser*, 17.6.1944, p.7
248 Major P.S. Wakefield's Diaries
249 *Leicester Mercury*, 20.5.1944, p.6
250 *Ibid* 20.7.1944, p.6
251 *Ibid* 27.6.1944, p.5
252 *Ibid* 20.7.1944, p.1 and 21.7.1944, p.8
253 NA: WO 199/3348
254 LRO: Misc 140/1
255 *Ibid*
256 Interview: John Bevis, 30.6.2003
257 Original manuscript via Jim Briggs with additional detail from Woodward, p.41–42
258 Interview: Bernard Spiers, 28.1.2003
259 LRO: DE 819/5
260 Interview: Jack Cox, 17.12.2002
261 Interview: Albert Purchase, 4.11.2002
262 *Leicester Mercury*, 30.11.1944, p.1 and p.6
263 *Ibid* 9.10.1981
264 Whiting, p.52
265 *Leicester Mercury*, 27.11.1944, p.3
266 Interview: Ray Elgood, 14.12.2003
267 *Leicester Mercury*, 4.12.1944, p.3
268 *Loughborough Monitor*, 7.11.1944, p.5
269 *Leicester Mercury*, 4.12.1944, p.3
270 *Leicester Advertiser*, 9.12.1944, p.8
271 *Lincoln, Rutland and Stamford Mercury*, 8.12.1944
272 Crook, 1998, p.90
273 Original manuscript by the late Albert Squires, via his wife, Mavis Squires
274 Interview: Ray Elgood, 14.12.2003
275 Original manuscript via Jim Briggs with additional detail from Woodward, p.43–44
276 *Leicester Mercury*, 7.6.1946, p.5
277 *Ibid* 8.6.1946, p.1
278 *Leicester Advertiser*, 12.5.1945, p.3
279 Quorn Home Guard Archive
280 *Ibid*
281 LRO: DE 819/6C
282 LRO: DE 1738
283 *Leicester Mercury*, 6.11.1944, p.4
284 Interview: Harry Gudger, 14.11.2002
285 *Leicester Mercury*, 21.5.1945, p.5
286 *Ibid* 22.8.1975. NB: The British Legion became the Royal British Legion in 1971
287 *Ibid* 2.8.1975
288 Communication with George McGilvery, 11.11.2004
289 Interview: Tony Smith of Oadby RBL, 11.11.2004
290 http://www.britishlegion.org.uk/membership/index.asp
291 See website: www.irish-guards.co.uk/recent.htm
292 *Leicester Mercury*, 26.5.1977
293 *Ibid* 5.12.1980
294 Ogilvy-Dalgleish, p.9
295 LRO: Misc 1361

296 LRO: DE 3620/29
297 Ogilvy-Dalgleish, p.9/10
298 Ogilvy-Dalgleish, p.11
299 'C' Company, 6th. (Quorn) Battalion, 2nd Anniversary Bulletin No. 18, June 1942
300 Harwood, p.4
301 LRO: DE 2263/3
302 'C' Company, 6th. (Quorn) Battalion, 2nd Anniversary Bulletin No. 18, June 1942
303 Osborne, p.53
304 Osborne, p.97
305 Ogilvy-Dalgleish, p.11
306 *Leicester Mercury*, 31.7.1940, p.1
307 Ogilvy-Dalgleish, p.11
308 Via Tom Elliott
309 *Ibid*
310 Letter: Dick Elliott, 11.12.2004
311 Ogilvy-Dalgleish, p.16/17
312 Interview: Leslie Furnival, 19.8.2003
313 Ogilvy-Dalgleish, p.30
314 *Ibid*, p.44
315 Interview: Ray Elgood, 14.12.2003
316 'C' Company, 6th. (Quorn) Battalion, 2nd Anniversary Bulletin No. 18, June 1942
317 Interview: Aneurin Owen, 9.12.2002
318 Letter: John Swan, 17.6.2003
319 Ogilvy-Dalgleish, p.55/56
320 MacKenzie, p.102
321 NA: WO 166/1222
322 NA: WO 166/6751
323 Interview: Eric Smith, 18.12.2002
324 *Leicester Mercury*, 24.3.1942, p.5
325 Author's emphasis
326 *Consolidated Instructions to Invasion Committees in England and Wales* July 1942, HMSO, p.19
327 *Leicester Mercury*, 15.2.1972
328 *Ibid* 28.4.1942, p.4
329 Ogilvy-Dalgleish, p.56
330 Letter from Wigston ARP Sub-Controller 1.2.1943 (via Roger Miles)
331 Quorn Home Guard Archive
332 LO
333 via Mr and Mrs W. Ruth Smith
334 via Roger Miles
335 LRO: DE 4368/83–87
336 via Mr M.J.M. Lea
337 LRO: DE 1381/393
338 Ogilvy-Dalgleish, p.56
339 LRO: DE 2263/7
340 LRO: Misc 140/1
341 Ogilvy-Dalgleish, p.48
342 Interview: Ken Allsopp, 11.8.2003
343 Leaflet: 'Invasion and Industry', August 1942 (via Roger Miles)
344 NA: WO 166/6751
345 LRO: DE 819/5
346 NA: WO 199/1532
347 NA: WO 199/1531
348 *Loughborough Monitor*, 12.11.1942, p.6
349 LRO: Misc 140/1
350 *Ibid*
351 NA: WO 166/10871
352 Original manuscript by the late Albert Squires, via his wife, Mavis Squires
353 Interview: Ken Allsopp, 11.8.2003
354 Interview: Bernard Spiers, 28.1.2003
355 Interview: Arthur Kirkpatrick, 13.1.2003
356 via Tom and Dick Elliott, December 2004
357 See Appendix A: Leicestershire and Rutland Home Guard Order of Battle 1940
358 Information from www.chapter-one.com/award.asp?vc=1201; www.anzacday.org.au/education/medals/vc/details/symons.html and www.awm.gov.au/units/people_681.asp
359 Information from www.chapter-one.com/award.asp?vc=281 and www.homeusers.prestel.co.uk/stewart/leiceste.htm
360 *Loughborough Monitor*, 30.11.1944, p.12
361 Interview: Sir David Attenborough, 13.2.2003
362 Information via Anton Rippon
363 *Leicester Mercury*, 6.7.1942, p.8
364 Ogilvy-Dalgleish, p.59
365 Ogilvy-Dalgleish, p.8
366 LRO: Misc 140/1
367 LRO: DE 819/5
368 *Loughborough Monitor*, 7.12.1944, p.5
369 Ogilvy-Dalgleish, p.62
370 Steppler, p.149
371 *Leicester Mercury*, 1.12.1944, p.6
372 LRO: Misc 140/1
373 Interview: Horace Gamble, 19.12.2002, originally published in *British Railways Illustrated* Volume 9, June 2000, p.384–388
374 Interview: Horace Gamble, 20.12.2002
375 Quoted in Holloway, p.214
376 Original manuscript via Jim Briggs with additional detail from Woodward, p.29–43
377 Skillen, p.xi
378 Some information drawn from Beaumanor and Garats HaY Amateur Radio Society website at www.beaumanor.hosted.pipemedia.net
379 Kay Staddon 11.11.2003
380 Nicholls, p.101
381 Interview: Peter James, 11.8.2003
382 Nicholls, p.101
383 Interview: Peter James, 11.8.2003
384 Nicholls, p.103
385 Interview: Peter James, 11.8.2003
386 *Leicester Mercury*, 11.5.1976
387 Interview: Bill Stevenson, 10.12.2003

388 Whittaker, p.128
389 Holloway, 1949, p.115
390 Ibid p.216
391 Quoted in Lewis, p.59
392 www.cwgc.org/cwgcinternet/casualty_details.aspx?casualty=2651959 and Alison England and Martin Mace
393 Wisbech Standard, 18.7.41
394 Isle of Ely and Wisbech Advertiser, 23.7.1941
395 NA: WO 166/1300
396 Interview: Frank Cooke, 19.7.2003
397 Interview: Ray Elgood, 14.12.2003
398 Ogilvy-Dalgleish, p.46/47
399 Ibid p.34
400 Interview: David Salmon, 22.1.2003
401 Interview: Jim Tailby, 2003
402 Lucas, p.79–81
403 Ogilvy-Dalgleish, p.51
404 Leicester Mercury, 11.5.1976
405 LRO: Misc 140/1
406 Interview: Dennis Underwood, 17.12.2002
407 Ogilvy-Dalgleish, p.45
408 Interview: Alan Clare, 13.11.2003
409 LRO: Misc 140/1
410 Leicester Mercury, 7.8.1943, p.6
411 Ibid 21.11.1997, p.10 and internet
412 Interview: Henry Shipley, 2005
413 Leicester Mercury, 18.5.1944, p.3
414 Not to be confused with Home Guard Auxiliers, members of the secret British resistance organisation, the Auxiliary Units
415 404,000 women served part-time and full-time in CD at its peak in 1942.
416 NA: WO 166/10974
417 Daily Mail, 1.12.1951, p.2
418 From June 1943, Major Whaley became 2nd i/c of the 1st (Rutland) Battalion
419 Interview: Edith Eayrs, 29.11.2003
420 Leicester Mercury, 7.12.1942, p.3
421 Loughborough Monitor, 16.4.1942, p.10 et al
422 Interview: Bill Tollington, 16.12.2003
423 NA: WO 166/10974
424 Major P.S. Wakefield's Diaries
425 Leicester Mercury, 1.10.1999
426 LRO: DE 2263/9/1
427 NA: WO 166/14516
428 LRO: DE 2263/10/1
429 Ogilvy-Dalgleish, p.56
430 Interview: Allan Hopcraft, 14.6.2003
431 Leicester Mercury, 12.2.1942, p.6
432 LRO: DE 2263/10/2
433 Loughborough Monitor, 15.10.1942, p.1
434 Leicester Mercury, 15.9.1992
435 Ibid
436 Interview: Dennis Underwood, 17.12.2002
437 Loughborough Monitor, 7.5.1942, p.7
438 Ibid 26.3.1942, p.10
439 Ibid p.7
440 LRO: DE 819/5
441 Interview: Norman Bazeley, 8.2003
442 NA: WO 199/3348
443 Leicester Mercury, 13.1.1943, p.1
444 Whittaker, p.104
445 Interview: Derrick G. Malyon, 19.12.2002
446 Leicester Mercury (undated)
447 Ibid (undated)
448 Interview: Robert Reay, 7.11.2002
449 NA: WO 166/11206
450 Interview: Derrick G. Malyon, 19.12.2002
451 Interview: Robert Reay, 7.11.2002
452 NA: WO 166/11206
453 NA: WO 166/14646
454 Dobinson, passim
455 NA: WO 166/11206
456 NA: WO 166/14646
457 The original manuscript states 'No. 4 Projectors', but evidence suggests this may be a typographical error as this weapon was not introduced for almost another year.
458 'AA Training Instruction Serial VI: 'Z' AA Artillery', September 1942
459 Dobinson, p.300
460 Norman, p.126
461 Chamberlain & Gander, p.52
462 NA: WO 166/14646
463 Ibid
464 Boynton, p.22
465 NA: WO 166/14646
466 Ibid
467 Leicester Mercury, 12.12.2002, p.14
468 Norman, p.124
469 Army Report No. 226 of 2.11.1944, quoted in Dobinson, p.397
470 Interview: J.T. Clarke, 27.1.2003
471 Interview: John Greaves, 17.12.2002
472 Mills and Carney, p.87
473 Leicester Mercury, 19.10.1996
474 NA: WO 166/11206
475 Ibid
476 Ibid
477 Ibid
478 NA: WO 199/1481
479 NA: WO 166/10974 and via Jon Mills
480 NA: WO 199/400 and Mills and Carney, p.86
481 NA: WO 166/14516
482 NA: WO 166/14427
483 Loughborough Monitor, 21.9.1944, p.1
484 Via Russell W. Barnes, 17.4.2003 and Lowry and Wilks, p.91
485 NA: WO 199/66
486 Lowry and Wilks, p.103–106
487 Via Adrian Westwood.

488 Via David Blair.
489 Interview: Peter James, 11.8.2003
490 Interview: Fred Whitford.
491 Interview: Norma Deeming.
492 Interview: Wendy Warren, 2003
493 Ogilvy-Dalgleish, p.28
494 Quoted in MacKenzie, p.107
495 Ibid p.116
496 Letter: Mrs Anne Cooper, 26.2.2005 and interview, 17.3.2005
497 Leicester Mercury, 11.9.1964
498 See Lowry and Wilks, p.113–116
499 LO: 355.35
500 Harrison, p.91–92
501 Interview: Allan Hopcraft, 14.6.2003
502 'C' Company, 6th. (Quorn) Battalion, 2nd Anniversary Bulletin No. 18, June 1942
503 Holloway, p.105
504 LRO: DE 819/5
505 Interview: Wendy Warren, 2003
506 LRO: DE 3548/2
507 Leicester Mercury, 13.10.1944, p.10
508 Ibid 8.9.1964
509 Ogilvy-Dalgleish, p.53
510 Holloway, p.152
511 Ogilvy-Dalgleish, p.33
512 Leicester Mercury, 23.5.1980
513 LRO: DE 819/5
514 Interview: John Greaves, 17.12.2002
515 Shaw, p.37
516 Letter: Horace Gamble, 19.12.2002
517 Leicester Mercury, 11.9.1998, p.9
518 Interview: Leslie Furnival, 19.8.2003
519 Letter: Jim Briggs, 10.11.2003
520 Ogilvy-Dalgleish, p.39/40
521 Original manuscript by the late Albert Squires, via his wife, Mavis Squires
522 Interview: Ray Elgood, 14.12.2003
523 Interview: Wendy Warren, 2003
524 Leicester Mercury, 26.5.1977
525 Major P.S. Wakefield Diaries
526 Interview: Harry Gudger, 14.11.2002
527 Loughborough Monitor, 30.11.1944, p.12
528 Interview: Wendy Warren, 2003.
529 Loughborough Monitor, 27.2.1941, p.11
530 Ibid 4.9.1941, p.10
531 Ibid 12.11.1942, p.10
532 Ibid 28.5.1942, p.1
533 Original manuscript via Jim Briggs with additional detail from Woodward, p.33
534 LRO: Misc 140/1 and Background detail from Mills and Carney, passim
535 LRO: Misc 140/1
536 Ibid
537 Mills and Carney, p.47
538 LO 355.35
539 LRO: Misc 140/1
540 Ibid
541 Ibid
542 LRO: Misc 140/1
543 Ibid
544 Interview: Eric Smith, 18.12.2002
545 Major P.S. Wakefield's Diaries
546 Ibid
547 LRO: DE 819/5
548 LRO: Misc 140/1
549 Major P.S. Wakefield's Diaries
550 'War Vocabulary of Clothing and Necessaries 1942, (August 1943)' quoted in Mills and Carney, p.149
551 LRO: Misc 140/1
552 Mills and Carney, p.7
553 Ibid p.10
554 Ogilvy-Dalgleish, p.20/21. Ogilvy-Dalgleish is proven correct, but not in the way he imagined. As only about 2,000 of these badges must have been originally struck, they have now become highly sought after by collectors. As a result, many copies have been restruck since the war. They are deceptively difficult to tell from the original.
555 Hathern Local History Society, p.52 and Interview: Bill Tollington, 16.12.2003
556 Mills and Carney, p.43
557 Much of the technical data in the following chapter is drawn from Gander, passim
558 The general timeline is based on LRO: Misc 140/1
559 Leicester Mercury, 13.10.1994, p.10
560 Harrison, p.90
561 Ogilvy-Dalgleish, p.13
562 Interview: Jim Tailby, 2003
563 Gander, p.17
564 LRO: DE 819/5
565 LRO: DE 4952/17
566 Ogilvy-Dalgleish, p.30
567 Ibid p.8
568 Ibid p.30
569 Interview: Jim Tailby, 18.9.2003
570 LRO: Misc 140/1
571 LRO: DE 3620/43
572 LRO: DE 3548
573 LRO: DE 819/6
574 Original manuscript by the late Albert Squires, via his wife, Mavis Squires
575 Interview: Dennis Booth, 28.11.2002
576 Interview: Peter James 11.8.2003
577 LRO: DE 3548/2
578 Ibid
579 Ibid
580 Data in this section is largely derived from Ashworth, passim
581 Ogilvy-Dalgleish, p.14/15
582 Interview: Bill Tollington, 16.12.2003

583 LRO: DE 3548
584 MacKenzie, p.92
585 E.g. 'North Midland District Home Guard Mobile Section' leaflet c.1943
586 LRO: DE 3548
587 'North Midland District Home Guard Mobile Section' leaflet c.1943
588 Ogilvy-Dalgleish, p.15
589 *Leicester Mercury*, 29.1.1997, p.10
590 Correct description in Holloway, p.127
591 Bishop, p.273
592 LRO: Misc 140/1
593 LRO: DE 3548
594 Via Wendy Warren.
595 Interview: Leslie Furnival, 19.8.2003
596 LRO: Misc 140/1
597 Interviews with Lady Rosamund Hanworth and Chris Shepheard
598 *Ibid*
599 Interview: Ray Elgood, 14.12.2003
600 Finch, p.248
601 Interview: Allan Hopcraft, 14.6.2003
602 MacKenzie, p.94
603 Interview: John Greaves, 17.12.2002
604 LRO: DE 3548
605 Home Guard Instruction No. 51, Part IV: *The Organization of Home Guard Defence*, Nov. 1943, p.16
606 MacKenzie, p.95
607 Ruddy, p.24
608 Interview: Fred Parr, 14.1.2003
609 Interview: Ray Elgood, 14.12.2003
610 (Ed.) Carswell, p.30
611 Ogilvy-Dalgleish, p.55
612 Interview: John Greaves, 17.12.2002
613 Listing compiled from author's field research and Defence of Britain Database website at www.ads.ahds.ac.uk/catalogue
614 McCamley, p.119
615 MacKenzie, p.121
616 McCamley, p.10
617 Interview: Bill Tollington, 16.12.2003
618 Gulvin, p.32
619 Interview: John Swan, 17.6.2003
620 *Ibid*
621 Interview: Mr M.J.M. Lea
622 Major P.S. Wakefield's Diaries
623 *Ibid*
624 Interview: Ray Elgood, 14.12.2003
625 *Leicester Mercury*, 28.7.1941, p.6
626 *Ibid* 12.2.1942, p.4
627 Longmate, p.76
628 Interview: Ray Elgood, 14.12.2003
629 Interview: Harry Gudger, 14.11.2002
630 Interview: Allan Hopcraft, 14.6.2003
631 No. 3 Section, No. 13 Platoon, 4th (Central Leicester) Battalion Magazine, No. 8, December 1941, p.8
632 Interview: Robert Reay, 7.11.2002
633 Holloway, p.114
634 Major P.S. Wakefield's Diaries
635 Major P.S. Wakefield's Diaries
636 Interview: Albert James Purchase, 4.11.2002
637 Interview: Bill Tollington, 16.12.2003
638 Interview: Aneurin Owen, 9.12.2002
639 Letter: John Bevis, 30.6.2003
640 Interview: John Greaves, 17.12.2002
641 Interview: Robert Beardsley, 13.1.2003
642 LRO: DE 2263/5
643 Ogilvy-Dalgleish, p.64
644 Whittaker, p.121 and Newarke Houses Museum, Leicester
645 NA: WO 166/6751
646 Quorn Home Guard Archive
647 By February 1944, it was: Chairman: Mr Lister L. Ward, Craddock Drive, Quorn. Deputies: Rev. W.E. Pilling, The Vicarage, Quorn. Mr F.W. Bailey, Loughborough Road, Quorn.
648 All awards have been cross-referenced with the Home Guard awards page at www.home-guard.org.uk/med.html. Again, the author would be interested to know if any other names have inadvertently been left of the above list.
649 Hickman, p.33
650 Ogilvy-Dalgleish, p.61

Cartoon from the Quorn Home Guard's Stand Down programme.